Analyzing
Financial
Statements

Fifth Edition

Analyzing Financial Statements

Clifton H. Kreps, Jr.
Wachovia Professor of Banking
University of North Carolina
Chapel Hill, North Carolina

and

Richard F. Wacht
Professor of Finance
Georgia State University
Atlanta, Georgia

AMERICAN INSTITUTE OF BANKING

 AMERICAN
BANKERS
ASSOCIATION

1120 Connecticut Avenue, N.W.
Washington, D.C. 20036

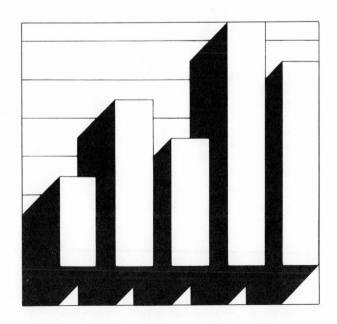

Contents

Figures and Tables

Figures

Tables

Preface

This, the fifth edition of the American Institute of Banking textbook *Analyzing Financial Statements,* is more than a mere revision of the work contained in the earlier editions. It is, in fact, a completely new and unique text in which emphasis is placed on the proper use of accounting information in the commercial bank credit decision.

The earlier editions concentrated about equally on the nature and origins of the accounting data, formats and methods of presentation of the data in financial statements, and the proper interpretation of the data in statement analysis. In planning the fifth edition, however, the American Bankers Association's Education Policy and Development group permitted us to create a text that would assume that the reader possessed an adequate working knowledge of the principles of accounting. This enabled us to concentrate more fully on the methodology of financial statement analysis as employed in bank credit decisions and to illustrate more clearly the ways in which the level and nature of business activity influence the results presented in the financial statements.

The approach we use in acquainting the student with the basic principles of financial statement analysis is one that encourages active participation by the student in the analysis of business activity as revealed in the balance sheet, income statement, and funds flow statement of the firm. Each of the principles, tools, and techniques is explained in the text and then illustrated within the context of simple yet realistic business settings. The companion workbook problems and cases permit the student to benefit from "hands-on" problem-solving experiences that further reinforce the principles of statement analysis and their application. We encourage the use of these problems and cases; it is obvious that the student cannot become a skillful credit analyst without practice, practice, practice.

Acknowledgements

In developing the text materials and designing the approach to presenting these materials, we received much assistance from many quarters. Not all our debts to others can be adequately acknowledged here, but the principal ones at least must be enumerated.

We are indebted to Glen Jent, Cissel Gott, and Barbara Paull of the ABA Education Policy and Development group and Diane Sloan of the AIB Student Services Division for their assistance in planning, text revision, and production. The manuscript review committee likewise deserves our gratitude for their many constructive suggestions. Members are: Rodney Cornwall, Vice President, Seattle-First National Bank, Seattle, Washington; Robert J. McCoy, Senior Vice President, First National Bank and Trust Company, Joplin, Missouri; A. James Grant, Senior Vice President, Exchange Bank and Trust Company, Dallas, Texas; William Heillier, Vice President, First National Bank of Atlanta, Atlanta, Georgia; George F. Fields, Vice President, Shawmut County Bank, N.A., Cambridge, Massachusetts; Warren P. Rothe, Senior Vice President, Suburban Trust Company, Hyattsville, Maryland; and M. Camper O'Neal, Jr., American Security Bank, N.A., Washington, D.C.

Stephen G. Timme, Georgia State University, contributed substantially to the development of the text and workbook materials, and Arvind Mahajan, also of Georgia State University, rendered invaluable assistance in the preparation of the end-of-chapter questions and workbook problems.

The University of North Carolina at Chapel Hill, Georgia State University, and our faculty colleagues have been most generous in helping create a climate favorable to the completion of this text. We also acknowledge a debt of gratitude to Trudy Kaplan of the ABA Publications and Printing Department for her assistance in transforming the manuscript into the bound volume.

Finally, Jeanette Wacht and Linda Edwards labored tirelessly and uncomplainingly as they typed and retyped the various drafts through which the manuscript passed until the final version emerged. Without their efforts, the project would never have been completed.

While we are indeed grateful to all those named above, we must ourselves bear final responsibility for the quality of the product. Thus, we are culpable for all errors of whatever sort that may have crept into our work. We hope these are few and that they will find a forgiving readership.

Clifton H. Kreps, Jr.	Chapel Hill, North Carolina
Richard F. Wacht	Atlanta, Georgia
	June 1978

Chapter 1

Objectives of Financial Statement Analysis

Bankers, businessmen, investors, tax authorities, and business regulatory agencies all use different standards for judging the performance of the businesses in which they are interested. Some of those standards may be political or social, such as those that seek to ensure equity in wages and employment opportunities or adequate concern with environmental protection, but most are financial and are applied to the financial condition and performance of business firms as revealed in financial statements. Of the various financial statements in common use, the balance sheet, the income statement, and the flow of funds statement are probably the most important. The information they contain may be analyzed intensively, by the firm itself for internal managerial purposes and also by interested outside observers. Those may include short-term creditors, such as trade creditors and banks; intermediate- and long-term creditors, such as banks, commercial finance companies, and bondholders; and present and potential investors in the firm's common and preferred stock.

The preparation and presentation of financial statements thus provides a basis for evaluating business performance. The process of evaluation constitutes *financial statement analysis*. Its raw material includes not only the data in the statements but also all relevant information available from other sources. It involves careful study of all the revealed financial "facts." The analyst attempts, through the use of established principles of financial statement analysis based on sound logic, to draw correct conclusions from the body of information at his disposal. In this sense he practices the scientific method, but neither business administration nor accountancy is a science; neither, therefore, is financial statement analysis.

Its results may be distorted by defective data as well as by improper application of the principles and tools of analysis. That is a useful piece of information to keep in mind. More to the point, however, is the observation that the results of the analysis of business performance through financial statements are deemed by various parties to be so significant and interesting that the "art" of financial statement analysis is widely and extensively practiced throughout the business and financial communities. That is, in fact, the reason we turn our interest to it here.

Basic Objectives of Statement Analysis

Before the analyst can begin properly to analyze a firm's financial statements, he should know and be able to define clearly the end-product he is seeking. Only if he is fully aware of his objectives—both interim and ultimate—can he focus his attention on the relevant considerations with which he should deal. Establishing objectives is therefore essential to the process of conducting a truly effective and efficient analysis: effective in that the conclusions reached will be not only correct but also most useful for the purposes of the analysis; efficient in that the analyst will achieve his results with a minimum expenditure of time and effort.

In general, financial statement analysis has three basic objectives with respect to a given business enterprise: *evaluation* of past and current financial condition; *diagnosis* of (and prescription of remedies for) any existing financial problems; and *forecasting* of future trends in the firm's financial position. Regardless of who is doing the analysis or what firm he is analyzing, these three objectives are always paramount, although their relative importance may vary from analyst to analyst and, for a given analyst, from one situation to another.

EVALUATION

A pervasive question that every financial analyst is seeking to answer when examining the financial statements of a business firm is, How did the firm perform over the period for which statements are available? In most cases, however, merely answering that question correctly should not bring the analysis to an end, since the answer says nothing about the future. For example, a potential trade creditor may evaluate a firm's historical performance, possibly with perfect accuracy, and accept or reject its application for credit seemingly on the basis of that evaluation alone. But obviously some assumptions about the firm's future performance must, explicitly or implicitly, weigh importantly in the credit-extension decision. Often the assumption is simply the implicit and potentially dangerous one that the future will be an image of the past.

In "real life" there are at any time many firms that historical analysis will reveal as poor performers but that are entering phases of improved profitability and greater value as credit customers to trade suppliers. To deny those firms access or increased access to trade credit solely on the basis of "the record" would surely be a very shortsighted way of doing business.

At the other extreme, there are also at any time many established firms with excellent financial track records that are beginning, for any of a number of reasons (technological changes, lack of successor management, changes in consumer tastes, for example), to lose their status as going concerns. For trade suppliers to begin or continue to extend credit to those firms on the liberal terms suggested by "the record" would again reflect a serious error in business judgment.

All of which is to say that the evaluation of a firm's past and current financial statements is an extremely valuable and useful exercise, because it tells us, in financial terms, where the firm has been and where it is. And for some purposes that is all we need to know. But for most purposes it is not enough, and an answer is required to another paramount question that financial analysts continually ask: In financial terms, where is the firm likely to be going from here?

To answer that question, of course, is to achieve the third basic objective of financial statement analysis, *financial forecasting.* Before discussing that subject, however, let us examine the second basic objective, *diagnosis of financial problems.*

DIAGNOSIS

In a relatively few instances the evaluation of financial statements may be considered an end in itself. Business managers, for example, may set performance goals, such as target rates of return on assets, gross profit margins, or inventory levels, for comparison with actual results at the end of an operating (accounting) period. If the goals are met, the assumption that all's well may be justified, and the financial analyst may choose to go no further. But if a firm's operating goals are not met, something more than evaluation becomes necessary—i.e., diagnoses of the failures to meet targeted goals that evaluation has revealed.

Diagnosis implies prescription; and its true purpose is not only to seek the causes of the financial problems that statement analysis uncovers but also to suggest remedies for them. In fact, recommending solutions to financial problems discovered through statement evaluation is at least as important a responsibility of the financial statement analyst as defining those problems.

But it is here that the financial analyst's responsibility ends and the responsibility of those charged with the financial management of the firm begins. Armed with the diagnoses and prescriptions supplied by financial statement analysis, the financial managers can correct past errors of omission and commission while seeking their continuing objective of maintaining the firm's financial condition within the relatively

3

close tolerance suggested by sound principles of financial management and demanded by potential suppliers of funds.

FORECASTING

The third basic objective of financial statement analysis is *forecasting* future trends in the firm's financial and underlying operating conditions. To achieve that objective, the financial statement analyst must answer the question: How and why will the firm's financial statements change over some specified future period? The period specified may be of any duration but is usually near-term, ordinarily not longer than six months or a year and most often a quarter for single-period forecasts. Careful financial planning often involves *concurrent forecasting*, for periods of from three months to as long as ten years (although the degree of validity—the probability index—that can be attached to business and economic forecasts decreases very rapidly as the time is extended). All the forecasts are carefully reviewed and revised each quarter, so that the firm employing concurrent forecasting always has an updated road map of the "most probable" path toward its future objectives—a valuable aid in the process of current decision making.

The answer to the "why" part of the forecasting question is at least as important as the answer to the "how" part. It is largely embodied in the assumptions the analyst must make about the future course of the firm's operations and future changes in the business and economic environment in which the firm operates.

Financial statement analysis alone cannot generate all the information needed to make those assumptions. It can give a detailed picture of a business firm's current financial position. It can also, through comparative statement analysis, show the historical track over which the firm came to its present position. All this information is essential to the task of estimating the firm's "most probable" future prospects and performance. But to complete that task, the information provided by the analysis of the firm's financial statements must take into account the management's expectations about the firm's future, as expressed in performance goals and objectives. Since those expectations reflect management's own forecast of the firm's future, the probable accuracy of the forecast must be assessed by reference to information, externally obtained, about prospects for the firm's industry in particular and for the business community and the economy in general.[1] From a review of that information, the financial statement analyst can form his own conclu-

---

1. Such information is readily available from a wide variety of sources, some of which are listed in the bibliography at the end of this volume. It consists of informed judgments expressed by academic , business, and government economists and other close and continuous observers of the business and economic scene about the future course and levels of business and economic activity.

sions concerning the "most likely" future business scenario and either accept or modify management's own forecast accordingly.

With the appropriate future dimension thus supplied, the financial statement analyst may perform what is possibly his most important task—the preparation of *pro forma* financial statements. These *project* the firm's financial position from what it is to what it is expected to be at some chosen future time, reflecting all the assumptions that have been made about the shape of things to come.

Pro forma financial statements are of great value to various groups. Their value to a firm's management may largely be inferred from what has been said. They quantify and make explicit the goals and objectives of management's operating policies and thereby provide an extremely useful control and a reference point for keeping operations "on track" during the period they cover. Divergences of actual from projected results require both explanations and, where appropriate, remedial actions; thus the firm's financial statement analysts may expect continual opportunities for diagnosis and prescription.

Moreover, other groups besides management are interested in a firm's expected future performance and may make their own financial forecasts for it, sometimes informally but often through the same process that leads to the preparation of pro forma statements. Bankers and other short- and intermediate-term lenders (trade creditors, commercial finance companies, insurance companies) may do so to monitor the firm's continuing ability to service and repay its debts; actual or potential equity investors may do so to satisfy themselves of the firm's continuing ability to pay dividends or the possibilities of capital gains from holding its stock; and if the firm is in a regulated industry, such as a public utility, public regulatory agencies may do so in fulfilling their mandate to provide the firm, through rate regulations, with an adequate but not excessive return on its investment.

Preparation of pro forma statements marks the end of a cycle in the financial forecasting process, but the process itself is a continuous one. With the passage of time, forecasts become outmoded; they must be reviewed and reformulated, and pro forma statements based on the reformulated forecasts must again be projected into the future. (Et cetera, ad infinitum!) But because financial forecasting is a continuously rewarding process, it is widely practiced by all the groups—management, creditors, stockholders, regulators—who have an interest in the financial future of particular business firms.

INTERRELATIONS AMONG BASIC OBJECTIVES

It should be clear from the preceding discussion of the three basic objectives of financial statement analysis—*evaluation* of past and current financial conditions; *diagnosis* of, and prescription of remedies for, financial problems; and *forecasting* of future trends in financial conditions—that they are highly interrelated. Yet achieving them requires separate and different analytical *processes.* Evaluation requires that data from a firm's financial statements and from other sources be disassembled and grouped homogeneously for purposes of analysis. Diagnosis delves deeply into particular, narrowly defined areas by disassembling the data even further. Finally, forecasting examines all the bits and pieces of data, introduces additional data relevant to future prospects, and recreates the statements on a pro forma basis, exhibiting the financial conditions expected at some future date.

These interrelations suggest the complexity of financial statement analysis in general. Further to compound the difficulty, moreover, various financial statement analysts have unique sets of objectives, which they seek for different particular purposes. Some of those are discussed in the next section.

Unique Sets of Objectives

We have been examining the objectives of financial statement analysis in very general terms; that is, we have implied that all financial statement analysts, regardless of where they work or what their responsibilities are, will pursue the basic objectives of evaluation, diagnosis, and forecasting. That is probably true; but it is also true that some of them pursue unique sets of objectives that derive from the particular function the analyst is performing for his firm and from the particular characteristics of the firm and of the industry of which it is a part.

In this examination of some unique sets of objectives, the major emphasis is on those ordinarily pursued by financial statement analysts in commercial banks in support of their institutions' commercial lending activities. But brief attention is also given to some other unique sets of objectives.

OBJECTIVES OF STATEMENT ANALYSIS FOR COMMERCIAL LENDING

In earlier years commercial bank credit analysts generally aimed their analyses at only two of the three basic statement analysis objectives—evaluation and forecasting. They evaluated a commercial loan applicant's financial position to determine the degree of his *credit-worthiness,* or right of access to bank credit. Since the borrower's credit-worthiness also depended on his ability to service and repay his loan as scheduled, an attempt was made, if necessary, to forecast, or assess, the extent of that ability. However, commercial bankers dealt principally in "productive credits"—short-term, seasonally self-liquidating loans to businessmen and farmers—and application of the second test was seldom necessary. For borrowers seeking only productive credits, a satisfactory current financial condition was adequate proof of credit-worthiness.

In more recent years, however, commercial bankers have greatly extended the scope of their lending operations. They have become deeply involved, for example, in making intermediate-term loans ("term loans") to businessmen and farmers, mortgage loans to businessmen, farmers, and homeowners, and instalment loans to consumers. All the newer kinds of loans share a major characteristic: the borrower's ability to repay his loan depends, not on his current financial condition, but on his anticipated future income. Today's broader range of loans has thus caused bank credit analysts to shift their emphasis away from the evaluation of current financial position[2] toward forecasting ability to pay, which has become the principal criterion of borrower credit-worthiness.

Another change in banker views about lending has also had a significant impact on the objectives of financial statement analysis as seen by commercial bank credit analysts. That is the growing recognition by bankers that most of their business borrowing customers are relatively small, highly dependent on commercial banks for their external funding requirements,[3] and rather inefficiently managed. In short, they need all the help they can get from their banks, and that help can usefully take the form of informal management counseling as well as necessary credit accommodation.

What this implies is that *diagnosis* of the financial problems of smaller business borrowers and the prescription of cures for those problems now constitute an important element of commercial bank credit analysis, one that was formerly almost totally ignored.

The bank credit analyst's diagnosis of a small borrower's financial problems and his recommendations for solving them have their place in the borrower's credit file for several reasons. Some of the problems may be so serious, for example, as to have a significant effect on the terms and conditions on which the bank can make credit available to the borrower. In extreme cases, correction of the problem may be a necessary condition for the granting of any credit. And while for many pervasive financial problems of small businesses (e.g., inadequate equity capital) there may be no ready cure, others (e.g., inefficient use of working capital arising from loose accounts receivable policies) are more readily remediable. The lending officer handling the account can tactfully urge the small business borrower to adopt the credit analyst's problem-solving

---

2. Except, as before, for seasonally self-liquidating loans; but those now constitute a very small proportion of total commercial bank loans.

3. Since their smallness bars them from the national money and capital markets, and their few alternative fund sources—such as factors and commercial finance companies—are much more expensive than banks.

7

recommendations on the perfectly reasonable premise that by doing so he will make his business enterprise more viable and himself a more valuable customer to the bank.

STATEMENT ANALYSIS BY OTHER INTERESTED PARTIES

Financial statement analysis is obviously not the exclusive province of commercial bank credit analysts. In fact, it is engaged in for a variety of reasons by other interested parties, including trade creditors, bondholders, equity investors, and the managements of business firms.

Trade Creditors

A trade creditor is interested primarily in the liquidity (degree of "cashness") of the firms to which he extends credit. His claim is usually relatively short-term,[4] and he judges the ability of a debtor firm to pay that kind of claim by analyzing its current position, although he may give some attention to the adequacy of cash flows to maintain short-term liabilities on a current basis. Trade suppliers approach the financial statements of their actual or potential credit customers in much the same way bankers analyze requests for productive credits; i.e., current financial position is the principal test of credit-worthiness, and forecasting ability to pay is reserved for special cases. Except with respect to bankruptcies and other workout situations, the trade supplier has little interest in diagnosing his credit customers' financial problems.

Longer-Term Creditors

In contrast to the debt claims of trade creditors, those of bondholders and term-lending commercial finance companies are intermediate (two to five years) or long term (six years or longer). Accordingly those creditors are interested in the same thing as commercial banks making term loans, mortgage loans, and consumer instalment loans—ability to repay out of anticipated future income. Their analyses of the financial statements of present or would-be borrowers are focused on forecasting relatively long-term profitability and from such forecasts assessing the degrees of risk in extending or retaining longer-term credits. The profitability forecast determines the maximum longer-term debt the firm can safely place in its capital structure; the assessment of risks weighs heavily in the determination of loan maturity, interest rate, and other terms and conditions written into the bond indentures or term loan covenants to protect the lenders from loss.

---

4. Trade credit terms ordinarily require payment in no more than 90 days, more usually 30 or 60 days, depending on the length of the current asset turnover (the inventory to receivables to cash cycle) of firms in the trade. Discounts are often offered for prompt payment.

Equity Investors

Actual and potential stockholders are also generally much more concerned with anticipated future earnings and their stability than with past or current financial conditions. Their analyses of individual firm financial statements seek the answers to such questions as: Will future earnings be adequate not only to service and retire debt but also to continue and even increase dividends, while providing for the retention of enough earnings to fund the firm's continued steady growth? Or, in a nutshell, what compounded annual rate of return will an investment in this firm's stock yield over time?

Business Management

Finally, it is obvious that a business firm's management is, or certainly should be, much more intensely interested in the results of the detailed and continuous analysis of its financial statements than any group of outsiders (creditors, and in this sense even stockholders) could possibly be. There are many reasons for this interest.

The ultimate objective of business financial management is to maximize the present value of the owners' equity (common stock). That objective is sought in two ways: attempting to maximize present and future earnings; and attempting to increase the stability of future earnings and thus reduce the degree of risk associated with investing in the firm's stock.

In pursuing these goals, management needs and seeks all the help it can get, and it can get considerable help from the close and continuous analysis of its financial statements. Forecasting—concurrent budgeting through pro forma statements, for example—can help to delineate management's path toward its financial objectives; detailed evaluation of current statements can cast up actual and potential financial problems; and diagnosis of those problems can lead to the prescription of remedies. Thus financial statement analysis is a valuable management tool for providing more effective control of operations, improving present and future profitability, and keeping the business enterprise on track through time. Small wonder that it is so widely employed. It is essential to the information generating and processing necessary for sound business and financial decision making.

The Plan of the Book

The process involved in gathering a relevant body of data, organizing and analyzing it, and presenting conclusions derived from it—the process of financial statement analysis—can and must be standardized in the interests of consistency, efficiency, and pedagogy. Thus general guidelines have been developed for the process to provide a necessary frame

9

of reference for the neophyte. That framework of principles and tools of financial statement analysis is presented in subsequent chapters as follows:

Part I (Chapters 2-4, on "Financial Statement Analysis and Accounting") examines the raw material of financial statement analysis—financial accounting data. The discussion assumes that the reader has a working knowledge of the principles of financial accounting; starting from this assumption, it examines accounting principles and data as they relate to the needs and objectives of the financial statement analyst. Part II (Chapters 5-7, on "Financial Statements and Business Funds Flows") traces the flow of funds—the lifeblood of business—through the financial accounts of the business firm and consequently through the firm itself under various operating and economic conditions. Its purpose is to focus attention on the fact that financial accounting involves a translation of the realities of business operations into monetary measurements by way of the financial statements. And it emphasizes that financial statement analysis attempts to gain insight into those business realities through a proper interpretation of this accounting translation.

Part III (Chapters 8-11, on "Tools of Financial Statement Analysis") discusses in detail each of the principal tools of financial statement analysis, arranged in order of increasing complexity, from ratio analysis through the preparation of pro forma financial statements. The chapters of Part IV (12-18, on "The Technique of Financial Statement Analysis") illustrate the proper use of the tools by the financial statement analyst as he pursues his objectives of evaluation, diagnosis, and forecasting.

The central theme of this book is statement analysis from the point of view of the commercial banker. It emphasizes the tools and techniques most useful to the banker-analyst in pursuing the bank's objectives as they relate primarily to the commercial lending function. It also examines the other objectives of statement analysis, since these too will be of occasional use to the bank credit analyst and lending officer, especially if they are called on to play the role of management consultants for their business customers.

Whenever possible, the point of view taken is that of the commercial bank financial statement analyst engaged in credit analysis in support of his institution's commercial lending function. To use this point of view consistently and continuously, however, would leave the reader with a highly warped perspective. And it is the authors' intention to present a complete and well-rounded discussion of financial statement analysis that may nevertheless be of particular value to commercial bankers.

Questions

1-1 What is financial statement analysis and what is its fundamental purpose?

1-2 What are the three basic objectives of statement analysis?

1-3 Do you feel that a financial institution should accept or reject a loan application merely on the basis of an evaluation of past performance?

1-4 Specifically, when can the evaluation of financial statements be considered an end in itself?

1-5 Define diagnosis as it relates to financial statement analysis.

1-6 What are pro forma financial statements? Who uses them?

1-7 Briefly explain the unique objectives of statement analysis for each of the following:
   a. Commercial bankers
   b. Trade creditors
   c. Long-term creditors
   d. Investors
   e. Management

11

Part I

Financial Statement Analysis and Accounting

Chapter 2

The Generation of Accounting Data for Statement Purposes

Financial decision making requires a broad array of data, including much that is nonfinancial—economic, social, political, and legal information, for example. However, the most important quantitative data used by financial decision makers in a business enterprise are the financial data presented in the enterprise's financial accounting reports—its balance sheet, income statement, retained earnings statement, and sources and uses of funds statement.

The importance of those statements can be measured by the frequency of their use both by insiders and by interested outside parties. Owners, creditors, managers, and others spend considerable time reading and analyzing the financial statements of firms in which they are interested, and they demand timely reports on both an interim and an annual (audited) basis.

The reasons for the popularity of the statements are simple. First, the statements are *objective*—they report the results of actual historical events. Second, they present *quantitative* data that can be measured, compared, and manipulated arithmetically. Finally, they are *expressed in dollars*—a common denominator familiar to everyone and especially convenient for comparison with data on other business firms (or any other real or financial asset). In short, financial accounting data, expressed in dollars and presented in the financial statements of business enterprises, provide the basic ingredient—*the raw material*—for business financial decision making of every kind.

This chapter and the next examine the nature of accounting data, the way they are prepared and presented, and the limitations on their use in financial statement analysis.

Accounting data are sometimes spuriously precise—not nearly so accurate as their appearance in formal financial statements makes them appear. But the efforts of the accounting profession over many years have made most of today's financial accounting data, if generated in

15

conformity with generally accepted accounting principles, sufficiently reliable to be useful in financial statement analysis.

However, accounting data cannot be used intelligently in such analysis unless the analyst thoroughly understands the processes through which financial statements are developed and presented. The required level of accounting understanding sometimes transcends the "working knowledge of accounting principles" with which the reader is presumably equipped. Hence the discussion that follows.

The Purpose of Accounting

The basic purpose of accounting is to translate the economic activities of business enterprise into quantitative terms, using the standard monetary unit—the dollar—as the common unit of measure. Business and financial accounting had its formal beginnings in the fourteenth century in response to the needs of entrepreneurs for financial summaries of the results of their activities.[1] Such summaries, to be useful to businesses as going concerns through time, required the development of a more or less formal set of rules for recording (in monetary terms), classifying, and presenting the results of the activities of the business and their cumulative effects on its wealth (capital position) and economic viability. Those rules[2] are still being developed by the accounting profession, in response to changing economic and social circumstances. For example, accountants are now concerned with such problems as how to deal with inflation in a systematic way and how to place a monetary value on the work force of a business enterprise (the problem of valuing "human capital").

But in spite of continual changes in the body of generally accepted accounting principles, the basic purpose of accounting remains constant. That purpose, detailed in *Accounting Research Study No. 1*,[3] may be summarized as follows:

1. To measure the value of the resources held by the accounting entity
2. To present the value of the claims against and the interests held in those resources
3. To reflect all changes in the values of resources, claims, and interests from one period to the next
4. To express those values in monetary terms

---

1. Simple household, institutional, and trading accounts were kept much earlier, of course, as witness the records of the ancient Greeks relating to *oikonomia* (economics), which to them meant managing the affairs of a household.

2. They are, of course, the "generally accepted principles, applied on a basis consistent with that of the preceding year," to which public accounting firms refer when certifying the statements of business enterprises whose accounts they have audited.

3. Maurice Moonitz, "The Basic Postulate of Accounting," *Accounting Research Study No. 1* (New York: American Institute of Certified Public Accountants, 1961).

This purpose is carried out in accordance with accounting rules that govern the *recording, measurement,* and *presentation* of the data. Those rules are classified as accounting *principles* and *conventions* (also called *postulates* or assumptions). In addition, since business enterprise is subject to a wide variety of influences, the rules allow for the exercise of *personal judgment* in the application of the principles and conventions.

RECORDING THE DATA

The procedures for recording accounting data are governed by the principle of double-entry bookkeeping, a system based on the duality of every business transaction. For example, if a business is extended credit by one of its suppliers for the purpose of procuring inventory, it acquires an asset (inventory) in exchange for a claim (accounts payable) against the entity. Moreover, the asset and the claim, or liability, are recorded as equal in value.

Under the double-entry system, all transactions are recorded and then classified under one of four general headings: assets, claims (including liabilities and equities), revenues, and expenses. In general, when an entity acquires an asset, the counterbalancing accounting entry will include one or more of the following:

1. An increase in a liability
2. An addition to the equities (owners' capital)
3. A decline in another asset

The disposition of an asset will result in one or more of the following:

1. A decrease in a liability
2. A deduction from the equities
3. An increase in another asset

Increases or decreases in claims against the entity will be offset by opposite and equal changes in other claims, identical changes in asset accounts, or some combination of the two.

When an entity receives revenue, the offsetting transaction will result in one or more of the following:

1. An increase in assets
2. A decrease in liabilities
3. A ~~decline~~ increase in the equities

Conversely, when the entity incurs an expense, it will also see one or more of the following:

1. A reduction in assets
2. An increase in liabilities
3. An addition to equities

The business activities of the accounting entity are recorded in this manner continually in the form of *journal entries.* Periodically those entries are collected and summarized in one or several *ledgers,* which together contain all the business entity's asset, liability, equity (capital), and income and expense accounts. Those include a *summary income* (expense) or *profit-and-loss* account, into which all the individual income and expense accounts are closed at the end of each accounting period. The net debit (income) or credit (expense) balance in that account—reflecting net profit or loss for the period—is then closed into the appropriate equities (capital) account, which is usually called *retained earnings.*

After thus closing the books at the end of an accounting period, the balances of all the "open" accounts (assets, asset reserve, deferred charge, liability, equity, and deferred credit) and all the accumulated income, expense, and net profit (loss) detail in the profit-and-loss account are transferred to what may be termed the grand summaries—the *financial statements.* In producing such summaries, the accountant must follow established rules that govern the assembly and appropriate display of the data collected.

OBJECTIVES OF ACCOUNTING STANDARDS

The preparation of financial statements from accounting data is governed by rules called accounting *standards,* which include conventions and generally accepted accounting principles. The purpose of the rules is to endow the financial statements and the information they contain with attributes intended to maximize their usefulness to those who must base decisions on them.

Desirable Attributes

Accounting data in the form of financial statements are used by different people for different purposes. Thus the statements should be clear, complete, comprehensive, and of general purpose. Trade creditors, prospective investors, and business managers must be readily able to satisfy their needs for financial information from a single set of statements produced by a firm's accountants. Moreover, the information should be relevant to each; that is, the statements should provide needed data directly and conveniently.

A firm's financial statements should also be objective, that is, free from any influence of concerned individuals or interests. They should be subject to verification through audit and completely reliable. Otherwise their usefulness for financial decision making will be greatly reduced.

A given firm's current financial statements should possess historical, i.e., *intertemporal* comparability with its statements as of earlier dates. They also should be comparable, both currently and historically, with statement data generated for other firms. Such comparability ensures that differences in operating results arise from differences in circumstance, not merely from differences in accounting methods.

Finally, the "current" data should indeed be timely, since the further in time financial information is removed from the events that produced it, the less useful it is to those who wish to rely on it in making financial decisions. The statements should be prepared and distributed to all potential users as soon as possible after the end of the accounting period.

Conventions

The desirable attributes enumerated will not characterize a firm's financial statements unless structure and uniformity are introduced into the process of generating and manipulating the accounting information on which they are based. Accounting *conventions* provide the needed structure and uniformity and are, indeed, the underlying tenets of accounting. Some of the more important of those conventions relate to entity, accounting periods, continuity, conservatism, consistency, and full disclosure.

Entity. Accounting theory assumes that the results of only one major business operation should be shown in one set of financial statements. That is the convention of entity. There are a few traditional exceptions, usually involving a group of related companies engaged in the same type of business operation but legally separate. The majority of such cases involve corporations, and such corporate statements are referred to as *consolidated.* A primary reason for preparing consolidated statements is that the combined data are more meaningful to users than the data from each of the related entities would be.

Accounting Periods. The desirable attributes of timeliness and comparability, which require that accounting data be prepared and presented at frequent and more or less standard intervals, lead to the convention of reporting by accounting period. While comprehensive reports are generally prepared only at annual intervals, more frequent intervals (e.g., quarterly or semiannual) are used for interim reporting.

This convention permits a business year to be defined as a 12-month period other than a calendar year. For example, a wholesale boat dealer in New England may elect to end his business year on September 30, since his inventories and accounts receivable reach their low points on that date. The boat dealer is then better able to determine whether the seasonal expansion in those assets can be "shrunk down" again at a reasonable profit, and his year-end statements become more relevant for purposes of historical comparison.

Continuity. Although financial statements are prepared only periodically, business operations go on continuously. The convention of continuity assumes that those operations will also go on indefinitely; consequently the costs of long-lived assets may properly be spread over the many accounting periods that constitute their useful lives, without regard to current market or liquidation values. Similarly the current

19

(due within one year) portions of long-term liabilities are shown in statements as short-term liabilities, to separate the effect of short-term debts on the liquidity of the firm from the effect of long-term debts on its solvency.

Conservatism. The convention of conservatism is based on the proposition that, given the risks and uncertainties inherent in business operations, it is better to err on the side of caution in estimating the outcomes of future events. In conformity with that convention, accountants do not record income until it is realized but take account of losses as soon as they can reasonably be foreseen. The valuation of inventories at "the lower of cost or market" is a corollary of the convention, stating that the value of inventories may never exceed cost but that any reduction in their current market value must immediately be recognized.

At times the convention of conservatism conflicts with that of consistency, in that gains and losses are not handled in the same manner. In all such cases the convention of conservatism takes precedence, to achieve the desirable attribute of objectivity.

Consistency. The convention of consistency requires that both the presentation of accounting data in financial statements and the underlying methods of generating them be consistent over time to preserve the desirable attribute of intertemporal statement comparability. When a material change in any of the accounting principles employed is made, the fact of the change, its effect, and the reason for making it must be fully and immediately disclosed. There is also an underlying, though sometimes rebuttable, presumption that any change in accounting principles employed is always in the direction of generating better accounting data, providing for fairer presentation of the data, or permitting fuller disclosure.

Full Disclosure. Full disclosure does not mean that the whole mass of accounting data generated by the firm's accountants during the year should be included in the firm's annual (audited) financial statements. It means that sufficient information should be presented in such a way as to avoid misleading anyone using the statements. In other words, not only accountants but also and especially business financial managers, as well as actual and potential investors and creditors, business regulatory agencies, and all others interested in a particular firm, should be able to derive conclusions significant to their own interests from an inspection of the firm's financial statements.

Generally Accepted Accounting Principles

Accounting standards and conventions establish the framework in which the generation and presentation of accounting data occur. So-called generally accepted accounting principles (GAAP) are established within that framework and provide answers to such questions as: How are assets to be properly valued? When are liabilities to be shown as having been incurred? How should the accounting recognition of revenues, expenses, and profits and losses be timed? What formats for the presentation of financial statements are most appropriate?

The principles are not embodied in any authoritative written code, containing mutually exclusive methods of procedures for dealing with accounting data. They exist mostly in the minds of accountants, as "received doctrine" they have come to know during their years of training for and practice of professional accountancy. Changes in the GAAP are communicated to practitioners largely through professional publications.

The generally accepted principles are seldom dogmatic. For example, they often go only so far as to state equally satisfactory alternative methods of recording accounting transactions. Table 2-1 shows a partial list of transactions for which two or more methods are deemed generally acceptable.

The importance of this table for users of financial statements is its implication that the starting point for any statement analysis should be an investigation, if one is possible, of the principles underlying the data presented. The financial analyst should not take such data at full face value before "going behind" them to ascertain whether any data adjustments are required to conform the statements to his particular needs and interests. Sometimes the analyst will have an adequate supply of facts at his disposal to make such an investigation; at other times he will not. At those other times, he will be able to do no more than acknowledge and accept the possible existence of *accounting risk* in his work.

Accounting risk is defined as the inherent risk that conclusions derived from financial statement analysis may be faulty because of the existence of alternative accounting principles and possible variations in *personal judgments* about the application of those alternatives. It raises the possibility that differing interpretations may be given to the same body of data because different generally accepted accounting principles have been used to generate and present it. The analyst cannot avoid that risk; he can only attempt to minimize it, by informing himself as completely as possible about which alternatives have been used in a given situation and keeping the information constantly in mind as he proceeds with his analysis. Admittedly that is no easy task; but several of the chapters that follow deal with the reduction of accounting risk in the analysis of financial statements.

21

Table 2-1

GENERALLY ACCEPTABLE ALTERNATIVE METHODS FOR HANDLING SELECTED ACCOUNTING TRANSACTIONS

Revenue Recognition
  At time of sale
  After sale:
    Completed contract
    Percentage completion
    Instalment sales

Inventory value
  Specific identification
  Average:
    Simple
    Weighted
    Moving
  Last-in, first-out (LIFO)
  First-in, first-out (FIFO)
  Standard cost

Subsidiary operations
  Consolidate
  Do not consolidate:
    Equity basis
    Cost basis

Depreciation
  Straight-line
  Sum-of-years'-digits
  Units of output
  Fixed percentage declining balance
  Cost basis:
    Actual cost
    Replacement cost
    Retirement cost

Business combinations
  Purchase
  Pooling of interests

Intangible assets
  Capitalize cost
  Expense cost

Leases
  Capitalize lease payments
  Expense payments

PRESENTING THE DATA

The efforts of the business accountant in creating and recording the data that measure the economic activities of his firm culminate in the periodic preparation of financial statements. Accounting standards, conventions, and generally accepted principles govern the process leading to statement preparation and also the form and content of the statements, which summarize the results of the firm's economic activities for an accounting period. The following sections deal with each of the three basic statements—the income statement, the balance sheet, and the statement of sources and uses of funds.

The Income Statement

The income statement details the determination of net income; it shows both the total *revenues* realized and all the *costs* incurred in producing those revenues. The income statement format shown in Table 2-2 separates the cost of goods sold from selling and administrative expenses. Deducting both of those from the revenue from sales determines the firm's operating income. The firm may have sources of income other than sales and deductions from income other than cost of sales and selling and administrative expenses. They are generally either unrelated to the normal operations of the business or episodic or both; hence they are grouped separately.

The accountant's function in preparing the income statement is, first, to ascertain the kinds and amounts of revenue received during the period, and then to determine the kinds and amounts of costs that should be deducted from revenue for the period. The costs assigned to the period are regarded as having *expired* and are designated as *expenses* in the income statement. *Unexpired* costs are designated as *assets* on the balance sheet, because they will benefit the operation of the business in future periods. Any excess of revenues over costs—net income—appears on the balance sheet as an addition to retained earnings.

The Balance Sheet

The assets listed in the balance sheets are *deferred* or *unexpired* costs, except for cash and such claims to cash as accounts receivable and investments in securities. The assets representing unexpired costs will eventually appear in the income statements as deductions from revenues

Table 2-2

**INCOME STATEMENT
ST. JOHN PULP AND PAPER CORPORATION
for the years ended December 31, 1978 and 1977**

	1978	*1977*
Net sales	$4,695,833	$5,650,945
Cost of sales	3,689,920	4,121,565
Gross profit	$1,005,913	$1,529,380
Selling and administrative expenses	204,688	212,523
Operating income	$ 801,225	$1,316,857
Other income		
Interest earned	$ 10,315	$ 9,410
Sale of salvage	9,346	20,621
Miscellaneous	17,063	25,070
	$ 36,724	$ 55,101
Other deductions		
Bond interest	$ 33,000	$ 35,000
Loss on equipment sold or retired	39,359	—
Miscellaneous	5,658	3,344
	$ 78,017	$ 38,344
Income before provision for income taxes	$ 759,932	$1,333,614
Income taxes	421,002	698,651
Net income	$ 338,930	$ 634,963
Earnings per share	$.847	$1.587

23

received in future periods. Thus it is important that these deferred charges against future income be properly stated in the balance sheet.

Liabilities are sums owed to creditors. Their values as shown in the balance sheet are fixed as to amount and maturity either by contract, as in the case of notes or bonds payable, or by customary trade practice, as in the case of accounts payable. The capital (stockholders' equity or partnership or proprietor's capital) represents the ownership interest in the business. It comprises the initial investment of the owners plus any reinvested (undistributed) earnings not paid out as dividends.

Table 2-3 illustrates a common form of balance sheet. Items are listed in descending order of liquidity for assets and ascending order of matur-

Table 2-3

BALANCE SHEET
ST. JOHN PULP AND PAPER CORPORATION
December 31, 1978 and 1977

Assets	*1978*	*1977*
Current assets		
Cash	$ 495,522	$ 642,895
Marketable securities, at cost which approximates market	475,000	464,399
Accounts receivable, less allowance for losses—$5,000	141,846	95,990
Inventories	455,640	393,705
Prepaid expenses	84,289	26,748
Total current assets	$1,652,297	$1,623,737
Other assets		
Advances to pulpwood cutters	$ 60,088	$ 51,122
Employees' accounts	16,508	15,128
Cash value of life insurance	62,225	58,000
	$ 138,821	$ 124,250
Property, plant, and equipment		
Land—plant site	$ 26,064	$ 26,064
Timber and timberlands	1,105,414	1,098,006
Buildings	940,123	973,595
Machinery and equipment	3,973,862	4,230,487
Construction	155,359	85,399
	$6,200,822	$6,413,551
Less accumulated depreciation and depletion	2,682,369	2,790,258
	$3,518,453	$3,623,293
Deferred charge (unamortized bond expense)	$ 22,567	$ 24,071
Total Assets	$5,332,138	$5,395,351

Table 2-3

BALANCE SHEET
ST. JOHN PULP AND PAPER CORPORATION
December 31, 1978 and 1977

Continued

Liabilities	*1978*	*1977*
Current liabilities		
Accounts payable	$ 179,701	$ 226,014
Accrued expenses	45,478	99,971
Accrued federal and state income taxes	101,475	152,812
Current maturities of long-term debt	50,000	50,000
Total current liabilities	$ 376,654	$ 528,797
Long-term debt		
First mortgage 4% serial bonds	$ 750,000	$ 800,000
Total Liabilities	$1,126,654	$1,328,797
Stockholders' Equity		
Common stock, $5 par value Authorized: 500,000 shares Issued and outstanding:		
400,000 shares	$2,000,000	$2,000,000
Other paid-in capital	500,000	500,000
Retained earnings	1,705,484	1,566,554
Total Stockholders' equity	$4,205,484	$4,066,554
Total liabilities and Capital	$5,332,138	$5,395,351

ity for liabilities and equity. On the asset side, for example, the most liquid asset, cash, is listed first, followed by the less liquid current assets and then the more permanent fixed assets. On the liabilities side, those liabilities with the shortest maturities are shown first, followed by long-term debt and finally by owners' equity.

The practice of showing assets on the left side of the balance sheet and liabilities and equity accounts on the right is an application of the *accounting equation:*

Assets = Liabilities + Capital (Net Worth)

The balance sheet and the accounting equation on which it is based reflect the proposition that, at any given time, the assets of a business are equal in value to the total funds used to acquire them. The sources of funds are of two types, either external, such as short- and long-term liabilities, or internal (ownership), such as paid-in capital and retained earnings.

The Statement of Sources and Applications of Funds

The statement of sources and applications of funds (sometimes called the statement of changes in financial position or, more colloquially, the "where got-where gone" statement) shows changes in the kinds and amounts of all sources of funds during a given period and details the uses to which all the funds were put. A typical sources and uses of funds statement is shown in Table 2-4. This important statement is discussed more fully in Chapter 10; the basis for its preparation and the reasons for its importance to the financial statement analyst are outlined in Chapters 5 through 7.

Audited and Unaudited Statements

The examination by independent certified public accountants of the records of a firm's business and financial transactions during an accounting period, leading to the independent auditors' certification of the financial statements, is the best assurance available to the financial

Table 2-4

**STATEMENT OF SOURCES AND APPLICATIONS OF FUNDS
ST. JOHN PULP AND PAPER CORPORATION
for the years ended December 31, 1978 and 1977**

	1978	*1977*
Funds provided		
By profits		
Net income	$ 338,930	$ 634,963
Add income charges not requiring funds		
Depreciation	287,720	293,600
Depletion	86,593	97,692
Bond expense amortized	1,504	1,504
Loss on equipment sold	39,359	—
Total funds provided by profits	$ 754,106	$1,027,759
By proceeds from sales of property	19,671	—
Total funds provided	$ 773,777	$1,027,759
Funds applied		
To increase in working capital	$ 180,703	$ 290,738
To increase in other assets	14,571	11,521
To reduction in long-term debt	50,000	50,000
To payment of dividends	200,000	200,000
To purchase of property and equipment	328,503	475,500
Total funds applied	$ 773,777	$1,027,759

statement analyst of the reliability of the data the statements contain. He must always remember, though, that at all times and in all situations the financial statements of a business are primarily the representations of its management. The certified public accountant's task is to review the accounting records and systems of a business, to make such tests and checks of them as he deems appropriate, and finally to state in writing (subject to such qualifications as he may find necessary) whether in his opinion the firm's financial statements have been prepared in conformity with generally accepted accounting principles and fairly present the financial condition of the business on the date of the statements.

THE ACCOUNTANT'S CERTIFICATE

The purpose of an independent certified public accountant's audit of a business firm's records is to enable him to express an opinion on the validity of the firm's financial statements; the form and nature of that opinion should be carefully considered by the financial statement analyst. The CPA's opinion, sometimes called the auditor's certificate, or report, accompanies the financial statements. A firm's independent outside auditor may suggest and probably has suggested to the firm's management how, in his judgment, financial statements should be prepared. But he can only suggest; the final decision must always be made by management. To evaluate the firm's statements properly, therefore, the financial statement analyst should be fully aware of the nature of the CPA-client relationship.

The suggestions of the CPA to management will be based on his analysis of the firm's financial records in the light of generally accepted accounting principles. His opinion will indicate whether or not the firm's statements, as finally prepared, reflect a proper application of those principles. It will set out any reservations he has about the adequacy of his examination and the extent, if any, to which he differs with management about the way statement data are presented. Any such auditor's reservations should be considered by financial statement analysts, who must decide for themselves, in view of all other considerations, whether they are sufficiently material to reflect on the reliability of the statements.

An unqualified opinion by a reputable firm of CPAs is regarded by some financial statement analysts as more significant than a detailed outline of the steps taken in the examination of the statements. Competent, experienced CPAs can obtain a "feel" of statement accuracy from firsthand observation of and familiarity with a business, while the outside analyst would have to be an expert accountant to determine whether the detailed auditing procedures undertaken were sufficient to establish the accuracy of the statements. Accordingly each analyst should learn the meaning of the various forms of accountants' certificates and attempt to determine the relative competence of the CPA firms whose opinions accompany financial statements he is interested in analyzing.

SCOPE OF THE CPA'S EXAMINATION

In their examination of a business firm's books, CPAs seldom make a complete audit of every transaction that has occurred during an accounting period. They base their opinions on a number of more or less standard tests and checks and on their general observations of the firm's accounting methods and systems. Thus, in reviewing an audit report, the statement analyst should be careful to read all comments made by the CPA, particularly those outlining the nature and scope of the methods used to verify the statements. From those comments the analyst may draw his own conclusions as to whether the existence, ownership, and correct valuation of every asset have been reasonably established, the inclusion of all liabilities has been ensured, and the operating results have been satisfactorily verified. Unless the opinion states that a particular procedure has been omitted, the financial statement analyst is generally justified in assuming that reasonable and appropriate tests have been made of the items appearing in statements.

TYPES OF OPINIONS

If, after all tests deemed necessary and appropriate have been made, a CPA feels that a business firm's statements fairly present its current operating results and financial position, he will issue an unqualified, or "clean," opinion, stating that fair presentation has been achieved. From a finanical statement analyst's point of view, that is the best kind of opinion to have attached to any set of statements he is interested in analyzing.

The implication of a CPA's clean opinion for a set of financial statements is that, in his professional judgment, all items appearing in the statement are not only correctly valued but also properly classified. That is a very important implication for the financial statement analyst to understand and keep in mind; it would be a grave mistake to think that CPAs carrying out audits are concerned only with the accuracy of dollar amounts.

For example, in the case of the current asset section of a balance sheet, a CPA's clean opinion may be interpreted as follows:

1. The CPA has made such tests of the item included in current assets as, in his professional judgment, he deemed necessary.
2. On the basis of those tests, he in effect asserts that there is a high probability that the current asset section contains all asset items, including cash, that can reasonably be expected to be used in current operations or converted into cash.
3. The conversion of current assets into cash will occur within the normal operating cycle of the business or at least within one year of the balance sheet date.

On the other hand, if he feels that the statements are not fair representations of the firm's financial position, the CPA will give a negative opinion (deny certification), stating in writing his reasons for doing so. Occurrences of that kind are rare, however; the client seldom wishes his statements to bear a negative opinion. Typically, then, the client will follow the CPA's suggestions for improving accounting methods and statement adequacy so that fair presentation is achieved.

More frequently the CPA will for some reason not perform all the accounting tests he deems necessary for a clean opinion. He will then issue a qualified opinion, identifying the areas left untested. Perhaps he was unable to test the valuation of the ending inventory, for example. If he feels that value is a significant piece of information for statement purposes, he will state that he was unable to test it and therefore cannot say with assurance that it is fairly presented.

UNAUDITED STATEMENTS

Business firms ordinarily prepare interim, unaudited statements for internal management purposes, which are frequently submitted to lending institutions—for example, in connection with requests for credit accommodations—because they contain more recent information than the latest available set of audited statements.

However honest and well-intentioned a business management may be, there is always the strong possibility that it will lean toward the optimistic side in preparing its financial statements for credit purposes. The old generalization that a man's possessions are worth more to him than to anyone else is applicable here. An independent, outside verification of account values is needed to obtain an objective viewpoint.

There is even greater danger that unaudited statements may be misleading and misrepresentative through lack of knowledge of accepted accounting principles and procedures or lack of appreciation of the importance of observing those principles and procedures closely in preparing statements. In all honesty, fixed-asset expenditures may be improperly capitalized, some accrued expenses may not be taken into account in figuring earnings or stating liabilities, and the cost-or-market rule may be improperly applied in valuing inventories.

The financial statement analyst or bank lending officer confronted with a firm's unaudited statements should, if possible, review them very carefully with its management, to determine whether proper accounting procedures were followed in preparing them. In his study of the statements, the analyst should remain aware of possible unconscious or unintentional misrepresentations. In addition, unaudited statements used for external purposes should always be signed ("attested to") by an officer of the firm to establish responsibility for the representations contained in them. For obvious reasons audited statements are always preferable to unaudited ones for purposes of financial statement analysis.

Questions

2-1   Why are accounting data often referred to as the raw material for statement analysis?

2-2   What is the purpose of accounting and what are its objectives?

2-3   List the desirable attributes of financial statements and accounting data.

2-4   What roles do accounting conventions and principles play in achieving the overall objectives of statement analysis?

2-5   What is the entity convention?

2-6   When the conventions of conservatism and consistency are in conflict, which takes precedence and why?

2-7   Does the existence of accounting principles enable the financial statement analyst to avoid having to dig deeply behind the figures presented in the financial statements?

2-8   What is accounting risk?

2-9   What are the three basic financial statements? What information does each contain?

2-10   Of what significance is the accounting equation?

2-11   Briefly outline the three types of auditor's opinion.

2-12   How can an analyst make the best use of unaudited statements when audited financial statements are unavailable?

Chapter 3 Limitations of Accounting Information

The purpose of this chapter is to dispel any illusions of absolute precision that may be attributed to accounting information (and hence financial statement data) by examining several important limitations of such information. These include the use of the dollar as the common unit of measure, the extent to which accountants' personal judgments enter into the data-generation process, constraints imposed by the accounting period convention, and the possibility that false information may creep into the accounting records.

The Dollar as Common Unit of Measure

One of the most important limitations of accounting information arises from the use of the dollar as the basic unit of measure in recording information and preparing financial statements. The need for a common unit of measure is obvious enough; a firm must be able to know and compare the values of its various stocks of assets, sources of funds, and flows of products and materials, and for those purposes some common denominator of value is essential. For performing that function, moreover, the nation's standard monetary unit—the dollar—is the only practical choice. But the immense convenience afforded by its use is subject to a significant disadvantage: the value, that is, the purchasing power, of the dollar has been far from constant; in fact, it has been falling consistently (i.e., prices have been steadily rising). That development has seriously compounded the problem of distinguishing properly between accounting (historical cost) asset values and current market values. (A second, less serious problem stems from a rather widespread but false impression that asset values listed on financial statements represent market values.)

31

VARYING PURCHASING POWER OF THE DOLLAR

All of us know about the changes in price levels (downward, or deflationary and upward, or inflationary) caused by changes in the quantity and hence the value of money. Business firms, like the rest of us, are adversely affected by price-level inflation: they find the prices they pay for everything—raw materials and supplies for manufacturing firms, finished goods inventories for trading concerns, and the price of labor (wages)—constantly increasing. They naturally do what they can to offset cost increases, by trying to increase their cash inflows; and what they can do, besides attempting in all ways to increase their business efficiency (productivity), is to increase the prices of the goods and services they sell. Thus the effects of a long period of steadily rising prices permeate the accounting records of all business enterprises, at best seriously distorting them and at worst completely destroying their usefulness (until adjusted for price changes) for any intertemporal comparison, whether of fixed assets, earnings, or long-term capital.

Fixed Assets

Any firm that began purchasing fixed assets—building and equipment—in periods when asset prices were lower and has continued to acquire such assets over the years will find that its fixed asset account contains a mixture of dollar values, which vary with the different times when assets were acquired. Suppose a firm located in the Southeast constructed a new plant in 1971 that cost $1 million. Five years later it expanded its market to include the Southwest and built a plant there identical in all respects with its Southeastern one except that it cost $1.5 million. A strict nominal cost comparison would indicate that the new plant is half again as large as the old one; but that is obviously not true, since the two are by definition identical. The greatly increased cost of the new plant results solely from an increased price level—a decreased value of the dollar, accounting's "standard" unit of measure.

Similarly, whatever the amount in dollars of the firm's current cash holdings, each dollar of cash held has a different, smaller value than any dollar expended for fixed assets had at the time those assets were acquired.

Earnings and Price Inflation

Inflation has a double-edged effect on earnings. First, unless a firm's earnings grow at a rate at least as high as the inflation rate, the firm will be left with progressively less purchasing power, either to reinvest in the business or to distribute to stockholders as dividends. Second, because of steadily rising costs (inflated values) of new fixed assets, a firm's depreciation allowance also rises steadily. Thus two firms whose sets of fixed assets are identical except that they were acquired at different times and at different costs will report different earnings and generate different cash flows, solely as the result of differences in the timing of fixed asset acquisition.

For example, suppose that 1978 earnings of the two manufacturing plants of the preceding illustration were reported separately, as in Table 3-1. The depreciation for each plant is charged at 10 percent of asset cost, or $100,000 for the Southeast plant and $150,000 for the Southwest plant. Since sales and operating expenses are identical for both plants, both report earnings before depreciation and taxes of $500,000. The tax rate is assumed to be 50 percent.

It can be seen from Table 3-1 that the incremental investment of $1.5 million returned profits of $25,000 less than the 1971 investment of $1.0 million. This inflation-induced reduction in earnings prevents direct comparison of the two regional operations. The different dollar amounts they have invested in identical sets of fixed assets lead to different allowances for depreciation, different amounts of net income, and the apparent paradox that a larger dollar investment in fixed assets yields a smaller net dollar return.

It is possible, though not always easy, to restore interfirm comparability by restating historical balance sheet and income statement information in current dollar terms. Accounting theorists have spent much time and effort developing the methodology for such restatements, but the process is not nearly so widely used as it should be, even by financial statement analysts.

Capital Accounts

The value of long-term capital funds—long-term debt and equity capital—is stated on the balance sheet simply as the number of dollars invested whenever capital funds were acquired. Capital accounts thus resemble fixed-asset accounts in that stated dollar amounts really represent some mixture of dollars of various values (purchasing powers). Since the price level has been rising more or less steadily since the late

Table 3-1

**COMPARISON OF EARNINGS OF THE SOUTHEAST
AND SOUTHWEST PLANTS**

	Southeast Plant	*Southwest Plant*
Earnings before depreciation and taxes	$500,000	$500,000
Depreciation	100,000	150,000
Earnings before taxes	$400,000	$350,000
Taxes, at 50 percent	200,000	175,000
Net income	$200,000	$175,000

1930s, a firm organized in 1950 will have stated initial paid-in capital in terms of the value of the dollar at that time; and its retained earnings will have been taken into its accounts at the steadily declining annual dollar values prevailing for the years 1950 to date, say 1978. If it were to suffer an operating loss in 1979, the nominal amount of that loss would be subtracted from the firm's capital accounts in terms of dollars of lesser "real" value than any of those "accumulated" there. In current dollar terms, any long-established firm's capital accounts, like its fixed-asset accounts, will always tend to be undervalued.

ACCOUNTING VALUES AND MARKET VALUES

The word *value* has many shades of meaning when applied to real or financial assets. The committee on terminology of the American Institute of Certified Public Acountants has given the following definition of value for accounting purposes in the institute's *Accounting Research Bulletin No. 9:*

> Value: As used in accounts signifies the amount at which an item is stated, in accordance with the accounting rules or principles relating to that item. Generally book or balance sheet values (using the word "value" in this sense) represent cost to the accounting unit or some modification thereof; but sometimes they are determined in other ways, as for instance on the basis of market values or cost of replacement, in which case the basis should be indicated in financial statements.

The value of any item given on the balance sheet of a business firm must be in terms of dollars, but that value is assigned with the accounting rule judged by the accountant to be most appropriate for that particular item under the circumstances. Accounting value is therefore hardly a definitive concept. Morever, it may bear little relation to other definitions of value used in business.

To illustrate, a building owned by a business may have many different types of values, depending on the point of view used in establishing its value. For example, the building has an accounting value based on historical cost—its original cost, less depreciation to date, plus any capitalized expenditures made to increase its usefulness. It has a market value—the price it would currently bring if sold—and an assessed value for local property tax purposes. The building also has a replacement value, the cost of reproducing it if it were destroyed by fire, for example. This might but need not equal its current market value.

Likewise the going concern value of a whole firm may differ from its net worth (net asset value). It is the capitalized value of future earnings that is purchased when a firm is sold; and usually, when a firm's net earnings are capitalized at an appropriate interest rate, the value obtained will exceed the firm's net asset value. There are several reasons for this. First, as noted, net assets are shown in the balance sheet at historical costs; hence net worth is understated in current dollar terms. Second, in a going concern the factors of production—land, labor, capital, and management—have been assembled and combined into a profitable operation, but only land and capital—the firm's accounting assets—are shown on its balance sheet.

Conversely, and obviously, if a going concern "stops going" (i.e., if its net earnings become net losses), its market value will decline correspondingly, possibly below the market value of its net assets or even below their historical cost. The market value of a total enterprise simply cannot be ascertained from inspecting its balance sheet, which contains only vague clues to its future earnings prospects.

Use of Accounting Judgment

The personal judgments exercised by accountants in generating accounting information for use in business financial statements should always be taken into account in analyzing such statements. Although the accounting procedures employed in statement preparations are subject to the standards and conventions defining generally accepted accounting principles, the accountant has considerable latitude in selecting from among them the particular ones he considers applicable under various sets of circumstances. And their income-level and asset-valuation implications will differ from those of others he might have chosen. A few illustrations may make this point clearer.

VALUATION OF INVENTORIES

The accountant is free to select from any one of several "generally accepted" methods of valuing inventories. The two most important methods are first-in, first-out (FIFO) and last-in, first-out (LIFO). Inventories valued on the FIFO basis when acquired may nevertheless be valued at the "lower of cost or market" value for balance sheet presentation. LIFO inventories are always carried at cost.

The difference between FIFO and LIFO can be illustrated by considering as inventory a pile of coal. If newly purchased coal is piled on top and coal sold is taken from the bottom, we have a typical case of FIFO; the coal first purchased is the coal first sold, and what remains consists of the most recent purchases. But if the coal sold comes from the top of the pile, a LIFO situation results: the last coal purchased is the first coal sold, and what remains consists of the least recent purchases.

In a period of rising prices, the use of FIFO marks up old inventories when they are sold at current market prices, increasing earnings by an "inventory profit" factor. Under LIFO, however, this inventory profit is not realized; both earnings and inventory values are lower, since current purchases of inventories are sold at current prices.

35

ALLOWANCES FOR BAD DEBTS

Accountants' judgments may also differ with regard to estimating allowances for doubtful accounts—bad debts—the valuation reserves applied against accounts receivable. Generally accepted accounting principles prescribe historical bad debt loss rates as the basis for estimating future bad debt losses. But specific methods of calculating historical rates are not prescribed, and significant variations from historical loss patterns are permissible under varying economic conditions. Bad debt loss rates used to establish "appropriate" allowances for doubtful accounts may not always be historical, therefore; they may reflect accountants' expectations about future economic conditions. Net income level and accounts receivable values will naturally differ according to whether past or expected future bad debt loss rates are employed.

DEPRECIATION OF FIXED ASSETS

Accounting principles permit accountants to use either *constant* or one of several *accelerated* rates of depreciation on fixed assets. The accountants' exercise of their choice among acceptable methods of depreciation obviously affects both income levels and the balance sheet values of depreciable fixed assets.

In addition to permitting the exercise of accounting judgment in the selection of depreciation methods, accounting principles further allow (1) the use of values other than original cost in calculating periodic depreciation charges; (2) discretion in the choice of time period (asset life) over which an asset's depreciable value is to be recovered; and (3) use of one depreciation method for income-tax purposes and another in published financial statements.

The Accounting Period

The so-called accounting period convention, requiring the preparation and presentation of financial statements at frequent and more or less standard intervals, may sometimes limit the usefulness of accounting data for financial statement analysts.

For example, the standard reporting period for audited statements is 12 months (not necessarily a calendar year, however; a fiscal year may be used). When a firm's operating cycle coincides at least roughly with a period of such length, a 12-month reporting basis yields generally satisfactory results. Some industries, however—commercial construction, shipbuilding, whiskey distilling, for example—have operating cycles longer than 12 months. For them, therefore, specialized accounting and reporting methods and techniques, such as percentage-of-completion accounting for long-term contracts, have had to be devised. Otherwise firms in such industries could not conform to a 12-month accounting period convention.

Because they use specialized methods and techniques, however, these firms' financial statements are different and will appear "strange" to financial statement analysts unaccustomed to dealing with them. They are; and only by acquiring a full understanding of their unusual characteristics can the analyst hope to interpret them correctly.

STATEMENT DATES

Business firms are free to select the beginning and ending points of their 12-month accounting periods, subject only to: (1) the practical consideration that their published reports reflect as favorably as possible on the firm's financial condition; and (2) the accounting convention of consistency, which requires that the data represented in the statements be free from such inconsistencies as might be introduced in a seasonal firm, for instance, by changing accounting periods and hence reporting dates.

The general constraints do not really bear on the problem of statement comparability between otherwise similar firms that happen to have accounting periods ending on different dates. Nor do they at all address the problem of calculating industry norms—averages for all firms in an industry, with which individual firm data may be compared—since they leave open the possibility that the firms in an industry may be using different accounting periods and statement dates.

False Statements

When an analyst receives a set of audited financial statements for review, he may generally assume that they provide a true picture of the firm's current financial position and the financial results of its most recent operations. Sometimes, however, though fortunately rarely, such an assumption may prove to be unwarranted. In a few instances, a firm's accounting records may have been doctored, either to conceal defalcation or to delineate a more favorable financial condition for the firm than its management has actually been able to achieve.

The analyst cannot usually detect the presence of false or intentionally misleading data. His general assumption of reliability for a firm's financial statements rests on his belief in the integrity of the firm's management and in the expertise of the outside accountants who audited the firm's books. He need not suspect fraud every time a questionable statement item catches his eye. But neither should he forget that embezzlers and other swindlers do exist in the business community, albeit in small numbers, or that basically honest business managers, under the pressure of circumstances, sometimes feel compelled to practice financial deception.

Nevertheless, financial statement analysis is not detective work. Neither, for that matter, are the careful audits of business financial records performed periodically by independent CPAs. Such audits are not conducted on the premise that they are expected to uncover fraud; sometimes they do, but unexpectedly. And proper financial statement analysis proceeds from a similar premise: fraud is not what the financial statement analyst is looking for; it is, in fact, what he is least likely to find.

Questions

3-1 List some of the more important limitations of accounting data relative to financial statement analysis.

3-2 What are the advantages and the disadvantages of using the dollar as the common unit of accounting measure?

3-3 How may accounting value be defined when applied to assets listed on a balance sheet?

3-4 How can an accountant's personal judgment distort the factual basis of accounting data? Give two examples.

3-5 What kinds of problems does the use of the accounting period convention pose for a financial statement analyst?

3-6 With how much confidence can an analyst employ the figures in audited financial statements?

Chapter 4

Financial Statement Analysis: An Overview

This chapter presents general guidelines for financial statement analysis and a survey of the principal analytical tools. These are fitting subjects with which to conclude the discussion of financial statement analysis and accounting, and their presentation here prepares the reader for the more detailed discussions in the chapters that follow.

General Guidelines For Financial Statement Analysis

The process of financial statement analysis encompasses four sequential activities:

1. Definition of analytical objectives
2. Assembly of relevant data
3. Analysis of data
4. Interpretation of results

Since the activities are sequential, a proper performance in each is essential to complete analytical success. The following sections examine the constituents of proper performance in each area.

DEFINITION OF ANALYTICAL OBJECTIVES

The first task the financial statement analyst must perform is to develop a clear understanding of his reasons for undertaking the analysis (i.e., what information he hopes to derive from it). Armed with this understanding, he can screen both the statement data and the range of analytical techniques for relevancy to his particular purposes and thus avoid unnecessary work.

The three basic objectives of financial statement analysis are: evaluation of statement information, diagnosis of revealed financial problems, and forecasting of future trends in statement data. Let us consider the case of a commercial bank credit analyst working in support of his institution's commercial lending function, as he seeks those objectives through analysis of the financial statements of a prospective borrowing customer. On the basis of his evaluation, supplemented by his diagnostic conclusions about the severity of and the remedies for any financial problems revealed, he must forecast whether a given loan request, if granted, will yield a "bankable" loan—one that will be repaid as scheduled. Furthermore, he must be prepared to justify his prediction by stating explicitly the degree of confidence he has in it. He cannot do that without identifying all the factors influencing his decision and the relative significance of each. Such concrete results will flow only from a well-structured decision-making process, which is possible only if its objectives are clearly understood.

Bank credit analysts know that, while successful retirement of short-term, seasonal loans (which generate their own repayment) depends primarily on the borrowing firm's sound current financial condition, the successful retirement of intermediate-term ("term") loans depends on the adequacy of anticipated future earnings and cash flows. Those cash flows arise primarily from normal business operations—business management's actions within its market environment. The bank credit analyst must know the future operating plans and estimated results of a firm seeking a term loan before he can predict future earnings and cash flows.[1]

Given those plans and estimates, future earning power remains a function of management's competence in using the firm's assets and adjusting the firm to its environment so that its plans will be successfully carried out. In the short run at least, cash flows depend on the nature of the business and the character, quality, and volume of assets employed, as well as on earning power. Thus the nature and size of the assets are also important elements in the bank's term loan decision, not least because asset pledges offer banks an element of protection against loss when term-borrowing customers face insolvency.

For a commercial bank credit analyst involved in commercial lending operations, then, *determination of ability to pay* is the overriding objective for which analysis of potential borrowers' financial statements is undertaken. Requests for short-term, self-liquidating credits may require no more than a review of current financial condition, to determine whether the ability to repay exists. Determining a potential term borrower's ability to pay out of anticipated future income requires a much more complex analytical process, one involving access to information not contained in the financial statements.

But the more complex process is much more characteristic than the simpler one of the work of financial statement analysts, as is evidenced

---

1. Ordinarily such information must be included in the term loan application and is automatically carried to the borrower's credit file.

by the requirements for successful analysis in such diverse areas as long-term lending, corporate security evaluation, and the internal management of business enterprise in general. But while the information being sought may be different (i.e., the stated objectives of the analyses may not be the same), the analytical techniques are highly standardized, and the analytical focus is generally on one or more of the following, sometimes overlapping areas of analytical interest: short-term liquidity and solvency, funds flow analysis, operating performance, long-term financial strength, and efficiency of asset utilization.[2]

ASSEMBLY OF RELEVANT DATA

With the objective(s) of the analysis established and the specific areas of inquiry defined, the analyst will know what data he needs to tell him what he wants to know. His information requirements depend, of course, on the particular analysis being performed.

Let us look at our bank credit analyst again, now attempting to assess a potential business borrower's ability to service and repay a term loan. In addition to past and current audited financial statements and any more recent unaudited interim statements, he will ordinarily request the borrowing firm to provide him with its projections of future operating results and the assumptions underlying these projections.

The analyst may wish to supplement the financial information supplied by the borrowing firm. A visit to the prospective borrower's place of business is often a helpful way of obtaining insight into a company's business practices and operating efficiency. And there are, of course, other means of obtaining information. The analyst may consult the company's creditors, its other banks of account, its outside accountants, its customers, and other firms in the same line of business. He may refer to reports of mercantile agencies (Dun and Bradstreet and others) and trade reports furnished by such groups as the National Association of Credit Men. Public records are also available to determine the recorded ownership of assets and the size and nature of recorded liens, judgments, and mortgages.

Information obtained through those channels does not supplant that provided by the firm itself but may provide a valuable supplement to it, even if it merely confirms what has already been learned from the potential borrower.

ANALYSIS OF DATA; INTERPRETATION OF RESULTS

Once having assembled all the information he deems necessary, the financial statement analyst can proceed to analyze and interpret it.

---

2. Each of these is considered at length in Part IV, "The Technique of Financial Statement Analysis."

Suppose that he is the bank credit analyst of our earlier illustration, seeking to judge the anticipated future income (ability to service and retire a term loan) of a potential borrower. He will project the annual results of the firm's operations over the period of time required to service and retire the loan (eight to ten years) and prepare a set of pro forma financial statements that will reflect the expected results of the firm's operations during the period and show its financial position at the end.

Tools of Statement Analysis

This introductory discussion of financial statement analysis concludes with a brief description of the various analytical tools it employs. Those tools are discussed much more extensively in Part III.[3] Here a bird's-eye view will suffice. Those treated include ratio analysis, comparative financial statements, sources and uses of funds statements, statements of variation in net income, cash budgets, and pro forma statements.

RATIO ANALYSIS

Ratio analysis involves the selection, computation, and interpretation of certain relationships between balance sheet and income statement items at a given time. The ratios are computed because they may illuminate the current operating results and the financial position of a firm. But ratio analysis, though it may yield interesting and useful analytical results, constitutes only the beginning of a complete financial statement analysis.

Ratio analysis is an excellent tool for locating some kinds of current operating problems that may, for example, be creating excessive needs for cash or otherwise reducing financial operating efficiency. It alone cannot always locate the *source* of such problems, however, or even determine their precise magnitudes. That is why it can be only an analytical first step and why additional steps must follow it.

COMPARATIVE FINANCIAL STATEMENTS

Ratio analysis compares selected balance sheet and income statement items. It is also possible to compare entire balance sheets and income statements intertemporally for the same firm, currently for different firms, or for a given firm and industry averages. Such comparisons reveal differences to be explained in major groups of accounts—assets, liability, net worth, revenue, and expense accounts. The explanations lie in the differences in individual accounts in each of the major groups.

An easy way to perceive these differences is to construct *common-size*

---

3. Part III is devoted exclusively to them.

statements, by reducing each statement item to an appropriate percentage—of total assets (liabilities and net worth) for asset, liability, and equity items; of sales (or other principal revenue source) for each income and expense account. The common sizing of financial statements standardizes them with respect to enterprise size and operating scale and permits direct comparison of the statements of large and small enterprises.

SOURCES AND USES OF FUNDS STATEMENTS

Another form of comparative statement analysis involves the preparation of sources and uses of funds statements. These use current income statement information in combination with data showing *changes* in balance sheet accounts during the accounting period covered by the income statements.

Sources and uses of funds statements answer such important questions as why a firm's net income of, say, $10 million as shown on its income statement, does not necessarily improve its cash position by the same amount. It shows how funds accruing to a firm through normal operations, together with any other funds generated internally or externally, have been allocated during a given accounting period between acquisition of additional assets and reduction of current and long-term liabilities.

STATEMENTS OF VARIATION IN NET INCOME

The statement of variation in net income is still another product of comparative statement analysis. In such a statement, all the factors affecting net income are divided into two groups, those decreasing net income and those increasing it. Appropriate values for each factor are determined through comparison of the two most recent income statements. Such statements of factors of increase and decrease in net income are highly useful to a firm's management for internal control purposes. They are also of considerable value to various outsiders—intermediate- and long-term creditors, stockholders, security analysts—with an interest in the firm's current and continuing profitability.

CASH BUDGETS

A cash budget details the estimated cash receipts and disbursements of a business over a budget period (a month, a year). It is a forward-looking tool of financial analysis. Ordinarily it shows a firm's expected cash position for each month of an annual budget period, indicating *whether, when,* and *by how much* a firm's anticipated cash holdings will differ from its estimated cash requirements. Such information provides a basis for prearranging the firm's seasonal line of credit with its bank. Indeed, if a firm does not voluntarily submit a cash budget in support of its seasonal loan request, its banker will almost invariably demand one.

PRO FORMA FINANCIAL STATEMENTS

Cash budgets forecast a firm's cash flows for a given budget period but do not reveal either the firm's entire operating results during the period or the impact of those results on its financial condition at the period's end. To obtain those larger pictures, pro forma statements must be prepared.

The preparation of a pro forma income statement and balance sheet for a given firm for a given future period (e.g., a year) shows the financial statement analyst both *how* and *why* the firm's financial position will be changed if the operating plans of the firm's management are successfully carried out. In those statements and the cash budget for the same period, the financial statement analyst has at his disposal the most complete representation he can possibly obtain both of the firm's "most likely" future financial condition and of its "most likely" path to that position. He may then choose to accept what he sees as adequate or test it further with any of the other analytic methods—ratio analysis, comparative statement analysis, income variation analysis, and sources and uses of funds analysis—before rendering his final judgment.

Summary

This chapter's brief exposition of general guidelines and principal tools of financial statement analysis is intended to provide the reader with a kind of preview of what is to follow in Parts III and IV of the book, which cover the tools and technique of financial statement analysis in greater detail. Preceding that discussion, however, and to make it more meaningful, the three chapters of the next section (Part II, "Financial Statements and Business Funds Flows") relate the arid accounting dollar values listed in a firm's financial statements to the lively and dynamic process of its actual business operations, in order to breathe life into the accounting data and provide the reader with a better feeling for what the accountants and the financial analyst are trying to do.

Questions

4-1 As a prospective analyst-decision maker, why should you follow a standardized approach to statement analysis?

4-2 List the four general steps outlined in the text for financial statement analysis.

4-3 You are a loan officer of a local bank and are approached by an established customer for a short-term loan. Should you formally define your objective before conducting the analysis? What would your objective be?

4-4 Answer question 3 above assuming the customer approached you for a long-term loan.

4-5 List the five areas of interest to financial statement analysts.

4-6 As a bank analyst assessing a firm's ability to repay a loan, what two initial informational choices are available to you?

4-7 From what sources besides the financial statements can an analyst gather information?

4-8 List the tools and methods available for performing the actual statement analysis.

4-9 Is past a good predictor of future when it comes to statement analysis?

Part II

Financial Statements and Business Funds Flow

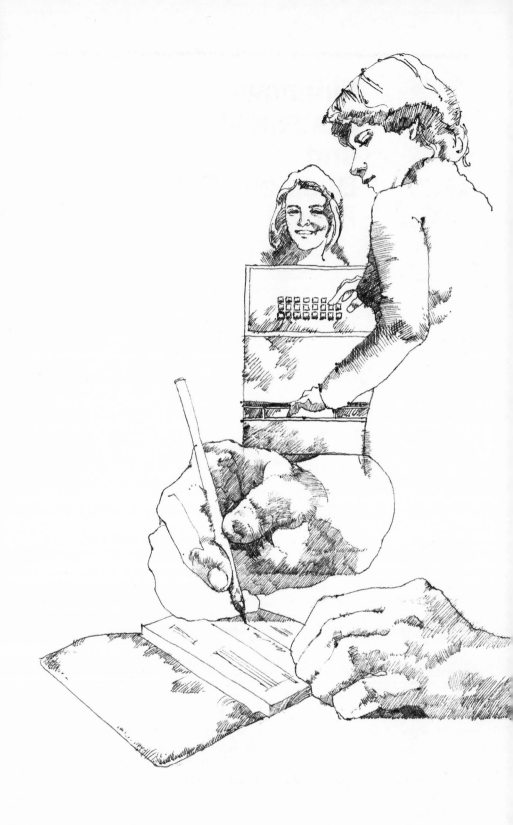

Chapter 5　The Flow of Cash Through the Business Firm

This and the next two chapters examine the nature and characteristics of business cash flows. The information presented serves as an introduction to both the tools and the methods of financial statement analysis. Toward that end, these chapters:

1. graphically portray the flow of funds into and through the business firm,
2. relate that portrayal of cash flow to the traditional form of presenting accounting data (the financial statements), and
3. illustrate how the firm's operating characteristics and its external environment influence business cash flows and hence the firm's financial statements.

The Graphic Approach

The purposes of the graphic approach are, first, to enable the student to *visualize* the flow of funds through a business firm. The figures presented in the financial statements, though more precise than graphic presentations, do not facilitate the conceptualization of the flow nearly so well. Second, the graphic approach better illustrates the *dynamic* nature of business operations. While statement analysis makes constant use of historical and pro forma statements for comparative purposes, the commonly used quarterly, half-yearly, and annual accounting reporting periods emphasize comparison of *static* business records and mask the true dynamic character of the conduct of business. The graphic analysis, however, permits the user to visualize the process as a *continuing* flow. Finally, this mode of presentation permits the student to assess management's role in *adjusting* cash flows, in anticipation of internally or externally induced changes in business conditions or in response to the financial problems that invariably arise in the life of a business firm.

In simple terms the graphic approach portrays the flow of cash

49

through the business as the process of converting cash into noncash assets and back into cash again. That process takes place on a continuous basis in almost all business firms. It is depicted here as a circular flow—without a beginning or end—and is characterized as capital, or funds, *circulating* between related sets of assets and liabilities. This description of funds flow is a little oversimplified, because there are so many routes over which a dollar may travel and so many breaks in the flow through which it may leak out and be lost forever to the business. Nonetheless, the concept of a circular flow is useful; along with certain refinements, it is used here to facilitate the presentation of a rather complex subject.

Circular Flows of Cash

If the circular flow of each dollar through a business could be timed, a wide range of observations would be recorded. Some dollars would take only a few days to return to the form of cash after being converted into some noncash asset; others would take many years to complete the cycle. The dollars that return in the shortest period (within one year) are generally referred to as *working capital*, and the route they take through the business is described as the *short cycle*.

The short cycle involves only current assets, which are made up of cash and all the assets that will be completely converted into cash within the normal operating cycle of the business, generally one year. They include inventories, accounts receivable, short-term investments, and certain prepaid expenses. Those assets are constantly being extinguished and renewed in the conversion process. For example, as inventory is sold, it ceases to exist as inventory and becomes either cash or accounts receivable. However, the aggregate amount of inventories does not change significantly since the firm continues to convert cash into inventories to replace those sold. Hence the *stocks* of current assets remain fairly constant under normal conditions while the flows of funds between related asset stocks continues at constant or changing rates.

The conversion of the cash invested in longer-lived (fixed) assets back to cash again takes longer than one year. This process is termed the *long cycle*. The fixed assets involved in the long cycle are buildings, machinery, office fixtures, vehicles, and so forth. They may be defined as assets that will not be completely used up or converted into cash in the ordinary course of business within one year.

Most kinds of fixed assets are partially converted into cash within one year, but the overall process of conversion generally takes many years. A manufacturing firm may expect that it will sell its entire inventory of finished goods in two to six months but knows that it will take several years to recover the cost of equipment purchased and used to manufacture that inventory. The costs of fixed assets are recovered by setting selling prices high enough to cover all costs—*including depreciation expense*—charged against current income. Here too stocks of assets remain fairly constant, rising when new equipment is purchased and falling relatively slowly under other circumstances. And cash flows generated through noncash depreciation charges against income provide for a constant conversion of fixed assets into cash—then back into fixed assets—for the profitable firm.

RELATIONSHIP TO THE FINANCIAL STATEMENTS

When the accountant closes the books of a firm, he measures the stocks of assets and liabilities and reports them in the balance sheet. He also measures the flows of cash and reports them in the income statement and the sources and uses of funds statement. The cash flow diagrams in this section of the book are merely graphic and dynamic portrayals of the three basic financial statements. The stocks are graphically portrayed as reservoirs or pools of cash that rise and fall as cash flows in and out of them. The flows of cash between related assets and liabilities are depicted as being carried through connecting pipes. The accountant must prepare three statements to reveal the information on the entire status and operating results of the business that is contained in one cash flow diagram. The following sections present the two basic components of the complete cash flow cycle—the short and long cycles—as separate cycles purely for expository purposes. Those component parts are then assembled into a diagram representing the complete cash flow of a manufacturing firm.

THE SHORT CYCLE: CURRENT ASSETS

Current assets were formerly called *circulating assets* to emphasize that such assets continually change form. They are associated with the short cycle, and the cash flow through them illustrated in Figure 5-1 is the conversion of cash into raw materials. In other words, the level of cash in the cash reservoir is drawn down by an outflow of cash through the purchases pipe as it flows into, and raises the level of cash in, the raw materials reservoir. The flow continues out of raw materials and pauses in work in process until the raw materials are converted into finished goods. The length of the pause is determined by the technology involved in the manufacturing process. The cash flow builds up in the finished goods inventory until that inventory is sold and thus converted either directly into cash or into accounts receivable. The buildup of cash flowing through the credit sales pipe remains in accounts receivable for the length of the credit period (or longer, if the firm's customers fail to pay on time). Upon collection of the receivables, the cash flows out of that reservoir and back into cash, where it started from.

This description depicts a lumpy flow of cash through the firm's assets, the levels in the several reservoirs rising and falling as cash flows through the business. In reality, the flow is smooth, in that cash flowing out of each reservoir is replaced almost simultaneously by cash flowing in. The cash in the asset reservoirs remains fairly constant at levels determined either by technology (as in work-in-process inventories) or policy (as in accounts receivable). Raw materials and finished goods inventories are maintained high enough to ensure steady flows into the manufacturing process and the marketplace respectively. An interruption in either flow is generally costly to the business through lost production or lost sales.

Let us examine the cash flow of a hypothetical firm, using Figure 5-1 to help visualize both the levels of the individual asset accounts and the rates at which cash flows between them. We will assume that the firm is new and is having difficulty keeping up with the demand for its product.

Figure 5-1

THE SHORT CYCLE: CASH FLOW THROUGH THE CURRENT ASSETS OF A MANUFACTURING FIRM

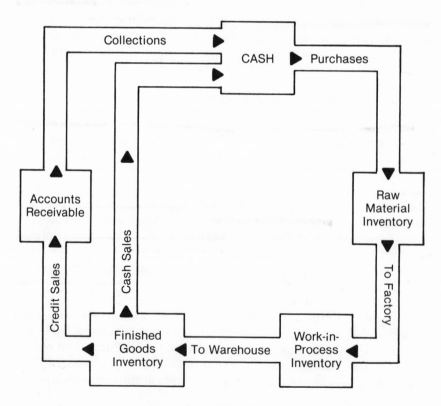

Because it is new, its suppliers demand cash payment for raw materials purchased, and it cannot raise additional cash from other sources; so it must work with minimum levels of raw materials and finished goods. It takes 10 days to manufacture its product and collects its receivables in 20 days after shipment; it thus takes 30 days for the firm to complete one cash flow cycle, from the stock of cash required to purchase raw materials to the point at which the cash is recovered from the collection of accounts receivable. Finally, let us ignore the existence of profits.[1]

To achieve a higher rate of sales, the firm must increase both its total production and the rate of cash flowing through all its assets. In terms of Figure 5-1, the level of the work-in-process reservoir must grow (since technology has fixed the production time at 10 days), to increase the supply of goods available for sale. The firm's only source of cash, however, is accounts receivable. If the level in the receivables reservoir can be reduced—by asking the firm's customers to pay more promptly, for example—the cash thus freed can be used to increase production and hence the rate of the circular flow of cash. When its customers pay more promptly (say, in 10 instead of 20 days), production can increase. However, because of the greater rate of sales, the level of the accounts receivable reservoir will not be cut in half: it will fall by an amount equal to the increase in the work-in-process inventory, and the cash flow cycle will be completed in less than 30 days. In other words, the firm now sells a greater volume of goods per period without any increase in available cash: it is using its assets more efficiently.

This example reveals the importance of the relation between stocks of assets and their associated cash flows in measuring business activity and efficiency. Later chapters show how these measurements can be obtained directly from the financial statements; here let us continue to develop the graphic analysis.

THE SHORT CYCLE: ADDING SOURCES OF FUNDS

Figure 5-1 presents the short cycle in its most basic form. The diagram and the example based on it are hardly realistic presentations of business cash flow, however, because they depict only the *uses* of cash and none of its *sources*. It is obvious that businesses often run short of cash; when they do, they often rely on banks or trade creditors for their temporary cash needs and on the sale of long-term securities for their permanent needs.

In addition, Figure 5-1 ignores the flows of cash associated with the payment of operating expenses (i.e., wages, utilities, supplies, and other manufacturing costs) and selling and administrative expenses. Those expenses are added to the cost of raw materials (along with some other

---

1. The cash flows available from profits, new equity funds, and long- and short-term debt are introduced in later sections of this chapter.

costs) in determining the selling price of finished goods. The short cycle in its expanded form is presented in Figure 5-2.

The cash flow of a manufacturing firm, as shown in Figure 5-2, is slightly more complicated than that of a mercantile or service firm. In a retail clothing store, for example, the inventory is purchased in an already salable form; consequently there are no processing costs and only one kind of inventory instead of three. In a service firm, such as an accounting firm, there may be no salable inventory and therefore no need for trade credit or raw materials purchases. The flow consists simply of a cash requirement for operations that flows directly into the

Figure 5-2

EXPANDED SHORT-CYCLE CASH FLOW OF A MANUFACTURING FIRM

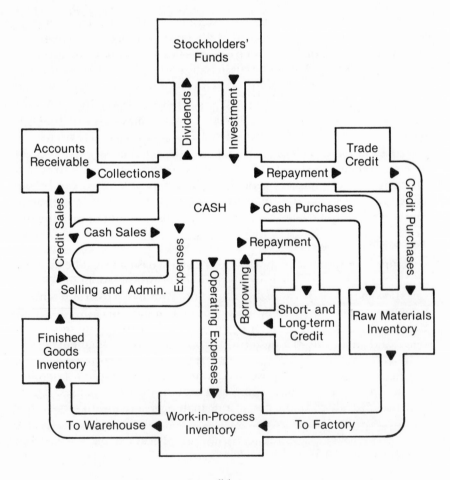

cash sales and credit sales pipes in the same way that selling and administrative expenses do in Figure 5-2. The stockholders' funds and the long- and short-term credit flows remain as shown in the figure, however.

Continuing with our previous example, let us assume that the firm finds a supplier willing to extend it credit on the purchase of raw materials. The firm can increase production by shifting its purchases to the new supplier and need not tighten the terms under which it extends credit to its customers. In terms of Figure 5-2, the firm can increase accounts receivable and all three inventories to the higher levels required to support the higher rate of sales, all without experiencing a commensurate decline in cash. The trade credit reservoir will inject a sufficient amount of cash flow into the system to enable it to grow; however, the trade credit must be repaid in cash within the time specified by the creditor. If the firm does not repay on time, it may lose its source of credit and raw materials and have to reduce its rate of sales to the former level in order to survive. The same effect can be obtained by injecting cash into the system through the short-term credit reservoir or stockholders' funds.

After a firm increases its sales, obtaining a balance in the circular cash flow is complicated by the need to increase the rates of flow through both the operating expense and the selling and administrative expense pipes. Thus the injection of trade credit funds may not be sufficient to permit the firm to grow at the desired rate. If the firm's cash reserve is not large enough to pay for the increased operating and selling expenses over the 30-day cash flow cycle, the firm will have to supplement its cash balance by borrowing or reducing the length of time its receivables are outstanding.

The relations between the flows of cash stocks of assets and the rate of sales must be comprehended fully, because they are at the heart of financial statement analysis. Stocks refer to the amount of cash the firm has invested in an asset account at a particular time. These stocks are represented by balance sheet accounts. The flows are represented by the revenue and expense accounts in the firm's income statement and by the funds flows in the statement of sources and uses of funds. Either flows or stocks by themselves will provide an incomplete description of the firm's activities and its size. For instance, an income statement indicates the value of the goods sold, the cost of the raw materials, labor, and other factors that have gone into producing those goods, and the amount of profit earned. However, those data alone do not tell much about the efficiency of production or whether the firm can continue to operate much longer. The information given by the income statement combined with that presented in the balance sheet gives a better picture of how well the firm is doing. Additionally, an idea of how well the firm is likely to do in the future can be developed from the stock and flow relationships evidenced in the historical statements. That is the aim of statement analysis.

THE LONG CYCLE

Most of the fixed assets owned by business firms are involved in the process of conversion into cash. The value of the assets is reduced as a result of their use in the production of the firm's goods or services, and the reduction in value is periodically charged against current income as an expense of operations. That expense, *depreciation,* is one the business expects to be able to recover through the sale of its products, just as it expects to recover the cost of the raw materials that go to make up the finished goods. Since fixed assets are not immediately used up in the same way that raw materials are, their costs (their purchase prices) are allocated through depreciation expense to each unit of finished goods produced. In pricing and selling its product, the firm hopes to recapture the immediate cash expenditures connected with its production, such as labor and materials, as well as depreciation, which represents cash that has been expended sometime in the past. The conversion of fixed assets into current assets and finally into cash—the long cycle—is illustrated in Figure 5-3. The conversion of fixed assets *directly* into cash is also shown in the figure, although it is not generally regarded as an operational cash flow.

The long cycle, as its name implies, reflects a slow process. By definition, the complete cycle—from initial investment to complete recovery of the cost of the asset—requires more than one year; however, the rate at which the process takes place varies with the nature of the asset. The costs of buildings are generally recoverable in 25 to 30 years, while the costs of vehicles may be recovered within 3 years. The methods used to determine the rates of recovery—that is, depreciation methods—likewise influence cash flows through the long cycle. The idea is to write off the value of the asset during its "useful life" and to charge the periodic write-offs against *current income.* As long as current income—earnings before taxes and depreciation—is equal to or greater than the charge for depreciation of fixed assets, "cash flows from depreciation" will be equal to the amount of the asset "used up" in the current period. Depreciation, in that sense, may be loosely termed a *source of funds.* As shown in Figure 5-3, the total cost of the fixed assets will be recovered as cash when the long cycle is completed. The following example illustrates this concept.

Abel Manufacturing Corporation's fixed assets are being depreciated at the rate of $10,000 per year. The firm sells strictly on a cash basis. Table 5-1 shows figures from the firm's income statement for 1978.

The company earned $15,000 for the year, but by how much did it increase its bank account balance? Its check stubs revealed total deposits, from sales, of $158,000 and checks written for a total of $133,000, including the tax payment to Uncle Sam. And the ending bank balance exceeded the beginning balance by $25,000, exactly $10,000 more than the

Figure 5-3

THE LONG-CYCLE CASH FLOW OF A MANUFACTURING FIRM

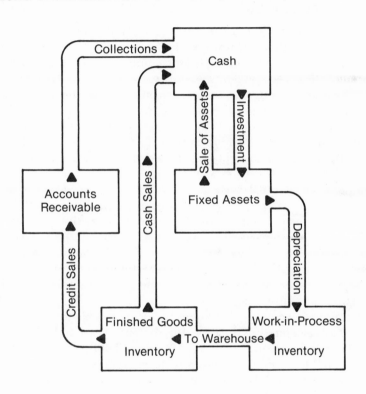

Table 5-1

ABEL MANUFACTURING COMPANY INCOME STATEMENT, 1978

Sales		$158,000
Manufacturing expenses (excluding depreciation)	$96,000	
Selling and administrative expenses	32,000	
Depreciation	10,000	138,000
Earnings before taxes		$20,000
Taxes		5,000
Net income		$ 15,000

net income figure.[2] Since the net income figure is calculated by subtracting *all* expenses from sales and the cash balance by subtracting only *cash
expenditures* from cash sales, the extra $10,000 in the bank results from
deducting depreciation expense from current income without having to
write a check for it. Depreciation is a *noncash expense,* and it gives the appearance of providing funds over and above the net income figure reported on the income statement.

Methods of Depreciation

Cash flows in the long cycle can be greatly affected by the choice of
depreciation methods. Three of the most widely used methods are
straight-line, double declining balance, and sum-of-the-years'-digits.

Straight-line depreciation allows the cost of the asset, less salvage
value, to be spread out evenly over its economic life. The yearly charge is
calculated by subtracting the asset's salvage value from its total initial
cost; the result is then divided by the asset's economic life. For example,
if a machine with a ten-year life costs $110,000 and has a $10,000 salvage
value, the charge for straight-line depreciation in each of the ten years is
($110,000 − $10,000)/10 = $10,000.

Double declining balance is a method of *accelerated depreciation.* It allows the firm to recapture a greater proportion of the cost of the asset in
the early years of the asset's life than is possible with the straight-line
method. The annual rate of depreciation is double the yearly rate of
straight-line depreciation. Unlike the straight-line rate, though, the
double declining balance annual rate is applied to the asset's full purchase price less accumulated depreciation after the initial year; that is,
salvage value is ignored.

The first two years' depreciation under the double declining balance
method is calculated as follows: for the first year, $110,000 × .2 =
$22,000; for the second year, ($110,000 − $22,000) × .2 = $17,600. Although double declining balance will decrease taxes in the early years of
an asset's life as compared to straight-line and thereby increase the cash
flow in the long cycle, in later years straight-line depreciation will provide the higher depreciation charges and hence larger cash flows.

The sum-of-the-years'-digits is another accelerated depreciation
method. The first step in its calculation is to determine the sum of the
years of the asset's life. In the example given, the sum is 55.[3] That
number is used as the denominator in a fraction the numerator of which
is the asset's remaining expected life. The depreciation in the preceding

---

2. It is assumed here that there are no changes in the balance sheet accounts other than
cash, net fixed assets, and profits (income) retained in the business.

3. The following formula is useful in calculating the sum of the years of asset life: $n[(n + 1)/2]$, where n is the life of the asset. In the above example, we get $10[(10 + 1)/2] = 10 \times 11/2 = 10 \times 5.5 = 55$. If the asset's life were 20 years, then $20 \times 21/2 = 20 \times 10.5 = 210$.

example for the first year would be ($110,000 − $10,000) × 10/55 = $18,182; for the second year it would be ($110,000 − $10,000) × 9/55 = $16,364.

Table 5-2 compares the annual depreciation charges for each of the three methods. Note that the accelerated methods lose their cash flow advantages over the straight-line method in the fifth and sixth years in this example.

Table 5-2

**COMPARISON OF DEPRECIATION METHODS
FOR A MACHINE COSTING $110,000 AND HAVING A TEN-YEAR LIFE
AND A SALVAGE VALUE OF $10,000**

Year	Straight-Line	Double Declining Balance	Sum-of-the-Years'-Digits
1	$ 10,000	$22,000	$ 18,182
2	10,000	17,600	16,364
3	10,000	14,080	14,545
4	10,000	11,264	12,727
5	10,000	9,011	10,909
6	10,000	7,209	9,091
7	10,000	5,767	7,273
8	10,000	4,614	5,455
9	10,000	3,691	3,636
10	10,000	$ 2,953	$ 1,818
	$100,000	$98,189	$100,000

Depletion and Amortization

Depending on the nature of the fixed asset, the periodic reduction in its value may be called depreciation, *depletion,* or *amortization.* Depreciation is the name given to the reduction in asset value due to wear and tear in use and to the action of the elements on its physical makeup—quite simply, to the passage of time. Depletion is the term applied to the exhaustion of such natural resources as oil, gas, gravel, and stone. In effect, the land that supports the resources is reduced in value. That is not the same as if the firm depreciated the land it had built a plant on. A new plant can be built on the same land as an earlier one and be as productive, but building a new oil-drilling rig on an oil field whose supply of oil has been depleted would not be lucrative. Therefore, as the resource is extracted from the land, it becomes an inventory of the firm that will be converted into cash as it is sold. Thus the long cycle is applicable here, too.

Finally, amortization, like depreciation, is the name given to the decrease in the value of an asset solely by reason of the passage of time. Depreciation, however, relates to tangible fixed assets, amortization to certain types of intangible assets, such as patents, copyrights, goodwill, and "start-up" or organization cost. The treatment of depletion and amortization in accounting and the analysis of their associated cash flows are very similar to those of depreciation; so their definitions are all that need to be mentioned here.

THE COMPLETE CASH FLOW CYCLE

When Figures 5-2 and 5-3 are merged and the realities of profits, losses, taxes, bad debts, and other minor cash flow losses are taken into account, the complete cash flow cycle of a manufacturing firm can be depicted as in Figure 5-4. This figure appears complex at first glance; however, compared with the actual cash flow of a multiproduct, multiplant corporation that draws on hundreds of trade suppliers and a dozen or so commercial banks for its short-term credit needs, it is quite straightforward. It should provide some insight into the complexities of the complete circular flow of cash through a business. An analysis of the funds flowing along the various paths will show where a buildup of cash occurred (sources of cash); where the firm increased its investments in current or fixed assets (uses of funds); where the volume of the circular flow was increased (sources of cash); and where the volume of the circular flow was decreased and how the reduction occurred (uses of funds). Through the careful analysis of all those changes and their interrelations, the student can form judgments concerning the positive or negative aspects of the decisions reached in the firm during the period. Then on the basis of the past experiences of the company, its projected future performance, and the conditions existing within its economic environment, he will be better able to see what corrective actions may be needed and better able to judge the credit-worthiness of the company.

The Importance of the Graphic Approach

The graphic representation of the cash flow cycle forms the basis for the further discussions of cash flow presented in Chapters 6 and 7. It is important that the nature of the stocks and flows of cash depicted in the figures in this chapter be thoroughly understood. Moreover, the material in Chapters 5 through 7 forms the basis for a thorough comprehension of the methods of financial statement analysis and hence is essential to the efficient and effective application of the tools of analysis.

The concept of cash flow has been introduced in this chapter. The next chapter examines the influence of management policy on the firm's operations, and Chapter 7 examines the effects of the business environ-

Figure 5-4

COMPLETE CASH FLOW OF MANUFACTURING FIRM

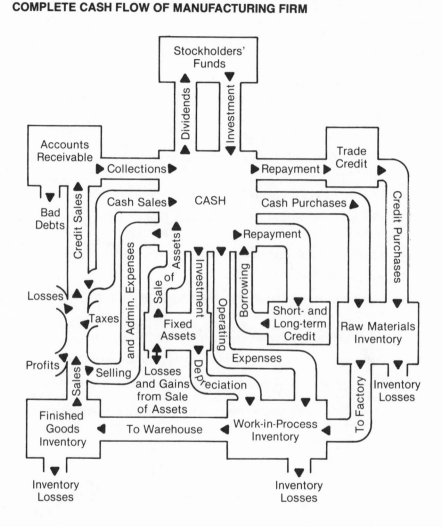

ment on its operational cash flows. Without that fund of background information, the financial condition or performance of a business firm cannot be accurately appraised. In other words, a financial statement analyst must learn to think like a businessman before he can evaluate business performance effectively. The true test of excellence in financial statement analysis is not whether the statement analyst can *detect* or *measure* cash flows but rather how well he can *interpret* the meanings of those trends and flows as they relate to his analytic objectives. The

graphic approach presented here is designed to facilitate the interpretation of the results of statement analysis by providing the analyst with a
visual framework for use in his work.

Questions

5-1   In what way does the graphic portrayal complement the traditional approach of presenting accounting data and the flow of funds through the
business firm? *can visualize flow - illustrates dynamic nature of bus. op.*

5-2   Define the term *working capital.*

5-3   What items are included in a firm's current assets? How are they related to
the short cycle?

5-4   What sources of funds are included in the short cycle?

5-5   Why is the analysis of the circular cash flow of a manufacturing firm
somewhat more complicated than that of a mercantile or service firm?

5-6   What are fixed assets? How are they related to the long cycle?

5-7   What is depreciation? *reduction in asset value due to passage of time*

5-8   Explain the three most common methods of depreciation. How do their
effects on a firm's cash flow differ? *straight line, double declining, sum of the totals*

5-9   In what sense is depreciation a source of funds? *can affect cash flows & net income*

5-10 Distinguish between depreciation, depletion, and amortization.

5-11 The complete cash flow cycle is a graphic portrayal of accounting stocks
and flows. Which of the basic financial statements present accounting
"stocks" and which present the "flows"? How does the diagram in Figure
5-4 represent stocks and flows?

Balance sheet - stocks
Income statement - flows
shows build-up of cash, increased investments, volume increases & reduction

Chapter 6

Management Policy and Cash Flow

This chapter continues the discussion of business cash flow by examining some of the internal factors that cause imbalances in the flows of cash through the firm and hence create situations in which managers must make decisions. The diagrams presented in Chapter 5—especially Figure 5-4—will be helpful in the discussion of this topic. The reader is encouraged to refer to those diagrams as often as necessary.

Causes of Imbalances in the Circular Flow

If, at the end of the year, the cash inflow of a firm balanced the cash outflow exactly, management's job would be greatly simplified. Unfortunately this seldom, if ever, happens. What is more, in most business firms there are times during the year when cash outflows exceed inflows by an amount sufficient to prevent the firm from meeting its regular financial obligations unless management takes steps to secure additional funds. Those imbalances may result either from external causes over which the firm has no control or from management's internal policy decisions. Some examples of external causes are a seasonal demand for the firm's product and the economic environment in which the firm operates. Those influences on cash flows are more fully described in the next chapter.

The internal influences on imbalances, including changes in the firm's manufacturing, purchasing, or selling policies, form the major topic of discussion in this chapter. The chapter examines the characteristics inherent in the cash flows of profitable, unprofitable, growing, and declining firms and discusses the effects of changes in management policy on those flows.

PROFITABLE FIRMS

We will define a profitable business firm as one that has proved financially successful but has no plans for expanding either the scale or the scope of its operations. That kind of firm has a natural tendency to accumulate excess cash. As illustrated in Figure 5-3 in connection with the discussion of depreciation cash flows, each year the firm will accumulate additional cash equal to the amount of its after-tax profit *plus* the charges for depreciation (and depletion and amortization, where applicable). But the accumulation of cash is by no means guaranteed, because cash can be lost from the circular flow even by a business that is operationally and financially sound.

The most common reasons for the loss or removal of cash from the circular flow of a profitable business are the payment of dividends to the owners, the repayment of borrowed funds, and the replacement of fixed assets. Those, for the most part, are proper uses of funds for a well-managed and profitable business.

Other reasons are equally important to the business but not so noticeable because the resulting losses are relatively small. Perhaps the most important, for some firms at least, is the cash outflow resulting from inventory losses caused by theft, deterioration, breakage, or carelessness in the manufacturing process. It is quite possible for a financial statement analyst, realizing the significance of those cash outflows, to suggest ways to prevent them by such means as greater security and tighter quality control. Bad debt losses, easing of accounts receivable collection efforts, and overpurchase of inventories also create drains on cash, as do any losses taken on disposition of fixed assets. These are all substantially controllable by management. It should be recognized that such drains on cash—even if almost imperceptible month by month—can, if unchecked, create serious imbalances in the circular flow of cash.

The only justifiable reasons for the firm to *add* to the amount of cash circulating through the profitable business are (1) to correct imbalances caused by cash drains and (2) to make an expansion of operations possible. The cash added will usually come from borrowing or the sale of additional stock and occasionally from the sale of fixed assets. It is quite normal, however, for the profitable firm to *remove* excess cash from the circular flow (when it exists after the payment of debt service charges and dividends) and invest it in, for example, marketable securities or real estate. It may then convert those nonoperating assets into cash if the circular flow becomes inadequate to support current or expanded operations.

The financial manager of a profitable corporation that has neither the opportunity nor the intention of expanding its operations probably plays a very good game of golf or tennis, since he has ample time to devote to either sport. That is stretching the truth, of course, because executives seldom have so few problems that they can spend most of their time away from their jobs. But compared with the problems that exist in firms that are operating "in the red" or that are growth oriented, the problems of the stable but profitable corporation are indeed few. A look at the cash flow problems of the other kinds of firms will illustrate this point.

UNPROFITABLE FIRMS

We will define the unprofitable firm in the conventional manner as a firm whose operating revenues fail to cover its operating expenses. We will also assume for present purposes that this type of business is not interested in expanding its operations. Firms that operate in the red fall into two groups with respect to their cash flows. The first group consists of firms that add to their cash balances even though they lose money year after year—railroads, airlines, and shipping companies, for example. The reason they can continue operating and even *pay dividends* to their owners is that they usually have high depreciation and amortization charges. Those charges are often very difficult to cover entirely with revenues because, for government-regulated firms, the rates they charge for their services are fixed by law and severely limited by competition. Such firms usually have no trouble covering out-of-pocket expenses, but their noncash charges are only partially covered by sales revenues. Thus they can continue to operate and pay their bills, and the partial coverage of depreciation expense provides for the accumulation of excess cash balances that can be withdrawn from the circular flow. An example will help illustrate how this happens.

Suppose the Bless Shipping Company's depreciation charges total $800,000 per year on its transportation equipment. Its 1977 income statement, shown in Table 6-1, reports a net loss of $300,000 for the year; however, Bless Shipping has covered all its out-of-pocket expenses plus $500,000 of its $800,000 depreciation charge out of revenues. Its balance sheet will show an increase of $500,000 in cash (other things remaining constant), which is provided through the long cash flow cycle. Even though Bless incurred an operating loss, it may have sufficient cash to meet all its financial obligations and still pay dividends.

Table 6-1

BLESS SHIPPING COMPANY INCOME STATEMENT, 1977

Sales		$2,500,000
Deduct: Operating expenses	$1,600,000	
Administrative expenses	400,000	
Depreciation	800,000	
Total expenses		2,800,000
Net loss		(300,000)
Add depreciation		800,000
Net cash provided by operations		$500,000

65

Eventually, however, the loss position of such businesses will cause them to face severe financial problems. That will usually occur when the fixed assets on which the depreciation charges have been based must be replaced. If all the cash generated by the depreciation charges were conserved by the loss firms, it would be inadequate to replace their fixed assets, even if price increases are ignored, because the firms' yearly operating losses would have prevented the complete recovery of the original cost of the assets. For example, if the Bless Shipping Company managed to break even from now on and set aside all the cash flow generated by its depreciation charges, it would come up $300,000 short when it came time to replace its fully depreciated equipment. The firm would need to borrow the difference between the cash on hand and the replacement cost of the asset. Even if that could be arranged, the loan would require higher cash outflows in subsequent years for interest payments and the repayment of the loan principal. The demise of these firms is inevitable unless they can in some way make revenues cover both out-of-pocket and fixed charges and thereby return to a profitable basis of operation.

The second group of unprofitable firms are in a far worse financial condition than the first group. This group consists of business firms that are unable to sell their goods at prices high enough to cover their out-of-pocket expenses, to say nothing of their noncash charges.

Let us revisit Bless Shipping to see how the cash flow of a firm is affected by these operating conditions. Assume that because of higher fuel and labor costs, Bless's operating costs rise to $2.1 million and its administrative costs escalate by $200,000 during 1978. The results of operations at the higher levels of cost are shown in Table 6-2. The firm's cash balance declined by $200,000, and its depreciation charges were not even partially covered by revenues. If such losses continue, the firm must repeatedly pump money into its circular flow in amounts equal to the cash drains being experienced. It will certainly have to look to outside sources of funds for the replacement of fixed assets when that becomes necessary.

Table 6-2

BLESS SHIPPING COMPANY INCOME STATEMENT, 1978

Sales		$2,500,000
Deduct: Operating expenses	$2,100,000	
Administrative expenses	600,000	
Depreciation	800,000	
Total expenses		3,500,000
Net loss		$(1,000,000)
Add depreciation		800,000
Net cash provided by operations		$ (200,000)

Firms in this group of loss corporations generally find it extremely difficult to raise the funds they require to survive because potential lenders do not see how cash can be generated from operations to repay loans. The owners will also be reluctant to contribute more cash to the venture; they will probably begin looking for a profitable corporation that may be interested in purchasing the firm as a *tax loss corporation*. [1] But a firm with significant losses and little hope of being made profitable within a relatively short time will not be very attractive even for that purpose.

In spite of the dismal prospects these unprofitable firms present to the financial statement analyst, they should not be immediately disregarded as hopeless cases because the analyst may be able to diagnose the causes of the cash imbalances. For example, the losses may result from inefficiencies in operations or administration. In our first example, the Bless Shipping Company had only to cut out-of-pocket costs by a little more than $300,000 to return its operations to a profitable basis. Obviously in the second example Bless would need to cut out-of-pocket costs considerably more; but if ways could be found to trim the budget, the firm might eventually begin operating in the black. Exchanging its current stock of transportation equipment for another more fuel-efficient stock might be the answer, in which case a lender might easily be persuaded to extend long-term credit to the firm.

EXPANDING FIRMS

A profitable firm that is rapidly expanding its scale of operations is likely to experience an acute shortage of cash with which to expand its inventories, meet higher operating expenses, and carry the larger quantity of accounts receivable that will be generated out of increased sales. That increase in the volume of the circular flow—the short cycle—is usually accompanied by an expansion in the firm's investment in fixed assets, which intensifies the need for cash during the expansion phase. Not only must the firm keep its existing operations in balance, but it must also seek ways to supplement the circular flow of cash in order to support expansion *and* keep the firm from expanding beyond the cash flows predicted at the new level of production and sales.

The financial manager must first look within the firm for the cash he needs to expand operations. Possible internal sources include the sale of temporary investments and a reduction in the dividends paid to the owners. Efforts may also be made to speed up the collection of accounts

---

1. A profitable corporation may acquire another firm that has a tax loss, operate it as a subsidiary, and present a consolidated tax return that uses the acquired losses to reduce overall corporate income-tax liability. The purchasing corporation, naturally, hopes that the tax savings thus realized will provide a net increase in its cash flow.

receivable and trim inventories through better management. But in spite of these efforts to generate funds from internal sources, the firm will probably need to resort to outside sources of financing.

When outside funding is obtained, the firm must begin balancing the known *future cash outflows* it will incur in servicing the newly acquired debt or equity funds with its expected *future cash inflows* from expanded operations. For example, Figure 5-4, which depicts the complete flow of cash through a manufacturing firm, shows that each external source of funds—stockholders' funds, trade credit, and short- and long-term credit—has a cash drain associated with it. If the cash drain required to repay the long-term credit obtained to finance the firm's expansion exceeds the additional cash inflow the expansion will provide, the firm will experience either a decrease or a slower rate of increase in its circular flow of cash. If that situation continues, the net cash drain due to the expansion that will occur with each cash flow cycle will deplete the firm's cash balance. Or at least the cash drain will keep the balance from increasing at the rate necessary to support the subsequent planned growth of the firm. It should be clear that the financial statement analyst, when examining growth-oriented businesses, must give attention to both present and future cash flows.

One other point deserves consideration: a clear parallel may be drawn between the financial condition of the losing (shrinking) firm and that of the expanding firm. Both experience net cash drains as a result of their operational characteristics, and without proper control both may find themselves in serious financial difficulty as a result of those drains. Clearly, the reasons for their problems are different—one may be termed a "good" trend and the other a "bad" trend—but unless the conditions causing those trends are ameliorated, both firms could fail.

DECLINING FIRMS

The declining firm is defined as one whose product is losing its popularity or becoming obsolete. An example is a subsidiary of an electronics corporation that has supplied the parent firm and other manufacturers with vacuum tubes used in television sets, radios, phonographs, and various types of electronic testing equipment. Its sales began to fall years ago as a result of advances in solid-state electronics that eliminated the need for vacuum tubes in radios and often in electronic devices. It currently is producing at minimum levels for the tube replacement market. What happened to its cash flow as the firm's management began to plan for the orderly contraction of its operation?

As sales began to drop, management reduced raw materials purchases and lowered production by gradually reducing its labor force. Accounts receivable fell in proportion to the decline in sales, and inventories fell as the rates of production and purchases declined. The firm also reduced its marketing effort, and the parent firm began hiring the salesmen and other executives who were willing and able to make the transition. In terms of Figure 5-4, the cash investment in the firm's current assets was reduced, cash outflows for purchases, operating expenses, and general administrative expenses were likewise reduced, and the firm's cash balances rose steadily.

As sales continued to fall, the firm removed some of its equipment from the production process and sold it; it thereby reduced its investment in fixed assets and increased its cash balance even further. Meanwhile, the firm began repaying its borrowed funds with its surplus cash and investing the remainder in marketable securities pending the parent company's decision on the ultimate disposition of the remaining assets.

As sales declined further, the firm's profits disappeared; it could no longer cover depreciation charges and operating expenses out of revenues from sales and investment income. However, its cash balances continued to increase, at a diminished rate, as funds continued to flow in from the liquidation of assets. Finally the parent firm decided to level off production at a point below break-even to maintain a supply of vacuum tubes for its replacement needs and to take advantage of the tax losses the subsidiary was providing. The excess cash built up by the subsidiary was transferred to the parent company, and efforts were made by the subsidiary to become profitable at the new, lower level of operations.

In summary, the declining firm, if properly controlled, will generate cash surpluses until it is no longer able to cover out-of-pocket expenses for operations. At that point the surplus cash should be disposed of, generally in one of two ways. It can be paid to the owners (after the claims of any remaining creditors have been satisfied) in the form of a *liquidating dividend,* or it can be used to enter another line of business in which some measure of success is likely to be achieved.

Changes in Management Policy

Implicit in the preceding discussion of profitable, unprofitable, expanding, and declining firms is the fact that certain management policies remained unchanged as the firm's operational characteristics changed. Although it is convenient to make that assumption for expository purposes, it is not particularly realistic. This final section of the chapter examines how changes in certain management-controlled policies affect cash flows. The cash flow effects of changes in accounts payable, accounts receivable, and research and development policies are examined as representative of many more such management policies.

ACCOUNTS PAYABLE

When a business firm applies for and receives credit from a supplier, it is generally granted the industry's customary credit terms. Those terms may involve a cash discount for prompt payment. For example, a firm may be granted terms of 2,10/net 30 on its credit purchases; that is, if the firm pays within 10 days of the date of the invoice, it may deduct 2 percent from the total invoice as a cash discount. If it cannot pay within the discount period, the face amount of the invoice must be paid by the 30th day.

If a firm that formerly paid its trade credit on the last day of the net period decides to take advantage of the cash discount, its cash balance will fall by an amount equal to 20 days' purchases (30 days minus 10 days times average daily purchases of inventory). If the excess cash is available, cash flows in later periods will increase by the amount of cash outflow saved by taking the discounts on purchases (i.e., profits will increase). If the firm does not have the cash, it may borrow it provided cash flows are adequate to repay the loan without having to miss discounts.

ACCOUNTS RECEIVABLE

The other side of the accounts payable coin is accounts receivable. The firm that extends credit generally does so to maintain its sales volume in the face of competition. Any change it makes in its credit terms will therefore very likely affect its sales volume.

For example, if the firm decides to seek a larger share of its market by lengthening its credit period, say from 30 to 60 days, its cash flow pattern will be altered by two opposing forces. First, by doubling the length of the credit period, the firm will double the size of the receivables arising from sales to its present customers. Any new customers attracted by the more liberal credit terms will also add to the stock of accounts receivable, which will increase more than twofold. Second, the increased rate of sales will increase the rate of collection of accounts receivable, but the firm will have to wait 60 days for that to happen. Moreover, it will see its collection rate fall to near zero for 30 days after the new credit terms go into effect, assuming, of course, that all its customers take immediate advantage of the longer credit period. Thus the firm will starve itself for cash before the new, larger cash flows materialize.

Finally, if the firm is successful in gaining a greater share of the market—that is, if the competition does not match its credit terms—its rate of production, rate of raw materials purchases, and base stock of inventories may all have to increase to keep up with the increased sales rate. Consequently the firm will experience the same cash flow problems as those associated with the *expanding firm.*

RESEARCH AND DEVELOPMENT EXPENDITURES

Research and development (R&D) expenditures are generally classified as general administrative expenses and treated as a *fixed cost* of operations. The benefit to the firm from research and development programs is seldom immediate, and some firms consequently reduce such expenditures when cash is tight and reinstate them when cash flows improve. Other firms behave differently, however, attaching more importance to the impact of those *current* expenditures on *future* cash flows.

When research and development programs are successful, they generally either provide the firm with some competitive edge with respect to existing products or technology or give it a head start on the competition with respect to new products. In either instance, the firm will usually need to make an additional cash investment, generally in fixed assets, before it can achieve the desired results from the new discovery. That, of course, places the firm in the position of being an *expanding firm*. Since the firm intends to lead its competition in the marketplace, it hopes to take on the characteristics of the *profitable firm* as well, with its attendant surplus cash flows. But those future benefits are neither certain nor necessarily immediate; consequently the firm that establishes a research and development program must be willing to commit the necessary cash over time in support of the program. It must also be able to generate sufficient cash, from either internal or external sources, to take full advantage of the fruits of the program. Otherwise the initial cash outlays will be counted as an unnecessary leakage in the circular flow.

Questions

6-1   What is meant by imbalances in the circular flow of funds? Why do such imbalances demand management's immediate attention?

6-2   What kind of cash drains can an analyst find in an operationally and financially sound and profitable firm?

6-3   Why do profitable firms have a tendency to accumulate cash? When would such a firm's management consider injecting more cash into its circular flow?

6-4   Describe the two groups of unprofitable firms. Give an example of each, distinguishing the characteristics of their cash flows by referring to their revenues, costs, and depreciation expenses. How would you make them viable again?

6-5   Why do expanding firms normally experience cash shortages, and what sources of funds are available to alleviate the shortages?

6-6   Why should an analyst pay special attention to both the present and the future cash flows of a growing firm?

6-7   Are there any similarities in the reasons for the typical financial condition experienced by loss firms and growing firms?

71

6-8 What is a declining firm? Trace the implications on cash flows of management's orderly contraction of such a firm's operations.

6-9 Suppose a firm's suppliers begin to offer cash discounts for prompt payment. How would that affect the firm's cash flows?

6-10 Why would management follow a liberal accounts receivable policy? How would instituting such a policy change the firm's cash flow pattern?

6-11 A firm has allocated a larger budget for its research and development program for the current year. How would that action affect its present and future cash flows?

Chapter 7

Business Environment and Cash Flow

What the graphic analysis of cash flow presented in the previous chapters has failed to show explicitly are the complexities added to the circular flow of cash by seasonal, cyclical, and competitive influences. Those influences work primarily through the firm's sales efforts and pricing policies, but they may also have a direct influence over almost any aspect of a firm's operations. When they do, they tend to change the patterns of cash flow considered normal in light of the firm's history. It may be necessary to recommend that appropriate allowances be made in the firm's operations to compensate for such changes.

Seasonal Fluctuations

Wide variations in the cash flows of many businesses occur because of seasonal swings that affect their sales efforts. A firm involved in the production of Christmas tree ornaments is an extreme example. Toy sales likewise peak during the calendar year-end selling period; sales of camping and outdoor sports equipment are highest during the spring and summer. Businesses engaged in the manufacture and sale of products subject to significant seasonal influences have cash flows characterized by periodic surpluses and deficits. By way of contrast, businesses able to produce and sell at constant rates throughout the year find their cash requirements relatively uniform from month to month, other things being equal.

But as almost all financial officers can testify, other things are not usually equal. On the contrary, it seems that "other things" take a devilish kind of pleasure in being unequal, sometimes in the most subtle ways. Therefore it can be said that *all* firms are subject to seasonal influences of one kind or another that have direct effects on their cash flows.

Seasonality in business operations, no matter what the source, requires the financial statement analyst to be very careful in analyzing the relations between the firm's stocks and flows of cash, so that the comparisons give a true description of the firm's financial status and operations. We will examine some of the commoner kinds of seasonal influence to see how they can distort the relation between stocks and flows when the firm is examined at different points in its operating cycle.

SEASONAL SALES

Given the assumption that a firm will find it desirable to produce at a more or less steady pace throughout the year, a decidedly seasonal sales pattern will cause the firm to run short of cash during the period of slack sales and accumulate surpluses of cash immediately after its peak selling period. During the slow season, the firm will pump cash into raw materials and through the operating cost pipe, but the circular flow will stop temporarily in the finished goods inventory. If at that point in the firm's yearly operations, the level of inventory on hand were compared with the cost of goods sold to date, it would appear that the amount of inventory held was too large in proportion to the level of sales. Conversely, if a comparison were made immediately after the firm's peak selling season, when inventory is probably at its lowest level, a stock and flow analysis would lead to the conclusion that the firm's inventory management was extremely efficient, as indicated by the relatively small investment in inventory. Therefore extreme care must be used in interpreting comparisons of the stocks and flows of a firm with a seasonal sales pattern.

The typical pattern of stocks and flows of a seasonal business may be described as follows. When seasonal sales begin to pick up, the finished goods inventory will be converted into accounts receivable, but the cycle will not be completed until after the peak sales period. The buildup of cash surpluses will take place only after the receivables have been collected. At that point, even after repaying its short-term creditors, the firm will usually find itself with a surplus of cash. The cash can be converted into an investment in short-term securities, which will be liquidated during the succeeding seasonal upswing as the need for cash to purchase inventories increases.

It must also be recognized that seasonal businesses require skillful managers. For example, an accurate projection of sales is crucial to seasonal operations. If actual sales fall below management's projections, the firm may find itself holding a high level of slow-moving inventory at year-end, when inventories are supposed to reach minimum levels. Those higher than expected inventories will prevent the completion of the cash conversion process. The firm may thus find it necessary either to finance the higher inventory levels from outside sources or to sell the inventory at low, after-season prices to generate the cash needed to repay trade creditors or bank loans.

SEASONAL PURCHASES

Some businesses are subject to seasonal patterns in the timing of their purchases of raw materials. The tobacco industry is a good example of such a business. Raw tobacco is available on the market for only about three months each year, between July and September, during which the manufacturers must purchase enough to supply their needs for the entire year. Because the consumption of tobacco products remains fairly constant throughout the year, accounts receivable do not fluctuate appreciably, and the conversion of those receivables into cash occurs at a steady rate throughout the year. The cash inflow from the collection of receivables must be allowed to build up in the cash account to provide for investment in raw tobacco when it becomes available. In this kind of seasonality, the firm may have a surplus of cash before its purchases of raw materials, but it may also have a severe cash deficit after those purchases, which must be offset by an inflow of cash from outside sources. The cash flow from the collection of accounts receivable must then replenish the system with a sufficient amount of cash to repay the outside funds and rebuild the cash accounts in anticipation of the next tobacco harvest.

SEASONAL PAYMENTS ON ACCOUNTS

A seasonal pattern most prevalent in firms engaged in retail sales made largely on credit (oil companies, department stores, furniture shops) is associated with the payment habits of consumers. There are four brief periods during the year in which a relatively large volume of consumer spending takes place—just before Easter, during summer vacation periods, just before school starts in the fall, and at Christmas. During those peak periods, numerous families overextend themselves, partly because of the nature of the season (e.g., Christmas) and partly because of the easing of credit terms by retailers as they encourage extensive consumer purchases in order to clear out large inventories. Very often the consumer receives credit from several sources; after reaching his credit limit on each source, he finds himself obligated for much more than he has the ability to repay on the customary credit terms. As a result, he may become selective in the payments he makes afterward until he can catch up.

During postpeak buying periods, retail businesses are likely to experience a drop in their rates of collection of accounts receivable, which increases the number of days it takes the investment in accounts receivable to be converted to cash. Although that can cause a severe cash shortage, it may not be so severe for the period after Christmas. Since sales are at annual highs for many retailers during the Christmas season, the level to which accounts receivable have been increased can overshadow a relatively significant fall in the collection rate. Hence the slowing of cash inflows may not be detected or, if it is, may not matter.

75

But any reduction in the collection rate adversely affects the flow of cash into the firm's cash reservoir. It is because of this seasonality of payments that the analyst must be careful when comparing accounts receivable with sales at different times during the year. If the analysis is conducted quarterly or monthly, certain allowances should be made for the seasonal collection patterns evident in past periods. Management should always strive to shorten the basic short cash flow cycle to ensure the ready availability of cash when needed.

SEASONAL PATTERNS IN THE LABOR FORCE

Summer vacations take a toll on the flow of cash. Most businesses find it difficult to maintain production during the summer months when absenteeism runs high and most employees request their vacations. Even with careful planning, some businesses find it necessary to pay overtime premiums to their employees in order to meet delivery dates, and others hire temporary help who are generally less efficient than the workers they replace. The result, of course, is a greater than normal flow of cash into the work-in-process reservoir through operating expenses during that period.

A number of businesses solve the problem by closing down entirely for some period each year. In that way they give all their employees vacations at one time, except for selected maintenance personnel who can then repair, replace, and otherwise improve the firm's equipment without interfering with production. Many businesses are unable to do that, however, for technological reasons. For example, it takes a basic steel producer about two weeks to heat its massive melting furnaces to the proper temperature or to shut them down without destroying them in the process. Consequently it is uneconomical to close down such an operation for vacations or for any other reason.

Cyclical Fluctuations

Almost all business firms experience some of the effects of the alternate waves of expansion and contraction of economic activity during what is called the *business cycle*. Although such waves have been taking place at least since the eighteenth century, cyclical changes cannot be predicted as precisely as seasonal influences can be measured. Nevertheless, sufficient allowances must be made for these fluctuations so that the firm experiencing their effects will be reasonably well prepared to cope with them.

CLASSIFICATION OF FIRMS

Not all firms respond in the same way to fluctuations in the business cycle. Business firms can be classified according to the effect a change in the business cycle is likely to have on their operations. Four classes of firms have been identified: *growth, cyclical, defensive,* and *cyclical-growth* firms.

Growth firms can be thought of as those that have high growth in earnings; they are often relatively free from the direct effects of the business cycle. Most firms in this class are associated with industries in which a major breakthrough in production or design technology or a major service innovation has just emerged. Recent examples of such industries are those associated with the manufacture and sale of citizen's band radios and mobile homes and those using a marketing strategy based on warehouse retail showrooms.

Cyclical firms are those that are most affected by the business cycle. During expansion they enjoy great prosperity in both sales and asset growth; during contraction they usually suffer the most. This type of firm usually deals with consumer and manufacturer durable goods. The reason for their close association with the peaks and troughs of the business cycle is simply that the purchase of the products they manufacture is considered postponable when business and employment prospects are bad and becomes highly desirable when economic conditions improve.

Defensive firms are those hurt least during a business cycle contraction. This type of industry is associated with the production or processing of goods essential in the lives of most people, such as those related to basic needs for food and shelter.

Cyclical-growth firms have characteristics of both cyclical firms and growth firms. The industries in which they operate are characterized by periods of tremendous growth, followed by periods of stagnation or even decline. This pattern is usually brought about by major changes in technology within the industry.

The business cycle and its effects on the firm's operation can be seen primarily and most dramatically in those firms falling into the *cyclical* class. The student may find it helpful to refer to Figure 5-4 as we discuss that class of firm.

CYCLICALLY SENSITIVE FIRMS

During the contraction phase of the business cycle—recession—the sales of a cyclically sensitive business firm decline. As sales drop, production is cut and purchases of raw materials are curtailed. The outflows of cash for operating expenses and general selling and administrative expenses decrease, as does the amount of cash invested in work in process, finished goods, and eventually accounts receivable. With a reduction in purchases of raw materials, the firm also finds the amount of its outstanding short-term credit decreasing. The firm is supporting a lower level of sales with a lower level of inventory and accounts receivable.

77

Conceivably, the relations between the stocks of, and the cash flows into and out of, receivables and inventory could remain constant in spite of the decrease in sales, leaving the firm initially with a surplus of cash generated by both a reduction in cash outflows for salary and operating expenses and a proportional reduction in its accounts receivable and inventory.

If the recession is expected to last long, the firm may postpone plans to add or replace fixed assets. That will reduce or eliminate another cash outflow (investments in fixed assets), while depreciation allowances continue to contribute to the growth of cash by way of the long cycle. A business may thus give a misleading appearance of financial strength in a period of reduced economic activity.

This description of the contraction phase of the business cycle makes the major assumption that the firm, even with a reduced level of sales, can still cover its out-of-pocket expenses and fixed charges. But note how two firms manufacturing the same product and having the same level of assets, out-of-pocket expenses per unit, and annual depreciation charges may perform in a contraction phase.

Assume that the only difference between the firms is in the way each has financed its operations. Firm A is conservatively operated. Its owners have always tried to limit its reliance on borrowed money. They have $1,000,000 outstanding in long-term debt, carrying an interest rate of 10 percent per year. The creditors receive annual principal payments of $100,000. Firm B is more aggressive than A and has $3,000,000 outstanding in long-term debt, with a 10 percent interest rate and principal repayments of $300,000 per year.

Assume further that both firms have earnings before interest, depreciation, and taxes of $500,000. Table 7-1 presents an operating summary of the results of a recession year. Firm A's expenses include $200,000 depreciation plus $100,000 interest as a result of its long-term debt. At a tax rate of 50 percent, that gives Firm A after-tax earnings of $100,000. Its cash balance has increased by its after-tax earnings plus its depreciation charge, or by $300,000. After it repays $100,000 on the debt principal, its final cash balance has increased by $200,000.

Firm B, on the other hand, pays $300,000 in interest. It therefore has zero profits, its cash balance has increased only by the amount of the depreciation charge, $200,000, and it must still pay $300,000 for debt reduction. After making the repayment, Firm B finds its cash balance reduced by $100,000 at the end of the year.

As the recession grows worse and sales revenues decline further, both firms will continue to find it difficult to cover their fixed charges of depreciation, interest, and debt repayment; however, firm A can obviously weather a prolonged worsening of the business cycle contraction much better than firm B. This example illustrates the importance of profits in

Table 7-1

OPERATING RESULTS OF TWO FIRMS DURING A RECESSION

	Firm A	*Firm B*
Earnings before interest, depreciation, and taxes	$500,000	$500,000
Less:		
Depreciation	200,000	200,000
Interest	100,000	300,000
Earnings before taxes	$200,000	$ 0
Taxes (50%)	100,000	0
Earnings after taxes	$100,000	$ 0
Add depreciation	200,000	200,000
Cash flow	$300,000	$200,000
Debt repayment	100,000	300,000
Net cash flow	$200,000	$(100,000)

helping to sustain cash flows. It also illustrates that a firm that breaks even in a profit sense can experience a reduction in available cash through debt repayment.

EXPANSION

When the economy recovers and the expansion phase of the business cycle begins, cash requirements expand rapidly, and any surpluses a firm may have accumulated, assuming the contraction did not cause a severe cash drain on its resources, are quickly used up. Not only do inventory and receivables require funds with which to expand, but investment in new fixed assets, seemingly called for by the optimistic climate of the boom period, tends to exceed the firm's (noncash) depreciation charges.

As noted in Chapter 6, too much expansion may eventually drain the resources of even a profitable firm. Thus the cash outflows and inflows associated with expansionary projects must be carefully analyzed if the firm is to avoid the perils associated with the expansionary phase of the business cycle.

The expansion stage can also give the firm the false impression that it is doing better than it really is. That is, a firm's dollar sales may be increasing along with those of similar firms, but industrywide the firm's sales as a percentage of its product market may actually be falling. There could be many reasons for this phenomenon. It may or may not be significant, however; to know, one must first determine how the firm's increasing or decreasing share of the market could affect its future cash inflows.

It is interesting to note that the cash balance carried by a business is inversely related to the state of the economy; that is, cash is short when times are good and plentiful when times are bad. Another paradox is worthy of mention: a profitable firm in a growth industry that is moving into its peak season during a period of economic expansion is quite likely to find itself in serious financial difficulty. Why? Because all the internal "plus" factors that the firm has working for it are compounding the externally created cash drain it is experiencing. Yet to be added to the firm's expansionary seasonal and cyclical problems is another—price increases that generally accompany upward movements in economic activity levels.

INFLATION

Price increases, especially if they are widespread throughout the economy, exaggerate each step of the circular flow of cash. Raw material prices are inflated, as are those of labor and other operating needs. Those increases inflate the amount of cash required to carry finished goods inventories and usually boost their selling price. That in turn means that accounts receivable will also absorb more cash. The only relief from this cash drain is the hope that profits will increase as well. The analyst may also discover that in inflationary times a firm may purchase larger amounts of raw materials than seem necessary. A possible reason for stockpiling inventory is the firm's expectation that purchase prices will rise even higher. The firm will weigh the cost of future price increases against the cost associated with holding a larger inventory. If it finds that buying more is the less expensive alternative, inventories will rise, provided that the necessary amount of cash or outside financing is available. If, however, a firm's projection of future raw material prices proved wrong, it would soon be holding an inventory worth less than its purchase price and would be faced with an inventory write-down. This would eventually become a cash drain as the goods reached the market at prices below the original cost plus carrying charges.

If profits do not increase, the added cash investment in inventories and accounts receivable may create cash shortages that cannot be easily overcome without instituting cost reduction programs. Such programs are aimed at reducing operating expenses; they may take the form of reducing the number of employees, for example. Although many cost reduction schemes can and do cut fat from the operating budget, some are shortsighted, and their effects on cash flows are felt in future periods as the firm continues to grow.

Temporary solutions, such as short-term borrowing, will not succeed in halting cash drains caused by inflation-induced imbalances in cash flows. Short-term borrowing may help to carry the larger dollar amounts of inventory and accounts receivable for a little while; but since the debt must be repaid, that solution will result in higher cash outflows in later periods. It might be feasible for the firm to continue to borrow, but as inflation continues to increase costs and hence the values of assets held, the firm's outside sources of short-term borrowing will not be available for other business purposes. Inflation calls for continuing inflows of cash to offset the higher investment in assets. In dealing with cash flow imbalances caused by inflation, a firm must overcome the cash shortage through either increased selling prices or cost reduction programs, both of which may add to profits.

Competition

Competition among business firms affects their cash flows in many ways. The most obvious, of course, is that the firm with a competitive edge will sell more than its competitors. Other things being equal, that firm will increase its circular flow at the expense of other firms in the market. The following sections discuss several forms of business competition, ranging from price competition to more subtle forms, such as absorption of freight charges by the seller.

PRICE COMPETITION

Cutthroat competition, often manifested by price wars, will reduce the cash flows of everyone (except the consumer). As prices fall, profits fall and may eventually disappear. Those firms with sufficient staying power, provided by an adequate cushion of cash or the ability to raise capital, will win any price war simply by outlasting the financially weaker firms. Price wars are often initiated unintentionally by one firm in achieving a higher level of sales. The reaction of competitors in matching or exceeding price cuts precipitates overreaction by others. For some products, for which there is excessive production capacity, prices will be lowered to create greater demand and reduce excess capacity. If the response to that kind of price reduction does not get out of hand, the producers may find that their cash flows will increase as excess capacity begins to disappear.

ADVERTISING

Another obvious form of competition is advertising. A large advertising campaign will need an immediate cash outflow (for selling and administrative expenses), but it may be some time before the campaign will produce the cash inflow hoped for from an increase in sales. If the competition is keen enough, the campaign may not produce an increase in sales but may simply prevent a decline as a result of the competitors' selling efforts. In such a situation, there can only be a decrease in the net cash inflow.

The decision to undertake the advertising campaign may be justified, however, on the grounds that the cash outflow for financing it will be smaller than the cash outflow associated with the decline in sales that might occur if the campaign is not undertaken. In this case, the firm is faced with the task of *minimizing* cash *outflows* rather than maximizing cash *inflows*.

Another kind of advertising, usually combined with a low selling price, is associated with a product that requires multiple purchases over a period of time. An example is the safety razor. The design of the basic razor is changed periodically as a result of new technology. The new razors are produced and sold, possibly below production cost, causing an immediate cash drain. But as replacement blades suitable only for use with the newly designed razor are purchased in future periods, the previous cash outflows are recovered many times over, possibly before competitors can duplicate the designs in their new products.

WARRANTIES AND GUARANTEES

Another major cause of imbalances in cash flows from competitive influences is related to warranties and guarantees. The automotive industry offers an excellent example of internal decisions fostered by such influences. In the 1960s, Chrysler Corporation introduced a change in new-car warranties from the standard one-year or 12,000-mile to a five-year or 50,000-mile limit. Chrysler was able to maintain its advantage alone for a full year before the other major automobile producers followed suit. The immediate effect was a rather dramatic increase in sales for Chrysler—and in net cash inflows during the first year. But subsequent years saw Chrysler's sales advantage disappear as the five-year warranty became universal in the industry. On top of that, the frequency with which all the automobile producers—Chrysler included—had to stand behind the warranty policy and provide free services and repairs began to create real problems. The result was a significant drain on cash. With the introduction of the 1971 models, all major automobile producers returned to the one-year or 12,000-mile warranty. Since 1975 some producers have begun to return to extended warranties, indicating an increase in this form of competition (and perhaps also a better-built product).

Fortunately not all such innovations turn out so badly. However, the automobile warranty case does serve to underline the fact that the managers of business firms must often adopt policies they do not like simply because the competition has left them little choice. Moreover, cash positions of some other firms in the industry may not be so comfortable as that of the innovator. A decision by those firms to follow the competition may be doubly onerous.

CREDIT TERMS

Another form of nonprice competition is related to the credit terms a seller offers his customers. If a firm's credit terms are lengthened for certain customers who have cash flow problems or for all customers in the hope of increasing sales, the firm extending the credit can expect to carry a higher level of accounts receivable for a given level of sales. As in price competition, if competitors follow that practice, the greater level of sales may not be obtained, but the cash investment in receivables will still be increased, leaving the firm worse off.

ABSORPTION OF DELIVERY CHARGES

One more form of nonprice competition worth mentioning is the absorption of delivery or installation costs in connection with the sale of a firm's product. If the seller pays for the delivery, it can expect cash outflows for operational expenses to increase. The firm hopes, of course, that the increase in cost will be offset by an increase in profits resulting from an increase in sales.

Advances in Technology

A major change in a firm's pattern of cash flows can be caused by a change in the technology used in, or associated with, the firm's product. An example of a change in technology that, while not rendering existing products obsolete, had the effect of making them less desirable, oc-curred in the camera industry. Before the introduction of an affordable single-lens reflex camera, cameras based on the range-finder principle dominated the market. Technological changes made it possible to offer single-lens reflex cameras in relatively lightweight and inexpensive models. The market for range-finder cameras shrank, and the single-lens reflex camera soon dominated the thirty-five-millimeter camera market.

Technological advances include changes in production technology as well as in products. A current example of cost-saving production technology is that associated with light-emitting diodes, especially in LED watches. As more manufacturers entered the market, prices began to drop. But as some manufacturers gained a technological production edge, other producers were forced to leave the market because they could no longer produce and sell at competitive prices and still operate profitably.

With changes in production technology, the firm may be forced to purchase newer fixed assets if it is to remain competitive. It should be noted that the lower selling prices associated with a new cost reduction process may at times reduce unit profits; however, the firm hopes to speed up the cash flow cycle through higher sales, thereby generating greater cash inflows per period. The danger is that, if technology is changing rapidly, the newly purchased fixed assets may soon become obsolete, and the high volume of sales needed to cover the fixed costs associated with them may not materialize.

83

In short, the conduct of business is a dynamic process subject to serious risks that may take the form of changes in the economy, price and nonprice competition, technology, the attitude of government regulatory authorities, and the structure of labor and supply markets. Each of those changes will affect a firm's cash flows in unique ways and cause management to take decisive action to correct the imbalances that result. If possible, management must also anticipate change and take action beforehand to prevent potential imbalances from occurring. The financial statement analyst must likewise use his tools of analysis in both a descriptive and a prescriptive manner. That is, he should be able to trace the cash flow effects of the various internal and external changes the firm has faced historically and, more important, be able to predict the likely effect on the firm's future operations of changes he anticipates. The tools of financial statement analysis available to accomplish those related tasks are presented and discussed in the following chapters.

Questions

7-1 List the five external influences that may create imbalances in the circular flow of cash in a business firm.

7-2 In what way do the cash flow characteristics of firms susceptible to seasonal influences differ from those of firms immune to such influences?

7-3 What are some common seasonal influences? Briefly describe how they cause imbalances in the flow of cash.

7-4 Into what four categories can business firms be classified relative to the ways in which their operations are influenced by economic cycles?

7-5 Explain why financial leverage influences cyclically sensitive firms' cash flows when the economy is in a recession.

7-6 Trace the effects of a business expansion on the cash flows of a cyclically sensitive firm.

7-7 How may a firm susceptible to cyclical influences protect itself against the adverse influences of price inflation?

7-8 What price and nonprice weapons do firms have in their arsenal to compete with each other? What effect do these competitive weapons have on their cash flows?

7-9 How do changes in technology affect firm's cash flows?

7-10 Why should an analyst be concerned with the external factors that influence cash flows?

7-11   With the aid of Figure 5-4, trace the cash flow effects on a manufacturer of wood paneling of a cut in the supply of raw materials due to an embargo by the exporting country. If the firm had sufficient raw material for one month, what would happen if the embargo extended beyond that period?

Part III

Tools of Financial Statement Analysis

Chapter 8   Ratios

Ratios are among the best known and most widely used tools of financial statement analysis. The reasons for their popularity as a means of assessing the performance and financial conditions of business firms are that (1) they are easy to compute, (2) they are quantitative measures that can be used in intertemporal and interfirm comparisons, and (3) they provide a convenient means for disclosing information that cannot readily be detected through an examination of the components of the ratio. Unfortunately, the apparent convenience and ease of their application often overshadow the fact that the use of ratios in financial statement analysis is hardly a mechanical process. Those who feel that it is—and their number among all those employed as statement analysts is surprisingly large—have a tendency to overrate the significance of ratios and to ignore the basic principles governing their application. While it is terribly easy to compute a ratio and compare it to one or another "standard ratio," interpreting its meaning and relating it to the objectives of the inquiry are far more complex.

The purpose of this chapter is to present and discuss only the technical aspects of constructing and examining financial ratios. The *application* of ratio analysis in the context of the various aspects of financial statement analysis is discussed in Part IV.

This chapter begins by examining some of the principles that govern the use of ratios in statement analysis, including selection of the relationships, interpretation of the ratios, and proper use of standards for comparison. The second part of the chapter analyzes the components and the basic meanings of some of the most commonly used financial ratios.

Principles of Ratio Analysis

Ratio analysis involves the selection and interpretation of the relationships between and among various balance sheet and income statement

89

items at a given time. The ratios should not be considered ends in themselves, however. They are computed because they say something about the operations and the current and historical financial positions of the firm. The principles that govern the use of the ratios help to ensure that the information the analyst obtains from them will be both *accurate* and *relevant* to his objectives.

SELECTION OF THE RELATIONSHIPS

In selecting balance sheet and income statement items to be compared, the analyst must first make certain that the ratio he has selected expresses a relationship that is significant both in absolute terms and in terms of his objectives in analyzing the firm's financial statements. Some financial statement analysts tend to relate almost every balance sheet and income statement item to every other item. Many ratios created in this way have no logical bases, and their inventors can offer no logical explanations of what such ratios are supposed to indicate about the firm's operations or financial position. Moreover, when an analyst computes and tabulates the hundreds of possible combinations of items in the financial statements, he not only wastes valuable time but also runs the risk of losing truly significant ratios in the mass of numbers he produces.

Illogical Comparisons

Blatantly illogical comparisons are easily recognized and therefore should easily be detected and rejected by even the most inexperienced analyst as having no value in financial statement analysis. Examples of such ratios are dividends to fixed assets, accrued wages payable to accounts receivable, and cash to net worth. Other illogical relations are not so easy to detect, however, because the items constituting the ratio may at first glance *appear* to be related.

For example, an illogical ratio that has been often proposed is that of liabilities to sales. In this ratio, the average liabilities figure is compared with the total dollar volume of sales during the period. As we will soon see, relationships do exist between sales and inventory (inventory turnover) and between sales and accounts receivable (receivables turnover), but there is no reason why the average amount of money due the firm's creditors should be in any definite proportion to dollar sales, especially when the liabilities probably include amounts owed for items other than the purchase of raw materials or merchandise.

Various comparisons of statement items with *net working capital* are frequently cited as valid ratios, but they are defective on either of two bases. First, net working capital—the excess of current assets over current liabilities—cannot be split into components made up of cash, accounts receivable, or inventory. Hence the ratio of inventory to net working capital cannot be interpreted as showing the proportion of working capital "tied up" in inventory, as is sometimes alleged. If the user of the ratio is attempting to determine whether or not the inventory is at a satisfactory level, he might better use the ratio of inventory to cost of goods sold or the ratio of inventory to total current assets. Those are much more direct than the ratio of inventory to net working capital and hence more easily interpreted.

The second reason net working capital ratios are illogical is that the analyst will find it impossible to specify an optimum level for a firm's year-end net working capital figure. That is because so many factors directly affect the firm's current assets and current liabilities during a year. For example, an increase in net working capital is generally considered favorable; however, an increase in current assets (and therefore net working capital) can be the result of poor inventory management or lax accounts receivable collection policies, both of which reflect poor management. Conversely, a decrease in net working capital may be caused by large profits, which increase the firm's tax liability, coupled with increased efficiency in the management of receivables and inventories and a reduction in long-term debt outstanding—all favorable factors. Under these latter circumstances, the meaning of the ratio of, say, sales to net working capital (the net working capital turnover ratio) becomes obscured by the effects of the firm's balance sheet changes, which are for the most part unrelated to the level of sales.

Relevant Comparisons

Relevant ratios are those that compare items that bear a clear and logical relation to each other, a relation that should be simple and readily understandable. Ratios computed with items related only vaguely or in a complex or confusing way should be avoided. Furthermore, to ensure that the ratios are relevant to his purposes in examining the financial statements, the analyst must first decide what he wants to know about the firm and then formulate an approach that will yield the information he is seeking.

Let us say that the financial administrator of a business firm applies for a 90-day bank loan. A bank loan officer would have little interest in the firm's earnings projections over the next one to five years, because repayment of the loan will come not from long-run earnings but from the collection of existing accounts receivable and those created during the next two months. In other words, the loan officer is interested in the current position of the firm, specifically whether the current assets are of such a nature and sufficient in relation to operational cash needs and current liabilities to enable the firm to pay its obligations on time.

If, instead of short-term borrowing, the financial administrator thought it more appropriate to acquire noncurrent debt, the analysis of the firm's long-run earnings would take precedence over that of the current position. The analyst would also be concerned with the degree of risk associated with the firm's operations and capital structure. The ratios that would interest the analyst would be those involving liabilities, capital, and income.

INTERPRETATION OF THE RATIOS

After the analyst has computed a ratio, he must interpret its meaning. This aspect of ratio analysis is obviously more difficult than selecting the relevant combination of financial statement items (constructing the ratio) and dividing one number by another; it requires an intimate knowledge of both general business practice and the particular operating and financial characteristics of the firm being analyzed. The analyst's task in interpreting a ratio is to decide whether it indicates a satisfactory relation between the items being compared.

Although the interpretation of each financial ratio involves examining the items that make it up in the light of specifically related elements of accounting risk, economic conditions, managerial practice, and so forth, there are certain generally applicable principles that will aid in proper interpretation. Those principles are applicable to almost all ratios and provide a useful framework within which to begin the task of interpreting the ratios.

First, there are five ways the value of a ratio can increase:

1. The numerator increases while the denominator falls $(\frac{\uparrow}{\downarrow})$.
2. The numerator increases while the denominator remains constant $(\frac{\uparrow}{\bullet})$.
3. The numerator increases by an amount greater than an increase in the denominator $(\frac{\uparrow}{\uparrow})$.
4. The numerator remains constant while the denominator falls $(\frac{\bullet}{\downarrow})$.
5. The numerator falls by an amount less than a decrease in the denominator $(\frac{\downarrow}{\downarrow})$.

Likewise, there are five ways the value of a ratio can decrease and three ways it can remain constant. Thus it is inappropriate to label a change in a ratio either favorable or unfavorable unless the change was caused by a *set* of favorable or unfavorable changes in its components.

For example, an increase in the ratio of net profits to sales is generally looked on as a favorable trend; however, if both sales and profits declined (as in number five), the analyst could hardly say that the trend was favorable. Similarly, an increase in the ratio accompanied by a sales decline (as in numbers one and four) would not be interpreted nearly as "favorably" as that resulting from an increase in both sales *and* profits (as in number three). Thus the underlying causes of the change in a ratio impart different shades of meaning to its interpretation.

Second, the analyst should always be aware of whether the ratio is a *percentage* ratio (the net profit to sales ratio), a *turnover* or *"times"* ratio (the sales to accounts receivable ratio), a *"pure"* ratio (the current assets to current liabilities ratio), or a *converted* ratio (the average collection period, which is 365 divided by receivables turnover). Recognizing the classification of the ratio he is working with will help the analyst interpret its meaning more readily. For example, many beginning analysts have difficulty in determining the meaning of the ratio of earnings before interest and taxes to interest expense until they learn that it is called "times interest earned." Being a "times" ratio, it measures the number of *times* earnings before interest and taxes *cover* the firm's interest charges (usually on long-term debt).

The analyst should also select the form of the relationship that is most familiar to him and consequently most comfortable. The converted ratios are excellent examples: the accounts receivable turnover ratio is a times ratio that indicates the number of times per period the average dollar value of accounts receivable is converted into cash (collected). It may be *converted* into what is called the collection period by dividing 365, the number of days in a year, by the turnover. Inventory turnover can be converted by the same procedure into the number of days required to sell the dollar value of the average inventory. If the analyst finds it more convenient to use the times ratios, he need not convert them into their alternative forms since the two forms present identical information.

Finally, the analyst should not feel that he is absolutely bound to use the figures contained in the financial statements in computing ratios. As we have seen in earlier chapters, the strict application of accounting conventions and irregular or unusual events that occasionally occur in business operations can often distort certain income statement and balance sheet accounts. Consequently, the ratios calculated from the distorted data will not reflect the true picture of activity or financial condition. In such cases, when the analyst is certain of the facts, he should adjust the data before beginning his analysis.

For example, suppose a firm increased its year-end inventory to double its normal level in preparing to fulfill a contract for the production of a special order early in the next fiscal year. A failure to adjust the inventory figure would reduce the firm's inventory turnover probably to a dangerous level and inflate its accounts payable seemingly beyond a reasonable amount—even though none of the payables were past due. The result would be a false picture of the firm's current financial position and the efficiency of its inventory management.

Of course, after he makes the appropriate adjustments in the data, the analyst must not ignore the causes of the distortions. He should assess their impact on future operations. In the preceding example, the special order may improve next year's profits and result in greater cash inflows—provided that management is able to handle the special contract without disrupting normal operations.

STANDARDS FOR COMPARISON

The selection of a proper benchmark, or standard, against which measured actual performance can be compared, is just as critical as the selection of the appropriate ratio for a specific type of analysis. A ratio standing alone is generally meaningless until it is compared with a standard that has meaning for the firm to which it is applied.

The three most common kinds of standards used in ratio analysis are (1) absolute, (2) historical, and (3) industry standards. *Absolute standards* are those that have become generally recognized as desirable regardless of the company, the industry, the time, the stage of the business cycle, or the objectives of the analysis. The classic examples are the 2:1 standard for the current ratio and the 1:1 standard for the acid-test ratio. Those particular standards have become so deeply imbedded in the practice of statement analysis that they will probably never be cast aside, even though they and other absolute standards are not very meaningful benchmarks. It is doubtful that an independent or absolute standard exists that is desirable in all cases.

The firm's own past performance produces a continuous set of *historical standards* that can be used with considerable confidence and provide a high degree of comparability. On the assumption that the past is indicative of the present and the future, those standards can help the analyst determine whether a firm's position in any area is improving or deteriorating. If the past does not reflect the future, as in a situation where a firm has just consummated a merger with another firm in another industry, the historical standards must be set aside or, if possible, adjusted to take account of the changes that have taken place.

Industry standards are widely used in ratio analysis.[1] Many trade associations prepare detailed balance sheet and income statement ratios by size of firm and by geographic location. Dun and Bradstreet's annual publication, *Dun's Review and Modern Industry,* contains 14 ratios for 72 lines of business activity. But the problem in using industry ratios (or making ratios for similar companies) is that no two business firms are exactly the same. Variations in accounting methods can lead to significant differences in the ratios. For example, one firm may set "other operating income" against "other operating expense" and report the net as a smaller income or smaller expense item than the unadjusted figures would show. That method would make ratios prepared with those figures inconsistent with those of the rest of the industry. In addition, the vari-

---

1. See the appendix to this chapter for two examples of reports containing industry average ratios.

ability of the product mix, geographic location, corporate objectives, and most other conditions under which businesses operate lessens comparability even among firms of equal size in the same industry. Marked differences between a company's ratios and the industry average would "prove" nothing. They should, however, serve to raise questions concerning the policies that affect the ratios being studied. Although there may be sufficient reasons for such differences within a firm, constant review with the aid of industry standards often proves well worth the effort.

A fourth standard, internally established goals, or *target ratios,* must also be mentioned here. They are especially useful for newly organized businesses and other firms whose unique products or operations put them in a class by themselves. Target ratios may also be used by more ordinary businesses to improve certain aspects of their operations. For example, suppose a firm's collection policies are producing satisfactory results by historical and industry standards, but management feels that the firm's investment in accounts receivable is too large. A target ratio of credit sales to average accounts receivable may be established by management to reduce the firm's relative investment in receivables to a level it considers more appropriate. The major difficulty in using target ratios, of course, is in determining the level at which the target should be set.

Commonly Used Financial Ratios

Some of the most commonly used financial ratios are presented and briefly discussed in the following sections. The list by no means exhausts all the ratios that can be calculated from a set of financial statements, nor does it necessarily include all the "most important" ratios that have ever been used by practicing financial statement analysts. It is presented to provide a sound basis for the application of this important tool to the analysis of financial statements. The ratios are divided into three groups: balance sheet ratios, income statement ratios, and ratios using data from both financial statements.

BALANCE SHEET RATIOS

Balance sheet ratios, as the name implies, express relationships among balance sheet items. They are used mainly to analyze the financial position of the company at a given time. They deal with relationships between owners and creditors and between sources and uses of funds, and they help measure the billpaying ability of the firm. The balance sheet of the Franklin Cutlery Company, shown in Table 8-1, provides data from which ratios presented in this chapter are computed.

Table 8-1

BALANCE SHEET
FRANKLIN CUTLERY COMPANY, INC.
December 31, 1978

Cash	$ 8,257	Notes payable (bank)	$ 7,500
Accounts receivable (net)	42,370	Notes payable (other)	4,650
Inventories	36,324	Accounts payable	31,223
Prepaid expenses	725	Accrued expenses	2,484
Current assets	$ 87,676	Current liabilities	$ 45,857
Fixed assets (net)	19,825	Long-term debt	15,000
		Total liabilities	$ 60,857
		Common stock	20,000
		Retained earnings	26,644
		Total capital (owners' equity)	$ 46,644
Total assets	$107,501	Total liabilities and capital	$107,501

Current Ratio

The current ratio is computed by dividing current assets by current liabilities. Franklin Cutlery, with $87,676 of current assets and $45,857 of current liabilities, shows a current ratio of 1.91:1.

$$\text{current ratio} = \frac{\text{current assets}}{\text{current liabilities}} = \frac{\$87,676}{\$45,857} = 1.91$$

In other words, for every dollar of current debt, the firm has $1.91 of current assets. This ratio is a useful measure of the ability of a firm to meet its short-term financial obligations only if the firm is in danger of having to liquidate its assets. It should be kept in mind, however, that it is not an absolute measure of debt-paying ability in a "going concern." A firm without any cash may be able to convert its accounts receivable quickly into cash or borrow to repay its current creditors. In any event, a going concern will not liquidate its current assets entirely unless it intends to cease its operations. Similarly, as long as it continues to operate, the firm will always carry current liabilities on its balance sheet. Except when a firm misses cash discounts for prompt payment, accounts payable are generally a costless source of funds; thus a firm is ill advised to repay this form of credit before its maturity date.

A company having a current ratio of 2:1—the traditional absolute standard—may be in satisfactory condition, but a "satisfactory" current ratio by itself does not establish that fact conclusively; a current ratio of 2:1 merely indicates that the company's current assets could shrink to 50 percent of face value before the firm's current creditors lost their margin of safety in case the firm experienced financial difficulty. Of much more importance to the current creditors in assessing the short-run financial viability of the firm are the quality of the trading assets and the experience of operating hazards faced by the firm.

The Quality of the Trading Assets. The quality of the trading assets has a most important bearing on the adequacy of the current ratio. If receivables and inventory are of high quality and liquidity, a low current ratio may be acceptable. If those assets are slow and questionable, the current ratio should be correspondingly higher. To illustrate the influence of the quality of the current assets on the adequacy of the current ratio, consider the following examples.

Suppose the current ratios of a manufacturing company and a retail jewelry company are 1.5:1 and 2.5:1 respectively. An inspection of the manufacturer's accounts receivable reveals that the firm's trade customers are all credit-worthy and that the accounts are in excellent condition with rapid turnover. The manufacturer's inventory has been conservatively valued, and its raw materials and finished goods are considered stable, of high quality, and thus highly marketable. For the manufacturing company, a current ratio of 1.5:1 appears to be entirely adequate because of the quality of its trading assets; that is, the firm's current assets are likely to maintain their market values at least at the book values shown on the balance sheet.

Inspection of the retail jewelry company shows its current assets to be in a somewhat less than desirable condition. The company's receivables are mostly instalment notes and are widely distributed; that is in some circumstances desirable but in almost all circumstances means costly collection expenses. The business records show that few customers pay their instalments at the store; collections are often made by company representatives through monthly or weekly calls. Still further investigation reveals that many accounts are in arrears and historical charge-offs for bad debts have been substantially above industry norms. The inventory appears to be composed mostly of high-priced and slow-moving items, and its overall valuation is questionable. In this instance, the higher than "standard" current ratio of 2.5 would be considered entirely too low since, if the firm were liquidated, the creditors would probably be hard pressed to generate sufficient cash from the sale of the firm's assets to satisfy all claims. Moreover, there appears to be more than a remote chance that the jewelry store will fail. Thus an even higher current ratio is required to achieve an adequate margin of safety for the firm's creditors.

Operating Hazards. The operating hazards of a business will also influence the analyst's opinion of the adequacy of the current ratio. A company that has demonstrated its ability to operate profitably in good and bad times may have less need for a high current ratio than a company that for years has alternated between one or two years of profitable operations and several years of large operating losses. Finance companies, for example, usually operate profitably in good and bad times; hence under normal conditions a relatively low current ratio is satisfactory for such companies.

Some industries are considered "feast or famine" industries, their profits being exceptionally good or their losses large depending on the position in the trade cycle. A relatively high current ratio is desirable for companies having such trade characteristics, since allowances must be made for the weakening of working capital through operating losses. That weakening results in a further reduction of current asset coverage of current liabilities. When examining any business firm, the analyst naturally endeavors to consider the probable operating conditions in the immediate future, a step that is particularly necessary when weighing the advisability of extending credit to companies in feast or famine industries.

Acid-Test Ratio

A ratio that is a more severe test of the current position and is not affected by the quality of a business's inventory is the acid-test ratio. The acid-test, or quick, ratio is computed by dividing the *quick current assets* by current liabilities. Quick current assets consist of cash, marketable securities, and notes and accounts receivable. The term *quick* is used to describe those asset categories because they either are cash or can quickly be converted into cash to meet pressing financial obligations. Inventories are excluded from quick current assets since, even if they are of high quality, they are not always readily convertible into cash without financial loss.

Franklin Cutlery's acid-test ratio is computed as follows:

$$\text{acid-test ratio} = \frac{\text{cash} + \text{accounts receivable}}{\text{current liabilities}} = \frac{\$8,257 + \$42,370}{\$45,857} = 1.10$$

or 1.10:1. Traditionally an acid-test ratio of 1:1 has been considered favorable; at this level every dollar owed by the firm is backed by one dollar of quick (cash and near-cash) assets.

The fallacy in this interpretation of the ratio is that accounts and notes receivable are not necessarily convertible into cash at face value and on very short notice because of the quality considerations mentioned. Other factors can also alter the adequacy of the ratio. For example, a need may arise for additional legitimate borrowing beyond the amount of the quick current assets held at any given time, such as short-term financing of inventory required to fill a special order or short-term construction loans that will be replaced by long-term debt when construction is completed. Thus, as for the current ratio, a realistic standard for the acid-test ratio will vary from firm to firm, industry to industry, and season to season.

Liabilities to Capital

The relationship between liabilities and capital is generally expressed by two ratios: current liabilities to capital (or owners' equity) and total liabilities to capital, also called the debt to net worth ratio. These ratios measure the degree of protection from loss afforded to the firm's creditors by the owners' investment; the higher the ratios, the less protection creditors have.

"Proper" proportions of debt to net worth may vary from industry to industry, but the important criterion is that total debt should be kept within manageable limits. For stable industries and firms, debt can usually be safely increased beyond "acceptable" standards and a real advantage obtained for the stockholders by *trading on the equity,* or employing *financial leverage* in the capital structure. These are terms given to the practice of borrowing funds to make investments that will earn profits at a rate higher than the interest rate on the borrowed funds. As a result, the rate of return on the small equity investment may be proportionately rather large.

There are dangers to trading on the equity, however. Just as this practice tends to magnify the earnings under profitable circumstances, it also tends to magnify the losses if the firm enters a period of depressed economic activity. The burden of the debt—interest payments and the repayment of the principal—during such periods is a common cause of financial difficulties among highly leveraged firms.

The ratio of current liabilities to capital for Franklin Cutlery is 0.98:1. It indicates that current creditors and the owners are supplying approximately equal funds to the business. The ratio of total liabilities ($60,857) to owners' equity for the firm is 1.30:1, indicating that the firm's current and long-term creditors are supplying 30 percent more funds than the owners. The calculations of the ratios follow:

current liabilities to capital

$$= \frac{\text{current liabilities}}{\text{owners' equity}} = \frac{\$45,857}{\$46,644} = 0.98$$

total liabilities to capital

$$= \frac{\text{total liabilities}}{\text{owners' equity}} = \frac{\$60,857}{\$46,644} = 1.30$$

Franklin Cutlery's ratios of liabilities to capital are fairly high; but since the firm's investment in fixed assets is relatively small, that condition is not necessarily unsatisfactory. The greatest losses in value in case of forced liquidation or bankruptcy generally come from the sale of fixed assets. When that investment is small, the risk of large liquidation losses becomes less important; consequently, the ratios of liabilities to capital can become larger than the usual rule-of-thumb maximum of 1:1.

The significance of the ratio is illustrated when it is compared to the firm's historical ratios and the ratios of other firms in the same industry. The ratio of total liabilities to owners' equity should prove more stable than the ratio of current liabilities to owners' equity. As stated previously, a high ratio is not always indicative of higher risks. Risk is more a function of the types of assets owned by the firm than of the firm's capital structure. A firm may experience a dramatic increase in its ratio of current liabilities to owners' equity, but if the current claims are against high-quality, easily marketable inventories and readily collectible receivables, the increase can be overshadowed by the type and quality of the assets. The analyst must, therefore, have a thorough understanding of the relevant characteristics of the industry in which the firm operates and a specific knowledge of the quality of the assets owned by the firm.

Fixed Assets to Net Worth

Many analysts consider the fixed asset to net worth ratio important since it shows the proportion of fixed assets financed by the owners of the firm. The ratio is computed by dividing the company's net fixed assets (gross fixed assets less reserves for depreciation) by the owners' equity. For Franklin Cutlery, the ratio of fixed assets to net worth is computed as follows:

$$\frac{\text{fixed assets}}{\text{net worth}} = \frac{\$19,825}{\$46,644} = 0.43$$

Franklin Cutlery's ratio is 43 percent, indicating that the firm's owners have supplied all the capital for the fixed assets and an additional contribution to the current assets. In this case, even though the creditors have invested more in the business than the owners, the creditors have (theoretically at least) supplied none of the investment required to purchase the risky fixed assets. Thus the creditors are protected to the extent that they can rely on the more salable current assets for repayment in case of liquidation. Generally, an increase in this ratio is an unfavorable sign, because an upward trend indicates that a smaller proportion of the permanent assets—including permanent working

100

capital—is being financed by the owners. It is desirable, especially from a creditor's point of view, that the owners supply *all* the permanent assets; consequently, a fixed-assets-to-equity ratio of 1:1 indicates that the firm is totally dependent on outside sources for its permanent working capital needs.

Comparisons of this ratio with that of other firms or with historical standards can be difficult because of differences in the age of the fixed assets, the methods of depreciation, and the extent to which the fixed assets are leased. A firm that has recently purchased a large amount of fixed assets has almost certainly increased its ratio of fixed assets to equity, unless it financed its purchases with an equally large amount of equity capital. Similarly, a firm using accelerated depreciation would find its fixed-assets-to-equity ratio falling more rapidly than that of a firm employing the straight-line method. Finally, a firm that leases most of its fixed assets would have an extremely low ratio that would defy comparison even with other firms that lease their fixed assets. Again the analyst must make appropriate inquiries into the nature of the firm's fixed assets before he can properly interpret the comparative analysis of this ratio.

Owners' Equity to Total Assets

The ratio of stockholders' equity to total assets is ranked in importance with the current ratio by many financial statement analysts. It is of special interest to long-term creditors in assessing the long-run solvency of a firm. Generally speaking, the higher the ratio, the stronger the long-run financial position of the firm; a rising trend indicates that a larger proportion of the company's resources have been obtained from the owners in the form of capital stock and earnings retained in the business.

The calculation of the equity to total assets ratio is as follows:

$$\frac{\text{owners' equity}}{\text{total assets}} = \frac{\$46,644}{\$107,501} = 0.43$$

Franklin's ratio is 43 percent, a rather low ratio when considered in isolation from other indicators. But, as mentioned, the relatively small investment in fixed assets and the firm's strong current position tend to lessen the significance of the rather low value.

When comparing the percentage of total assets supplied by owners' equity with historical percentages, the analyst should remember that the firm may have undergone considerable internal changes from year to year. For example, a firm may have begun to diversify into other industries or change its capital structure to take advantage of the benefits of financial leverage. Furthermore, because of depressed stock prices a firm may temporarily be using short-term debt instead of common stock to finance an expansion of fixed assets, with the intention of issuing stock as soon as the market price improves. Thus any general statement concerning the acceptable amount of equity invested in a business is inappropriate. Further, since fixed assets often constitute a large portion of total assets, the age of the fixed assets, the method of depreciation used, and the extent of leasing will also affect the ratio of owners' equity to total assets.

Debt to Net Worth

The ratio of total indebtedness of a company to its net worth is one of the most important capital structure ratios employed in financial statement analysis. It measures the riskiness of the firm's capital structure in terms of the relative proportions of the total funds supplied to the firm by the owners and outside creditors. The ratio's numerator is sometimes defined to exclude short-term debt; however, the most conservative and best practice is to consider all liabilities, both current and noncurrent, as debt in calculating the ratio of debt to net worth.

INCOME STATEMENT RATIOS

Table 8-2 presents Franklin Cutlery's income statement for the year ended December 31, 1978. The ratios that follow, used primarily to analyze the profitability of a firm's operations, are computed from the data in that table.

Operating Ratio

Of particular interest to the analyst is the relationship between operating expenses and net sales. It provides a general indication of how efficiently the firm has been operated. The most commonly used ratio is the operating ratio, which is computed by dividing total operating expenses by net sales. Total operating expenses include all costs except financing charges and income taxes; that is, they include the cost of goods sold as well as selling, general, and administrative expenses. The ratio for Franklin Cutlery is computed as follows:

$$\text{operating ratio} = \frac{\text{cost of goods sold} + \text{operating expenses}}{\text{net sales}}$$

$$= \frac{\$126,831 + \$57,505}{\$193,625} = 0.95$$

Table 8-2

**INCOME STATEMENT
FRANKLIN CUTLERY COMPANY, INC.
for Year Ended December 31, 1978**

Net Sales (on credit)		$193,625
Beginning inventory	$ 65,359	
Purchases	97,796	
	$163,155	
Less: ending inventory	36,324	
Cost of goods sold		126,831
Gross margin		$ 66,794
Operating expenses		
Selling and delivery	$ 14,540	
Salaries	26,423	
Other	16,542	
		57,505
Operating margin		$ 9,289
Other expenses		
Interest on long-term debt	900	
Loss from sale of property	2,025	
Other	1,700	
		$ 4,625
Earnings before taxes		4,664
Taxes		1,026
Net Income		$ 3,638

Franklin Cutlery's operating ratio indicates that 95 percent of the firm's dollar sales for the year were consumed by operating expenses.

The difference between the operating ratio expressed as a percentage and 100 yields the ratio of operating income to net sales, or the operating profit ratio. In the example, it is 100 − 95 = 5 percent. Obviously, the lower the operating ratio, the higher the rate of operating profits and, by inference at least, the more efficient the operations of the firm. It would seem that the operations of Franklin Cutlery are not very efficient.

Like most ratios, this one is not very informative unless it is compared with the firm's historical performance or with firms in the same industry. Many trade associations collect such data from their members and publish the results to make interfirm comparisons possible. When comparing a firm's current operating ratio with historical ratios, the analyst must keep in mind that the ratio can reflect nonrecurring expenses. For example, the current operating ratio for the Franklin Cutlery Company

103

may be noticeably higher than past ratios; that would warrant further investigation. The analyst may discover, for example, that the ratio has increased as a result of management's decision to treat as operating expenses the installation and start-up costs of some recently acquired equipment designed to improve the efficiency of the firm's production process. Consequently the analyst may choose to ignore the present operating ratio and anticipate significant future improvement.

Net Profit Margin

An increase in the total dollar profits of a manufacturing or a trading concern can be brought about only by (1) an increase in the profit element in each dollar of sales, (2) an increase in total dollar sales more than sufficient to offset the effect of any decline in the profit element in each dollar of sales, or (3) some combination of the two. If a business can increase its dollar sales while maintaining the same profit element in each dollar of sales, its earnings are bound to increase. If dollar sales decline, the profit element in each dollar of sales must increase if earnings are to increase or be maintained at historical levels.

These rather obvious and elementary statements should indicate why it is helpful for the analyst to determine and follow the proportionate size of the profit element in the sales of a firm from period to period and from company to comparable company. That size is represented by the ratio of net profit after taxes to net sales.

Franklin Cutlery's net profit margin is:

$$\frac{\text{net income}}{\text{net sales}} = \frac{\$3,638}{\$193,625} = 0.0188$$

or 1.88 percent of sales. For every dollar of sales, the firm realizes 1.88 cents in profit. That figure by itself is not very informative. The analyst must view the size and the trend of the net profit margin in relation to the various operating and economic factors affecting the performance of a business.

A wholesale dealer, for example, may handle a large volume of sales with a relatively small capital investment in receivables, inventories, and fixed assets; a very low profit-to-sales ratio may yield satisfactory earnings in relation to the capital employed. A manufacturer of a costly product with only a moderate sales volume but with expensive production facilities and heavy working capital requirements must show a considerably higher ratio of net profit to net sales if an adequate return is to be earned on the capital invested.

Whether the ratio is satisfactory or unsatisfactory also depends, of course, on the size and trend of the ratio for that company over time and on a comparison with the ratio for the same year for other concerns having approximately the same sales volume and operating in the same

field under comparable conditions. More than just a few years should be
used in such a comparison to avoid inappropriate conclusions from
scanty data. For example, net profit is easily influenced by such irregular
occurrences as a price war, a labor strike, or a temporary excessive
demand for the product. Furthermore, a smaller ratio or a downward
trend need not necessarily be subject to criticism so long as total dollar
profits are large or increasing. Business management is generally more
interested in dollar profits than percentages, although the achievement
of an adequate percentage of return on sales or invested capital cannot
be totally ignored.

Net Profit Before Income Taxes to Net Sales

Income taxes are an operating charge over which management has
little or no control. Since income tax rates vary over time (for example,
the surtaxes levied in the late 1960s temporarily raised corporate tax
rates above the current 48 percent maximum), the ratio of net earnings
before income taxes (EBT) to net sales is followed with interest by many
analysts.

The ratio of net profit before income taxes to net sales for Franklin
Cutlery is

$$\frac{\text{EBT}}{\text{net sales}} = \frac{\$4,664}{\$193,625} = .02409$$

or 2.41 percent.

The difference between it and the ratio of net profits after income
taxes to net sales is one measure of the impact on profits of changing tax
rates.

Times Charges Earned

Ordinarily, the noncurrent liabilities of a business are paid not from
the normal seasonal conversion of inventories and receivables to cash
but from the earnings made on the conversion process. Such earnings
must be sufficient to meet all periodically maturing payments of principal and interest on noncurrent debt, or the business may find itself in
financial difficulties.

Debt is still debt whether it is current or noncurrent, and failure to
service any part of the noncurrent debt may cause long-term debt to
become immediately payable in full. It is therefore wise for current
creditors to make certain that the size and trend of past earnings before
interest and taxes indicate that a comfortable margin of profits over debt
service requirements will be maintained in the future.

The times charges earned figure is computed by dividing earnings
before interest and taxes (EBIT) by interest charges. For Franklin Cut-

lery, EBIT is calculated by adding earnings before taxes ($4,664) and the interest charges ($900):

$$\text{times charges earned} = \frac{\text{EBIT}}{\text{interest charges}} = \frac{\$5,564}{\$900} = 6.2$$

EBIT is the dollar amount of earnings available for payment of interest (and other fixed charges) associated with long-term obligations. The ratio is useful in determining the ability of the firm to meet those fixed payments without impairing its operations. Before-tax earnings are more relevant than after-tax earnings because interest expense is deductible for tax purposes.

Whether the times charges earned ratio is acceptable obviously depends on the nature of the business and the current economic environment. For example, a ratio of three times charges earned for a producer of consumer luxury goods may be acceptable if the prevailing economic environment is healthy and the projected outlook is one of continuing growth; future profits will increase the coverage of debt service charges. However, the same ratio may be unacceptable for the same firm if the economy is slowing down and the economic forecast indicates a decline in GNP. In that case, the firm's future profits are in danger of disappearing very rapidly, since luxury goods are the first to feel the effects of economic recession. Further, the coverage ratio of three does not offer much protection for creditors.

RATIOS USING DATA FROM BOTH FINANCIAL STATEMENTS

The following ratios use figures from both the income statement and the balance sheet. They are, in general, efficiency ratios used by management for control purposes and by investors and creditors as gross measures of managerial competence. It should be noted that, when constructing ratios that include figures from both financial statements, the figures from the balance sheet are normally converted into averages (of the figures appearing on the last two balance sheets) for the period covered by the income statement. The average figures are more representative of the entire period in which sales, income, and expenses occur than are the year-end figures from the most recent balance sheet.

Receivables Turnover

The receivables turnover, also known as the collection ratio or the sales to receivables ratio, measures the relation between credit sales made during a period and the average volume of accounts receivable outstanding over the same period.

Before trying to analyze an asset of any kind, the analyst should be sure of the exact nature of the account total he is dealing with. It is unsafe to assume that the receivables shown in a balance sheet are owed by trade customers without some specific assurance to this effect. The total may include accounts and notes of stockholders, directors, officers, partners, employees, subsidiaries, or affiliates or receivables arising from transactions other than the sale of merchandise in the regular course of business to a disinterested clientele. If the receivables shown as current assets do not carry clearly descriptive account titles or if the analyst has any reason to question the makeup of the asset, he should satisfy himself that he is dealing only with true trade receivables before he makes an attempt at analysis.

Similarly, it is pointless for the analyst to begin an appraisal of receivables if he has any reason to feel that the asset total is not honestly and accurately stated. If he has reasonable confidence in the management of a business and there are no obviously suspicious circumstances, he is usually justified in relying on the integrity of the amount reported. His best assurance, however, is to know that the receivables have been independently audited by a reputable CPA using tests that include direct communication with the debtors.

The relation between accounts receivable and sales can be expressed in either of two ways: (1) the number of times during the period (usually a year) that the average accounts receivable are collected (the receivables turnover):

$$\text{receivables turnover} = \frac{\text{credit sales}}{\text{average accounts receivable}}$$

or (2) the average number of days that uncollected sales are outstanding in accounts receivable (the average collection period):

$$\text{average collection period} = \frac{365}{\text{receivables turnover}}$$

The analyst will find that the little extra work of converting a receivables turnover ratio into days will be more than repaid by the added meaning given to the expression of the relationship in this way. A slowing in the average collection period from 37 days to 44 days is more easily grasped than a decline in the turnover from 10.00 to 8.28 times per year.

The receivables turnover figure expresses the average collection experience of the business throughout the year. It is a more accurate indicator of the average length of time required for receivables to be turned into cash than the ratio of sales to year-end accounts receivable. That ratio shows merely the extent to which sales for the year remain uncollected and is useful primarily in gauging the condition of the balance sheet figure as of a given date. Since the turnover of receivables is a measure of the efficiency of a firm's credit and collection policies throughout the year and of the quality of average receivables, it is more significant to the credit analyst than the ratio of sales to year-end receivables, particularly from the standpoint of a going concern.

From the income statement in Table 8-2 we obtain Franklin Cutlery's credit sales; since all sales were made on credit, we use the total sales. To obtain the average accounts receivable, we divide the sum of accounts receivable at year-end (from the balance sheet) and accounts receivable at the beginning of the year (say, $27,763) by 2:

average receivables turnover
$$= \frac{\$193,625}{(27,763 + \$42,370)/2} = \frac{\$193,625}{\$35,067} = 5.5 \text{ times}$$

$$\text{year-end receivables turnover} = \frac{\$193,625}{\$42,370} = 4.6 \text{ times}$$

To determine how long the average accounts receivable are outstanding, we divide 365 (days in a year) by 5.5 (the receivables turnover). We find that the average receivables were outstanding for 66 days, or about two months, during 1978. If the terms of sale are net 30 days, one-half of the receivables are apparently past due. And, since the year-end receivables figure is greater than the average for the year, the current collection period of 79 days (365/4.6) is even worse.

Inventory Turnover

The relation of the cost of sales to the average inventories of a period is commonly called the turnover of inventories. It shows the number of times that average inventories are turned or converted into accounts receivable (or cash, to the extent that the firm's sales are not on credit) during the year. Hence it reflects on the quality of inventories throughout the year and on the purchasing and merchandising efficiency of business management. The ratio is computed by dividing cost of goods sold for the current year by the average inventory.

In computing the average inventory, the use of daily or weekly totals provides a more accurate figure than an average of beginning and ending inventories for the period. But an average of month-end inventories is usually made to suffice, and when only the opening and closing inventories for a year are given, the average inventory is obtained by dividing the sum of the beginning and ending inventories by 2.

A few financial statement analysts use net sales rather than the cost of goods sold in computing the ratio. However, since the cost of sales is available from the firm's income statement, there is, in most instances, no reason why the analyst should not relate inventories (which are stated in terms of their cost to the firm) to a factor based on a comparable concept of value (that is, on sales at *cost* rather than cost plus markup).

Moreover, the ratio of cost of sales to inventories is a more reliable index of the relative heaviness of inventories than the ratio using net sales, since it eliminates the extraneous influence of varying margins of profit.

Relating year-end inventories to the cost of sales for a period gives the analyst some idea of the relative heaviness of total inventories at year-end, which may be interpreted as a reflection of their quality and liquidity. However, the inventory total shown at the close of business on the final day of a fiscal year is not necessarily characteristic of that maintained throughout the year. If the analyst wants a more reliable index of the merchandising ability of a business from period to period or in relation to other comparable concerns, he must use an average of inventories throughout the year.

Using the figures in the income statement (Table 8.2), we find that the Franklin Company's inventory turnover during 1978 was 2.5:

$$\text{inventory turnover} = \frac{\text{cost of goods sold}}{\text{average inventory}} = \frac{\$126,831}{(\$65,359 + \$36,324)/2} = 2.5$$

Ordinarily, the higher the rate of inventory turnover, the larger the amount of profit, the smaller the amount of working capital tied up in inventory, and the more current the stock of merchandise. If the rate is unusually low compared with that of past periods, with that shown by other concerns in the same line, or with what all the attendant conditions reasonably appear to suggest, the analyst should conduct a further investigation.

In the Franklin Cutlery case, let us first assume that the industry average is higher than 2.5. Under those circumstances, it would be desirable to determine why Franklin's rate does not equal or exceed that of the industry. The slow turnover could be the result of inferior merchandise, overbuying or stockpiling for future sales increases, increase in prices over the year, or a change in production or inventory policies. A rapid inventory turnover (above the industry average) could result from a decline in prices over the period, a shortage of materials (due to strikes, for example), higher sales than anticipated, or a contemplated reduction in sales. It is difficult to determine which of these reasons have affected Franklin Cutlery's turnover, but since the firm's *ending* inventory is less than its *average* inventory, it appears that its turnover rate is increasing.

If the turnover is abnormally high, the analyst should consider the possibility that ordinary purchases may have been intentionally postponed until after the statement date as window dressing.

Operating Asset Turnover

Theoretically at least, all the operating assets owned by a business are acquired to produce profits and are presumably essential to the production of income. Hence many analysts feel it is significant to consider and follow the relation between the total funds invested in the operating assets of a business and the annual sales income produced by the employment of those assets.

The ratio of sales to operating assets (those used in the normal operation of the business) is generally referred to as operating asset turnover and is a measure of how effectively the assets of the business are being used to generate sales. The ratio is computed by subtracting all nonoperating assets, such as long-term investments and real estate not used in the business, from total assets and dividing the firm's net sales for the year by this figure. Generally, the higher the ratio, the smaller the investment needed to generate sales, and the more efficient the firm's operations.

Franklin Cutlery's operating asset turnover is the same as its total asset turnover, since its balance sheet lists no nonoperating assets:

$$\text{operating asset turnover} = \frac{\text{net sales}}{\text{operating assets}} = \frac{\$193,625}{\$107,501} = 1.8 \text{ times}$$

The ratio of 1.8 times indicates that Franklin Cutlery's assets are producing almost twice their value in annual sales. In other words, for every $1 invested in operating assets, the firm produces $1.80 in net sales.

Here again the ratio has little or no significance when used by itself and must be compared with those of other concerns or with the same concern's historical ratios. Clearly, it is desirable that a business have a large and increasing ratio of dollar sales to funds tied up in the relatively permanent assets it must acquire and manage to produce sales revenues. Ordinarily, then, a high ratio in comparison with that of other similar concerns is favorable, and an upward trend in the firm's ratio over time is a sign of operating improvement.

Care and discretion are advisable in using and interpreting a firm's operating asset turnover. Many concerns elect to rent or lease some of the operating assets they need. They may have no funds, or a smaller proportion of their funds, tied up in assets and may thus avoid or reduce the annual cost of owning and maintaining such properties. However, they must obligate themselves to pay others periodically for the essential use of rented or leased properties, and that may not always be as advantageous financially or as satisfactory for other reasons as owning the fixed assets. Hence in many instances the comparison of a firm's operating asset turnover with that of another firm, even in the same industry, is inappropriate.

Therefore the standard of judgment almost has to be the historical performance of the firm. That is because no two firms operate in exactly the same way, have the same number of machines in identical buildings or employ workers of equal productivity. Within the company an increase in the ratio from one period to another can only be interpreted favorably since it indicates that total assets are being employed more effectively in the production of sales income. However, as with other ratios that have little or no value except when used in comparisons, it is highly important that each factor used in the computation of the ratio for one period be closely comparable in method or basis of valuation with the same factor used in the computation for another period. Therefore in some instances the existence of a high or increasing ratio may not automatically have favorable implications.

Since the operating assets of a business may fluctuate considerably during a year as receivables, inventories, and related liabilities expand and contract seasonally, the use of average operating assets, when an average is available, is preferable to the use of year-end assets in the computation of the ratio. In the absence of monthly or other interim balance sheets, total assets at the beginning and end of the year may be averaged to come a little closer to the figure desired.

Return on Investment

The *return on investment* is not a single ratio but a number of ratios, each of which measures the return on a particular type of investment. The following are the most important of those ratios as computed for Franklin Cutlery:

$$\text{return on total assets} = \frac{\text{EBIT}}{\text{total assets}} = \frac{\$5,564}{\$107,501} = .052, \text{ or } 5.2 \text{ percent}$$

$$\text{return on permanent assets} = \frac{\text{EBIT}}{\text{total capitalization}} = \frac{\$5,564}{\$61,644}$$
$$= .090, \text{ or } 9.0 \text{ percent}$$

$$\text{return on equity} = \frac{\text{net income}}{\text{stockholders' equity}} = \frac{\$3,638}{\$46,644} = .078, \text{ or } 7.8 \text{ percent}$$

The return on total assets provides a measure of the productivity of the capital employed in the business from all sources—short-term debt, long-term debt, and equity. The return on permanent assets eliminates the short-term investment and emphasizes the earnings available from the long-term capital investment. Both these ratios use EBIT (earnings before interest and taxes) as the numerator since interest payments are part of the total "residual earnings" that are divided between investors and creditors. The return on equity relates net income to stockholders' equity. The ratio is most significant when the book value of net worth is close to the market value of the stock since new capital is raised at market prices rather than at book value.

The return-on-investment ratios recognize the value of invested capital to the business and the fact that business capital is almost never made available to firms in unlimited amounts. They therefore put a premium on the efficient use of invested capital by pointing out areas in which management can improve the performance of the capital invested in the business and thereby make the best possible use of this scarce resource.

As in the case of other ratios computed from book values recorded on the balance sheet, interfirm comparisons may be misleading. For example, a firm working with fairly new and lightly depreciated assets would have a relatively lower return on total assets than another firm with the same level of sales but with heavily depreciated assets. Differences in depreciation and inventory valuation methods may also result in significantly different earnings, and hence ratios of return on investment, for two otherwise comparable firms. The use of before-tax earnings in computing the ratios isolates the effects of tax "management" from the firm's overall operating performance. Using the before-tax figure also eliminates the effects on the ratios of changes in income tax rates. Moreover, when analyzing companies that have tax losses carried forward, the analyst will experience difficulty in restating earnings after taxes on a comparable basis. The before-tax figures are thus generally both more meaningful and easier to work with.

Use of the Ratios

The ratios we have discussed are summarized in Table 8-3. The analyst will find it helpful to employ all those ratios and perhaps others at one time or another. However, there is much more to the application of ratio analysis than the production of a series of ratios according to specific formulas. It should be noted that some ratios can be computed on both a before- and an after-tax basis (for example, profit margin and return on assets), and other ratios may be modified to emphasize different aspects of the firm's operations. The mechanics of ratio construction are not as important as the proper interpretation of the ratios *as constructed*. In other words, an analyst must exercise proper care in interpreting the new meaning of a ratio he elects to modify.

Similarly, although each of the ratios we have examined is of some specific value in interpreting the financial condition and operating results of the company, some of them are of much greater importance for one particular objective of financial statement analysis than for others. Like all tools of analysis, ratios should not be thought of as mechanical men that can be wound up and set on a table to perform. Nor is ratio analysis a technique that will automatically reveal all the strengths and weaknesses of the firm being analyzed. Rather, ratios are an integral part of the total process of financial statement analysis. In other words, an analyst should not perform ratio analysis as an end in itself; it is used to *complement* the other tools of analysis and to *supplement* the information the other tools provide.

Table 8-3

SUMMARY OF RATIO ANALYSIS

Balance Sheet Ratios	*Formula*	*Computed Value*
Current	$\dfrac{\text{current assets}}{\text{current liabilities}}$	1.91:1
Quick or acid test	$\dfrac{\text{cash + accounts receivable}}{\text{current liabilities}}$	1.10:1
Liabilities to capital (debt to net worth)	(a) $\dfrac{\text{current liabilities}}{\text{owners' equity}}$	0.98:1
	(b) $\dfrac{\text{total liabilities}}{\text{owners' equity}}$	1.30:1
Fixed assets to net worth	$\dfrac{\text{fixed assets}}{\text{owners' equity}}$	43 percent
Owners' equity to total assets	$\dfrac{\text{owners' equity}}{\text{total assets}}$	43 percent
Income Statement Ratios		
Operating	$\dfrac{\text{total operating expenses}}{\text{net sales}}$	95 percent
Net profit margin	(a) $\dfrac{\text{net income}}{\text{net sales}}$	1.88 percent
	(b) $\dfrac{\text{EBT}}{\text{net sales}}$	2.41 percent
Times charges earned	$\dfrac{\text{EBIT}}{\text{interest charges}}$	6.2 times
Other Ratios		
Receivables turnover	$\dfrac{\text{credit sales}}{\text{average accounts receivable}}$	5.5 times
Average collection period	$\dfrac{365}{\text{receivables turnover}}$	66 days
Inventory turnover	$\dfrac{\text{cost of goods sold}}{\text{average inventory}}$	2.5 times

113

Table 8-3

SUMMARY OF RATIO ANALYSIS

Continued

Operating asset turnover	$\dfrac{\text{net sales}}{\text{operating assets}}$	1.8 times
Return on investment:		
(a) total assets	$\dfrac{\text{EBIT}}{\text{total assets}}$	5.2 times
(b) permanent assets	$\dfrac{\text{EBIT}}{\text{total capitalization}}$	9.0 percent
(c) equity	$\dfrac{\text{net income}}{\text{stockholders' equity}}$	7.8 percent

As we shall see in Chapters 12 through 18, ratio analysis is an important part of each statement analysis module from measuring short-term liquidity to performing financial forecasts. We will reserve further discussion of it and the interpretations of the individual ratios until then.

Sources of Data for External Ratio Comparison

The most commonly used source of industry average ratios is *Key Business Ratios,* published by Dun & Bradstreet. The publication covers 125 lines of business, including 71 manufacturing and construction categories, 30 categories of wholesalers, and 24 categories of retailer establishments. Key business ratios for 11 lines of retailing are illustrated in Table 8A-1.

For each line of business—classified by Standard Industry Classifications (SIC)—*Key Business Ratios* lists 14 key ratios. It also lists the number of different firms used in calculating each ratio (a figure found in parentheses to the right of the line of business classification in the table).

Three figures are listed for each ratio: the median and the upper and lower quartiles. The figures in bold type in the table are *median* ratios. The median is the middle ratio (or the average of the two middle ratios) of a series of ratios calculated for the individual businesses in a particular group. It represents the typical ratio for all the firms in that specific line of business, in the sense that a ratio larger than the median has the same probability of occurring as a ratio smaller than the median. The median is preferred to a simple average (or *mean*) because most of the ratios are not normally distributed; that is, the *averages* of the ratios contained in Table 8A-1 are likely to be significantly higher or lower than their respective *medians*. Consequently, using the mean would introduce an upward or downward bias when used in comparisons.

The figure found above the median figure is the ratio that represents the *upper quartile,* and the figure beneath the median represents the *lower quartile*. The upper and lower quartiles are the middle ratios between the median ratio and the highest and the lowest ratios, respectively. The upper quartile figure, for example, is the typical ratio for firms in the upper half of the sample. This method of presenting industry averages provides the analyst with both a measure of central tendency (the median) and a measure of the range of observations about the median (the

115

Table 8A-1

DUN & BRADSTREET REPORT FOR SELECTED INDUSTRIES

Line of Business (and number of concerns reporting)	Current assets to current debt	Net profits on net sales	Net profits on tangible net worth	Net profits on net working capital	Net sales to tangible net worth	Net sales to net working capital	Collection period	Net sales to inventory	Fixed assets to tangible net worth	Current debt to tangible net worth	Total debt to tangible net worth	Inventory to net working capital	Current debt to inventory	Funded debts to net working capital
	Times	Percent	Percent	Percent	Times	Times	Days	Times	Percent	Percent	Percent	Percent	Percent	Percent
5531 Auto & Home Supply Stores (59)	3.75	4.38	15.57	29.60	5.27	8.53	**	7.3	10.6	32.1	65.0	62.2	44.4	16.0
	2.01	2.83	9.09	13.51	3.60	5.26	**	5.5	22.0	64.0	99.6	96.9	100.0	39.3
	1.52	1.37	4.63	6.90	2.60	3.47	**	3.9	48.5	109.3	161.4	142.3	164.0	71.9
5641 Children's & Infants' Wear Stores (49)	4.73	4.52	18.52	19.74	5.87	6.35	**	6.7	6.6	30.8	67.9	72.7	33.3	22.1
	2.50	1.67	7.18	10.87	4.10	4.85	**	4.7	14.1	55.2	113.6	106.7	58.2	32.2
	1.88	0.55	1.92	2.75	2.79	3.33	**	3.9	30.5	98.5	162.0	137.3	104.5	62.6
5611 Clothing & Furnishings, Men's & Boys' (222)	4.35	4.38	16.02	17.89	4.93	6.00	**	5.9	5.2	27.0	62.8	62.3	39.7	11.1
	2.64	2.30	8.18	10.10	3.30	3.87	**	4.4	11.9	49.2	114.5	90.7	67.3	22.4
	1.77	0.91	3.14	3.36	2.28	2.57	**	3.4	25.5	104.8	185.1	132.3	100.7	61.1
5311 Department Stores (275)	4.33	3.32	10.11	13.40	4.56	6.01	**	6.9	11.9	24.3	50.6	59.6	42.7	18.1
	2.82	1.89	5.65	8.18	3.32	4.11	**	5.3	33.9	43.6	91.8	81.4	68.9	41.7
	2.01	0.77	2.34	2.86	2.44	2.97	**	4.2	59.1	68.7	140.2	113.3	97.7	72.3
Discount Stores (212)	2.63	2.52	15.26	19.03	8.79	11.00	**	7.7	15.6	48.3	89.6	106.2	54.5	22.0
	2.02	1.35	9.10	10.72	6.13	7.50	**	5.0	32.1	81.1	147.9	146.7	70.3	41.2
	1.58	0.62	4.23	5.01	4.41	4.95	**	3.9	53.9	130.7	227.9	198.6	90.8	73.2

Discount Stores, Leased Departments (53)	2.90	3.70	14.22	15.21	7.89	9.23	**	6.1	12.0	45.4	78.7	99.7	47.5	17.2
	2.12	1.41	8.86	9.14	5.58	5.71	**	4.4	24.8	81.6	149.8	132.8	68.5	42.5
	1.60	0.56	3.03	3.42	3.67	4.52	**	3.5	41.2	143.7	191.5	189.4	89.7	54.0
5651 Family Clothing Stores (103)	5.11	4.55	15.69	16.93	4.91	5.52	**	5.8	6.2	22.7	74.4	53.7	34.4	17.0
	3.16	1.99	8.55	10.13	3.24	3.57	**	4.4	12.7	42.7	107.5	85.2	56.3	41.7
	2.27	0.73	2.14	2.36	2.46	2.42	**	3.5	28.6	68.5	157.6	119.2	87.8	55.5
5712 Furniture Stores (175)	4.80	4.82	13.28	15.38	4.90	5.72	29	6.8	4.3	29.3	57.9	32.9	62.4	9.7
	2.51	2.37	7.73	8.00	2.76	3.11	96	4.5	10.7	58.6	102.0	75.6	89.7	24.2
	1.77	1.09	3.26	3.36	1.77	1.72	198	3.4	24.4	125.2	213.9	123.0	133.5	60.7
5541 Gasoline Service Stations (77)	3.31	6.45	23.45	82.55	5.35	16.06	**	27.3	23.6	19.9	35.1	42.1	84.3	23.5
	1.90	4.66	16.28	41.67	3.62	8.01	**	13.0	44.1	34.7	73.1	70.2	151.2	62.6
	1.45	1.57	6.42	14.52	2.18	5.37	**	7.7	64.8	71.8	121.0	120.4	233.6	111.2
5411 Grocery Stores (144)	2.43	1.68	13.13	32.61	15.48	31.40	**	21.3	38.1	34.2	80.3	80.6	65.0	39.2
	1.76	0.89	9.61	18.44	11.27	20.48	**	15.5	71.8	65.3	127.2	134.2	88.0	77.4
	1.37	0.39	4.29	8.86	7.25	12.57	**	12.0	99.3	103.6	188.6	227.7	117.1	155.2
5251 Hardware Stores (91)	6.80	5.06	12.38	17.92	4.26	5.06	**	5.7	6.9	14.7	37.5	59.3	25.8	13.3
	3.53	2.73	7.69	9.10	2.64	3.57	**	4.1	17.0	30.0	95.7	86.8	51.4	28.4
	2.08	0.94	2.95	4.41	1.69	2.40	**	3.1	36.5	62.3	151.0	116.5	83.6	72.5

**Not computed. Necessary information as to the division between cash sales was available in too few cases to obtain an average collection period usable as a broad guide.

Reprinted by permission of Dun & Bradstreet, Inc.

117

Table 8A-2

TROY REPORT FOR SELECTED INDUSTRIES
ALAMANAC OF BUSINESS AND INDUSTRIAL FINANCIAL RATIOS, 1976 EDITION*
Manufacturing: Fabricated Metal Products, Except Machinery and Transportation Equipment:
Cutlery, Hand Tools, and Hardware

SIZE OF ASSETS IN THOUSANDS OF DOLLARS (000 OMITTED)

Item Description for accounting period 7/72 through 6/73	A Total	B Under 100	C 100 to 250	D 250 to 500	E 500 to 1,000	F 1,000 to 5,000	G 5,000 to 10,000	H 10,000 to 25,000	I 25,000 to 50,000	J 50,000 to 100,000	K 100,000 and over
1. Total receipts (in millions of dollars)	3635.5	75.5	56.9	112.9	140.3	545.5	532.2	418.0	339.3	352.8	1061.7

Selected operating factors in percent of net sales

	A	B	C	D	E	F	G	H	I	J	K
2. Cost of operations	61.4	66.3	61.2	64.6	69.3	68.5	66.2	64.2	63.8	62.7	51.0
3. Compensation of officers	1.6	2.9	9.1	8.4	2.6	2.5	1.5	1.3	.8	.6	.5
4. Repairs	1.3	2.0	.7	.5	—	1.0	1.1	.9	1.5	1.8	1.7
5. Bad debts	—	—	—	.5	—	—	—	—	.6	—	—
6. Rent on business property	.8	1.3	1.3	.8	—	.5	.6	.5	2.1	.8	.8
7. Taxes (excl. Federal tax)	3.1	2.9	3.8	2.6	2.7	3.1	2.8	3.2	3.1	2.9	3.2
8. Interest	.9	.8	.7	1.0	—	.7	.6	1.1	1.2	.6	1.1
9. Deprec./Deplet/Amortiz†	2.6	3.0	3.0	2.1	1.6	1.9	1.8	3.5	2.7	3.0	2.9
10. Advertising	3.3	.6	1.4	1.4	.6	1.0	1.5	2.1	1.5	1.7	8.0
11. Pensions & other benef plans	2.1	2.4	2.8	1.4	1.2	1.9	1.9	1.9	1.2	2.0	2.9
12. Other expenses	14.8	15.6	12.9	12.4	11.1	12.3	14.6	14.8	12.7	11.3	19.1
13. Net profit before Tax	7.8	1.9	2.9	4.3	9.7	6.4	7.3	6.3	8.7	12.5	8.6

118

Selected Financial Ratios (number of times ratio is to one)

14. Current ratio	2.6	1.3	2.5	2.0	2.9	2.6	3.8	2.2	1.7	3.3	2.7
15. Quick ratio	1.1	.9	1.3	1.2	1.4	1.3	1.6	1.0	.7	1.2	1.2
16. Net sls to net wkg capital	3.6	48.6	6.3	4.6	4.2	3.9	3.0	3.7	5.6	2.8	3.4
17. Net sales to net worth	2.0	19.0	3.4	3.3	3.0	2.4	2.2	2.2	2.5	1.5	1.6
18. Inventory turnover	3.1	11.1	3.7	4.5	2.8	3.3	3.7	3.5	2.4	2.6	2.8
19. Total liab to net worth	.5	1.3	.6	.9	.6	.5	—	.7	.9	—	.6

Selected Financial Factors in percentages

20. Current liab to net worth	34.3	103.6	36.6	68.1	37.8	37.7	26.5	46.8	59.7	23.1	28.2
21. Inventory to curr assets	46.1	29.1	44.7	39.6	48.3	47.3	55.5	49.5	48.7	54.7	36.0
22. Net income to net worth	11.9	42.4	14.2	12.3	21.2	9.6	10.3	6.3	14.6	11.5	13.7
23. Retained earn to net inc	49.7	53.0	79.8	91.6	86.3	54.6	81.8	15.5	21.7	77.8	34.6

† Depreciation largest factor

*Leo Troy, copyright © 1976 Prentice-Hall, Inc.

119

upper and lower quartile ratios).

Another source of external ratio data is the Troy *Almanac of Business and Industrial Financial Ratios.* It provides both selected average ratios and a partial common-size, composite income statement for firms in over 75 industries. An example of this report is presented in Table 8A-2.

The Troy report differs significantly from the Dun & Bradstreet report in that Troy subdivides the industry by asset size and reports only one figure—the mean—for each subdivision.

Questions

8-1   What is the purpose of ratio analysis?

8-2   What are the reasons for the popularity of ratios as tools of financial statement analysis?

8-3   List the criteria that should be used in selecting the combination of balance sheet or income statement items that will make up a given ratio.

8-4   Why are net working capital ratios considered illogical?

8-5   What are the five ways in which the value of a ratio can increase? Decrease?

8-6   If a ratio does not change in value, can the analyst assume that the firm's operating characteristics have remained constant?

8-7   What is a *percent* ratio? a *times* ratio? a *converted* ratio?

8-8   Is it ever permissible for the statement analyst to adjust the figures in the financial statements before computing ratios?

8-9   Should an analyst expect the firm he is analyzing to conform closely to industry or historical standards?

8-10 In examining the current ratio of a business firm, why must the analyst also look into the quality of the firm's trading assets and likely operating hazards?

8-11 The ratio of fixed assets to net worth is probably one of the most difficult ratios for which to obtain a reasonable standard for comparison. Why is this true?

8-12 Table 8-2 lists Franklin Cutlery Company's purchases for 1978 as $97,796, or about $268 per day ($97,796/365=$268). When year-end accounts payable of $31,223 are divided by average daily purchases of $268, the resultant figure is 117 days ($31,223/$268). What does that ratio mean?

8-13 If a ratio compares favorably with a reasonably good standard, is the task of the analyst relative to that particular aspect of the firm's operations ended?

8-14   Should all the ratios listed in this chapter be computed for each firm being
        analyzed? Should more ratios ever be used?

Chapter 9

Comparative Financial Statements

In his analysis of the financial statements of current or potential borrowing customers, the credit analyst must usually go beyond and behind the ratios discussed in Chapter 8 in order to assure himself that his analysis and interpretation of the data are as accurate and meaningful as possible. Ratios are excellent tools with which to locate actual or potential problem areas that may be creating an artificial need for cash, diverting funds from essential operations, or reducing operational efficiency. But ratio analysis alone cannot always locate the *source* of the problems or determine their severity. A thorough analysis of the financial statements of a business firm requires that ratios be supplemented with other analytical tools.

This chapter presents and discusses what is generally referred to as *comparative statement analysis,* in which interfirm and intertemporal comparisons of a firm's financial statements form the basis for an assessment of its historical performance. We will also examine a variation of comparative financial statement analysis—common-size analysis—in which a company's statement items are reduced to a common size (usually a percentage of total assets in balance sheet analysis and a percentage of sales in income statement analysis). Finally, we will examine the use of index numbers to isolate and analyze trends in balance sheet and income statement data.

Balance Sheet Analysis

The balance sheet records the financial condition of a company at the close of business on a single day. It is a financial snapshot of a dynamic organization whose condition has changed, for better or for worse, since the previous balance sheet date. The picture of the firm's financial condition revealed in its latest balance sheet is valuable in analysis, because it provides data helpful in assessing the firm's financial health on the statement date. However, the fact that the statement reveals no indications of financial difficulty implies nothing with respect to the company's condition before the statement date, nor does it give assurance that the company will be in a position to discharge its future obligations in a manner satisfactory to its creditors.

Although it may be tempting to interpret a strong financial condition shown by a balance sheet as clear evidence of a firm's continuing financial strength, such an assumption may be incorrect for at least three reasons:

1. A single balance sheet may not reflect a typical condition.

2. A single balance sheet does not show whether a company's financial condition is stronger or weaker than it was at the previous statement date.

3. The trend (upward or downward) in a company's financial condition may be as important as its present condition.

A balance sheet reports the firm's financial condition as of a given date even if that condition is unique. It may reflect an unusually strong or an unusually weak condition, for example. The figures can show a very small indebtedness, a strong cash position, and a highly liquid current position even when that condition has not existed before and may not occur again. Conversely, the balance sheet may reflect high indebtedness, a poor cash position, and an unsatisfactory current position even when that condition is atypical. It is unwise to base one's judgment of a firm's past or future financial condition on a single balance sheet.

One balance sheet does not indicate whether a company's financial condition improved or deteriorated during the year (or other period) ending on the balance sheet date. The changes in financial condition that took place during that accounting period may have been minor, or they may have been large enough to change the firm's financial condition entirely. For example, the sale of an issue of stock late in the fiscal year, the proceeds of which are still being held largely in cash, may significantly influence the firm's balance sheet proportions, possibly giving the appearance of a strong financial condition at the statement date. Similarly, the payment of long-term debt before its scheduled maturity may result in a temporary reduction in the firm's working capital, yielding a poor current position. If the analyst has no other data with which to compare the current statement, he may mistakenly assume that any condition he observes is normal for that firm. But it may not be at all, since the changes in a firm's financial condition during an accounting period cannot be discerned from the end-of-period balance sheet. The financial condition on the statement date alone is all that the balance sheet reflects.

Finally, the trend of a company's financial condition is often more important than its condition at the statement date. No company can survive continuing adversity, and few experience perpetual prosperity. The direction in which a company is moving and the rate at which its financial condition is changing are often much more important than its condition on a single statement date. Statements for a number of years must be compared to identify relevant trends clearly.

Since a balance sheet may reflect an atypical situation, the financial statement analyst will find it useful to conduct comparative analyses of the firm's position. The following sections describe several means by which such comparisons may be made: *internal* and *external* comparisons, for example, including increase-decrease analysis and comparative and common-size statement analysis.

INTERNAL BALANCE SHEET COMPARISON

Internal comparison is the intertemporal comparison of the balance sheets of a single company, in which the company's historical financial position serves as its standard of performance. Its success is evidenced by its past growth and its present liquidity and financial strength, in relation to its situation on selected earlier dates. The standard methods by which a company's present condition can be compared with its past record are the increase-decrease method and certain methods of balance sheet comparison (in either dollar or common-size form).

Increase-Decrease Method

The increase-decrease method is one of the simplest and oldest methods of balance sheet comparison. All that is required is that the analyst obtain at least two consecutive balance sheets. The simplicity and speed of the method contribute to its frequent use. The comparison generally involves only mental calculation, although at times a complete and more careful comparison is made for the permanent record. This method is helpful not only in comparing a statement with that of the previous year but also in comparing it with a statement prepared many years earlier. It is variously called the "increase-decrease method," the "where got-where gone statement," the "sources and application of funds statement," and "summarizing balance sheet changes." Strictly speaking, however, a source and application of funds statement is customarily used to trace the sources and disposition of *all* funds rather than net differences between two balance sheets. Thus the method's alternative names are not altogether accurate.[1]

The increase-decrease method is illustrated in Table 9-1. The balance sheets represent the latest audited reports of the Good Day Manufacturing Company.

---

1. The sources and application of funds statement is discussed in Chapter 15.

Table 9-1

COMPARATIVE BALANCE SHEETS
GOOD DAY MANUFACTURING COMPANY, INC.
December 31, 1977 and 1978

Assets	1977	1978	Increase	Decrease
Cash and marketable securities	$ 6,000	$ 8,000	$ 2,000	—
Accounts receivable (net)	26,000	31,000	5,000	—
Inventories	26,000	33,000	7,000	—
Total current assets	$ 58,000	$ 72,000	$14,000	—
Property, plant, and equipment	87,000	98,000	11,000	—
Less accumulated depreciation	35,000	40,000	5,000	—
Net fixed assets	$ 52,000	$ 58,000	$ 6,000	—
Total assets	$110,000	$130,000	$20,000	0

Liabilities and Capital	1977	1978	Increase	Decrease
Accounts payable	$ 17,000	$ 23,000	$ 6,000	—
Accrued federal and other taxes	14,000	17,000	3,000	—
Total current liabilities	$ 31,000	$ 40,000	$ 9,000	—
Long-term debt	10,000	13,000	3,000	—
Pension fund reserves	11,000	13,000	2,000	—
Total liabilities	$ 52,000	$ 66,000	$14,000	—
Capital stock	31,000	31,000	—	—
Retained earnings	27,000	33,000	6,000	—
Total stockholders' equity	$ 58,000	$64,000	$ 6,000	—
Total liabilities and capital	$110,000	$130,000	$20,000	0

Proof

Increase in assets	$20,000
Decrease in liabilities and capital	0
Total	$20,000
Decrease in assets	0
Increase in liabilities and capital	$20,000
Total	$20,000

The illustration shows that Good Day's assets grew by $20,000 during 1978: current assets increased by $14,000, presumably as a result of an increase in sales; new property, plant, and equipment worth $11,000 were purchased; and the reserve for depreciation increased by $5,000. To support the additional assets the balance sheets show an increase in retained earnings of $6,000, the additional funds ($14,000) being supplied by creditors. As can be seen, creditors supplied more than twice as much of the additional funds as stockholders.

Table 9-1 demonstrates that the increase-decrease method is helpful in two ways: (1) it shows what changes have occurred during the period in each account appearing in the balance sheet, and (2) it enables the analyst to see at a glance the net changes in all balance sheet accounts, some resulting in the acquisition of funds and others reflecting the application of those funds to the purchase of assets or the reduction of liability or capital accounts. That information discloses the nature of the differences in the two statements. It is a means to an end, not an end in itself; in other words, the comparison is merely one step in the analysis of a statement, not the complete analysis. While it does not enable the analyst to express an opinion regarding the financial strength of a company, it adds to his understanding of its mode of operation and helps him to determine relative improvement or retrogression in its financial position.

Comparative Balance Sheet Form

When more than two years of data are available to the analyst, he will find it convenient to "spread" the firm's financial information on a comparative balance sheet form, or *spread sheet*. The transcription of the balance sheet to the standardized spread sheet forms used by all banks and most credit-granting institutions is one of the first steps in intelligent financial statement analysis. The form makes possible a proper classification, in a consistent manner from year to year, of all balance sheet accounts and enables the analyst to observe the changes occurring from year to year and over a period of years in individual statement items and groups of items. Ratios can be more easily computed and recorded, and trends can readily be observed.

The comparative balance sheet form (spread sheet) for the Good Day Manufacturing Company is shown in Table 9-2. The firm's balance sheets for the five consecutive years from 1974 to 1978 have, been recorded on the form.

Table 9-2 shows several obvious balance sheet trends. Retained earnings increased steadily over the five-year period from $11,000 to $33,000. However, total liabilities increased from $22,000 in 1974 to $66,000 in 1978, suggesting that creditors have provided a substantially larger amount of the total funds employed than stockholders—exactly twice as much. The larger indebtedness was apparently required to support the growth of the firm's receivables and inventory, which together increased by $38,000 over the five years.

Common-Size Statement

Some analysts reduce the balance sheet to common size and follow the changes that occur in each account in relation to total "footings" (that is, either total assets or total liabilities and capital) from year to year. Total

Table 9-2

COMPARATIVE BALANCE SHEET FORM (SPREAD SHEET)
GOOD DAY MANUFACTURING COMPANY, INC.

Assets	*December 31, 1974*	*December 31, 1975*	*December 31, 1976*	*December 31, 1977*	*December 31, 1978*
Cash and marketable securities	$ 3,000	$ 4,000	$ 5,000	$ 6,000	$ 8,000
Accounts receivable (net)	14,000	18,000	21,000	26,000	31,000
Inventories	12,000	15,000	19,000	26,000	33,000
Total Current Assets	$29,000	$37,000	$45,000	$58,000	$ 72,000
Property, plant, and equipment	$50,000	$70,000	$76,000	$87,000	$ 98,000
Less accumulated depreciation	20,000	28,000	31,000	35,000	40,000
Net Fixed Assets	$30,000	$42,000	$45,000	52,000	58,000
Liabilities and Capital					
Accounts payable	$ 5,000	$ 7,000	$10,000	$ 17,000	$ 23,000
Accrued federal and other taxes	8,000	12,000	13,000	14,000	17,000
Total current liabilities	$13,000	$19,000	$23,000	$ 31,000	$ 40,000
Long-term debt	4,000	3,000	6,000	10,000	13,000
Pension fund reserves	5,000	7,000	8,000	11,000	13,000
Total liability	$22,000	$29,000	$37,000	$ 52,000	$ 66,000
Stockholders' equity					
Capital stock	$26,000	$31,000	$31,000	$ 31,000	$ 31,000
Retained earnings	11,000	19,000	22,000	27,000	33,000
Total stockholders' equity	$37,000	$50,000	$53,000	$ 58,000	$ 64,000
Total Liabilities and Capital	$59,000	$79,000	$90,000	$110,000	$130,000

assets are considered equal to 100 percent each year (as are total liabilities and capital), and each balance sheet account is stated in relation to that total. Since the total always sums to 100 percent, the statements prepared in this manner are referred to as "common size." This form of comparative statement enables the analyst to see at a glance the balance sheet trends and the proportionate changes taking place in the individual accounts from year to year.

The comparative common-size balance sheets for the Good Day Manufacturing Company are shown in Table 9-3. As can be seen from the table, cash and net accounts receivable as a percentage of total assets have remained fairly stable over the five-year period. Inventories have fluctuated but appear to be increasing in relation to total assets. Even though net fixed assets have been increasing in actual dollar amount, they have been decreasing as a percentage of total assets (from 51 percent in 1974 to 45 percent in 1978).

The statements also show that the percentage of funds provided by accounts payable has increased consistently over the past five years (from 8 percent in 1974 to 18 percent in 1978). The increase in that item alone explains well over half the five-year increase in total liabilities (from 37 percent in 1972 to 51 percent in 1976). Finally, the percentage of retained earnings to total assets has remained fairly stable over the period, and the relative importance of liabilities as a source of funds has steadily increased; thus the owner contribution to the total funds employed in the business has declined from 63 percent in 1974 to 49 percent in 1978.

These trends and changes, so easily discerned from the common-size figures, are not at all clear from the dollar figures presented in Table 9-2. For example, Table 9-2 indicates that retained earnings increased each year; however, the common-size figures clearly show that their relative importance as a source of funds remained constant from 1976 through 1978.

Comparison of common-size statements of a firm over a specific period can be valuable, as the preceding illustration has demonstrated. However, the analyst should avoid forming hasty conclusions based on the interpretation of the various account proportions and possible trends. As we have seen, a balance sheet item may remain unchanged in dollar amount over time but, because total assets are growing, become progressively smaller in proportion to its base. Because proportions can change with a change either in the individual account or in its base, the interpretation of a common-size statement comparison requires the analyst to examine both the dollar amounts used in computing the proportions and the reasons for the changes in the proportions. For example, a downward common-size trend in fixed assets may be the result of an absolute decline in the assets' value or a rate of growth of

Table 9-3

**COMPARATIVE COMMON-SIZE BALANCE SHEET
GOOD DAY MANUFACTURING COMPANY, INC.**

	December 31, 1974	*December 31, 1975*	*December 31, 1976*	*December 31, 1977*	*December 31, 1978*
Assets					
Cash and marketable securities	5%	5%	6%	5%	6%
Accounts receivable (net)	24	23	23	24	24
Inventories	20	19	21	24	25
Total Current Assets	49	47	50	53	55
Property, plant, and equipment	85	88	84	79	76
Less accumulated depreciation	(34)	(35)	34	32	31
Net fixed assets	51	53	50	47	45
Total Assets	100%	100%	100%	100%	100%
Liabilities and Capital					
Accounts payable	8%	9%	11%	15%	18%
Accrued federal and other taxes	14	15	14	13	13
Total current liabilities	22	24	25	28	31
Long-term debt	7	4	7	9	10
Pension fund reserves	8	9	9	10	10
Total liabilities	37	37	41	47	51
Capital stock	44	39	34	28	24
Retained earnings	19	24	25	25	25
Total Stockholders' Equity	63	63	59	53	49
Total Liabilities and Capital	100%	100%	100%	100%	100%

their dollar amount slower than the growth of the firm's total assets. The distinction between those two possibilities is often important to the analyst.

EXTERNAL BALANCE SHEET COMPARISON

Previous sections have shown the importance of balance sheet comparison in financial statement analysis and have pointed out (1) the benefits to be derived from comparing the latest balance sheet with that of the preceding year to ascertain the improvement or retrogression that occurred during the year, (2) the value of reviewing comparative statements over a period of years to determine the trends in evidence, and (3) the usefulness of trends in internal comparison. Those are all helpful methods to use in determining the "going concern" status of a company at the statement date and the probability of its continuance; they are all used in internal comparison.

External comparison recognizes the importance of other measuring devices. It calls for comparison of the statements and ratios of one company (1) with the statements and ratios of another company in the same line of business and (2) with the statements and ratios of a group of companies in the same line of business. While it is valuable to know how well a company has performed in comparison with its past record, its performance in relation to other companies in the same line of business is sometimes more significant. Even though a company makes an excellent showing when its past record is used as a yardstick, its financial experience may appear mediocre when compared with the record of its competitors.

For example, a carpenter who makes one window screen on Monday, two on Wednesday, and three on Friday appears to be doing exceedingly well if his production is tested by internal comparison alone. But if the average carpenter can make ten window screens a day, the record of the first carpenter is far from satisfactory. His low production makes him expensive to employ, even at half the wages paid to skilled carpenters whose production may be eight or ten times greater.

There are no infallible tests in statement analysis, and external comparison is no exception to this rule. External comparison can be helpful if it is used only as a means of opening the door to further inquiry and not as a means of providing definitive solutions to business problems.

Many factors may distort the comparison of one company with another in the same line of business or with a trade statement. A partial list of them follows:

1. Differences in the functions performed. Some manufacturers start with the raw product and carry it through to the finished article; others purchase semifinished parts and assemble them. Both are termed manufacturers, but the differences in the functions performed cause differ-

131

ences in their statements. Some wholesalers handle all the merchandise they sell; others have a large volume of "drop shipments," eliminating both the inventory item on their balance sheets and a great deal of handling expense. Both are wholesalers. Some retailers sell only on a cash-and-carry basis; others supply credit and delivery service. Both are retailers.

2. Differences in fixed assets. One company may own its building, while a competitor may rent. One company may have purchased its fixed assets at a time when prices were high, and others when prices were depressed. Those factors cause differences in comparison that may penalize one firm (relative to another) when it applies for credit accommodation, for example.

3. Differences in accounting methods. As mentioned in Chapter 3, if the accounting methods and policies of two concerns are not similar, the differences will greatly distort the results obtained by external comparison.

Before methods of external comparison can be employed in the analysis of a company's statement, figures of the trade or of other companies in the same line must be available. There are several yardsticks that may be used. A credit department that receives statements from several customers in the same line of business can make good use of those statements in external comparison. Even if the department has only two customers in the same line, their balance sheets may be compared. If the analyst has available the statements of a number of companies in the same industry, a trade statement, though limited in scope, can be prepared. Outside sources from which complete trade statements can be obtained are listed and discussed in the appendix accompanying this chapter.

Several methods are used in external comparisons. They include the balance sheet common-size statement, the trade common-size statement, and trade ratios.

The Balance Sheet Common-Size Statement

The common-size statement can be used to good advantage in the comparison of two companies greatly different in size. Assume that the analyst has received and desires to compare the statement of the Good Day Manufacturing Company, Inc., for December 31, 1978, with the statement of Nature, Inc., for the same date. The balance sheets for the two firms are shown in Table 9-4. Although a comparison of the dollar amounts of the two statements is helpful, it is difficult to draw worthwhile conclusions from the data in that form because of the size disparity of the figures. When the two balance sheets are reduced to a common denominator, however, their comparative analysis becomes easier through the resultant statement *proportions*. The *common-size* statement is

Table 9-4

COMPARATIVE BALANCE SHEETS OF TWO FIRMS
GOOD DAY MANUFACTURING COMPANY, INC., AND NATURE, INC.
December 31, 1978

Assets	*Good Day*	*Nature, Inc.*
Cash and marketable securities	$ 8,000	$ 11,000
Accounts receivable (net)	31,000	86,000
Inventories	33,000	92,000
Total Current Assets	$ 72,000	$189,000
Property, plant, and equipment	$ 98,000	$229,000
Less accumulated depreciation	40,000	132,000
Net Fixed Assets	$ 58,000	$ 97,000
Total Assets	$130,000	$286,000
Liabilities and Capital		
Accounts payable	$ 23,000	$ 57,000
Accrued federal and other taxes	17,000	23,000
Total Current Liabilities	$ 40,000	$ 80,000
Long-term debt	13,000	26,000
Pension fund reserves	13,000	17,000
Total Liabilities	$ 66,000	$123,000
Capital stock	$ 31,000	$ 94,000
Retained earnings	33,000	69,000
Total Stockholders' Equity	$ 64,000	$163,000
Total Liabilities and Capital	$130,000	$286,000

prepared by reducing the statement items to percentages of total assets, which for each firm are set equal to 100 percent.

In Table 9-5 the balance sheets of Good Day and Nature have been reduced to common size: the dollar amount of each balance sheet item of Good Day is divided by its total assets, $130,000, to obtain the percentage relation of each to the total. Similar computations are made for Nature's balance sheet accounts to derive its common-size statement.

The common-size statements facilitate the comparison of the two firms by eliminating the effects of their disparity in size. It is easy to see that Good Day has a smaller proportion of its total assets in current assets and a larger proportion invested in fixed assets than Nature. Good Day's current liabilities are also a larger proportion of its total sources of funds. That can lead the analyst to the conclusion that Good Day's current position, when compared with that of Nature, is not as favorable as it could or should be. The common-size statement also readily reveals the fact that Nature has secured a noticeably greater proportion of its total funds from capital stock than Good Day, which might indicate that Good

Table 9-5

**COMPARATIVE COMMON-SIZE BALANCE SHEETS OF TWO FIRMS
GOOD DAY MANUFACTURING COMPANY, INC. AND NATURE, INC.
December 31, 1978**

Assets	*Good Day*	*Nature, Inc.*
Cash and marketable securities	6%	4%
Accounts receivable (net)	24	30
Inventories	25	32
Total Current Assets	55	66
Property, plant, and equipment	76	80
Less accumulated depreciation	(31)	(46)
Net fixed assets	45	34
Total Assets	100%	100%

Liabilities and Capital		
Accounts payable	18%	20%
Accrued federal and other taxes	13	8
Total current liabilities	31	28
Long-term debt	10	9
Pension fund reserves	10	6
Total Liabilities	51	43
Capital stock	24	33
Retained earnings	25	· 24
Total stockholders' equity	49	57
Total Liabilities and Capital	100%	100%

Day's equity accounts have not kept pace with the growth of the company over the past five years.

The Trade Common-Size Statement

The common-size statement may also be used in comparing a company's balance sheet with those of a number of firms by way of the *trade common-size statement*. The trade common-size statement may be prepared by summing each figure contained in the balance sheets of a number of companies in an industry to form one large dollar trade statement, which is then reduced to a common size in the usual way. For example, all the cash accounts of all the companies are summed to obtain the total cash held by all the companies in the trade. All accounts receivable are added, all inventory figures are added, and so on. Since the statement of a very large company can dominate the trade statement, it is customary to omit the statements of very large firms, especially if the proportions vary greatly from those of the "average firm" and would thus distort the trade statement unduly.

Alternatively, the trade statement can be constructed by first reducing each of the statements used to a common size, adding those common-size statements together, and reducing the consolidated statement to a common-size basis. This approach eliminates much of the difficulty arising from the distortion of the final results by one very large company; however, it is much more difficult and time-consuming and thus is less frequently used.

When the trade common-size statement is available, a firm's balance sheet can be compared with it exactly as the common-size balance sheets of Nature and Good Day Manufacturing Company were compared. That method is often employed, although many analysts prefer to prepare a statement having the same dollar footings as the company under analysis and the same proportions as the trade common-size statement. It is then possible to compute the exact dollar amount by which each item of the subject company is over or under that of the trade. Such a comparison is shown in Table 9-6, which compares the December 31, 1978, balance sheet of Good Day with the trade common-size statement for the same date.

The trade common-size statement is shown in column (5) of Table 9-6. In column (1) are listed the dollar balance sheet figures of Good Day. The trade statement having the same dollar footings as Good Day but the same proportions as the trade common-size statement is shown in column (2). Each trade dollar figure was computed by multiplying Good Day's total assets of $130,000 by the trade common-size percentage figures found in column (5). For example, the cash figure of $6,500 was obtained by multiplying the total of $130,000 by 5.0 percent (the cash percentage in the trade common-size statement). Each item in column (2) was computed in the same fashion.

This format makes it possible to observe the actual dollar differences between the statement items of Good Day and the trade proportions. For example, Good Day has proportionately less invested in accounts receivable and inventory, and much more invested in fixed assets than the average firm in the trade. Further, it has a heavier indebtedness, mostly noncurrent, than the "trade."

Weaknesses in the Trade Statement. The way a trade statement is prepared frequently causes the conclusions derived from a comparative analysis to be subject to question. Insufficient sampling, differences in accounting methods and asset valuations among firms in the trade (as well as differences in their functions, territories, and customers), and variations in the mechanical means by which the trade statement is prepared all raise doubts whether the resulting statement is typical. Nevertheless, the trade common-size statement is helpful if it is not considered the final and absolute authority. When used as a general guide, a comparison of the proportions of a firm and the trade can

135

Table 9-6

COMPARISON OF BALANCE SHEET WITH TRADE COMMON-SIZE STATEMENT
GOOD DAY MANUFACTURING COMPANY, INC.
December 31, 1978

	(1) Good Day	(2) Trade $ Figures	(3) Over Trade	(4) Under Trade	(5) Trade Common Size %
Assets					
Cash and marketable securities	$ 8,000	$ 6,500	$ 1,500	—	5%
Accounts receivable (net)	31,000	37,700	—	$ 6,700	28
Inventories	33,000	39,000	—	6,000	30
Miscellaneous	—	3,900	—	3,900	3
Total Current Assets	$ 72,000	$ 87,100	$ 1,500	$16,600	67
Miscellaneous	—	2,600	—	2,600	2
Net fixed assets	58,000	40,300	17,700	—	31
Total Assets	$130,000	$130,000	$19,200	$19,200	100%
Liabilities and Capital					
Accounts payable	$ 23,000	$ 26,000	—	$ 3,000	20%
Accrued federal and other taxes	17,000	13,000	$ 4,000	—	10
Miscellaneous	—	2,600	—	2,600	2
Total Current Liabilities	$ 40,000	$ 41,600	$ 4,000	$ 5,600	32
Long-term debt	13,000	9,100	3,900	—	7
Pension fund reserves	13,000	6,500	6,500	—	5
Total Liabilities	$ 66,000	$ 57,200	$14,400	$ 5,600	44

Capital stock	31,000	41,600	—	10,600	32
Retained earnings	33,000	31,200	1,800	—	24
Total Stockholders' Equity	$ 64,000	$ 72,800	$ 1,800	$10,600	56%
Total Liabilities and Capital	$130,000	$130,000	$16,200	$16,200	100%

provide a starting point for an analysis, but the exact proportions must not be taken literally.

The common-size balance sheet comparison of two companies must likewise be accepted for what it is—a general test that only helps the analyst to place the firm's financial position in the context of the trade. The common-size statement shows the relation of each item to the total assets and *only to the total assets.* An unduly large item tends both to distort the relation of other items to the total and to inflate the total asset figure itself.

Trade Ratios

Many analysts consider trade ratios of greater help in external comparison than the common-size statement. They believe that the ratios are often more informative of trade proportions than those revealed in the trade common-size statements. Furthermore, the ratios of one large company cannot influence the final result to the same degree that its statement can affect the trade common-size statement as it is customarily prepared.

Trade ratios may be obtained from trade associations, Dun and Bradstreet, Inc., Robert Morris Associates, and others (see accompanying appendix). By a comparison of the subject company's ratios with those of the trade, some indication of the relative efficiency of management and of the company's credit strength may be obtained.

Income Statement Analysis

An income statement discloses the sources of all income, the costs and expenses, and the net profit or loss of a company for a specified period. Properly analyzed, it will tell the analyst much about the nature and profitability of the firm's operations for the period covered by the statement—but only for that period.

A single income statement, though an essential source of data for financial statement analysis, cannot be relied on too greatly for the same three reasons that a single balance sheet must be used with caution:

1. It may not be typical of the company's experience.
2. It does not show whether the results accomplished were superior or inferior to those of prior periods.
3. The trend of the company's operations is more important in analysis than the operating results attained in a single period.

A single income statement contains no information that shows whether operations were better or worse than those of previous periods since it tells the operating story for one year only. It does not reveal whether there was an increase or a decrease in sales, in manufacturing costs, in gross profit, in selling or administrative expenses, in other income or deductions, in income taxes, or in net profit. If the results were much better than those achieved during prior periods, the analyst cannot discern that from the single statement, nor can he deduce from it the cause of the improvement. Hence he is unable to give the management credit for the progress it may have made. If the results were less favorable than during prior periods, the analyst cannot detect that from the study of one statement alone.

INTERNAL INCOME STATEMENT COMPARISON

The company's past performance provides the yardstick by which the company's current operating performance is measured. Its current profitability is measured by its previous record as reflected in its past income statements.

Increase-Decrease Method

The increase-decrease method is also helpful in the comparison of two income statements of the same company. An illustration of the use of this method is shown in Table 9-7. The table presents the income statements of Good Day Manufacturing Company for the years ending December 31, 1977 and 1978. Through this method the changes in individual income statement accounts and in groups of accounts are brought into clear relief, and the analyst can quickly visualize the causes of the change in the net profit figure.

Comparative Income Statement Form

A comparative income statement form (spread sheet) is of invaluable aid in analysis, although for many years it was not considered necessary by credit analysts, who looked on the comparative balance sheet spread as a valuable aid. Most commercial banks today maintain a comparative spread sheet for the income statement as well. Many banks (and other credit-granting institutions) use detailed forms that also provide space for the reconciliation of earned surplus; others use an abbreviated form. The more elaborate forms yield much more information helpful in analysis, but the abbreviated forms contain all the data essential for the analyst to decide what sections of the statement, if any, should be investigated more closely.

Table 9-8 shows the comparative income statement spread sheet for the Good Day Manufacturing Company for the past five years. An examination of the table indicates the following:

1. Net sales have shown a decided upward trend since 1974.

2. Net income has also increased each year since 1974.

3. Total expenses have increased at a slower rate than sales, indicating that Good Day may be exercising a good deal of control over expenses.

4. Interest expense has remained constant, although total indebted-

Table 9-7

COMPARATIVE INCOME STATEMENTS
GOOD DAY MANUFACTURING COMPANY, INC.

	December 31, 1977	December 31, 1978	Increase Decrease*
Net sales	$250,000	$300,000	$50,000
Less cost of goods sold	163,000	192,000	29,000
Gross profit	$ 87,000	$108,000	$21,000
Selling expense	$ 21,000	$ 24,000	$ 3,000
General and administrative	12,000	15,000	3,000
Depreciation	10,000	11,000	1,000
Total expenses	$ 43,000	$ 50,000	$ 7,000
Earnings before interest and taxes	$ 44,000	$ 58,000	$14,000
Interest expense	1,000	1,000	—
Earning after interest	$ 43,000	$ 57,000	$14,000
Other income	1,000	1,000	—
Earnings before taxes	$ 44,000	$ 58,000	$14,000
Taxes	21,000	28,000	7,000
Net income	$ 23,000	$ 30,000	$ 7,000

ness has increased (see Table 9-2), indicating that the cost of outside funds to the company has decreased.

Common-Size Income Statements

The comparison in spread sheet form of Good Day's income statement in dollar amounts is obviously informative. The analyst can readily ascertain which income statement items have increased or decreased; however, he cannot easily conclude, for example, whether the cost of goods sold has increased or decreased in relation to the increased (or decreased) volume of sales. Comparison of a company's income statement in common-size form allows the analyst to determine whether the company is operating more or less efficiently at a higher or lower level of sales without having to undertake additional computations. It also allows him to detect any trends in various items over the period examined and compare the ratios of increase or decrease in those trends directly from the income statement itself.

The common-size income statement is prepared in much the same way as the common-size balance sheet. Net sales, if gross sales figures are not available, are used as the basis (i.e., set equal to 100 percent), and each item on the income statement is then divided by the sales figure to give that item's proportion of net or gross sales. Table 9-9 shows the spread sheet for Good Day in common-size form.

Table 9-8

COMPARATIVE INCOME STATEMENT FORM (SPREAD SHEET)
GOOD DAY MANUFACTURING COMPANY, INC.

Comparative Financial Statements

	December 31, 1974	December 31, 1975	December 31, 1976	December 31, 1977	December 31, 1978
Net sales	$140,000	$180,000	$210,000	$250,000	$300,000
Less cost of goods sold	81,000	108,000	132,000	163,000	192,000
Gross profit	$ 59,000	$ 72,000	$ 78,000	$ 87,000	$108,000
Selling expense	$ 18,000	$ 24,000	$ 23,000	$ 21,000	$ 24,000
General and administrative	8,000	10,000	11,000	12,000	15,000
Depreciation	6,000	8,000	9,000	10,000	11,000
Total expenses	$ 32,000	$ 42,000	$ 43,000	$ 43,000	$ 50,000
Earnings before interest and taxes	$ 27,000	$ 30,000	$ 35,000	$ 44,000	$ 58,000
Interest expense	1,000	1,000	1,000	1,000	1,000
Earnings after taxes	$ 26,000	$ 29,000	$ 34,000	$ 43,000	$ 57,000
Other income	1,000	1,000	1,000	1,000	1,000
Earnings before taxes	$ 27,000	$ 30,000	$ 35,000	$ 44,000	$ 58,000
Taxes	13,000	14,000	17,000	21,000	28,000
Net Income	$ 14,000	$ 16,000	$ 18,000	$ 23,000	$ 30,000

141

As can be seen from Table 9-9, the cost of goods sold increased in proportion to net sales in every year except the last. It can also be seen that the proportion of total expenses to net sales appears to be trending downward while net profit has fluctuated within a range of 8.6 to 10.0 percent.

EXTERNAL INCOME STATEMENT ANALYSIS

Like external balance sheet analysis, external income statement analysis offers a yardstick with which the credit analyst can measure a company's performance. The analyst may find that the firm's operations, though apparently outstanding when measured against its historical performance, are merely average or below average when compared to an outside standard of performance. Conversely, a company that appears by internal comparison to be of questionable quality may appear to be operationally efficient on the basis of external comparison.

Although external income statement analysis can provide the analyst with valuable information, that information is not obtained without some inherent weaknesses. For example, companies operating in the same line of business have different characteristics, are often located in different territories, are frequently subject to unlike conditions, and need not be expected to follow identical patterns in the production and sale of goods and services. Even if the major characteristics of each are similar, their operational patterns may not be the same. An automobile agency selling very high-priced cars performs the same function as an agency selling the lowest priced cars; yet there is a distinct difference in the product that may cause a difference in the financial statement proportions. A department store serving a population economically dependent on one agricultural crop may have a different record from a department store located in a stable, well-diversified industrial community. A wholesale hardware company with a large volume of heavy hardware will have a different record from a company with a small volume of heavy hardware. Both are engaged in the same line of business; but because of their individual characteristics, they are intrinsically different businesses.

Common-Size Income Statement

There are many factors that can and will interfere with the external comparison of one company with another or with a sample of firms in the same industry. They were discussed in connection with balance sheet analysis; so they need not be repeated here. However, as in the external analysis of common-size balance sheets, the analyst can compare the income statements of similar companies with different levels of sales by reducing each company's income statement to a common size. Table 9-10 compares the common-size income statement of the Good Day Manufacturing Company with that of Nature.

Table 9-9

COMPARATIVE COMMON-SIZE INCOME STATEMENT
GOOD DAY MANUFACTURING COMPANY, INC.

	December 31, 1974	*December 31, 1975*	*December 31, 1976*	*December 31, 1977*	*December 31, 1978*
Net sales	100.0%	100.0%	100.0%	100.0%	100.0%
Less cost of goods sold	57.9	60.0	62.9	65.2	64.0
Gross Profit	42.1	40.0	37.1	34.8	36.0
Selling expense	12.8	13.3	10.9	8.4	8.0
General and administrative	5.7	5.6	5.2	4.8	5.0
Depreciation	4.3	4.4	4.3	4.0	3.7
Total Expenses	22.8	23.3	20.4	17.2	16.7
Earnings before interest and taxes	19.3	16.7	16.7	17.6	19.3
Interest expense	.7	.6	.5	.4	.3
Earnings after interest	18.6	16.1	16.2	17.2	19.0
Other income	.7	.6	.5	.4	.3
Earnings before taxes	19.3	16.7	16.7	17.6	19.3
Taxes	9.3	7.8	8.1	8.4	9.3
Net Income	10.0%	8.9%	8.6%	9.2%	10.0%

143

As can easily be seen in Table 9-10, Good Day's cost of goods sold is noticeably higher than Nature's; however, Good Day's total expenses are lower. Good Day's net income as a percent of net sales (10.0 percent) is also lower than Nature's (12.2 percent). On the basis of these data alone, we would have to conclude that Nature is the more efficiently operated of the two firms.

Trade Common-Size Income Statement

Table 9-11 shows a comparison of the income statement of Good Day Manufacturing Company with a trade statement having the same level of sales as Good Day and the same proportions as the trade common-size statement.

As can be seen from Table 9-11, Good Day's cost of goods sold appears to be the major reason its net income differs significantly from the trade statement. It appears that Good Day has efficiently managed its other costs, such as selling and general and administrative expenses; however, the firm's net income is well below that of the average firm in the trade. The analyst should investigate further the reasons for Good Day's apparently higher than average cost of goods sold.

The Place of External Comparison in Income Statement Analysis

Comparison of the income statement of a company under analysis with trade statements (and possibly ratios) and with the financial data of other companies in the same line of business has an important place in

Table 9-10

COMPARATIVE COMMON-SIZE INCOME STATEMENTS OF TWO FIRMS GOOD DAY MANUFACTURING COMPANY, INC., AND NATURE, INC.

	Good Day	Nature, Inc.
Net sales	100.0%	100.0%
Less cost of goods sold	64.0	58.0
Gross Profit	36.0	42.0
Selling expense	8.0	9.0
General and administrative	5.0	6.0
Depreciation	3.7	4.0
Total Expenses	16.7	19.0
Earnings before interest and taxes	19.3	23.0
Interest expense	.3	.5
Earnings after interest	19.0	22.5
Other income	.3	1.0
Earnings before taxes	19.3	23.5
Taxes	9.3	11.3
Net Income	10.0%	12.2%

Table 9-11

**COMPARISON OF INCOME STATEMENT WITH TRADE
COMMON-SIZE STATEMENT
GOOD DAY MANUFACTURING COMPANY, INC.**

	Good Day	Trade $ Figure	Over-Under* Trade Figure	Trade Common Size %
Net sales	$300,000	$300,000	—	100.0%
Less cost of goods sold	192,000	171,000	$21,000	57.0
Gross Profit	$108,000	$129,000	$21,000*	43.0
Selling expense	$ 24,000	$ 24,000	—	8.0
General and administrative	15,000	18,000	$ 3,000*	6.0
Depreciation	11,000	12,000	1,000*	4.0
Total Expenses	$ 50,000	$ 54,000	$ 4,000*	18.0
Earnings before interest and taxes	$ 58,000	$ 75,000	$17,000*	25.0
Interest expense	1,000	3,000	2,000*	1.0
Earnings after interest	$ 57,000	$ 72,000	$15,000*	24.0
Other income	1,000	1,500	500*	.5
Earnings before taxes	$ 58,000	$ 73,500	$15,500*	24.5
Taxes	28,000	35,400	7,400*	11.8
Net Income	$ 30,000	$ 38,100	$ 8,100*	12.7%

financial statement analysis. Only through such a comparison can an intelligent idea of the relative progress of the company be obtained. The information derived from the comparison should be interpreted with care. Due allowance should be made for possible differences in functions, size, territory, accounting methods, customers, and products sold. No conclusions should be reached until those differences have been allowed for and until further investigation has satisfactorily explained the deviations of certain items from those of the trade or other companies. The analyst should always consider the possibility that the supposedly typical trade figures may not be truly typical; however, the general characteristics revealed by external analysis will prove beneficial as general guides in statement analysis.

The Importance of Trends

Operating results and the financial position of a firm fluctuate with conditions, but generally the balance sheets and statements of operations over time reflect trends in balance sheet items, sales, costs, expenses, and profits that are of great significance in attempting to analyze the likelihood of a company's future success. If sales have followed an upward trend over a given period, if costs and expenses have been held in line, and if profits, though varying with conditions, have been increasing in relation to sales, the vitality of the company is fairly well demonstrated. If an unfavorable trend has been in evidence for some years, the probability of improved operating results is questionable and becomes a matter for further analysis. Since the future is based on past operating performance (adjusted for expected future conditions), the operating trend enables the analyst to appraise the probable future success and solvency of a company. Consequently an assessment of the trends of selected items begins with a comparison of both balance sheets and income statements over a number of years. A helpful tool for such comparisons is the index-number trend.

INDEX-NUMBER TREND SERIES

The trend of a company's financial condition gives the analyst definite information about the likelihood of its future solvency and financial success. We speak of "the trend" as a single factor, and that is correct since from an overall standpoint the measure of whether a company improves or declines in financial strength is its operating income. Seldom, however, are all individual balance sheet and income statement trends favorable or unfavorable, and all of them must be considered and weighed in order to determine "the trend" of the firm. Since the individual movements must be considered, any comparative method that will bring each of them into clear relief should prove helpful. The index-number trend method of comparison does this effectively. It also shows the trend of one account in relation to the trend of all other accounts.

The statements of the Good Day Manufacturing Company that are used in this chapter were chosen because of the decided trends evidenced in their individual accounts. Table 9-12 shows a trend study of important balance sheet and income accounts. Only the more significant accounts are discussed here.

The computation of the trend percentage figures is simple. The first year is called the base year; each item appearing in the base year column (in this case 1974) is taken as 100 percent. For each subsequent year, the account is shown in relation to the base year. The percentage is computed by dividing the dollar amount in the account for 1975, 1976, and so on by the dollar amount in that account for 1974. For example, accounts receivable totaled $14,000 on December 31, 1974, the base year (see Table 9-12). On December 31, 1975, this item totaled $18,000. Dividing $18,000 by $14,000 gives a percentage of 128.6. That means that accounts receivable on December 31, 1975 were 128.6 percent of accounts receivable on December 31, 1974. Similarly the index for 1976 is calculated by dividing $21,000 by $14,000, yielding 150.0; and so on.

The analyst can examine the index number series (such as those in Table 9-12) to determine trends. Some of the accounts have had an uninterrupted upward trend—for example, accounts receivable, total current assets, stockholders' equity, net sales, and cost of sales. The figures for selling expenses rise and fall with no definite trend in evidence.

A statement made up of index numbers clearly reveals the trends of statement accounts when there are definite trends. The dollar figures also reflect the trends, but as a general rule the index number series not only indicate the trends but reflect their shapes more clearly. A review of the dollar accounts receivable in Table 9-12 indicates that the account has increased annually during the period. The percentage comparison tells the same story; in addition, it shows the extent of the increase each year over the base year. The analyst is interested in both the direction and the shape of the trend lines.

Although the trend of a balance sheet or income statement account is of interest to the analyst, it is meaningless by itself. The fact that accounts receivable have increased to 221.4 percent of the base figure during the five-year period is clearly informative, but it will have greater meaning if that item is related to other statement items. While receivables have increased to 221.4 percent of the base year figure, inventory has risen to 275.0 percent, and total current assets have climbed to 248.3 percent. Therefore, inventory represents a larger proportion than receivables of total current assets at the last statement date, indicating a reduction in the liquidity of the aggregate current assets.

Net sales have increased to 214.3 percent during the period, while accounts receivable and inventory have climbed to 221.4 percent and 275.0 percent, respectively. This comparison suggests that the firm is experiencing a slower collection rate and a somewhat heavier inventory than in the base year. Fixed assets have increased to 193.3 percent, but sales are up to 214.3 percent, reflecting a better sales-production relationship. Current assets have risen to 248.3 percent, current liabilities to 307.7 percent, and stockholders' equity to 173.0 percent, reflecting a smaller margin of current asset protection for the heavier indebtedness, which has increased at a faster rate than stockholders' equity. Fixed assets have increased at a faster rate than stockholders' equity. Cost of sales has climbed more rapidly than net sales, with a consequent narrowing of the gross profit margin. Total expenses have been under excellent control, increasing much less rapidly than net sales.

To better visualize the information presented in Table 9-12, Figure 9-1 and Figure 9-2 illustrate that information graphically for selected accounts. Translating the index numbers into graphic form is particularly helpful in seeing how the accounts have moved together over the five-year period.

Table 9-12

INDEX-NUMBER TREND SERIES FOR SELECTED ACCOUNTS
GOOD DAY MANUFACTURING COMPANY, INC.
Selected Accounts at and for the Years Ended
December 31, 1974-December 31, 1978

		1974	*1975*	*1976*	*1977*	*1978*
Accounts receivable	$	14,000	18,000	21,000	26,000	31,000
	%	100.0	128.6	150.0	185.7	221.4
Inventory	$	12,000	15,000	19,000	26,000	33,000
	%	100.0	125.0	158.3	216.7	275.0
Total current assets	$	29,000	37,000	45,000	58,000	72,000
	%	100.0	127.6	155.2	200.0	248.3
Net fixed assets	$	30,000	42,000	45,000	52,000	58,000
	%	100.0	140.0	150.0	173.3	193.3
Total current liabilities	$	13,000	19,000	23,000	31,000	40,000
	%	100.0	146.2	176.9	238.5	307.7
Stockholders' equity	$	37,000	50,000	53,000	58,000	64,000
	%	100.0	135.1	143.2	156.8	173.0
Net sales	$	140,000	180,000	210,000	250,000	300,000
	%	100.0	128.6	150.0	178.6	214.3
Cost of goods sold	$	81,000	108,000	132,000	163,000	192,000
	%	100.0	133.3	163.0	201.2	237.0
Gross profit	$	59,000	72,000	78,000	87,000	108,000
	%	100.0	122.0	132.2	147.5	183.1
Selling expenses	$	18,000	24,000	23,000	21,000	24,000
	%	100.0	133.3	127.8	116.7	133.3
Administrative expenses	$	8,000	10,000	11,000	12,000	15,000
	%	100.0	125.0	137.5	150.0	187.5
Total expenses	$	32,000	42,000	43,000	43,000	50,000
	%	100.0	131.3	134.4	134.4	156.3
Net income	$	14,000	16,000	18,000	23,000	30,000
	%	100.0	114.3	128.6	164.3	214.3

STRONG AND WEAK FEATURES

The preceding discussion has shown that the index-number trend series method of comparison has several advantages. It brings the trend of all statement items into clear relief more effectively than the dollar figures do; it reveals the trend of an account in relation to the trend of all other accounts. It does not take into account the internal statement relation and the quality of assets, except as reflected by the trends alone, information that is essential to an intelligent statement analysis. For example, the relation of current assets to current liabilities is more important than the trend of each taken independently. The trend method shows whether there has been an improvement in the relation of those items but does not reveal the exact relation.

To illustrate this point, suppose that a trend statement of current assets and current liabilities as illustrated in Table 9-13 shows the following:

Table 9-13

TREND OF CURRENT ASSETS AND LIABILITIES

		First Year	Second Year	Third Year	Fourth Year	Fifth Year
Current assets	$	200	250	300	400	500
	%	100	125	150	200	250
Current liabilities	$	100	130	140	150	200
	%	100	130	140	150	200

These figures clearly indicate that there has been an improvement in the relation between current assets and current liabilities, but until the analyst computes the current ratio of 2.50 on the fifth statement and compares it with the current ratio of 2.00 on the first statement, he cannot express an opinion about the adequacy of the current asset coverage. Furthermore, the trend percentage method can be misleading if the base figure is unduly small or large. A very small base figure will usually distort the trend percentage, and the degree of the *trend* might be misleading.

This method is particularly adapted to bringing trends into clear relief and helps the analyst compare the trends of individual accounts and groups of accounts. It must not be considered a complete method of analysis, for it needs to be supplemented by a comparison of the dollar amounts and by the computation of ratios that throw light on the relations of items and groups of items and on the quality of assets.

Analyzing Financial Statements

Figure 9-1

**INDEX-NUMBER TRENDS FOR SELECTED BALANCE SHEET ACCOUNTS
GOOD DAY MANUFACTURING COMPANY, INC.
December 31, 1974-December 31, 1978**

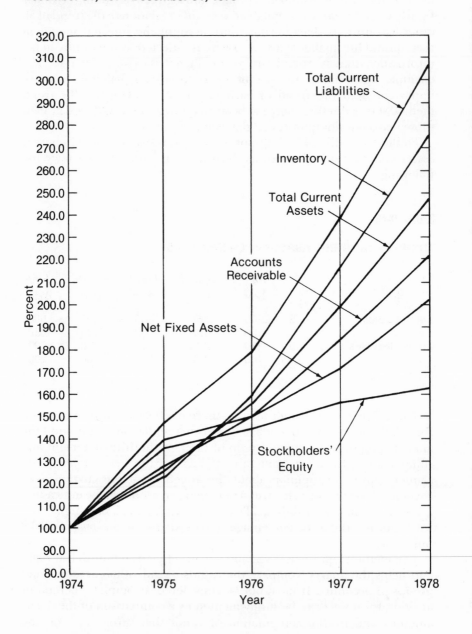

Figure 9-2

**INDEX-NUMBER TRENDS FOR SELECTED INCOME STATEMENT ACCOUNTS
GOOD DAY MANUFACTURING COMPANY, INC.
December 31, 1974-December 31, 1978**

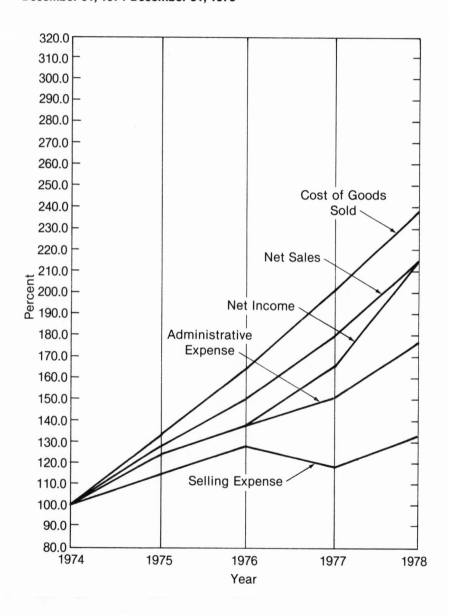

Appendix 9A Sources of Data for External Common-Size Statement Comparison

Financial reports for many industries are compiled by trade associations and, as demonstrated in Chapter 9, can be an important source of external data for comparison. Those reports can usually be obtained directly from the trade associations and often prove the best source of external data.

The Federal Trade Commission (FTC) and the Securities and Exchange Commission (SEC) jointly publish quarterly reports on various manufacturing companies. The reports, published approximately six months after the individual companies have made their financial reports available, provide data pertaining to both the income statement and the balance sheet. They include an analysis broken down by asset size and provide both ratios and common-size statements.

The Robert Morris Associates *Statement Studies* reports provide sixteen ratios and a common-size income statement and balance sheet for 306 lines of business. The reports are subdivided, as illustrated in Table 9A-1, into five groups by dollar amount of assets or contract revenues.

Common-size statements are provided only for categories in which ten or more firms have provided data; otherwise common-size data for that category are omitted. As in the Dun and Bradstreet reports, the RMA industry ratios are calculated and reported as the upper quartile, median, and lower quartile ratios. And to facilitate the conversion of the reported common-size statements into dollar amounts, the reports list total assets and total sales for all firms in each size classification.

Table 9A-2 illustrates a form provided as a part of the RMA *Statement Studies*[1] that facilitates the comparison of the reported industry data and the figures the analyst has calculated for one or more firms within that industry. That form has often been used as the basis for the spread sheets designed and currently used by many commercial bank credit offices.

---

1. Annual *Statement Studies,* 1977 edition.

Table 9A-1
SELECTED INDUSTRY REPORTS FROM ROBERT MORRIS ASSOCIATES

General Industrial Machinery & Equipment   *Manufacturers*   *Machine Shops—Jobbing & Repair*

	General Industrial Machinery & Equipment SIC # 3561 (64,66,67,69)					Machine Shops—Jobbing & Repair SIC # 3599				
	112(6/30-9/30/76)		178(10/1/76-3/31/77)			151(6/30-9/30/76)		150(10/1/76-3/31/77)		
ASSET SIZE	0-250M	250M-1MM	1-10MM	10-50MM	ALL	0-250M	250M-1MM	1-10MM	10-50MM	ALL
NUMBER OF STATEMENTS	21	78	132	59	290	86	139	65	11	301
ASSETS	%	%	%	%	%	%	%	%	%	%
Cash & Equivalents	7.6	7.4	7.5	8.9	8.5	8.9	9.1	7.7	6.0	7.1
Accts. & Notes Rec.—Trade (net)	31.4	28.1	26.4	26.9	26.8	26.1	24.0	23.9	26.2	25.1
Inventory	28.9	30.4	33.3	34.5	34.1	17.0	18.3	30.4	31.3	28.7
All Other Current	1.5	2.1	2.5	1.8	2.0	1.1	1.7	2.7	1.3	1.8
Total Current	69.4	68.1	69.6	72.1	71.4	53.1	53.1	64.7	64.7	62.7
Fixed Assets (net)	18.4	23.2	22.6	22.5	22.6	40.3	38.3	28.4	26.5	29.2
Intangibles (net)	3.5	1.1	.6	1.7	1.4	.5	1.1	.3	2.0	1.3
All Other Non-Current	8.6	7.5	7.2	3.7	4.6	6.1	7.5	6.7	6.7	6.8
Total	100.0	100.0	100.0	100.0	100.0	100.0	100.0	100.0	100.0	100.0
LIABILITIES										
Notes Payable-Short Term	21.4	9.3	6.7	3.2	4.2	8.9	7.7	4.1	2.1	3.8
Cur. Mat.-L/T/D	2.4	2.3	2.2	1.4	1.6	5.3	5.4	4.5	1.6	3.2
Accts. & Notes Payable—Trade	16.2	17.2	12.5	11.5	11.9	12.3	11.7	12.4	10.9	11.6
Accrued Expenses	6.4	6.9	7.6	0.9	8.6	6.3	6.9	7.5	9.0	8.1
All Other Current	13.1	4.9	6.2	3.9	4.5	6.4	3.8	5.6	2.8	4.0
Total Current	59.5	40.7	35.2	28.9	30.8	39.2	35.5	34.2	26.4	30.6
Long Term Debt	7.7	11.9	10.4	13.4	12.6	19.7	18.0	13.6	12.5	13.9
All Other Non-Current	6.5	1.7	2.1	2.2	2.2	4.2	1.6	4.5	.6	2.1
Net Worth	26.3	45.7	52.3	55.5	54.4	36.9	44.9	47.7	60.5	53.4
Total Liabilities & Net Worth	100.0	100.0	100.0	100.0	100.0	100.0	100.0	100.0	100.0	100.0

	1	2	3	4	5	6	7	8	9	10
INCOME DATA										
Net Sales	100.0	100.0	100.0	100.0	100.0	100.0	100.0	100.0	100.0	100.0
Cost Of Sales	71.6	69.7	75.4	71.1	64.8	69.9	69.3	71.5	69.9	64.6
Gross Profit	28.4	30.3	24.6	28.9	35.2	30.1	30.7	28.5	30.1	35.4
Operating Expenses	20.1	20.6	16.6	23.1	30.9	19.9	19.5	20.4	24.4	33.6
Operating Profit	8.3	9.6	8.0	5.9	4.3	10.2	11.2	8.2	5.7	1.7
All Other Expenses (net)	.7	.0	1.4	1.3	1.0	.5	.8	.3	1.2	1.7
Profit Before Taxes	7.0	9.7	6.6	4.6	3.3	9.7	10.5	8.4	4.5	.0
RATIOS										
Current	2.4 / 1.7 / 1.0	2.9 / 2.4 / 1.8	2.7 / 1.9 / 1.5	2.3 / 1.5 / 1.0	2.4 / 1.3 / .8	2.9 / 2.0 / 1.4	3.6 / 2.5 / 2.0	3.1 / 2.2 / 1.5	2.3 / 1.6 / 1.2	1.8 / 1.3 / .7
Quick	1.4 / .9 / .6	1.3 / 1.1 / .7	1.3 / .9 / .7	1.5 / .9 / .6	1.8 / .9 / .5	1.5 / 1.0 / .7	1.8 / 1.2 / 1.0	1.5 / 1.0 / .6	1.3 / .9 / .6	1.4 / .8 / .3
Sales/Receivables	31 11.7 / 44 8.3 / 57 6.4	41 8.9 / 47 7.8 / 69 5.3	34 10.8 / 49 7.4 / 66 5.5	31 11.7 / 43 8.5 / 55 6.6	27 13.4 / 42 8.7 / 54 6.8	39 9.3 / 51 7.1 / 65 5.6	49 7.5 / 60 6.1 / 74 4.9	41 9.0 / 51 7.1 / 64 5.7	41 11.1 / 51 7.9 / 64 6.1	34 10.7 / 40 9.1 / 58 6.3
Cost of Sales/Inventory	21 17.8 / 47 7.8 / 83 4.4	63 5.8 / 87 4.2 / 118 3.1	49 7.5 / 78 4.7 / 126 2.9	16 22.4 / 42 8.6 / 69 5.3	12 31.6 / 27 13.4 / 52 7.0	62 5.9 / 91 4.0 / 130 2.8	91 4.0 / 114 3.2 / 166 2.2	66 5.5 / 91 4.0 / 130 2.3	66 8.8 / 91 4.6 / 130 3.4	36 10.2 / 58 6.3 / 118 3.1
Sales/Working Capital	5.4 / 10.0 / INF	3.9 / 5.6 / 7.0	3.6 / 6.2 / 11.2	6.0 / 11.3 / -84.9	7.0 / 21.6 / -24.0	3.9 / 5.8 / 10.2	2.9 / 3.8 / 5.4	4.1 / 5.3 / 9.2	5.5 / 8.4 / 26.6	6.9 / 13.7 / -14.7
EBIT/Interest	9.4 / 3.9 / 1.7 (236)		10.7 / 5.2 / 2.4 (49)	8.8 / 3.6 / 1.6 (49)	8.1 / 3.2 / .9 (68) (111)	18.1 / 7.9 / 3.2 (218)	24.9 / 9.9 / 6.1 (45)	19.9 / 8.1 / 2.8 (96)	13.9 / 6.2 / 2.7 (62)	9.0 / 3.1 / -5.5 (15)
Cash Flow/Cur. Mat. L/T/D	4.4 / 2.0 / .8 (159)	36.2 / 11.6 / 2.6	5.8 / 1.9 / .8 (48)	3.8 / 2.2 / .9 (48) (76)	2.3 / 1.2 / .2 (24)	31.1 / 9.6 / 3.3 (175)	24.9 / 9.6 / 3.3	11.8 / 4.4 / 1.5 (43)	6.3 / 2.9 / 1.2 (83)	12.0 / 4.0 / 1.8 (41)

Table 9A-1

SELECTED INDUSTRY REPORTS FROM ROBERT MORRIS ASSOCIATES

Continued

Manufacturers

General Industrial Machinery & Equipment — SIC # 3561

	112(6/30-9/30/76) 0-250M	250M-1MM	178(10/1/76-3/31/77) 1-10MM	10-50MM	ALL
ASSET SIZE / **NUMBER OF STATEMENTS**	21	78	132	59	290
	%	%	%	%	%
Fixed/Worth	.3	.3	.3	.3	.3
	.6	.6	.4	.4	.5
	-1.2	1.1	.7	.6	.8
Debt/Worth	1.2	.8	.5	.4	.5
	2.4	1.4	.9	.8	1.0
	-5.6	2.7	1.9	1.4	2.0
% Profit Before Taxes/Tangible Net Worth	53.6	45.8	39.6	40.8	42.2
	(14) 18.4	(75) 18.9	(131) 29.1	(58) 29.2	(278) 25.8
	-.3	8.2	12.0	19.6	12.3
% Profit Before Taxes/Total Assets	20.5	15.4	20.7	18.7	19.5
	2.4	8.6	13.2	14.8	11.4
	-21.6	3.4	5.1	10.0	5.1
Sales/Net Fixed Assets	39.6	21.1	15.6	11.0	17.2
	12.2	10.8	8.3	7.1	8.7
	5.3	5.2	5.7	5.0	5.3
Sales/Total Assets	3.2	2.7	2.3	1.9	2.4
	2.3	2.2	1.9	1.6	1.9
	1.5	1.5	1.5	1.2	1.4

Machine Shops—Jobbing & Repair — SIC # 3599

	151(6/30-9/30/76) 0-250M	250M-1MM	150(10/1/76-3/31/77) 1-10MM	10-50MM	ALL
ASSET SIZE / **NUMBER OF STATEMENTS**	86	139	65	11	301
	%	%	%	%	%
Fixed/Worth	.5	.5	.4	.4	.5
	1.3	1.0	.6	.5	.9
	3.5	1.7	1.0	.6	1.8
Debt/Worth	.9	.6	.7	.5	.7
	2.1	1.2	1.1	.7	1.2
	6.5	2.9	2.0	1.3	3.0
% Profit Before Taxes/Tangible Net Worth	60.1	37.0	41.2	34.6	42.2
	(78) 18.7	(132) 19.9	25.9	33.6	(286) 21.0
	2.0	7.4	9.8	13.2	7.3
% Profit Before Taxes/Total Assets	16.7	15.8	19.8	22.8	17.6
	6.4	8.5	9.1	20.7	8.6
	-1.5	2.7	4.4	4.7	2.1
Sales/Net Fixed Assets	15.7	9.4	10.5	8.1	10.0
	4.9	5.0	6.4	7.2	5.3
	3.2	3.1	3.6	5.4	3.3
Sales/Total Assets	3.1	2.5	2.3	2.1	2.6
	2.3	1.9	1.6	2.0	2.0
	1.6	1.5	1.3	1.3	1.5

	1	2	3	4	5	6	7	8	9	10
% Depr., Dep., Amort./Sales	.7 2.2 (20) 6.4	.9 1.6 (74) 2.8	.9 1.4 (120) 2.2	1.0 2.1 (52) 2.9	.9 1.6 (266) 2.6	1.5 3.8 (81) 6.5	2.0 3.4 (128) 5.7	1.5 2.6 (62) 3.7	1.3 1.7 (282) 2.7	1.6 3.2 5.3
% Lease & Rental Exp./Sales	1. 2.3 (11) 4.4	.5 1.7 (38) 4.0	.5 1.0 (57) 1.6	.7 1.1 (17) 1.5	.6 1.1 (123) 1.5	1.8 3.1 (58) 4.8	1.2 2.0 (87) 3.3	.3 1.0 (34) 2.2	1.1 2.4 (184) 3.4	
% Officers' Comp/Sales	5.8 7.2 (15) 13.6	3.3 5.2 (42) 8.0	1.9 2.9 (46) 3.8		2.4 3.8 (104) 6.5	6.1 9.6 (57) 15.3	3.9 6.9 (91) 10.0	2.4 3.4 (35) 6.2	3.6 7.0 (183) 10.3	
Net Sales ($)	7267M	104200M	838688M	2254921M	3205076M	27245M	146935M	279998M	414866M	869044M
Total Assets ($)	3183M	48363M	456949M	1403779M	1912274M	11321M	72119M	156237M	236700M	476377M

© Robert Morris Associates 1977

M = $thousand   MM = $million

157

Table 9A-2

A COMPARISON OF RMA STATEMENT STUDY PERCENTAGE WITH CUSTOMER IN SIMILAR INDUSTRY

Name	Location		Robert Morris Code			
	Date		*Date*		*Date*	
	RMA	*Customer*	*RMA*	*Customer*	*RMA*	*Customer*
ASSETS						
Cash & Equivalents						
Accts. & Notes Rec.— Trade (net)						
Inventory						
All Other Current						
Total Current						
Fixed Assets (net)						
Intangibles (net)						
All Other Non-Current						
Total Assets	100.0%	100.0%	100.0%	100.0%	100.0%	100.0%
LIABILITIES						
Notes Payable-Short Term						
Cur. Mat.-L/T/D						
Accts. & Notes Payable— Trade						
Accrued Expenses						
All Other Current						
Total Current						
Long Term Debt						
All Other Non-Current						
Net Worth						
Total Liabilities & Net Worth	100.0%	100.0%	100.0%	100.0%	100.0%	100.0%
INCOME DATA						
Net Sales	100.0%	100.0%	100.0%	100.0%	100.0%	100.0%
Cost of Sales						
Gross Profit						
Operating Expenses						
Operating Profit						
All Other Expenses (net)						
Profit Before Taxes						
RATIOS						
Current						
Quick						
Sales/Receivables						
Cost of Sales/Inventory						
Sales/Working Capital						
EBIT/Interest						
Cash Flow/Cur. Mat. L/T/D						
Fixed/Worth						
Debt/Worth						

% Profit Before Taxes/ Tangible Net Worth	
% Profit Before Taxes/ Total Assets	
Sales/Net Fixed Assets	
Sales/Total Assets	
% Depr., Dep., Amort./ Sales	
% Lease & Rental Exp/ Sales	
% Officers' Comp/Sales	

Net Sales ($)	

As with any source of external data, caution should be used in drawing conclusions based on the comparison of an individual firm's financial position with data intended to reflect the typical position of a firm in a particular industry. The caveats associated with the use of industry average figures as a basis for comparison and concerning the interpretation of industry average figures are published by the RMA in its *Statement Studies*. They are reproduced below.

Interpretation of Statement Studies Figures

RMA recommends that *Statement Studies* data be regarded only as general guidelines and not as absolute industry norms. There are several reasons why the data may not be fully representative of a given industry:

(1) The financial statements used in the *Statement Studies* are not selected by any random or statistically reliable method. RMA member banks voluntarily submit the raw data they have available each year, with these being the only constraints: (a) The fiscal year-ends of the companies reported may not be from April 1 through June 29, and (b) their total assets must be less than $50 million.

(2) Many companies have varied product lines; however, the *Statement Studies* categorize them by their primary product Standard Industrial Classification (SIC) number only.

(3) Some of our industry samples are rather small in relation to the total number of firms in a given industry. A relatively small sample can increase the chances that some of our composites do not fully represent an industry.

(4) There is the chance that an extreme statement can be present in a sample, causing a disproportionate influence on the industry composite. This is particularly true in a relatively small sample.

(5) Companies within the same industry may differ in their method of operations which in turn can directly influence their financial statements. Since they are included in our sample, too, these statements can significantly affect our composite calculations.

159

(6) Other considerations that can result in variations among different companies engaged in the same general line of business are different labor markets; geographical location; different accounting methods; quality of products handled; sources and methods of financing; and terms of sale.

For these reasons, RMA does not recommend the Statement Studies *figures be considered as absolute norms for a given industry. Rather the figures should be used only as general guidelines and in addition to the other methods of financial analysis. RMA makes no claim as to the representativeness of the figures printed in this book.*

Robert Morris Associates
1432 Philadelphia National Bank Building
Philadelphia, PA 19107

Questions

9-1. What may the analysis of a single balance sheet reveal about a business firm?

9-2. Is an analyst safe in assuming that a firm will remain solvent if it is able to present a strong financial condition in its balance sheet? Why or why not?

9-3. Define the following terms:
1. internal balance sheet comparison
2. increase-decrease method of comparison
3. common-size balance sheet

9-4. What is the basic reason for comparing two balance sheets by the increase-decrease method?

9-5. Why do most banks "spread" a customer's statements as the first step in statement analysis?

9-6. What advantage does the common-size statement have over the comparative statement in dollar form?

9-7. Define external balance sheet comparison. How is it similar to internal comparison? How is it different?

9-8. Why must an analyst use caution when making interfirm or trade statement comparisons?

9-9. Explain how you would convert a trade common-size balance sheet into a statement having the same dollar footings as the company you are analyzing.

9-10. What are the major differences between internal comparisons of balance sheets and of income statements?

9-11. Insofar as the task of the analyst is concerned, why is the direction of the trend in operating results important?

9-12. Why is it important to determine both the direction and the shape of the trends of individual balance sheet and income statement accounts?

9-13. What information must be used to supplement the analysis of index-number trend series? Why?

Chapter 10 Statement of Changes in Financial Position

The statement of changes in financial position is generally considered one of the most important and useful tools of financial statement analysis. It is essentially an explanation of changes that have taken place in the financial position of a business over a given period as a result of its activities. It is used primarily by statement analysts to examine a firm's historical operations and explain how external influences and internal management decisions and policies have changed its financial position since the previous balance sheet date. It can also be used in conjunction with budgets and pro forma statements to detail the changes expected in the financial position of a business over the forecasted budget period.

Analysts increasingly rely on the statement of changes in financial position for information on a firm's financial history because it is a near perfect summary of both changes in financial position and results of the firm's operations. The analyst can readily determine, for example, why a net income of $4,000 shown on the income statement has not resulted in an increase of the same amount in the firm's cash balance. The funds flow statement, as it is sometimes called, clearly shows that the total funds acquired by a firm from all sources during a specific period (including those provided by the firm's net profits) rarely if ever wind up at year-end increasing only the firm's cash balance. The funds generated from those sources are constantly being redistributed by normal business operations among the firm's various assets and liabilities. The statement of changes in financial position picks up where the income statement leaves off in tracing the flow of funds into and among the accounts in the balance sheet. Thus the statement is an indispensable tool for summarizing the relation between the income statement and the balance sheet and tracing the operational flows of funds through the assets and liabilities of the firm.

This chapter presents the technical aspects of preparing the statement of changes in financial position, along with its useful variants (e.g., the statement of changes in net working capital and the statement of sources and uses of funds). The analysis and interpretation of the funds flow statement is discussed in Chapter 14.

Accounting Basis of the Statement

The basis for the preparation of the statement of changes in financial position is found in the accounting definitions of funds sources and uses. Sources are defined as "increases in liability and net worth accounts and decreases in asset accounts"; uses of funds are defined as "decreases in liability and net worth accounts and increases in asset accounts." In addition, certain more specific definitions of what must be included in the statement and the manner of their presentation are prescribed by the Accounting Principles Board (APB) *Opinion Number 19*. Some of the more noteworthy requirements for the statement's preparation and presentation outlined in this opinion are as follows:

1. The statement of changes in financial position is now a basic financial statement that must be furnished whenever a profit-oriented business entity issues financial statements that present both financial position (balance sheet) and results of operations (statements of income and retained earnings).
2. The statement of changes should be based on a broad concept embracing all changes in financial position. The recommended title of the "funds flow statement" was changed to reflect this broad concept. Thus all information concerning the financing and investing activities of a business enterprise should be included in the statement of changes, whether or not cash or working capital is affected by the transaction. Accordingly, transactions such as the following should be included:
   a. Assets acquired in exchange for capital stock or for long-term debt
   b. Exchanges of property
   c. Capital donations affecting noncurrent items
   d. Conversion of debt into equity
   e. Refinancing of long-term debt
   f. Issuance, redemption, or purchase of capital stock
   g. Dividends in kind (except for stock dividends and stock splits)
3. Items such as the following should not be netted against each other unless one item is immaterial:
   a. Acquisition and retirement of property, plant, and equipment.
   b. New long-term borrowings and repayment of long-term debt.
4. The statement should prominently disclose and appropriately describe working capital provided from or used in operations for the period:
   a. The effects of extraordinary items should be reported separately

from the effects of normal items in arriving at working capital or cash provided from or used in operations.

b. The statement should begin with income or loss before extraordinary items, if any, and add or deduct items recognized in that amount that did not use or provide working capital or cash during the period. As an acceptable alternative, the statement may begin with total revenue and deduct operating costs and expenses that required the outlay of working capital or cash. In either case, the subtotal should be followed immediately by the effect of extraordinary items on working capital or cash after being similarly adjusted for items recognized that did not provide or use working capital or cash during the period.

APB *Opinion Number 19* thus clearly delineates the intrinsic value of the statement, while setting forth certain requirements designed both to enhance its usefulness and to protect its value in financial statement analysis. The provisions of APB *Opinion Number 19* are applied in the following discussion of the preparation of the funds flow statement.

Preparation of the Funds Flow Statements

The preparation of the statement of changes in financial position is complex and requires a large amount of information, much of it not available routinely to the outside analyst. However, the analyst can usually obtain sufficient information from a published set of comparative financial statements to construct modified and less detailed versions of the statement that are nevertheless extremely valuable tools of analysis.

We will first show how the simpler versions of the statement of changes in financial position are prepared, then move on to the full-scale version of the statement. That approach will yield two important benefits. First, it will present a step-by-step plan for constructing the statement. Second, since the proper preparation of the statement is time-consuming and financial statement analysts often have too little time to accomplish their many analytical and interpretive tasks, the approach will provide the analyst with two time-saving, short-cut alternatives to the preparation of funds flow statements. Obviously, the short-cut versions do not provide the degree of detail found in the complete statement of changes in financial position.

We will illustrate the preparation of the various funds flow statements using the financial and operating data of the Sterling Yarn Company, a cotton yarn manufacturer, for the period December 31, 1977 through December 31, 1978. The firm's comparative balance sheet is presented in Table 10-1 and its income statement in Table 10-5. The funds flow statements that will be prepared for Sterling are (1) the statement of net

Table 10-1

**COMPARATIVE BALANCE SHEETS
STERLING YARN CORPORATION
for the Years Ended December 31, 1977 and 1978**

	December 31, 1977	December 31, 1978	Increase Decrease*
Assets			
Current assets			
Cash	$ 260,628.35	$ 149,073.31	$111,555.04*
Accounts receivable (net)	259,496.83	313,575.67	54,078.84
Inventory	676,323.16	1,081,362.84	405,039.68
Total current assets	$1,196,448.34	$1,544,011.82	$347,563.48
Fixed assets (net)	987,933.62	1,026,171.96	38,238.34
Investments	53,000.00	33,000.00	20,000.00*
Due from officers	10,278.91	20,512.31	10,233.40
Deferred charges	4,551.18	9,546.77	4,995.59
Total assets	$2,252,212.05	$2,633,242.86	$381,030.81
Liabilities and Net Worth			
Current liabilities			
Bank notes payable	$ 125,000.00	$ 570,000.00	$445,000.00
Accounts payable	37,207.11	89,133.72	51,926.61
Accrued taxes	504,384.16	269,286.37	235,097.79*
Other accruals	23,406.49	39,596.64	16,190.15
Total current liabilities	$ 689,997.76	$ 968,016.73	$278,018.97
Noncurrent bank loans	110,000.00	35,000.00	75,000.00*
Total liabilities	$ 799,997.76	$1,003,016.73	$203,018.97

Net worth			
Capital stock preferred	$ 400,000.00	$ 500,000.00	$100,000.00
Capital stock common	325,000.00	325,000.00	—0—
Capital surplus	367,291.48	377,291.48	10,000.00
Retained earnings	359,922.81	427,934.65	68,011.84
Total net worth	$1,452,214.29	$1,630,226.13	$178,011.84
Total liabilities and net worth	$2,252,212.05	$2,633,242.86	$381,030.81
Working capital	$ 506,450.58	$ 575,995.09	$ 69,544.51

167

working capital changes, (2) the statement of sources and applications of funds (sources and uses of funds statement), and (3) the statement of changes in financial position.

STATEMENT OF NET WORKING CAPITAL CHANGES

The statement of net working capital changes reports the effects of changes in noncurrent assets, noncurrent liabilities, and net worth over a given period on the firm's net working capital. A simple summary statement of net working capital changes between balance sheet dates will account exactly for the increase or decrease in a firm's net working capital and will provide a fairly comprehensive picture of the balance sheet effects of the net funds flows during the fiscal period. This form of the funds flow statement is the easiest to prepare since it uses the data provided by two consecutive balance sheets only.

The figures used in constructing the statement—the net increase or decrease in each balance sheet item over the period—are listed in the third column of Table 10-1. Sterling Yarn's net working capital on each balance sheet date has been computed by subtracting total current liabilities from total current assets and listed at the bottom of the table. The figures show that the firm's net working capital increased by $69,544.51 during the year; the statement of net working capital changes is designed to account for that increase and present the data in a form convenient for the analyst to use in tracing the firm's flow of funds. Thus the increases and decreases in the accounts listed in the last column of Table 10-1 are separated into those changes serving to increase working capital and those serving to decrease working capital. The following are the results of this classification:

A. Changes serving to increase working capital
   1. Decreases in noncurrent assets (in investments—$20,000)
   2. Increases in noncurrent liabilities (none)
   3. Increases in net worth accounts (in outstanding preferred stock—$100,000; in capital surplus—$10,000; in retained earnings—$68,011.84)
B. Changes serving to decrease working capital
   1. Increases in noncurrent assets (in net fixed assets—$38,238.34; in due from officers—$10,233.40; in deferred charges—$4,995.59)
   2. Decreases in noncurrent liabilities (in noncurrent bank loans—$75,000)
   3. Decreases in net worth accounts (none)

Those changes are summarized in a simple format in Table 10-2, which accounts exactly for the $69,544.51 increase in working capital shown in Table 10-1.

Table 10-2

**STATEMENT OF NET WORKING CAPITAL CHANGES
STERLING YARN CORPORATION
for the Year Ended December 31, 1978**

Factors serving to increase working capital		
Increase in outstanding preferred stock	$100,000.00	
Increase in capital surplus	10,000.00	
Increase in retained earnings	68,011.84	
Decrease in investments	20,000.00	
		$198,011.84
Factors serving to decrease working capital		
Decrease in noncurrent bank loans	$ 75,000.00	
Increase in net fixed assets	38,238.34	
Increase in due from officers	10,233.40	
Increase in deferred charges	4,995.59	
		128,467.33
Net increase in net working capital		$ 69,544.51

Although this simplified funds flow statement includes all the major elements needed to account for the change in net working capital, it lacks sufficient detail to enable the financial statement analyst to trace the complete cash flow cycle (described in Chapter 5)—or even the short cash flow cycle—through the various accounts of the firm; thus, although the statement is quickly prepared using only two successive balance sheets, it is little more than a general summary of the firm's major funds flows.

For example, the statement clearly indicates that the outstanding preferred stock increased by $100,000 but not whether that represents the total funds received by the company from the issuance of the stock. The stock may have been sold for an amount greater than its par value (at a premium) or an amount less than its par value (at a discount), if sale at a discount is permitted by state laws. Either a premium or a discount would have caused an increase or a decrease in the capital surplus rather than in the preferred stock account. Similarly, the statement does not reveal what brought about the increase in the capital surplus account or what was responsible for the net increase in retained earnings; the statement merely lists the net differences between additions and deductions and fails to provide details concerning the individual transactions that caused the net changes.

STATEMENT OF SOURCES AND APPLICATIONS OF FUNDS

In order to capture more detail concerning the funds flow of a business firm than is provided by the statement of changes in net working capital, the financial statement analyst must supplement the data provided by a set of comparative balance sheets with certain supporting data drawn mainly from the firm's income statement. Those data can then be used to prepare a statement of sources and applications of funds. Supplementary supporting data for Sterling Yarn Company are presented in Table 10-3.

Those data are used to make two basic adjustments in the statement of working capital changes. The first is designed to reveal what specific changes took place in the net worth section of the firm's balance sheet. Table 10-2 indicates under the heading "Factors serving to increase working capital" that preferred stock outstanding and the firm's capital surplus increased during 1978 by $100,000 and $10,000 respectively. Table 10-3 implies that both changes resulted from the sale of preferred stock, since it states that the cash proceeds from the sale amounted to $110,000. Table 10-2 also indicates that retained earnings increased by $68,011.84. That figure, according to the data presented in Table 10-3, is the result of the addition to retained earnings of the firm's 1978 profits (source of funds) less the sum of dividends paid and other deductions from retained earnings (uses of funds). The added detail is separated into "sources of funds" and "uses of funds" and presented in the sources and applications of funds statement for Sterling Yarn Corporation (Table 10-4) in the entries marked by a single asterisk.

The second adjustment relates to the change in the fixed asset account, the *net* amount of which is shown in Table 10-2 as a $38,238.34 increase. As the figures in Table 10-3 indicate, however, the increase in net fixed assets resulted from the combined effects of the deduction for depreciation charges of $82,753.16 and the purchase of $120,991.50 of new fixed assets. In order to show the full amount of the fixed assets purchases in the statement—an important bit of information concerning the firm's operations—the depreciation expense must also be shown. But rather than netting this figure against fixed assets, as is done on the balance sheet, this noncash charge against net income is accorded special

Table 10-3

SUPPORTING DATA FOR PREPARATION OF SOURCES AND APPLICATIONS OF FUNDS STATEMENT STERLING YARN CORPORATION for the Year Ended December 31, 1978

Net income per income statement	$124,706.81
Depreciation expense	82,753.16
Dividends paid	50,000.00
Fixed assets purchased	120,991.50
Other deductions from retained earnings (net)	6,694.97
Proceeds from sale of preferred stock	110,000.00

Table 10-4

**STATEMENT OF SOURCES AND APPLICATIONS OF FUNDS
STERLING YARN CORPORATION
for the Year Ended December 31, 1978**

Sources of Funds
  Funds from current operations
    Net income $124,706.81*
    Adjustments to net income for noncash items
      Depreciation expense   82,753.16**
  Funds generated from operations $207,459.97
  Funds from other business sources
    Sale of preferred stock   110,000.00*
    Decrease in investments   20,000.00
Total sources of funds $337,459.97

Applications of funds
  Decrease in noncurrent bank loans $ 75,000.00
  Purchases of fixed assets   120,991.50**
  Payment of dividends   50,000.00*
  Increase in due from officers   10,233.40
  Increase in deferred charges   4,995.59
  Other deductions from retained earnings (net)   6,694.97*
  Increase in net working capital   69,544.51
    $337,459,97

* entries detailing net worth adjustments
** entries detailing fixed asset adjustments

treatment in the preparation of the sources and applications of funds statement.

Since the depreciation charge reduced the firm's 1978 net income but (because it is a noncash expense) did not also decrease its cash account, we merely add it back to the net profit figure to determine the total of *funds provided by operations.* This adjustment, therefore, provides additional information about the firm's investment activities as well as its capacity to generate funds from operations. The adjusting entries are marked with a double asterisk in Table 10-4.

The increased information in the sources and uses of funds statement over that in the statement of net working capital changes is significant, but complete detail is still lacking. For example, the analyst may properly inquire into the nature of the other deductions from retained earnings and request additional supporting schedules so that he may determine what kinds of fixed assets were purchased and which investments were disposed of during the year. Those kinds of data are necessary to prepare the statement of changes in financial position.

171

STATEMENT OF CHANGES IN FINANCIAL POSITION

The preparation of the statement of changes in financial position requires a detailed income statement (Table 10-5), a statement of retained earnings (Table 10-6), and certain other supporting schedules, including a reconciliation of capital surplus, a schedule of investments, and a schedule of fixed assets.[1] The two adjustments discussed in connection with the sources and uses of funds statements are also required here; however, since this statement has to contain significantly more financial information than either the statement of changes in net working capital or the sources and uses of funds statement, the adjustments are carried out in greater detail.

Net Worth Adjustment

Beginning with the net worth adjustment once again, we find that the reconciliation of capital surplus of the Sterling Yarn Corporation (not illustrated) includes a $10,000 credit to capital surplus arising from the premium on the sale of preferred treasury stock (that is, the firm sold the stock for $10,000 more than its stated par value). Therefore, the selling price of the stock ($110,000) is listed in the statement of changes in financial position and accounts fully for the $100,000 increase in the par value of outstanding preferred stock and the $10,000 increase in capital surplus.

The adjustment for the factors that brought about the net increase in retained earnings uses the data contained in Table 10-6, the corporation's statement of retained earnings. The additions to retained earnings are sources of funds, and the deductions are applications of funds. Of course, the net profits are adjusted for the effects of certain noncash charges (i.e., the provisions for depreciation and amortization), as discussed earlier, but the other additions and deductions listed in Table 10-6 are entered without modification into the statement of changes in financial position as shown in Table 10-7.

The income statement lists bad debt expenses of $5,639.82. This expense is merely an *estimate* of bad debt losses and is charged to the *reserve* for bad debts. Although this expense, like depreciation, does not involve the expenditure of cash, it is excluded from the preparation of this statement because the accounts receivable figures shown in the balance sheets at the beginning and the end of the year are stated *net of the reserve for doubtful accounts;* hence any change in the amount of the reserve is automatically reflected in the book value of accounts receivable (and hence current assets), with a corresponding effect on the ending net working capital figure for the year. Thus, if the provision for

---

1. The supporting schedules are not illustrated here; however, the information useful in preparing the statement of financial position is detailed in the following discussion.

Table 10-5

**INCOME STATEMENT
STERLING YARN CORPORATION
December 31, 1978**

Gross sales		$3,663,977.68
Less: Returned sales and allowances		54,147.45
Net sales		$3,609,830.23
Cost of goods sold		
Inventory January 1, 1978	$ 676,323.16	
Purchases	3,205,292.60	
Freight on purchases	87,611.15	
Inventory December 31, 1978	1,081,362.84	
Cost of goods sold		$2,887,864.07
Gross profit on sales		$ 721,966.16
Less operating expenses:		
Selling	$ 118,125.75	
General and administrative	275,626.75	393,752.50
Gross operating income		$ 328,213.66
Depreciation	77,130.25	
Amortization	5,622.81	
Bad debt expense	5,639.82	88,392.88
Net income before taxes		$ 239,820.78
Federal income tax		115,113.97
Net income		$ 124,706.81

doubtful accounts were listed as an adjustment to net profit in preparing the statement, it would be counted twice—once in operations and once again in the change in working capital.

The statement of retained earnings also indicates that $9,363.63 of funds were provided by a refund of federal income taxes for the year 1977 and that $24,000 was applied to the payment of preferred dividends, $26,000 to the payment of common dividends, and $14,058.60 to the payment of additional income taxes applicable to the year 1976. Further, a $2,000 loss was sustained on the sale of the stock of the Milton Cotton Gin. A supporting schedule of the investments account (not illustrated) shows that the $20,000 decrease in investments was brought about solely by the disposition of the stock owned in this company, a transaction that gained the firm only $18,000 in cash. That information permits the analyst to account fully for the net increase in retained earnings and the decrease in investments shown by the summary statement (Table 10-2).

Table 10-6

**STATEMENT OF RETAINED EARNINGS
STERLING YARN CORPORATION
December 31, 1978**

Retained earnings, December 31, 1977		$359,922.81
Additions		
Net profit for the year (Exhibit C)	$124,706.81	
Refund of federal income taxes for the year 1977	9,363.63	
		134,070.44
		493,993.24
Deductions		
Dividends paid on preferred stock, 6%	$ 24,000.00	
Dividends paid on common stock, 8%	26,000.00	
Additional federal income taxes for the year 1976	14,058.60	
Loss on sale of stock of Milton Cotton Gin, Inc.	2,000.00	
		66,058.60
Retained earnings, December 31, 1978		$427,934.65

Fixed Asset Adjustment

The detailed schedule of fixed assets supporting the balance sheet (not illustrated) enables the analyst to perform the second adjustment. The schedule shows that the Sterling Yarn Corporation made the following fixed asset purchases (and additions to the cost value of these assets) during the year:

Purchase of land	$ 12,500.00
Purchase of machinery	84,260.51
Increase in cost value of buildings from renovations	24,230.99
Total	$120,991.50

The fixed asset schedule also reveals that patents with a total value of $84,342.15 are being carried as fixed assets. The only change in the reserve for depreciation during the year is the addition of the $77,130.35 depreciation charge to operations, and the increase in the reserve for amortization of patents reconciles exactly with the $5,622.81 charge to operations for this purpose. By deducting those amounts, representing reductions in the book value of net fixed assets, from the aggregate additions to the cost value of fixed assets (as previously determined), we can account fully for the increase of $38,238.34 in the net fixed assets during the year.

Table 10-7

STATEMENT OF CHANGES IN FINANCIAL POSITION
STERLING YARN CORPORATION
for the Year Ended December 31, 1978

Funds provided		
By net profit for the year	$124,706.81	
Add: Charges thereto not requiring funds		
Depreciation	77,130.35	
Amortization of patents	5,622.81	
		$207,459.97
By sale of preferred stock		110,000.00
By sale of stock of Milton Cotton Gin, Inc.		18,000.00
By a reduction in the value of investments		2,000.00
By refund of federal income tax for the year		
1977		9,363.63
Total funds provided		$346,823.60
Funds applied		
To payment of noncurrent bank loans		$ 75,000.00
To a loss on the sale of stock charged		
directly to retained earnings		2,000.00
To payment of dividends		
Preferred, 6%	$ 24,000.00	
Common	26,000.00	
		50,000.00
To expenditures on fixed assets		
Purchase of land	$ 12,500.00	
Purchase of machinery	84,260.51	
Additions to building	24,230.99	
		120,991.50
To increase in advances to officers		10,233.40
To increase in deferred charges		
Prepaid insurance	$ 3,846.22	
Prepaid interest	1,149.37	
		4,995.59
To additional income taxes for the year 1976		14,058.60
To increase in working capital		69,544.51
Total funds applied		$346,823.60

Unadjusted Data

The data contained in the comparative balance sheets presented in Table 10-1 enable us to complete the statement of changes in financial position. Here we find that $75,000 was applied to the reduction of noncurrent bank loans, $10,233.40 was used to increase advances to officers, $4,995.59 was absorbed by an increase in deferred charges ($3,846.22 of which was prepaid insurance and $1,149.37 prepaid interest), and $69,544.51 was applied to an increase in working capital. Those changes account for the application of all funds in the summary statement except for the increase of $38,238.34 in net fixed assets (already accounted for).

These data provide sufficient detail to explain the balance sheet changes over the period; thus, a detailed statement of changes in financial position can be prepared in the format illustrated in Table 10-7. This is a more complete, more accurate, and far more informative statement than the simple summary of net working capital changes in Table 10-2 or the sources and uses of funds statement in Table 10-4. But the statement is still incomplete in that the changes in the individual components of net working capital have not been presented in a convenient form. This defect can easily be remedied, however, simply by constructing a schedule similar to the one in Table 10-8 from the data in Table 10-1. The analyst may sometimes find the preparation of a schedule of changes in net working capital helpful, although he may deem it unnecessary if he has already compared the complete balance sheet in increase-decrease form, as shown in Table 10-1.

TREATMENT OF OPERATING LOSSES

Occasionally a financial statement analyst will examine a firm that has experienced operating losses. A net loss represents a drain on funds (a use) and must therefore be treated differently from profits in the statement of changes in financial position. One of two alternatives for record-

Table 10-8

SCHEDULE OF CHANGES IN NET WORKING CAPITAL
STERLING YARN CORPORATION
for the Year Ended December 31, 1978

	1977	*1978*	*Inc-Dec**
Current assets			
Cash	$ 260,628.35	$ 149,073.31	$111,555.04*
Accounts receivable (net)	259,496.83	313,575.67	54,078.84
Inventory	676,323.16	1,081,362.84	405,039.68
Total current assets	$1,196,448.34	$1,544,011.82	$347,563.48
Current liabilities			
Bank notes payable	$ 125,000.00	$ 570,000.00	$445,000.00
Accounts payable	37,207.11	89,133.72	51,926.61
Accrued taxes	504,384.16	269,286.37	235,097.79*
Other accruals	23,406.49	39,596.64	16,190.15
Total current liabilities	$ 689,997.76	$ 968,016.73	$278,018.97
Net working capital	$ 506,450.58	$ 575,995.09	$ 69,544.51

ing the loss is used, depending on the size of the loss in relation to other operational cash flows.

If the operating loss for the period is less than the noncash charges (for depreciation, for example), the operational funds flow section of the statement may be presented as follows:

Funds provided:
By operations
  Noncash charges to profit and loss:
    Depreciation $ 82,753.16
    Less: Net loss for the year   34,615.47
    Funds provided by operations $ 48,137.69

Alternatively, if the net loss *exceeds* the noncash charges, the entire computation must be shifted over to the *funds applied* section of the statement where the details may be presented as follows:

Funds applied:
To loss on operations
  Net loss per profit and loss statement $113,538.67
  Deduct noncash charges to profit and loss:
    Depreciation   82,753.16
    Funds applied to operations $ 30,785.51

In either case, all other entries and adjustments to the data presented in the firm's balance sheet, income statement, and supporting schedules are the same as described.

Alternative Statement Formats

Each of the statements discussed in this chapter is sufficiently flexible in content and arrangement to serve the particular needs of the analyst under varying circumstances. There is no one preferred format or method of treatment of the items included in the statements, nor is there any body of accounting theory that dictates what item will or will not be included in the statements when they are prepared, either by a firm's management for internal purposes or by an outside analyst analyzing the firm for his own or his employer's benefit. The major concerns of the analyst when he selects the format for the statement are (1) to meet his needs for information at the particular time, (2) to disclose the facts fully, and (3) to avoid conveying misleading information to others through the content or design of the statement. Nothing will prevent the analyst, for example, from including unusual or nonrecurring items in the report or treating ordinary items in an unusual manner. As long as such items are properly identified, the statement of changes in financial position, no matter what format is selected, will serve the purpose for which it was designed.

The statement formats most widely used can be classified under three general headings: (1) net working capital reports, (2) balanced reports, and (3) residual form reports. The net working capital reports, illustrated in Table 10-2, show the changes in net working capital as the balancing item, or the difference between the amounts of the sources and the uses of funds. The balanced report form, illustrated in Table 10-9, lists all sources of funds and then all uses, including either the total change in net working capital for the period (as either a source or a use, depending on whether it decreased or increased over the period) or the changes in the *individual* current asset and current liability accounts. The latter approach is used in Table 10-9.

The residual form report develops, as the final balancing item, some pertinent source or use of funds that management or the financial statement analyst wishes to highlight, generally for control purposes. For example, the changes in cash and marketable securities may be relatively important to a business with chronic cash problems. For firms that are undertaking long-range capital expansion programs, the analyst may wish to highlight "funds used for fixed assets purchased." The residual form report for Sterling Yarn is illustrated in Table 10-10, highlighting the firm's cash position. Note that the figures for cash and marketable securities have been included as separate items for the convenience of users.

Summary

Earlier discussions of the short and long cash flow cycles of a business firm (in Chapters 5 through 7) anticipated to some extent this chapter's discussion of the sources and applications of funds and the preparation of the statements designed to measure the flow of funds into and through a business enterprise. The cash and working capital resources of a firm are important indicators of its financial health. The ability of management to meet its firm's obligations as they become due and to expand its operations when the opportunity arises depends on adequate levels of liquid funds and cash flows. The statements of changes in financial position provide relevant information concerning those essential ingredients of financial success in convenient and easily interpreted formats. Moreover, they permit the interested outside financial statement analyst to examine the firm's major financing and investment activities and judge their impact on the firm's historical financial position.

While fragmentary information on sources and uses of funds can be obtained from comparative balance sheets and from income statements, a comprehensive picture of the firm's funds flows can be gained only from a statement of changes in financial position. That accounts for the growing importance and use of such statements in the analysis of busi-

Table 10-9

BALANCED REPORT FORM
STERLING YARN CORPORATION
Statement of Changes in Financial Position
for the Year Ended December 31, 1978

Funds provided		
By net income		$124,706.81
By depreciation		82,753.16
By sale of preferred stock		100,000.00
By increase in capital surplus		10,000.00
By sale of stock of Milton Cotton Gin, Inc.		18,000.00
By refund of federal income tax		
for the year 1976		9,363.63
By increase in bank notes payable		445,000.00
By increase in accounts payable		51,926.61
By increase in other accruals		16,190.15
By decrease in cash and marketable		
securities		111,555.04
Total funds provided		$969,495.40
Uses of Funds		
To expenditures on fixed assets		
Purchase of land	$ 12,500.00	
Purchase of machinery	84,260.51	
Purchase of building	24,230.99	$120,991.50
To payment of dividends		
Preferred 6%	$ 24,000.00	
Common	26,000.00	50,000.00
To payment of noncurrent bank loans		75,000.00
To increase in advance to officers		10,233.40
To increase in deferred charges		
Prepaid insurance	$ 3,846.22	
Prepaid interest	1,149.37	4,995.59
To additional income taxes for the		
year 1975		14,058.60
To increase in current assets		
Accounts receivable (net)	$ 54,078.84	
Inventory	405,039.68	459,118.52
To decrease in accrued taxes		235,097.79
Total funds applied		$969,495.40

ness operations. The preceding discussion is designed merely to acquaint the reader with the techniques of constructing the funds flow statements and with the various formats in which they appear. The more essential aspect of funds flow analysis—the *use* of the statements—is presented in Chapter 15.

Table 10-10

**RESIDUAL REPORT FORM EMPHASIZING CASH
STERLING YARN CORPORATION
Statement of Sources and Uses of Funds
for the Year Ended December 31, 1978**

Cash and marketable securities,			
January 1, 1978			
Cash		$100,628.35	
Commercial paper		53,333.32	
Repurchase agreement		35,555.58	
Treasury bills		71,111.10	
			$260,628.35
Add: sources of cash			
Net income	$124,706.81		
Depreciation	82,753.16		
Sale of preferred stock	100,000.00		
Increase in capital surplus	10,000.00		
Refund of federal income tax			
for the year 1977	9,363.63		
Sale of stock of Milton			
Cotton Gin, Inc.	18,000.00		
Increase in current liabilities	513,116.76	$857,940.36	
Subtract: uses of cash			
Purchase of fixed assets	$120,991.50		
Dividends paid	50,000.00		
Repayment of long-term debt	75,000.00		
Increase in noncash current			
assets	459,118.52		
Additional federal income			
taxes for the year 1976	14,058.60		
Increase in due from officers	10,233.40		
Increase in deferred charges	4,995.54		
Decrease in accrued taxes	235,097.79	$969,495.40	
Net increase (decrease) in cash			
and marketable securities			(111,555.04)
Cash and marketable securities,			
December 31, 1978:			
Cash		$ 44,282.84	
U.S. Government Treasury Bills		59,864.36	
U.S. Government Agencies		44,926.11	
Total Cash Account			$149,073.31

Questions

10-1. What are the general accounting definitions of sources of funds? Uses of funds?

10-2. Explain how a statement of changes in net working capital is constructed.

10-3. What supporting data are needed to enable an analyst to transform a statement of changes in net working capital into a statement of sources and applications of funds?

10-4. What two adjustments are generally needed to convert a statement of changes in net working capital into a sources and uses of funds statement?

10-5. Why is bad debts expense excluded from the "funds provided" section of the statement of changes in financial position?

10-6. How are operating losses treated in the preparation of the statements covered in this chapter?

10-7. What three criteria should an analyst keep in mind when selecting a format for analyzing funds flow?

10-8. Briefly describe the three most widely used formats employed for the statement of changes in financial position.

Chapter 11   The Tools of Financial Forecasting

From the point of view of the management of a business firm, *financial planning* may be described as a forward-looking appraisal of the financial aspects of an established business program, leading to decisions about the most effective course of action to be taken over a future period. It encompasses both the business plan and its translation into the funds needed to carry it out. It touches on the acquisition of those funds, control of their expenditure, appraisal of the results of the expenditures, and provision for the repayment of debt and the distribution of earnings to the owners of the firm.

The need to deal with the future financial aspects of a firm's operations is equally important to interested outside parties. Bankers, prospective investors, current and long-term creditors, and others must constantly look to the results of the firm's future operations for the satisfaction of their claims. The need to forecast thus becomes an essential part of financial statement analysis, and those who practice the art must be thoroughly conversant with the construction and use of the principal tools of financial forecasting—cash budgets and pro forma (projected) financial statements.

Although both cash budgets and pro forma statements can be used in short-term financial forecasts, the cash budget is generally considered the principal short-term forecasting tool because it provides a continuous picture of the firm's cash flows throughout the forecasting period. Pro forma statements, on the other hand, provide the analyst with the results of forecasted operations as of some future date; consequently, they are the more appropriate tool for projecting the results of operations over longer periods (that is, periods not less than one year). Although they can be equally useful in short-term forecasts, the amount of time and effort required to construct twelve monthly pro forma statements, for example, weighs heavily against their use in such forecasts.

The purpose of this chapter is to describe the methods by which cash

183

budgets and pro forma financial statements are prepared. We will begin by examining the cash budget and then present two approaches to constructing pro forma statements. The applications of these important tools of statement analysis are discussed in the final section of the chapter.

Cash Budgets

The cash budget, as its name implies, summarizes the estimated cash inflows and disbursements of a business over the budget period. It also shows the resultant cash position, generally on a monthly basis, as the budget period develops. It is the formal presentation in dollars of the expected circular flow of cash through the business as discussed and illustrated in Chapters 5 through 7. Its principal use in statement analysis is to predict *if, when,* and *by how much* the firm's cash resources are likely either to be greater than estimated requirements or to become insufficient to cover the checks it must write. Once those predictions have been made, the analyst can begin both to assess the firm's ability to handle short-term debt repayment and to diagnose the financial problems that may be interfering with its ability to generate adequate cash balances.

PREPARING THE CASH BUDGET

An outside analyst will find that preparing a cash budget for a firm is almost impossible unless he has the full cooperation of management. Since future operations depend largely on management's plans, the analyst must be aware of those plans and able to incorporate them into reasonably accurate estimates of the elements contained in four key areas of the cash budget: (1) revenues; (2) operating cash expenditures; (3) discretionary cash expenditures; and (4) financial transactions. The elements of those four key areas and the methods employed in developing forecasts for each are discussed in the following sections.

Revenues

Revenue sources may be classified under five general headings: (1) cash sales, (2) collection of trade accounts receivable, (3) collection of other accounts and notes receivable, (4) receipt of interest, dividends, rents, and royalties, and (5) cash sales of assets other than inventories. The first two sources are usually the most important in dollar amounts and also the most difficult to forecast accurately. The last three sources, being contractual, largely episodic, and for many firms relatively small or nonexistent sources of revenues, generally pose little problem to the analyst in forecasting their amounts and the timing of their receipt; consequently, an accurate revenue forecast depends most of all on how accurately the firm's sales and collection period are estimated.

Sales and Collections. Sales estimates for a future period should be derived by determining the quantity of each product likely to be sold in the period, applying to that quantity the price proposed for the product, and arriving at the total dollar sales figure. The estimate of the quantity of each product likely to be sold should be based on a detailed analysis of the quantities sold over the past three or four years. Such an analysis should be broken down by individual salesman, branch, geographic territory, and so on. Each salesman should be consulted for his estimate of the quantity of each product to be sold, and the salesmen's estimates should be assembled by branches and geographic territories to give an overall estimate of the sales of all products. A market survey service may be used to determine market demand and expansion possibilities in the light of the competition and general conditions to be faced in each present or prospective area; quantity estimates may be modified accordingly.

Other considerations that bear on the quantity of each product sold are (1) the unit price at which the product is to be sold, (2) the amount to be spent on advertising and promotional efforts, and (3) the general economic conditions likely to be encountered. The unit price proposed for each product (having been set with due consideration to the general price level and to competitive and economic conditions) is applied to the quantity estimates to compute the total dollar sales estimate for all products for the period.

The final sales forecast is usually a composite of several forecasts prepared by different methods to ensure that all factors affecting sales have been considered. The usual methods include an econometric, or statistical, forecast, in which past performance is projected into the future through trend analysis or other statistical approaches; a unit sales forecast generally prepared by the firm's own sales personnel; and a dollar sales forecast prepared by estimating the selling prices of the firm's products and relating them to unit sales forecasts. All the forecasts are compared to determine whether they produce a consensus. If they produce divergent results, they must be reconciled, usually by management. If they are in substantial agreement, the next step is to estimate the cash flow from the collections of the predicted sales.

First, it is necessary to separate cash sales from credit sales and to analyze the credit sales to determine the time lag between sales and collections. The effect of seasonal variations and general business conditions on collections and on the length of the collection period should particularly be noted. Unless a firm's list of customers changes dramatically from year to year, historical data will usually provide the basis for estimates of the proportion of each month's sales likely to be collected in that month and each month thereafter and how much the firm might expect its collections to change, given the forecast of business conditions over the budget period.

Second, other factors affecting collections must be taken into account. For example, returns and allowances must be estimated, especially if cash refunds must be made. The amount of cash discounts (if offered as part of the terms of sale) that customers are likely to take should be judged. The effects of any planned changes in either credit policy or collection policy must be estimated. Finally, the firm's bad debts experience must be brought into the picture, along with any expected deviations from historical norms resulting from changes in business conditions or in operating policies.

Other Cash Receipts. Most businesses receive cash during the course of their operations from sources other than the sale of their products or services, usually in relatively small amounts and at more or less regular intervals. When such sources exist, it is necessary to include them in the cash budget. Such receipts generally pose only minor problems in forecasting, because they have a minor impact on the overall cash budget. That does not mean, however, that such forecasts can be carelessly made, for even small errors can sometimes lead to major difficulties.

Cash Expenditures for Operations

The next set of forecasts needed in preparing the cash budget are forecasts of cash expenditures for operations. Their generally close relation to sales further emphasizes the need for an accurate sales forecast. Operating cash expenses include purchases of materials, payments for direct labor, and all other expenses (further classified as fixed, variable, and semivariable expenses).

Payment on Account for Purchases of Materials. The amounts paid and the timing of payments for raw materials or finished goods purchased for resale obviously have a direct relation to the sales volume a firm is able to achieve. Like the relation between sales and collections, however, this relation is not necessarily precise. It may be upset by a decision to increase or decrease the size of inventories carried, the use of level production by a firm whose sales are highly seasonal, or changes in technology or product mix, for example. Therefore, while the *volume* of sales for the forecast period will set the basic purchase requirements, the production schedule and inventory policies adopted will influence the timing and the ultimate quantity of goods purchased.

It is most likely that cash purchases will constitute only a small fraction of cash disbursements in the projected period. However, if some of the company's products use materials sold cash-and-carry, those cash disbursements must be estimated.

As for accounts receivable, there is a time lag between the arrival of materials (and the invoice) and the date when the actual cash payment is made. The length of the time lag is determined jointly by the credit terms extended by the supplier and the company's policy on the payment of its trade debts. For example, a firm that purchases its goods on credit terms of 2/10, net 30, may pay on the tenth day, the thirtieth day, or any other day after the invoice date it chooses, including a date after the account becomes past due.

Cash Payments for Direct Labor. The direct labor budget (if one has been prepared by management) provides the hours worked by employees in various job classifications. The conversion to dollars is relatively simple once the hourly rates of pay have been estimated for the budget period. To the estimate of direct wages must be added social security taxes, paid holidays, periodic payments into the retirement fund, payments for overtime, vacations, or payments in lieu of vacations.

If management has not prepared a direct labor budget, the historical relation between materials and direct labor costs (adjusted for relevant expected changes) may be used to forecast this expenditure. The analyst must, of course, recognize that purchases of materials relate to the period *following* their receipt, while wages paid relate to the period *preceding* their payment. The number of pay days per month (or other budget period) will also influence the size of the cash outflow for direct labor expenses.

Cash Disbursements for Other Operating Expenses. The remaining cash disbursements for operating expenses are usually listed in the cash budget under the heading of manufacturing, selling, and administrative expenses. They can also be classified as *fixed expenses, variable expenses,* and *semivariable expenses* for purposes of forecasting their timing and magnitude.

Fixed expenses are those expected to remain constant regardless of the level of production. They include property taxes, insurance, executive compensation, and most dues, fees, and service contracts. Although their level is independent of the level of production, they cannot be expected to remain constant forever. Property taxes and insurance costs change, especially when new fixed assets are acquired, and executive compensation can be expected to rise from year to year (at least in a profitable business). Thus the same degree of care must be given to estimating payments for fixed costs as is required for all other classes of expense.

Variable expenses are those expected to vary directly with the level of production or sales. Examples are packaging and shipping costs, salesmen's commissions, and certain preprinted production, sales, and administrative forms. A major problem likely to be encountered in forecasting such expenses arises from the changes that occur in their relative prices as the levels of production or sales change. If, for example, a 10 percent increase in dollar sales increases salesmen's commissions by 15 percent in one year and both the rate of commission and the selling price of the product are scheduled to be changed during the budget period, the effects of those changes on the relation between the two items must be reconciled before an accurate forecast of that expense can be made. Similarly, a change in the price of packaging materials will alter the relation between shipping costs and unit sales.

Forecasting problems associated with semivariable expenses arise from two sources. First, the relation between those expenses and the scale of operations may be either direct or indirect and may change at a changing rate. That is because semivariable expenses are in part fixed and in part variable. Second, changes in relative prices have effects on those expenses similar to their effects on the purely variable expenses. Examples of semivariable expenses are indirect labor, plant and equipment maintenance, and utilities.

Discretionary Cash Expenditures

Discretionary expenditures, as the name implies, are cash outlays for items that in management's judgment, are necessary to the profitable operation of the firm but can be postponed for at least a short period or can be increased or decreased without immediately impairing operations. Included in this classification are expenditures for research and development, for the introduction of new or the revamping of existing advertising campaigns, for the purchase of fixed assets, and for early payment of trade credit to take advantage of cash discounts.

In constructing this particular forecast for the cash budget, the financial statement analyst will have to rely solely on information provided by management. Forecasting discretionary expenditures on the basis of historical records is obviously unwise; such expenditures may be relatively large, and management has complete control over their timing.

Financial Transactions

Financial transactions constitute the last category of data used to construct the cash budget. Items normally found in this category are:
1. Issuance and retirement of capital stock
2. Issuance and retirement of long-term debt
3. Payment of interest on outstanding debt
4. Cash dividend payments
5. Purchase or sale of temporary or long-term investments

Most of those items are transactions controlled by management. Estimates of the timing and the amounts of certain of them can be quite accurate; for example, cash dividend payments and interest on long-term debt. But the decision to issue new stock or to retire long-term debt by purchasing outstanding bonds in the secondary securities market cannot always be forecast with precision because the actual funds involved in those transactions will depend on the market conditions that obtain when the stock is sold or the bonds repurchased.

The other financial transactions, such as contractual debt repayment, are firmly fixed in both amount and size as a result of the extant contract to make payment or repayment of specific amounts on predetermined days.

CASH BUDGET ILLUSTRATED

The Burkart Balsam Corporation, a small chemical processing and compounding firm, introduced a new chemical turpentine that in late 1978 became widely accepted in the marketplace. A recent marketing survey indicates that the demand for the new product will remain strong through 1979 and will help boost the overall demand for the company's other products. As a result, the company expects 1979 sales to total $419,600, a 10 percent increase over 1978 sales. The company expects sales in the next 12 months as follows:

Month	Estimated Sales	Month	Estimated Sales
January	$43,100	July	$26,200
February	40,400	August	26,200
March	41,800	September	30,800
April	34,000	October	33,600
May	30,300	November	42,100
June	25,300	December	45,800

At that level of sales, the firm's management believes a minimum working cash balance of $25,000 will be required throughout the year. Management also believes that the firm's growth will place a strain on its cash position that will probably require it to seek outside financing. Consequently, it decides to gather as much data as possible about its 1979 operations to be prepared to request financial assistance from its bank. It therefore assembles the data in Tables 11-1, 11-2, and 11-3, based solely on historical relations. In addition, management expects the following financial and discretionary transactions to take place during 1979.

The company plans to purchase $42,500 of new equipment during the year, for which it will pay $22,500 upon delivery in February and the remaining $20,000 after its final installation, probably in May. In addition to the cash outlay for new equipment, the company hopes to be able to repay a $10,000 bank loan incurred in 1978 and retire $8,000 of its long-term debt by making sinking fund payments of $4,000 each in June and December and paying the quarterly interest of $1,600 in March and June and $1,200 in September and December. In addition, the company

Table 11-1

WORKSHEET A
BURKART BALSAM CORPORATION
Estimates of Cash Collections
for the Months January-December 1979

	JAN	FEB	MARCH	APRIL	MAY	JUNE	JULY	AUG	SEP	OCT	NOV	DEC	TOTALS
Net sales	$43,100	$40,400	$41,800	$34,000	$30,300	$25,300	$26,200	$26,200	$30,800	$33,600	$42,100	$45,800	$419,600
Less cash sales (20% of net sales)	$ 8,620	$ 8,080	$ 8,360	$ 6,800	$ 6,060	$ 5,060	$ 5,240	$ 5,240	$ 6,160	$ 6,720	$ 8,420	$ 9,160	$ 83,920
Net credit sales	34,480	32,320	33,440	27,200	24,240	20,240	20,960	20,960	24,640	26,880	33,680	36,640	335,680
Collections													
1st month (50% of net credit sales)	$17,240	$16,160	$16,720	$13,600	$12,120	$10,120	$10,480	$10,480	$12,320	$13,440	$16,840	$18,320	
2nd month (30% of net credit sales)	10,200*	10,344	9,696	10,032	8,160	7,272	6,072	6,288	6,288	7,392	8,064	10,104	
3rd month (15% of net credit sales)	4,650*	5,100*	5,172	4,848	5,016	4,080	3,636	3,036	3,144	3,144	3,696	4,032	
Total collection from receivables	$32,090	$31,604	$31,588	$28,480	$25,296	$21,472	$20,188	$19,804	$21,752	$23,976	$28,600	$32,456	$317,306
Write-off for bad debts (5% of net credit sales)	$ 2,150†	$ 1,550†	$ 1,700†	$ 1,724	$ 1,616	$ 1,672	$ 1,360	$ 1,212	$ 1,012	$ 1,048	$ 1,048	$ 1,232	$ 17,324

*Collections from net credit sales of $31,000 and $34,000 for November and December 1978 respectively.

†Bad debts from net credit sales of $43,000 in October 1978, $31,000 in November 1978, and $34,000 in December 1978.

Table 11-2

WORKSHEET B
BURKART BALSAM CORPORATION
Monthly Cost and Expenses Estimates
for the Months January-December 1979

Materials...	15% of net monthly sales
Director labor.....................................	25% of net monthly sales
Factory overhead	
variable.....................................	10% of net monthly sales
fixed..	$1,000 per month
Selling expense...............................	15% of net monthly sales
Administrative expenses	
variable.....................................	5% of net monthly sales
fixed..	$1,500 per month
Federal income taxes......................	Quarterly payments of $2,500 in March and June, $2,000 in September, and $12,000 in December
Other taxes......................................	$5,000 in January and April and $10,300 in October

expects to declare and pay a cash dividend on common stock of $2,200 each quarter in January, April, July, and October.

The firm plans to sell $4,300 of obsolete equipment at book value in February, when the new equipment is delivered; $10,000 of securities the firm holds will mature during the same month.

The president of Burkart Balsam gathered up his worksheets and the list containing the other transactions and called on his banker with a request for a working capital loan. After discussing the firm's situation, the banker suggested that the president leave the data with him for a day or two so that he could prepare a monthly cash budget for 1979.

The cash budget prepared by Burkart's banker, shown in Table 11-4, is a compendium of the three worksheets and the list containing the other transactions. The form in which it is presented is fairly typical, but the form of the final section, "Financial transactions," was chosen by the banker to show Burkart's president how the firm's operating plans will probably affect both short-term credit needs (line 28) and idle cash balances. It highlights the availability of cash (line 26) and the ending cash balance (line 29), which the firm wishes to maintain as its minimum cash balance (about $25,000).

Worksheet A supplies all the information needed to fill in lines 1 through 4 in the budget. Note that the banker decided to omit from the cash budget the bad debt write-offs listed on the worksheet. The banker felt that the historical bad debt percentage of sales was inappropriate for use in 1979 since the economic outlook in chemicals was excellent and the firm had, at the banker's suggestion, made significant progress in

Table 11-3

WORKSHEET C
BURKART BALSAM CORPORATION
Estimates of Cash Payments for Material Purchases
for the Months January-December 1979

	JAN	FEB	MARCH	APRIL	MAY	JUNE	JULY	AUG	SEP	OCT	NOV	DEC	TOTALS
Materials purchased during month (15% of net sales)	$6,465	$6,060	$6,270	$5,100	$4,545	$3,795	$3,930	$3,930	$4,620	$5,040	$6,315	$6,870	$62,940
Payments													
1st month (50% of purchases)	$3,233	$3,030	$3,135	$2,550	$2,273	$1,898	$1,965	$1,965	$2,310	$2,520	$3,158	$3,435	$31,472
2nd month (50% of purchases)	3,000*	3,233	3,030	3,135	2,550	2,273	1,898	1,965	1,965	2,310	2,520	3,158	$31,037
Total payments	$6,233	$6,263	$6,165	$5,685	$4,823	$4,171	$3,863	$3,930	$4,275	$4,830	$5,678	$6,593	$62,509

*Remaining from purchase of materials in December 1978.

192

tightening up its credit and collection policies during 1977 and 1978.

The data for lines 5 and 6 of the budget are obtained from the list of transactions planned for 1979 and the firm's schedule of investments (not illustrated).

The banker based lines 9 through 16 on the data provided in Worksheets B and C; the figures in lines 17 through 21 were found in Burkart's list of planned financial and discretionary transactions. Although cash dividends (line 17) and purchase of fixed assets (line 20) are truly discretionary, they are nevertheless entered as if they were actual commitments. If management alters its plans after seeing the results of the cash budget, the figures can be altered and the effects on the cash flow noted.

From lines 23 and 24 in the "total" column the banker observes that the firm will experience a net drain of cash of $21,363 for the year. That loss is the result of the $42,500 capital expenditure, an unusually large outlay for the year. He is also able to determine that the existing bank loan (created in 1978) of $10,000 for working capital needs will be paid out in January and March in two equal payments. And the firm will have to begin to borrow from the bank again in May. Hence the additional entries in lines 27 and 28. Those entries indicate how the firm might wish to use the excess cash generated early in the year by collections of the fourth quarter's sales of the previous year and how the subsequent cash drains can be financed.

In May and June the firm will have to borrow a total of $13,000; in July, August, and September, it will repay a total of $7,000. It will reborrow that amount in October and repay another $6,000 in November. In December, because of a large tax payment, it will have to borrow another $10,000, leaving a total unpaid debt of $17,000 or $7,000 more than it started with on January 1, 1979. To the extent that the banker has confidence in the estimates on which the budget is based, he can use the data presented in lines 27 and 28 in assessing the firm's ability to repay its short-term debt while servicing its senior obligations and financing its continuing operations.

LIMITATIONS OF CASH BUDGETS

It is easy to see how such a tool as a cash budget may be indispensable when it comes to planning the amount and type of funds needs, repayment of debt, payment to the owners of the business, and efficient utilization of excess (idle) cash balances. But this tool, as indispensable as it may seem, is not without its limitations. First, errors in estimating the data that must be assembled before constructing the cash budget will obviously create inaccuracies in the cash forecast. Second, the time segments covered by the budget may be inappropriate. For example, if Burkart's receipts are concentrated near the end of each month, its debt service charges are due near the first, and its operating expenses are

Table 11-4

CASH BUDGET
BURKART BALSAM CORPORATION
for Year Ending December 31, 1979

	January	February	March	April	May
1. Sales forecast	$43,100	$40,400	$41,800	$34,000	$30,300
Receipts					
From operations					
2. Cash sales	8,620	8,080	8,360	6,800	6,060
3. Collections, accounts receivable	32,090	31,604	31,588	28,480	25,296
4. Total receipts from operations	$40,710	$39,684	$39,948	$35,280	$31,356
Other receipts					
5. Sale of fixed assets		4,300			
6. Income from investments	100		200		
7. Total other receipts	100	$ 4,300	$ 200		
8. Total receipts	$40,810	$43,984	$40,148	$35,280	$31,356
Disbursements					
For operations					
9. Raw materials	$ 6,233	$ 6,263	$ 6,165	$ 5,685	4,823
10. Direct labor	10,775	10,100	10,450	8,500	7,575
11. Factory overhead	5,310	5,040	5,180	4,400	4,030
12. Selling expense	6,465	6,060	6,270	5,100	4,545
13. Administrative expense	3,655	3,520	3,590	3,200	3,015
14. Federal income taxes			2,500		
15. Other taxes	5,000			5,000	
16. Total disbursements for operations	$37,438	$30,983	$34,155	$31,885	$23,988
Other disbursements					
17. Dividends	2,200			2,200	
18. Repayment of long-term debt					
19. Interest payment on long-term debt			1,600		
20. Purchase of fixed assets		22,500			20,000
21. Total other disbursements	$ 2,200	$22,500	$ 1,600	$ 2,200	$20,000
22. Total disbursements	$39,638	$53,483	$35,755	$34,085	$43,988
23. Net receipts (disbursements)	$ 1,172	$ (9,499)	$ 4,393	$ 1,195	$ (12,632)
24. Cumulative net effect on cash	1,172	(8,327)	(3,934)	(2,739)	(15,371)
Financial transactions					
25. Beginning cash balance	$32,500	$25,672	$26,173	$25,566	$26,761
26. Cash available	$33,672	$16,173	$30,566	$26,761	$14,129
27. Sale (purchase) of securities	(3,000)	10,000			
28. Borrowing (repayment) from bank	(5,000)		(5,000)		11,000
29. Ending cash balance	$25,672	$26,173	$25,566	$26,761	$25,129

194

Table 11-4

CASH BUDGET
BURKART BALSAM CORPORATION
for Year Ending December 31, 1979

	June	July	August	September	October	November	December	Total	
	$25,300	$26,200	$26,200	$30,800	$33,600	$42,100	$45,800	$419,600	1.
	5,060	5,240	5,240	6,160	6,720	8,420	9,160	83,920	2.
	21,472	20,188	19,804	21,752	23,976	28,600	32,456	317,306	3.
	$26,532	$25,428	$25,044	$27,912	$30,696	$37,020	$41,616	$401,226	4.
								4,300	5.
		100		200				600	6.
		$ 100		$ 200				$ 4,900	7.
	$26,532	$25,528	$25,044	$28,112	$30,696	$37,020	$41,616	$406,126	8.
	$ 4,171	$ 3,863	$ 3,930	$ 4,275	$ 4,830	$ 5,678	$ 6,593	$ 62,509	9.
	6,325	6,550	6,550	7,700	8,400	10,525	11,450	104,900	10.
	3,530	3,620	3,620	4,080	4,360	5,210	5,580	53,960	11.
	3,795	3,930	3,930	4,620	5,040	6,315	6,870	62,940	12.
	2,765	2,810	2,810	3,040	3,180	3,605	3,790	38,980	13.
	2,500			2,000			12,000	19,000	14.
					10,300			20,300	15.
	$23,086	$20,773	$20,840	$25,715	$36,110	$31,333	$46,283	$362,589	16.
		2,200			2,200			8,800	17.
	4,000						4,000	8,000	18.
	1,600			1,200			1,200	5,600	19.
								42,500	20.
	$ 5,600	$ 2,200		$ 1,200	$ 2,200		$ 5,200	$ 64,900	21.
	$28,686	$22,973	$20,840	$26,915	$38,310	$31,333	$51,483	$427,489	22.
	$ (2,154)	$ 2,555	$ 4,204	$ 1,197	$(7,614)	$ 5,687	$ (9,867)	$ (21,363)	23.
	(17,525)	(14,970)	(10,766)	(9,569)	(17,183)	(11,496)	(21,363)	(21,363)	24.
	$25,129	$24,975	$25,530	$25,734	$25,931	$25,317	$25,004	$ 32,500	25.
	$22,975	$27,530	$29,734	$26,931	$18,317	$31,004	$15,137	$ 11,137	26.
								7,000	27.
	2,000	(2,000)	(4,000)	(1,000)	7,000	(6,000)	10,000	7,000	28.
	$24,975	$25,530	$25,734	$25,931	$25,317	$25,004	$25,137	$ 25,137	29.

195

paid fairly evenly, the firm is likely to experience a chronic cash shortage at the middle of every month. That, of course, would increase its peak borrowing requirements over the amounts shown in line 28 of Table 11-4.

Finally, although the budget is usually prepared for a twelve-month period, it must be revised monthly for most firms. Business involves dynamic processes that are by definition subject to change and must therefore be adapted to any changes that occur. The changes are reflected in the cash flow patterns of the firm and hence in its cash budget. It is therefore totally inappropriate to require a business to adhere to its cash budget as originally drafted under such circumstances; instead, the analyst must adjust his figures—and often the financing and repayment plans as well—to fit the new circumstances. We will continue this discussion in more general terms later. Now, however, let us examine the method of constructing pro forma statements.

Pro Forma Statements

In addition to projecting the cash flow of a firm over time by way of the cash budget, it is often useful to prepare projected or *pro forma* income statements and balance sheets for selected future dates. As will be seen in the following sections, much of the information used in preparing the cash budget is also used in constructing pro forma statements. The following two sections discuss in detail how the estimates of the items that make up the pro forma statements are made and the assumptions that underlie the estimates.

The first section illustrates what we will call the *exact* method of estimating the future financial position and operations of the firm. While it is perhaps inappropriate to call any forecast exact, the name derives from the fact that the data from which such pro forma statements are constructed are individually estimated items, most of which appear in the cash budget. Thus the pro forma statements prepared by the exact method are actually extensions of the cash budgeting process.

The next section illustrates one of several *shortcut* methods of pro forma statement preparation. The method illustrated produces a forecast based on prior years' financial statement relations and account proportions of the firm being examined. That approach is admittedly less accurate than the exact method, but it is frequently used, especially by outside analysts who do not have access to the detailed forecasts prepared by management.

The Burkart Balsam Corporation's 1979 income statement and balance sheet will be projected by both methods. The data from its cash budget, prepared in the preceding section (Table 11-4), will be used extensively in illustrating the exact method. In addition, certain historical balance sheet and income statement data are required by both methods; those data are provided in Tables 11-5 and 11-6.

THE EXACT METHOD

The logical starting point in applying the exact method (as well as others) is the construction of the pro forma income statement, since the values of certain balance sheet accounts (e.g., inventories and retained earnings) depend on income statement figures. We will use the formats presented in Tables 11-5 and 11-6 for the pro forma statements and adjust them when necessary.

Table 11-5

COMPARATIVE BALANCE SHEETS AND SELECTED RATIOS
BURKART BALSAM CORPORATION
December 31, 1977 and 1978

Assets	1977	1978
Cash	$ 18,740	$ 32,500
Short-term securities	9,000	20,000
Accounts receivable (net)	38,760	21,620
Inventory	16,800	19,110
Total current assets	$ 83,300	$93,230
Investments	0	15,000
Fixed assets	60,000	58,800
Less accumulated depreciation	10,800	12,000
Net fixed assets	$ 49,200	$ 46,800
Other assets	14,850	14,450
Total assets	$147,350	$169,480
Liabilities and Equity		
Notes payable—bank	4,000	$ 10,000
Accounts payable	6,810	3,000
Accrued federal income taxes	1,860	2,500
Other current liabilities	2,000	3,540
Accrued property taxes	17,650	20,300
Total current liabilities	$ 32,320	$ 39,340
Long-term debt	64,000	56,000
Common stock	30,000	30,000
Retained earnings	21,030	44,140
Total liabilities and equity	$147,350	$169,480
Selected Ratios		
Accounts receivable collection period	33.3 days	20.6 days
Inventory turnover	12.2 times	12.0 times
Accounts payable/average daily purchases	39.1 days	19.8 days

197

Table 11-6

**COMPARATIVE COMMON-SIZE INCOME STATEMENTS
BURKART BALSAM CORPORATION
for the Years Ending December 31, 1975-1978**

	1975	*1976*	*1977*	*1978*
Net sales	100.0%	100.0%	100.0%	100.0%
Cost of sales				
Raw materials	16.3	17.0	15.5	14.1
Direct labor	26.3	28.4	27.5	25.0
Factory overhead	19.8	14.2	11.0	12.8
Cost of goods sold	62.4%	59.6%	54.0%	51.9%
Gross profit	37.6%	40.4%	46.0%	48.1%
Selling expenses	8.6	10.2	14.5	13.9
Administrative expenses	4.7	3.2	8.8	9.8
Bad debt expense	7.5	8.6	9.0	6.8
Operating income	16.8%	18.4%	13.7%	17.6%
Other expense (net)	7.0	6.8	6.5	6.0
Profit before taxes	9.8%	11.6%	7.2%	11.6%
Income taxes	2.8	3.0	3.2	3.5
Net income	7.0%	8.6%	4.0%	8.1%
Dividends paid	3.0%	2.8%	2.6%	2.0%
To retained earnings	4.0%	5.8%	1.4%	6.1%

Pro Forma Income Statement

The exact method of pro forma statement preparation is an extension of the cash budgeting process; therefore, we begin by pulling the figures from the "total" column in Table 11-4 and inserting them in the appropriate places in the pro forma income statement. The figures thus obtained are marked with an asterisk in the Burkart Balsam Corporation pro forma income statement presented in Table 11-7. The accounts not marked with an asterisk either were obtained from a different source or represent adjusted cash budget data. In either case, the sources of the data are provided in the last column of Table 11-7.

Cost of Sales. The figure for total disbursements for raw materials (line 9 in Table 11-4) cannot be used in the income statement because it does not represent total purchases based on the accrual method of accounting and it does not account for any inventory change contemplated for the end of 1979. If we assume that the firm wishes to increase its inventory commensurate with sales (that is, to about $21,150) we may determine the *cost* of materials as follows:

198

Beginning inventory	$19,110	(Table 11-5)
Purchases in 1979	62,940	(Table 11-3)
	$82,050	
Less estimated ending inventory	21,150	(estimated)
Cost of materials	$60,900	

Table 11-7

**PRO FORMA INCOME STATEMENT PREPARED BY THE "EXACT" METHOD
BURKART BALSAM CORPORATION
for the Year Ending December 31, 1979**

		Data source
Net Sales	$419,600	
Cost of sales		
Raw materials	60,900	adjusted cash budget figure
Direct labor	104,900*	
Factory overhead	53,960*	
Depreciation	3,750	Table 11-5 and new equipment
Cost of goods sold	$223,510	
Gross profit	$196,090	
Selling expenses	62,940*	
Administrative expenses	38,980*	
Bad debt expense	17,324	Table 11-1
Total expenses	$119,244	
Operating income	$ 76,846	
Less other expense		
Interest expense	5,600*	
Property taxes	20,300*	
	$50,946	
Plus other income		
Investment income	600*	
Profit before taxes	51,546	
Income taxes	18,242	22% of the first $25,000 and
Net income	$33,304	48% of the remainder
Dividends paid	8,800*	
To retained earnings	$24,504	

*Figures are taken directly from the cash budget.

Direct labor and factory overhead figures may be taken directly from the cash budget. Even more precise estimates of those costs may be obtained by adjusting each for any accruals; however, the adjustment does not usually result in significant changes in the figures since the beginning and ending accruals generally cancel each other out.

Finally, the depreciation figure may be obtained from a schedule of fixed assets or may be estimated from the preceding year's balance sheet. The latter method is used here. Table 11-5 shows an increase in the accumulated depreciation account of $1,200. The cash budget shows a fixed asset purchase of $42,500 and a disposal of $4,300 in fixed assets, the difference being a net increase of $38,200. Assuming straight-line depreciation over ten years at 10 percent per year, net annual depreciation charges for the net fixed asset purchase will be $3,820. Since the new equipment will be placed in service in May, a total of eight month's (or 8/12 of one year's) depreciation will be charged against income. Thus total estimated depreciation is the sum of $1,200 and $2,550 (8/12 × $3,820), or $3,750.

Operating and Other Expenses and Income. Selling and administrative expense figures are the same as those in the cash budget. Bad debt expense, a noncash charge against income, is obtained directly from Table 11-1, and the figures for the remaining income and expense items are taken from the cash budget.

The income tax figure was estimated using the prevailing tax rate of 22 percent of the first $25,000 of profits and 48 percent of the profit over that amount. The firm, of course, may be able to lower that tax figure by means discussed in earlier chapters; however, the tax liability calculated in this manner is a conservative estimate of what it will probably be required to pay.

Pro Forma Balance Sheet

Many of the figures needed to construct the pro forma balance sheet (using the exact method) can be taken directly from the "financial transactions" section of the cash budget and calculated from other cash budget and income statement data. In fact, the balance sheet must tie in precisely (that is, to the last dollar) with the other two financial statements, as we shall see.

Burkart Balsam Corporation's pro forma balance sheet for 1979 is presented in Table 11-8. The data source used to calculate each figure is listed on the right side of the statement.

Assets. The figure for cash is found in the last entry in the "total" column in the cash budget (line 29). In line 27 of that statement we find that the firm sold $10,000 in securities in February after purchasing $3,000 worth in January, leaving a net reduction in short-term securities

200

of $7,000. Table 11-5 shows a 1978 year-end balance of $20,000; thus the firm is expected to hold $13,000 in short-term securities at the end of 1979 ($20,000–$7,000).

Table 11-8

**PRO FORMA BALANCE SHEET PREPARED BY THE "EXACT" METHOD
BURKART BALSAM CORPORATION
December 31, 1979**

Assets

Cash	$ 25,137	Table 11-4
Short-term securities	13,000	1978 balance sheet less net sales of $7,000
Accounts receivable (net)	22,670	Tables 11-1, 4, 5, and 7
Inventory	21,150	Estimated
Total current assets	$ 81,957	
Investments	15,000	no change from 1978
Fixed assets	97,000	Tables 11-4 and 5
Less accumulated depreciation	15,750	Tables 11-5 and 7
Net fixed assets	$ 81,250	
Other assets	14,450	no change from 1978
Total assets	$192,657	

Liabilities and Equity

Notes payable—bank	$ 17,000	Tables 11-4 and 5
Accounts payable	3,431	Tables 11-3, 4, and 5
Accrued federal income taxes	1,742	Tables 11-4, 5, and 9
Other current liabilities	3,540	no change from 1978
Accrued property taxes	20,300	no change from 1978
Total current liabilities	$ 46,013	
Long-term debt	48,000	Tables 11-4 and 5
Common stock	30,000	no change from 1978
Retained earnings	68,644	Tables 11-5 and 7
Total liabilities and equity	$192,657	

The accounts receivable balance is calculated as follows:

Beginning accounts receivable	$ 21,620	(Table 11-5)
Credit sales	335,680	(Table 11-1)
	$357,300	
Less collections of receivables	317,306	(Table 11-4)
	$ 39,994	
Less bad debt expense	17,324	(Table 11-7)
Accounts receivable	$ 22,670	

The bad debt expense is, of course, a noncash deduction from revenues, and it is added to the reserve for bad debts, which has the effect of lowering the firm's accounts receivable balance.

The inventory balance was estimated previously for the cost of sales portion of the pro forma income statement; thus we simply enter that estimate ($21,150) into the balance sheet. The figures necessary to calculate the size of the fixed asset account are presented in lines 5 and 20 of the cash budget; old equipment will be sold at book value for $4,300, and new equipment costing $42,500 will be purchased. The net increase of $38,200 is added to the 1978 balance sheet figure of $58,800, giving a total fixed asset figure of $97,000. Accumulated depreciation will increase by the amount shown on the pro forma income statement, $3,750, to $15,750. Finally, in the absence of any mention of changes in either investments or other assets, we will assume the figures are the same as those reported in Table 11-5.

Current Liabilities.   The cash budget (line 28) shows that Burkart's bank loans will increase by $7,000 to $17,000 by the end of 1979. Accounts payable at year end 1979 may be calculated as follows:

Beginning accounts payable	$ 3,000	(Table 11-5)
Purchases	62,940	(Table 11-3)
	65,940	
Less payments on account	62,509	(Table 11-4, line 9)
Accounts payable	$ 3,431	

Accrued federal income taxes are calculated in much the same way:

Beginning accrued income taxes	$ 2,500	(Table 11-5)
Income taxes for 1979	18,242	(Table 11-7)
	20,742	
Less tax payments	19,000	(Table 11-4, line 14)
Accrued federal income taxes	$ 1,742	

Finally property taxes are assumed to remain unchanged from 1978.

Capital Accounts.   Long-term debt is being retired at the rate of $8,000 per year, according to line 18 of the cash budget. Therefore the 1978 figure of $56,000 will be reduced to $48,000 at the end of 1979. Common stock will remain unchanged from 1978 at $30,000, and retained earnings will increase by the amount shown in the pro forma income statement (that is, $44,140 + 24,504 = $68,644).

Once these figures have been assembled into the pro forma balance sheet shown in Table 11-8, the analyst may check his calculations for accuracy by determining whether total assets equal total liabilities plus equity. If the two sides of the balance sheet "balance" and the analyst has not resorted to "plugging" figures to ensure that outcome, he may be reasonably certain that his figures are accurate. The systematic method of construction of these three statements clearly illustrates their close interrelations and is the reason it is referred to as the exact method—the forecast itself is not guaranteed to be accurate, but the interrelations among the cash budget and pro forma statements are exactly specified.

THE SHORTCUT METHOD

As stated earlier, the shortcut method is most often used by outside analysts who must rely completely on published financial statements for the data on which they base their forecasts. To illustrate the method, we will base the 1979 pro forma financial statements on the Burkart Balsam Corporation data contained in Tables 11-5 and 11-6. As in the exact method, we will begin with the construction of the pro forma income statement.

Pro Forma Income Statement

So that we may compare the results obtained under the two methods, let us begin with the same sales forecast used in the exact method— $419,600. Normally, however, the analyst would have to estimate 1979 sales from an analysis of past trends, adjusted of course in light of whatever knowledge he might possess or acquire of the industry, the economic outlook, and competitive conditions.

Next, using a comparative common-size income statement, similar to that presented in Table 11-6, he will analyze past income statement relations over a reasonably long period, noting past trends and studying the more recent data to develop a pro forma common-size income statement for the forecasting period. He will also study the dollar figures (not illustrated), noting any apparent stability or trends in those data and, by applying his knowledge of industry price and cost movements for the period, make appropriate adjustments to the percentages and dollar figures.

Table 11-9 presents the 1979 pro forma income statement of the Burkart Balsam Corporation constructed by the shortcut method. Detailed explanations of how each of the items was estimated are contained in the last column of the table. Unlike the exact method where, after the cash budget has been prepared, there is only one figure possible for each item in the statements, the shortcut method permits each forecaster to prepare a unique set of statements based on his own interpretation of

203

Table 11-9

**PRO FORMA INCOME STATEMENT
PREPARED BY THE SHORTCUT METHOD
BURKART BALSAM CORPORATION
for the Year Ended December 31, 1979**

Net sales	$419,600	Ten percent increase over 1978
Cost of sales		
Raw materials	62,940	Combined effects of a downward trend and a recent price increase—15% of sales
Direct labor	109,096	Combined effects of increased efficiency from purchase of new equipment and a 12% wage increase—26% of sales
Factory overhead	57,098	Historic average of 13% of sales plus an increase in depreciation of $2,550 from new equipment purchase
Cost of goods sold	$229,134	
Gross profit	$190,466	
Selling expenses	62,940	Firm plans to increase rate of selling commissions—15% of sales
Administrative expenses	44,058	Upward trend—10.5% of sales
Bad debt expense	23,078	Improved economic conditions—5.5% of sales
Operating income	$ 60,390	
Other expense (net)	22,887	Unchanged from 1978
Profit before taxes	$ 37,503	
Income taxes	11,501	Tax rate of 22% of first $25,000 and 48% of remainder
Net income	$ 26,002	
Less dividend	$ 8,800	Unchanged from 1978
To retained earnings	$ 17,202	

how future conditions will affect the firm's operations. Consequently, it is quite likely that three analysts will produce three quite different forecasts from the same set of data. Hence, careful analysis of the data and intimate knowledge of both the business and its operating environment are essential to successful application of the shortcut method.

Pro Forma Balance Sheet

The 1979 pro forma balance sheet for Burkart is presented in Table 11-10, and the explanation for the estimates contained therein are listed in the right-hand column. The shortcut approach is different from that used in the exact method in that the balance sheet is *forced* to balance. That is accomplished by omitting the "notes payable-bank" account from the current liabilities section of the balance sheet and adding an "external" balance sheet account to act as a balancing or "plugged" figure. That account is found at the bottom of the balance sheet and is designated "external financing required (excess cash)."

As the explanation for the cash figure states, the minimum cash balance (in this case $25,000) is used to begin the construction of the pro forma balance sheet. All other assets, liability, and equity accounts are then estimated, and the two "sides" of the balance sheet are totaled. If total assets are greater than total liabilities and equity, additional (external) financing is required to "force" a balance, and the figure equal to the difference is placed in the external balance sheet account. However, if total assets are less than total liabilities and equity, the firm will have a surplus of cash over its minimum balance, and the difference is deducted from total liabilities and equity to force the balance sheet to balance. The balancing figure in Table 11-10 is positive, indicating that the firm will require $34,029 of external funds to finance its operations as forecast by the shortcut method.

COMPARISON OF THE EXACT AND SHORTCUT METHODS

When the results of methods are compared, we find significant differences, some of which are:

	Exact Method	*Shortcut Method*
Net income	$ 33,304	$ 26,002
Current assets	81,957	92,835
Notes payable less short-term securities	4,000	14,029
Total assets	192,657	203,535

The causes of these differences are quite easy to explain; the two methods simply use two different sets of assumptions, the assumptions underlying the shortcut method being less defensible than those used in the exact method.

The weaknesses of the shortcut method lie in the assumption that the firm's historical financial positions and operating characteristics as shown in published financial statements are accurate predictors of its future performance. That assumption is obviously weak; however, to the extent that the analyst can get management to help him modify the historical relations to reflect management's plans and external influ-

Table 11-10

**PRO FORMA BALANCE SHEET PREPARED BY THE SHORTCUT METHOD
BURKART BALSAM CORPORATION
December 31, 1979**

Cash	$ 25,000	Minimum cash balance requirement
Short-term securities	20,000	No change from 1978
Accounts receivable	28,740	Collection period = 25 days
Inventory	19,095	Turnover = 12 times (COGS/12)
Total current assets	$ 92,835	
Investments	15,000	No change from 1978
Fixed assets	97,000	Net increase of $38,200 in equipment
Less depreciation	15,750	Net increase of $3,750
Net fixed assets	$ 81,250	
Other assets	14,450	No change from 1978
Total assets	$203,535	
Accounts payable	$ 3,449	Accounts payable/average daily purchases (raw materials/365 as an estimate of average daily purchases) = 20 days
Accrued income taxes	2,875	1979 income taxes of $11,501 divided by 4 as an estimate of the quarterly tax liability
Other current liabilities	3,540	Unchanged from 1978
Accrued property taxes	20,300	Unchanged from 1978
Total current liabilities	$ 30,164	
Long-term debt	48,000	Reduction of $8,000 in principal
Common stock	30,000	Unchanged from 1978
Retained earnings	61,342	$44,140 + $17,202 (from pro forma income statement)
Total liabilities and equity	$169,506	Total assets minus total liabilities and equity
External financing required (excess cash)	$ 34,029	

ences, the shortcut method will produce more reliable forecasts than will otherwise be the case.

Using the Forecasts

Financial forecasts in the form of cash budgets and pro forma financial statements are used by the credit analyst to assess the credit-worthiness of applicants for commercial credit. They provide him with a means of gaining insight into the operating problems and financial requirements of the business he is analyzing. Specifically, they help him determine the amount of external financing the firm will require, the reasons the requested funds are needed, the length of time the funds will be employed by the firm, and the source of repayment the firm will rely on.

The analyst can also use the forecasts to maintain control over the credit once the loan has been granted by comparing actual results with the estimates at frequent intervals. Those comparisons allow the analyst to determine the causes of deviations from planned operations, appraise the dependability of future projections, and greatly increase his knowledge both of the ability and efficiency of the business management with which he is dealing and of the soundness of the credit extension in which he is involved.

It goes without saying that a failure to assemble careful and accurate estimates of transactions of any sort is likely to render the forecasts practically useless. If, for example, the analyst carelessly overlooks an entire step in a firm's manufacturing process in compiling the cash budget, he will predict a greater cash surplus (or a smaller cash deficit) than will most likely exist during the budget period. Borrowing in excess of the firm's capacity to repay may become necessary, which will further complicate the firm's financial position. Most important, however, both the financial analyst and management will have received an unpleasant "surprise," and that is exactly what the forecasting process is designed to prevent. Therefore, the reliability and usefulness of the cash budget and pro forma statements are highly dependent upon the accuracy of the estimates and the care with which the statements are prepared.

Furthermore, when forecasts are known to be merely "best guesses," as, for example, in periods characterized by unsettled conditions in supply markets or when a firm introduces an entirely new product, the financial analyst should be prepared for the worst, even though he may hope for the best. In such instances, more than one forecast should be prepared so that the analyst knows in advance the likely outcome of the worst combination of future events. Appropriate action can then be planned well ahead of an event everyone hopes will not occur.

For example, if the cash budget prepared under a pessimistic set of assumptions reveals that the firm's future cash deficit will exceed its borrowing capacity, the analyst will certainly want to warn the firm that it is risking insolvency and may even suggest that it arrange for additional permanent financing or adopt a more conservative operating plan for the period.

Thus, although accuracy in forecasting is always desirable, it is possible to develop good plans under conditions of uncertainty. That can be accomplished with a little extra effort by preparing as many as *three* sets of financing forecasts: (1) a "best" estimate, reflecting the most likely set of circumstances under which the firm will operate during the coming period; (2) a pessimistic forecast, based on the assumption that the worst outcomes will occur in those areas of the firm's operations subject to uncertainty; and (3) an optimistic forecast, based on assumptions opposite to those of the pessimistic forecast. All three forecasts are required when uncertainty exists since, as we saw in Chapter 6, even a very prosperous firm can find itself suffering financially from its good fortune. Of course, the method involved in each of the forecasts is identical; only the underlying assumptions are different.

Once the pro forma statements have been prepared, they must be tested for realism by examining account proportions (that is, reducing the statements to common size), developing sources and uses of funds statements, and computing and analyzing important financial ratios. Historical standards, especially those relating to high and low cycles, provide appropriate bases for comparison. If certain proportions or

Table 11-11

**EFFECTS OF SELECTED TRANSACTIONS
ON THE INCOME STATEMENT AND CASH BUDGET**

Transaction	Income Statement	Cash Budget
Cash sales	Yes	Yes
Collections of accounts receivable from previous periods	No	Yes
Credits sales to be collected in subsequent periods	Yes	No
Payment of wages earned in previous period	No	Yes
Cash payment for materials to be used in manufacturing next year's model	No	Yes
Advance payment from customer on order to be filled during subsequent periods	No	Yes
Instalment payment on purchase of fixed assets	No	Yes
Depreciation and amortization expenses	Yes	No
Quarterly tax payment on previous year's income	No	Yes
Purchase of short-term investments	No	Yes
Cash dividend payment to stockholders	No	Yes
Sale of company's stock or issuance of bonds	No	Yes
Bad debt expense	Yes	No
Repayment of loan principal to bank	No	Yes
Payment of current interest charges to bank	Yes	Yes
Cash sale of fixed assets at less than book value	Yes	Yes
Advance payment of fire insurance premium for subsequent periods	No	Yes

ratios appear to be unreasonable when compared to the standards, the assumptions underlying the estimates of the accounts involved should be carefully examined to determine whether they are at least defensible. If not, they should be discarded and replaced by more realistic ones, and the pro forma statements revised accordingly.

Finally, it is important to keep in mind the discussion in Chapter 5 of the flow of cash and the point made about the difference between the net income figure shown on the income statement and the net change in the firm's bank balance. Many cash expenditures are not included as expenses in the income statement; conversely, some items of expense appearing on the income statement do not require a cash outlay in the same period. Except under rather unusual circumstances, therefore, there will be a difference between the estimated profit for the budget period and the accumulation of cash in the firm's bank account. And this difference could be of crucial importance in financial forecasting; neglecting to take it into account could lead to wholly mistaken conclusions about the competence of the firm's management (or the soundness of the estimates on which the budget is based).

How certain transactions affect cash budget and pro forma income statements in different ways is illustrated in Table 11-11. The transactions selected for inclusion in the table should be sufficient to show why a firm's anticipated results from operations as presented in the income statement can be quite different from the results as shown by the cash budget for the same period.

Summary

The cash budget plays a central role in financial forecasting as conducted by a firm's management or by outside analysts who have close contact with management and are made aware of management's plans. Its principal purpose is to determine whether a firm's extant and anticipated cash resources are sufficient to finance its operating strategy. The information contained in the cash budget also forms the basis for developing pro forma income statements and balance sheets by what we have termed the "exact" method. Taken together, the cash budget and its related pro forma financial statements constitute the total financial plan for the budget period.

A shortcut method of constructing the pro forma financial statements was also illustrated in this chapter. This method relies on past percentage relations and key financial ratios for developing estimates of the individual balance sheet and income statement accounts.

Both forecasting methods are used to evaluate the firm's future performance and financial position. Bank credit analysts find them particularly useful in commercial lending for assessing the applicant's creditworthiness and ability to repay the amount of credit requested.

Questions

11-1.   What are the two basic tools of financial forecasting?

11-2.   What is a cash budget? What is its principal use in statement analysis?

11-3.   List the four primary divisions of a cash budget.

11-4.   Once a sales forecast has been developed, what is the next step in constructing the revenue portion of the cash budget?

11-5.   Discuss some of the factors that complicate the estimate of cash outflows for materials purchases.

11-6.   Define the following:
1. fixed expenses
2. variable expenses
3. semivariable expenses
4. discretionary expenses

11-7.   Discuss the limitations of the cash budget as a forecasting tool.

11-8.   What is the basic difference between the exact and the shortcut methods of preparing pro forma statements?

11-9.   Why is it advisable to list the source of the estimate for each balance sheet and income statement account when constructing a forecast?

11-10. What accounts are normally "plugged" to get the pro forma balance sheet to balance in the exact method? The shortcut method?

11-11. When pro forma statements developed by the exact and shortcut methods are compared, would you expect to observe material differences between them? Why?

11-12. How may the pro forma statements and cash budget be used in credit analysis?

11-13. Describe the technique used to forecast operating performance and the financial condition of a firm whose future is unsettled.

11-14. Why should pro forma statements be tested after they have been prepared? How should this be done?

Part IV

The Technique of Financial Statement Analysis

Chapter 12

A Basic Approach to Statement Analysis

We are now ready to describe the technique of financial statement analysis. Unfortunately no precise formula exists that is unconditionally guaranteed to work in all circumstances; however, the basic approach outlined here (and detailed in the remaining chapters of this book) provides a practical and highly useful framework particularly suited to credit analysis for commercial bankers. The approach focuses on the tools of statement analysis examined in the preceding chapters and encompasses both environmental and managerial factors affecting business operations. In short, the technique described here will permit the banker to conduct comprehensive analyses of business enterprises efficiently and effectively.

Need For a Structured Approach

You will recall that the three basic objectives of statement analysis are *evaluation, diagnosis,* and *forecasting.* The data contained in a series of annual financial statements of a business cannot by themselves provide sufficient information to reach valid conclusions in any of the three areas unless those data are placed in proper perspective vis-à-vis other kinds of basic credit information. Consequently, the financial statements must be examined within a carefully planned structure to achieve both the basic and the higher level objectives of the analyst.

Since the objectives vary both among those who are conducting analyses and among the firms being analyzed, the approach must be flexible enough to accommodate different objectives, yet structured enough to facilitate the speedy accomplishment of the analytical task. An example of a seemingly ageless structure that remains highly regarded by today's credit analysts is that provided by the *Cs of credit.* Another, suggested by more recent trends in the commercial banking industry, involves examining the firm for both credit-worthiness and managerial competence—the *dual function* of bank credit analysts. Finally, the structure we recommend is a *modular* approach centered on the *financial statements* and the *objectives* of statement analysis, which leads to the establishment of priorities for examining various aspects of a firm's financial condition and performance. Since this last structure is related to the other two, we shall briefly examine each.

THE Cs OF CREDIT

The classic approach to determining the credit-worthiness of individuals or business firms involves the structuring of *credit* analysis (as opposed to *statement* analysis) to examine the willingness and ability of the debtor to discharge his obligation in accordance with the terms of the borrowing agreement. The structure is defined as the three Cs of credit—*character, capacity,* and *capital.* Another important factor, a fourth C, has to do with *conditions*—general business conditions and conditions in the particular industry in which the company is engaged. Sometimes a fifth C, *collateral,* is added.

The place of statement analysis in this structure is not readily apparent. Beginning with the first C, we note that *character* refers to determination to pay; it is tested by hard times, poor business conditions, shortages of cash, and a lack of adequate credit. If good character is absent, further investigation is deemed inadvisable. It is impossible to measure character by statement analysis alone; however, certain clues to the character of business management may be provided by the statements.

Capacity refers to the ability of management to operate the business so that its obligations will be met routinely as they become due. The statements provide much evidence about capacity, but other information, such as the age, experience, and education of management, also bears on this aspect of credit-worthiness.

Capital refers to the adequacy of the funds employed in the business to enable it to operate efficiently in generating cash flows, and effectively in today's competitive business environment. While the financial statement figures provide much information about the size of the capital base and its efficient use, other data are required to form a complete picture of how a firm employs its available capital funds.

Conditions refers to the state of the economy and to environmental influences on the firm's financial health. *Collateral* refers to assets likely to retain their value in extreme circumstances, which may be pledged by the debtor to offset weaknesses in the firm's capacity, capital, or conditions. Financial statements throw some light on conditions and collateral, but other sources provide most of the information on them.

The weaknesses of this structure in providing guidelines for comprehensive *statement analysis* are (1) its emphasis on the *evaluation of credit-worthiness* to the exclusion of other objectives, and (2) its lack of coordination with the basic financial statements and the tools of analysis. In other words, if an analyst wished to examine the effects of expansion on a firm's financial condition and operations, the five Cs would not provide a logical starting point, nor would they permit him to judge what aspects of the business ought to be examined and in what order of priority. The structure they provide is thus not suited to the "management consultant" part of the banker's new dual function. But few experienced credit men would deny that the Cs of credit provide an excellent framework for *credit analysis*.

THE DUAL FUNCTION OF THE BANK ANALYSIS

In Chapter 1 we examined the new dual function of the bank credit analyst—not only credit and financial statement analysis but also *diagnosis* of financial problems of smaller business customers and prescription of cures for those problems. The banking industry's recent emphasis on the second function has been occasioned by a growing recognition on the part of banks and their commercial customers that it is in the best interests of both for the bank to provide financial advisory services to its business customers. While bankers have always performed such services, only recently has it been suggested that they be performed as a *routine* part of credit analysis, rather than only at the customer's request. Again, conclusions and recommendations about the financial condition of business borrowers are routinely formulated but communicated directly to the customer only on his request. Occasionally, however, such information is given *indirectly*; in the form of reasons why credit cannot be extended under existing conditions, for example.

Unfortunately, the structure for financial statement analysis suggested by the dual function of assessing credit-worthiness and managerial competence does little more than extend the framework provided by the five Cs of credit. This is, it increases the number of objectives by the addition of the second function, but it does not remove the two basic structural weaknesses of the Cs of credit. Here again, however, we cannot argue against the usefulness of the concept to the banking industry.

THE MODULAR APPROACH

The modular approach to *financial statement analysis* begins with establishing the objective or objectives of the particular analysis. It then permits the analyst to select certain areas (modules) of the firm's total financial picture that his analysis will emphasize to achieve his objective(s). Five modules have been identified:

1. Short-term liquidity and solvency
2. Funds flow

3. Operations

4. Long-term financial strength

5. Asset utilization

The relation between the modules and the financial statements is obvious.

Depending on the objectives set by the analyst, as few as one or as many as five modules will be examined in depth. Rarely, however, will an analysis involve only one module, since they are all highly interrelated. It is more likely that the objective of the analysis will determine its starting point and subsequent investigation will point to the direction in which it will proceed. In most cases—especially when a banker is performing his dual function—all five modules will be examined, but some will be accorded much more thorough treatment than others.

For example, suppose the owner of a small retail establishment applies to his bank for a short-term loan and asks for assistance in getting and remaining current with his suppliers. The banker's objectives in this instance are (1) to evaluate the short-term debt-paying ability of the customer and (2) to determine why the firm is having difficulty meeting its obligations. The modules the banker will begin with are short-term liquidity and solvency (to measure short-term financial strength) and funds flow (to locate possible imbalances in cash flows).

The selection of the modules also aids in the selection of the tools of analysis—in this case, liquidity and activity ratios, the statement of changes in financial position, and cash budgets. Finally, if the analysis of the chosen modules suggests that the firm's problem may be operational, the operations module is also analyzed, the appropriate tools being a comparative, common-sized income statement and certain income statement ratios. Once the analysis is complete, the banker must evaluate the data, interpret the results, and recommend courses of action for the bank and its customer.

While the modular approach may be subject to the criticism that it represents an artificial division of the firm's financial picture, it is nevertheless adaptable to any set of objectives and is easily coordinated with the financial statements and the tools of analysis. Similarly, the obvious interrelations among the modules enable the analyst to proceed in an orderly manner through either narrowly defined or comprehensive analyses without having to alter their structures.

In spite of these significant advantages, the modular approach is admittedly oriented toward the financial statements to the exclusion of other important information. Consequently, the analyst must look beyond the financial statements to complement his analysis of the modules he examines. Two Cs of credit—character and conditions—provide some guidance in this area. The following section presents the modular approach in an expanded format designed to overcome the problem presented by its orientation toward the statements.

Basic Approach to Statement Analysis

The modular approach sets out five modules related to financial statements from which the analyst selects those appropriate to his objectives. But before he can begin his analysis, he must acquaint himself with all aspects of the firm he is examining, the industry in which it operates, and the current economic conditions that may affect it and its operations. Without that information, the conclusions reached could be completely erroneous. Thus a certain amount of work, including information processing and analysis, must precede the examination of the modules. The basic approach to statement analysis recommended here consists of seven steps. They are, in order of performance:

1. Formulate a clear and thorough statement of the objectives to be achieved by the analysis.
2. Perform a thorough examination of the managerial, technical, and competitive nature of the firm being analyzed and the industry in which it operates.
3. Assess the business and economic conditions both within and outside the industry.
4. Select the modules to be examined and perform the analysis using the appropriate tools.
5. If forecasts are to be prepared, specify the assumptions on which the estimates and projections are based.
6. Interpret the results of the analysis, giving full weight to the qualitative and quantitative managerial, financial, technical, business, and economic conditions that prevail.
7. Formulate recommendations (achieve objectives) based on all of the above.

A careful reading of these seven steps reveals that they are a composite of the Cs of credit and the modular approach; the five Cs give us steps 2 and 3, and the modular approach provides steps 1, 4, and 5. Step 6 requires the analyst to interpret the results, and in step 7 the analyst achieves his objectives, including the performance of the banker's dual function. We have already examined step 1 in earlier chapters. The remaining chapters of this book deal with steps 4, 5, and 6—the analysis of the modules. The rest of this chapter examines the nature and sources of data needed to perform steps 2 and 3.

IMPORTANCE OF NONFINANCIAL DATA

Each business firm possesses certain unique, basically nonfinancial characteristics that make its financial position and operations different in some ways from other firms of its industry and size. Consequently, each firm must be carefully evaluated on its own merits and in light of its own environmental and operational characteristics. An example will help explain why this is true.

Suppose you were asked to evaluate two arts and crafts manufacturing firms as part of an annual review of active customer accounts. A brief examination of selected financial data taken from the recent statements of the firms (see Table 12-1) suggests that Wholly Hobbies is the better managed firm; its assets appear to be more efficiently employed. For example, its collection period and inventory turnover are better than Kustum Kraft's. However, if we add some nonfinancial information, the interpretation of the financial data can change dramatically.

For example, let us say that Kustum Kraft sells mainly to small, locally owned specialty shops in a large metropolitan area, most of which are proprietorships. Wholly Hobbies, on the other hand, has only two customers, who have contracted to purchase its entire output; both are large, national department stores and catalog chains.

With this information we can see that Kustum Kraft's collection period and inventory turnover appear more reasonable. Small proprietorships often require extended credit terms, since their sources of financing are limited. Their suppliers often carry them financially in order to retain their (profitable) business. Similarly, suppliers with many small customers located in a single area have to produce a greater variety of products so that each specialty shop can avoid stocking the same merchandise as every other shop in the area. This kind of merchandising often requires larger than normal inventories and results in a slower turnover.

The type of customer served by Wholly Hobbies makes its inventory turnover unreasonably long, unless a long time is required for the production process. An analyst would have reason to suspect that the firm is overstocking raw materials or having difficulty getting its customers to accept delivery of finished goods. Similarly, with only two

Table 12-1

SELECTED FINANCIAL DATA FROM ANALYSES OF TWO ARTS AND CRAFTS FIRMS

	Kustum Kraft, Inc.	*Wholly Hobbies, Inc.*	*Industry*
Current ratio	1.95:1	2.53:1	2.3:1
Collection period	63 days	40 days	35 days
Inventory turnover	4.5 times	5.2 times	5.0 times
Total assets	$1.12 million	$.98 million	—
Credit terms on sales	net 30 days	net 30 days	net 30 days
Total sales	$1.75 million	$1.90 million	—
Net profits	$165,000	$133,000	

customers, both well financed, it is difficult to explain why the firm's collection period is 40 days when its credit terms are net 30. It is possible that Wholly Hobbies may be "looking the other way" in order to retain the contracts; however, that is hardly necessary, given the dollar amounts involved in relation to the total resources of a national retail chain.

Finally, if Kustum Kraft's policies on receivables and inventory are as described, they appear to be working well. Note that its returns on both sales and total assets are higher than those of Wholly Hobbies by a wide margin. Since profit is generally accepted as a criterion of successful management, we would have to conclude, given the information on the two firms' clients, that Kustum Kraft is better managed. Such a conclusion may be premature, however.

Let us extend our analysis with the help of additional nonfinancial information: Wholly Hobbies' labor force is represented by a strong union, while Kustum Kraft's employees are for the most part either related to or close friends of the owners. The average wage paid by Wholly Hobbies is about 25 percent higher than that paid by Kustum Kraft. The conclusion that Kustum Kraft's receivables and inventory policies are profitable no longer appears appropriate in light of the new information. The firm's higher profits are probably the result of lower operating costs due to lower wages. This bit of speculation opens a wide range of possibilities for further analysis of Kustum Kraft, an analysis that will depend largely on gathering more nonfinancial information. At this point, however, all we can say about the firm is that its management is not necessarily as good or as bad as the limited financial data first indicated.

INFORMATION REQUIRED FOR A COMPREHENSIVE ANALYSIS

The preceding illustration clearly points out the need for an analyst to possess "business sense" along with the tools of analysis and the skills needed to apply them. One way for the inexperienced analyst to acquire business sense is by gathering as much data as possible concerning any businesses or industries he is assigned to analyze that he is unfamiliar with. He should do the data gathering before beginning the detailed modular examination of the financial statements.

The following outline presents some of the more important nonfinancial information that should be given attention in a comprehensive analysis of a business. In some investigations all these points should be checked fully; in others certain points may not require as careful an examination, since they may have little bearing on the analytic objectives. A review of the outline will show that the majority of the factors can be classified under the general headings of *character, capacity, capital,* and *conditions.*

221

   I. History of the company
- A. Date of inception
- B. Form of organization and changes (if any)
  1. Proprietorship: is it registered with the proper authorities?
  2. Partnership:
     a. Is it registered with the proper authorities?
     b. Terms of partnership agreement
  3. Corporation: articles of incorporation
- C. Past financial difficulties (if any)
  1. Bankruptcies
  2. Compromises
  3. Assignments, etc.
- D. Record of mergers or consolidations
- E. Summary of the company's past operating record

  II. Experience and ability of the company's management
- A. Ages of executives
- B. Business experience of executives
  1. With applicant
  2. With others
- C. Outside business affiliations (nominal financial interests) of executives
- D. Opinions about the integrity of management
- E. Outside financial interest of officers
- F. Provisions for management succession
- G. Insurance on the lives of executives

III. Exact nature of the company's operations
- A. Products handled or manufactured
  1. Staple
  2. Styled
  3. Consumer goods
  4. Capital goods
  5. Price stability
- B. Extent or nature of fabrication of products
- C. Selling methods employed
- D. Economic need for products
- E. Territory and customers served
  1. Agricultural
  2. Industrial
  3. Economic level
- F. Unusual hazards of business
- G. Buying and selling terms
- H. Sources of raw materials
- I. Proximity to labor supply, materials, and markets

    J. Labor situation
       1. Unionized
       2. Likelihood of unionization
       3. Wage scale
       4. Type of labor
    K. Importance of company in its industry
IV. Condition of the company's plant
    A. Location
    B. Condition of properties and machinery
       1. New or old machinery
       2. New or old buildings
    C. Plant layout
    D. Work flow
    E. Productivity: low-cost or marginal
    F. Insurance coverage of insurable risks
       1. Fire
       2. Fidelity
       3. Workmen's compensation
       4. Burglary
       5. Business interruption
V. Experience and opinion of banks of account and other banks regarding the company
    A. Account experience
       1. Date of inception
       2. Account balance and proportion to borrowings
    B. Loan experience
       1. Method of borrowing
       2. Line of credit
       3. Present debt
       4. Steadiness of loans
    C. General comments regarding:
       1. Management
       2. Financial condition
       3. Prospects
       4. Method of operation
VI. Trade opinions and ledger experience of concerns from which the company has been purchasing
    A. Manner of paying its bills
    B. Present outstanding bills and lines of credit (if any)
    C. Unjust claims (if any)
VII. Trade competitors' opinions (if advisable)
    A. Expression of critical viewpoint
    B. Reputation of the company
    C. General trade standing of the company

VIII. Conditions within and outside the industry
    A. General business conditions—position in the business cycle
    B. Conditions within the industry
       1. Economic justification of industry
       2. New, growing industry or old, dying one
       3. Competition with other industries
       4. Competition within industry
          a. Cutthroat
          b. Ethical
       5. Seasonal aspects of industry
       6. Industry price history
  IX. Extent and nature of government competition and regulation; effect of present or prospective legislation.

Each item in this outline could have a significant influence on the interpretation of the data produced by the analysis of the firm's financial statements. Thus, it is vitally important that the analyst become fully business-oriented before he becomes a business analyst.

SOURCES OF INFORMATION

Nonfinancial information may be classified as (1) information supplied by the firm being analyzed, and (2) information furnished by other sources. A large amount of information can be, and usually is, supplied by the firm being examined. If the analyst is satisfied of the integrity of the management, he can accept much of that information as accurate. At least some of it, however, must be confirmed from outside sources.

Information Supplied by Management

The information obtainable from management is discussed under three headings: (1) interviews, (2) plant inspection, and (3) the credit file (for the most part information originally obtained from the customer).

Interviews With Management. When a lending relation is established, as in commercial banking, the lending officer generally interviews the credit applicant as the first step in the process. Where the credit extension is merely part of another commercial transaction, as in selling merchandise or raw materials on credit, an interview with management may not take place. When an interview is appropriate, many important facts can be gleaned from discussions between the borrower and lender both at the lending officer's desk and at the applicant's place of business. Primarily, such discussions enable the analyst to evaluate the honesty and ability of management, and sometimes casual questions bring forth answers that give the analyst leads to be followed in gathering additional data and analyzing the relevant facts.

Early in the interview the lending officer should determine the purpose of the loan so that he can begin to establish the basic objectives of the analysis he will conduct. For example, if the proceeds of the loan will be used to purchase fixed assets, the need for long-term money will indicate what questions should be asked. If the loan is for working capital, either for seasonal use or for a specific transaction, the interview should be directed toward securing the information required for such a transaction for the company in question.

Information about the company's history can be derived from an intelligently conducted interview, and confirmed later through other sources. In addition, the analyst can learn much about the company's operations, including such matters as its principal products, its selling terms, the trade territory it serves, the character of its customers, the sources of its raw materials, its labor situation, and its standing in the industry.

The names of its principal competitors, outside interests of its officers, the name of the person or group who controls the company, relations with affiliated or associated companies, and the names of the principal banks of account should be determined in the interview. That kind of background information may shed light on the character of the management. In addition, financial information that would not normally be reflected in the firm's financial statements should be determined. For example, expansion plans (if any) and the proposed method of financing them, the method of borrowing, the customary peak indebtedness, the proposed peak debt, the high borrowing season, and the purpose of present borrowing all are matters to be determined through the interview.

The analyst can also learn something about the extent and nature of both seasonal variations in production and sales and the industrial cycle of the particular line of business. The extent to which these fluctuations coincide with those of the industry as a whole in the general business cycle is extremely important to the analysis.

During the interview the lending officer can tactfully obtain explanations that may clarify points on the applicant's financial statements that might otherwise be difficult to interpret and may give the analyst a more vivid picture of the applicant's business.

Plant Visits. Experience has shown that business executives who are reluctant to discuss their affairs at the banker's desk often display an entirely different attitude in their own offices or plants. In fact, most customers welcome a visit from a representative of the bank and are usually willing not only to discuss their problems with him but also to conduct him on a guided tour of their operations. Questions asked at the plant are generally regarded by the customer as evidence of interest on the part of the representative and hence are readily answered, although

225

the same questions asked at the banker's desk may be viewed as prompted by idle curiosity or by a disposition to be critical.

The analyst should not hesitate to ask questions while he is touring the customer's facilities. While he cannot expect to understand completely all the technical factors involved in complex manufacturing processes, for example, the clearer his understanding of the operations, the more precise his analysis and the more helpful his suggestions are likely to be, as he performs as a credit analyst or management consultant. The plant visit is helpful to the analyst for many reasons:

1. An insight into the method of operation enables him to interpret the customer's financial statements more intelligently than would otherwise be possible, as will be demonstrated in subsequent chapters.

2. Although he may not be an industrial engineer, he can nevertheless form a reasonably accurate assessment of the efficiency of operations. The arrangement of machinery and the flow of work through the plant usually throw light on the efficiency of management.

3. He can evaluate the quality of the product.

4. He can gain an impression of the attitude, efficiency, and treatment of the employees; good working conditions generally lead to increased efficiency.

5. He can acquire definite knowledge of the condition and salability of the inventory and its balance with respect to sales and production.

6. He can gain information on both the selling methods of a mercantile company and the manner of displaying its merchandise from touring the premises.

7. He can learn something about the nature, condition, and adequacy of the company's buildings and machinery.

8. Finally, he can gain some insight into the quality of the customer's accounting records.

Many bankers visit their customers' places of business at frequent intervals, to keep in closer touch with their clients' affairs and to serve them better. At times the banker is asked for his opinion on business matters and makes suggestions that result in reduced expenses and more efficient operations. Plant visits offer an excellent means of training young credit analysts, reducing the bank's losses on loans, and promoting a closer relation and mutual confidence between the bank and its customers.

The Credit File.   If the business firm is presently a customer of the bank (or supplier) for which the analyst is working, information about past payment habits, credit correspondence, the firm's financial and operating history, and memorandums of previous plant visits will generally be found in the credit files. The files will also include information from outside sources gathered in support of previous analyses. The credit file thus contains a wealth of historical information.

When the business is a new customer, the credit file may not exist, except when the bank or supplier has actively solicited the firm's business. The absence of a credit file is not too serious a disadvantage, however. Although it is always best to have as much information as possible on the credit applicant, the existence of a substantial credit file may persuade the analyst that assembling further information is not so important. He may consequently rely too heavily on *historical* data and fail to examine as thoroughly as he should the current condition of the firm. That obviously can lead to seriously erroneous conclusions regarding the financial health of the firm, since business conditions can deteriorate almost overnight. When no credit file exists, the analyst is compelled to dig deep for his information; but even when he has extensive credit information at his fingertips, he should dig just as deep into the firm's current status.

Information From Other Sources

The information supplied by the credit applicant enables the bank to assemble a fairly comprehensive file on the subject. Much of that information, however, must be confirmed by outsiders. Moreover, it is usually desirable to ascertain the opinions and experiences of others who have transacted business with the applicant or who are familiar with his affairs and trade practices.

It is always advisable for the bank to check with other banks that have had dealings with the company to learn their attitudes toward it. The inquiries should reveal at least on what basis loans have been granted and how they have been paid.

Often the bank finds it worthwhile to check with disinterested banks that may be able to divulge pertinent information about the customer. In some instances those banks can express only opinions of little value to the current investigation. In other instances they may have been offered the account and for valid reasons have declined to take it. The attitude of banks that do not have the account is often of vital importance.

The banker naturally makes inquiries of the firm's trade suppliers. Some banks write directly to the suppliers. Others obtain trade reports from mercantile agencies, which include the interchange bureaus affiliated with the National Association of Credit Management, The National Credit Office, and Dun and Bradstreet.

The manner in which the company is paying its bills is most important. If direct inquiry is made of suppliers, the following information should be obtained: (1) whether the company makes unjust claims; (2) whether it pays its bills within the discount period; (3) whether it occasionally deducts discounts to which it is not entitled; and (4) the high and low credit and the amount outstanding to particular companies.

The reports supplied by mercantile credit agencies are useful in confirming the company's history. A credit agency report includes information about the form of organization and the date of incorporation or inception, comments about the past business experience of the company's executives, and a brief summary of its past financial history. These facts, together with general comments on the company's method of operation, its selling terms, and perhaps a current financial statement, make up the body of the report. Usually a record of credit inquiries is included. Such reports are helpful because of their historical data, although most banks do not regard them as absolutely authoritative.

At times it is well to ask the principal competitors of the company about its standing in the trade, its method of competition, and the quality of its product, but this source should be used with caution. The analyst must realize that many competitors are unfair when expressing an opinion of another concern in the same line of business. But even though their opinions may be prejudiced, their expressed views may lead the analyst to investigate some point of great significance. A high recommendation of a competitor is usually the strongest kind of endorsement.

If the company sells its notes through a commercial paper broker, he also may furnish valuable data. The broker keeps in close touch with his customers by frequent visits to their plants or places of business, by obtaining regular statements, and by carefully watching the financial condition of each customer as well as the trends in its industry.

Among the general sources that can supply helpful information are trade association journals, newspapers, periodicals, directories, public records, and sundry statistical and reporting services. Newspapers, periodicals, and trade association journals furnish information on industrial trends, as well as comments on the specific company. Information about changes in products, selling methods, and manufacturing systems or about expansion plans, mergers, price changes, demand or lack of demand for the product, and many other matters can be obtained from careful reading of business magazines and the financial and business sections of daily metropolitan newspapers. All are important aids in the investigation of borrowers and potential borrowers and in keeping the bank in close touch with its customers.

Statistics published periodically by government agencies are valuable aids in credit work. The monthly *Federal Reserve Bulletin,* published by the Board of Governors of the Federal Reserve System, should be readily available and freely used by the analyst as a source of statistical data. Another equally useful publication is the monthly *Survey of Current Business,* published by the Office of Business Economics of the U.S. Department of Commerce.

Every analyst should check (or have checked for him) the public records to obtain information about the realty holdings of borrowers and any liens against those holdings. Any judgments, liens, and the like, should be known. In small communities that usually is not difficult. In larger communities the information can be procured through special agencies or from legal publications that specialize in the daily reporting of realty changes, liens, judgments, and other legal matters.

It is essential for the analyst to discover the extent and nature of government regulation of, or competition with, the credit applicant. In particular, he should learn what present or pending legislation may adversely affect the risk. Legislation is becoming more and more important in the extension of credit.

In summary, it may be said that the analyst should obtain all necessary information if he is to conduct a comprehensive analysis of a business firm that will achieve his established objectives. He should know what information is needed and where to get it. The major source of information is the applicant, but no outside source should be overlooked in the acquisition of data essential for the proper evaluation and intelligent interpretation of the financial statements of a business firm.

Questions

12-1. Why is a structured approach to financial statement analysis desirable?

12-2. What are the several Cs of credit?

12-3. What are the weaknesses of the analytical structure provided by the Cs of credit?

12-4. Describe the dual function of the bank analyst.

12-5. List the five modules, or areas, that describe the total financial picture of a firm being analyzed.

12-6. What is the major defect of the modular approach to statement analysis?

12-7. List the seven steps to statement analysis in the order of their performance.

12-8. Discuss the importance of nonfinancial data in financial statement analysis.

12-9. List nine important classes of nonfinancial data used in statement analysis.

12-10. What sources of information other than interviews with management, are generally available to the statement analyst?

12-11. Does the existence of a credit file of substantial size make the analyst's task easier? Explain.

Chapter 13

Module One: Short-Term Liquidity and Solvency (I)

Generally, the first concern of both management and any interested outside analysts is the short-term financial strength of the business, that is, its short-term liquidity and solvency. Many textbooks and practicing analysts combine the concepts of liquidity and solvency under the term *liquidity* and thus fail to distinguish between the operational cash flows, which provide liquidity, and the values of the firm's current assets in liquidation, which provide for the firm's solvency. A brief examination of these two concepts provides an excellent introduction to this first chapter dealing with the technique of statement analysis.

Distinction Between Liquidity and Solvency

The primary distinction between liquidity and solvency is that liquidity is a "going concern" concept and solvency is not. Liquidity has almost always been defined as the ability of the firm to pay its short-term obligations as they come due; the firm must possess adequate liquidity to remain in business. Solvency, on the other hand, is generally defined in terms of the relation between the total value of the firm's assets and its liabilities: *insolvency* occurs when the total liabilities exceed a *fair valuation* (instead of the *book* value) of its total assets. Admittedly, the insolvent firm is generally, but not always, illiquid as well; the firm's illiquidity is noted and precipitates activity among the firm's creditors that leads to the full disclosure of its weakened financial condition. However, even though the two are closely related and the terminology used interchangeably, it is useful for our purposes to draw the distinction because, unlike insolvency, illiquidity can usually be ameliorated.

CONSEQUENCES OF ILLIQUIDITY AND INSOLVENCY

The consequences of inadequate liquidity range from relatively minor inconvenience to very severe financial difficulties. For example, a firm that experiences a temporary shortage of cash to meet maturing short-term obligations may suffer only the inconvenience of notifying its banker and arranging for a loan. That of course will reduce the firm's profits by the amount of interest paid for the use of the funds. The firm may choose the alternative of delaying its payments to trade creditors until it collects its own receivables. The consequences of that decision may be a loss of cash discounts on purchases or a deterioration of its credit standing.

More serious consequences of illiquidity occur when the firm must either pass up profitable business opportunities or sell long-term investments or some of its operating assets at unfavorable terms to meet maturing obligations. In such cases, illiquidity is a symptom of some serious defect in the firm's operations that, if left unattended, will lead to insolvency. As the value of the firm's assets in relation to its total financial obligations shrinks, its ability to generate the profits and related cash flows needed to repay its debts diminishes, leaving the firm worse off. So long as the firm can continue to sell its assets, it remains liquid, but its solvency is impaired to the extent that the sale of the assets reduces its potential to earn profits.

The dividing line between serious and not so serious stages of illiquidity is conceptually very important but virtually impossible to identify. On the not so serious end of the spectrum, the symptom—illiquidity—can safely be treated, since the cause of the illiquidity is probably self-correcting. The passage of time may be all that is required to restore the firm's cash balance to its proper level. However, more serious causes of illiquidity require positive action by management, since treating the symptom will only hasten the ultimate demise of the firm. In these cases, liabilities grow, or at best are merely "rolled over," as the cause of the problem continues to drain cash from the circular flow. Hence, the *cause* of the illiquidity becomes the focal point of this statement analysis module.

SOME CAUSES OF ILLIQUIDITY AND INSOLVENCY

Management and interested outside analysts always monitor the firm's short-term liquidity for signs of cash flow problems. When such problems are spotted, the analyst begins searching for their causes.

One of the most common causes of short-term illiquidity is the lack of synchronization between the firm's cash receipts and its disbursements. Sometimes the time lag between the need for cash and its appearance in the cash balance is only a day or so. For seasonal businesses, however, the lag of receipts behind disbursements can be as long as nine or ten months. But most often, this kind of cash flow imbalance is self-correcting, and short-term illiquidity can be prevented or corrected either by maintaining a cash balance adequate to serve as a cash flow cushion or by keeping open (unused) lines of credit to be used when needed.

Sometimes the lack of synchronization is intensified by problems that are not self-correcting. For example, if policies on accounts receivable collection are inappropriate, the rate of sales per period will exceed the rate of collections, reducing the flow of cash into the firm and leaving it with a smaller cash balance with which to meet its recurring obligations. Similarly, when a firm purchases or manufactures more inventory than it is able to sell, the time lag between cash receipts and disbursements grows and is not self-correcting; management must take corrective action to restore the firm's cash flow balance.

Occasionally, cash flow problems are operations-induced. For example, a large order of merchandise may be returned because it is defective. The cash outflows for the costs of producing the goods must be absorbed by the cash balance or financed in some other way. Recurring operating losses produce a constant drain on cash flows and a continuing liquidity crisis, whereas nonrecurring losses may produce only a temporary illiquidity that will generally disappear as profits reappear. It is the non-self-correcting cash flow problems that seriously affect the firm's solvency. If those problems are not solved, they will erode the firm's liquidity and force it to use its assets defensively. That is, the assets may be auctioned off to maintain short-run liquidity rather than properly used to generate long-run profits.

We will examine the implications of operations-induced cash flow imbalances and the effects of long-run assets and liabilities on the financial health of the firm in later chapters. Here we will examine liquidity as revealed in the analysis of the current assets and current liabilities of the business firm.

Working Capital

Working capital refers to a firm's investment in current assets—cash, short-term securities, accounts and notes receivable, inventories, and prepaid expenses. *Net* working capital is defined as current assets minus current liabilities. Characteristically, current assets represent more than half the total assets of a business firm. Because they represent a large investment and the firm depends on their conversion for most, if not all, of its cash inflows, current assets and the way they are managed constitute the most important area of financial statement analysis.

Management of working capital is particularly important for small firms. A small firm may minimize its investment in fixed assets by renting or leasing its plant and equipment or by purchasing used equipment at low prices, but it cannot avoid making an investment in cash, accounts receivable, and inventories. Further, because small firms do not have ready access to sources of long-term financing, they must rely heavily on trade credit and short-term bank loans, both of which reduce net working capital as they provide funds for operating needs.

A firm whose sales are growing will need to provide for an additional investment in working capital. For example, if the firm's average collection period is thirty days and its credit sales average $1,000 per day, its investment in receivables amounts to $30,000. If sales increase by $100 per day, the investment in receivables will rise to $33,000. Sales increases produce similar *immediate* needs for additional inventories and perhaps for cash balances as well, all of which must be financed without delay.

CASH FLOWS AND ASSET STOCKS RELATED TO WORKING CAPITAL

The term *working capital* originated many years ago when agriculture dominated the U.S. economy and industry was largely confined to processing agricultural commodities. Firms purchased newly harvested crops, processed them, and sold them at more or less constant rates, ending up a year later at harvesttime with very low inventories. Bank loans with one-year maturities were used to finance both the purchase and processing costs and were retired with the proceeds of the sale of the finished product. That kind of bank loan was called *self-liquidating*, because the purpose for which it was requested (inventory purchase) generated the cash for its ultimate repayment.

The changes in the level of working capital of the food processor are shown graphically in Figure 13-1. There fixed assets are depicted as growing steadily over time while current assets follow the up-and-down pattern just described. Short-term working capital loans are used to finance current assets, and fixed assets are financed with long-term debt and equity capital.

As the economy became less dependent on agriculture, the production and financing cycles of the typical business changed. The aggregate investment in inventories increased to ensure a steady stream of goods to national markets, and the extension of trade credit between business firms gave rise to large investments in accounts receivable. It soon became apparent that current assets rarely, if ever, dropped to zero as the *annual production cycle* was replaced by the *continuous production process*. Those changes introduced the idea of the "permanency" of a portion of working capital invested in "permanent" inventories, "permanent" accounts receivable, and, to some degree, "permanent" levels of cash required for transactions. This newer idea of working capital is depicted in Figure 13-2.

The figure retains the notion of seasonal influences on working capital. The seasonal fluctuations may be sales related (as in a department store) or production related (as in tobacco manufacturing). Or they may have nothing to do with seasons but merely represent the use of excess

Figure 13-1

CURRENT AND FIXED ASSETS OF A FOOD PROCESSOR

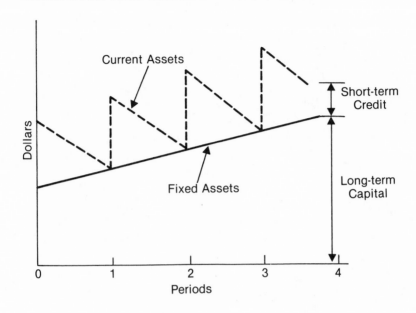

productive capacity to fill special orders. The diagram for firms whose operations are completely free of seasonal and irregular influences, however, would not contain the fluctuating current asset line; *all* their assets are permanent. Those firms continue to use short-term trade credit, but as a permanent source of financing: as suppliers' current invoices are paid, new purchases of inventory create new accounts payable. And accounts payable will grow apace with the growth in inventory requirements, making that source of financing as permanent as the current assets thus acquired. Figure 13-2 therefore properly includes the permanent portion of accounts payable in long-term capital.

Analyzing the Current Position

As the discussion of the short cash flow cycle in Chapter 5 suggested, the cash-to-cash cycle of a manufacturing firm begins with the acquisition of inventory (generally on credit), continues through the production process, finished goods inventories, and accounts receivable, and finally generates cash that is then used to repay the trade credit. Cash is also spent on selling and administrative expenses, which, with profits, are recovered through the markup over the cost of goods sold. Errors in judgment, mismanagement, or unexpected external influences can

Figure 13-2

PERMANENT AND FLUCTUATING ASSETS

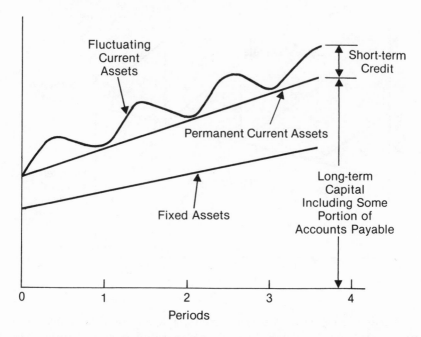

interrupt the short cycle and seriously impair the firm's liquidity. Thus the analysis of the current position centers on the careful examination of each component of the short cycle—cash, accounts receivable, inventories, and current liabilities—and its related cash flows. In addition, certain aggregate measures of liquidity are commonly employed in examining a firm's current financial condition. This chapter examines the aggregate measures of liquidity and discusses the degree of liquidity provided by a firm's investment in cash. Chapter 14 continues the presentation of module one by examining accounts receivable, inventories, and current liabilities.

AGGREGATE MEASURES OF LIQUIDITY

The best known measure of aggregate liquidity is the current ratio; however, as we saw in Chapter 8 and will emphasize in discussing the components of the current ratio in this and the following chapter, the analyst must exercise great care not to carry the interpretation of the current ratio beyond the conclusion that it measures the excess of dollars invested in current assets over dollars supplied by current creditors, tax liabilities, accrued expenses, and so forth. The trend of the current ratio may be revealing, but it should be remembered that a firm whose sales are declining is more likely to have a higher current ratio than a firm whose sales are rising. That is because a sales decline causes a firm to accumulate inventories involuntarily and thus cut back on its purchases. The net result is that the current ratio rises as current assets (inventories) increase and current liabilities (payables) decrease. The current liabilities of a growing firm, on the other hand, grow faster than its current assets. Its working capital position becomes strained, and its current ratio is likely to fall. Thus an analyst cannot measure "prosperity" with the current ratio.

The only valid measures of aggregate liquidity are those that assist the analyst in examining the *cash flow* of the firm. We have examined the cash flow measures that relate to individual current assets, and we will now examine two aggregate measures—the net trade cycle and the composition of current assets.

Net Trade Cycle

A firm desires to increase its rate of conversion of noncash assets into cash for two basic reasons: (1) for investment elsewhere, and (2) to pay its creditors. The net trade cycle measures the relation between the length of time cash is tied up in current assets and the length of time suppliers' funds are used to finance those assets.

For example, the following data are taken from the financial statements of the Cosse Supply Company:

Average daily sales	$ 2,500
Accounts receivable	105,000
Inventories	150,000
Accounts payable	25,000

Converting the receivables, inventories, and payables figures into the number of days' sales in each by dividing the total of each by average daily sales, we find:

Number of days' sales in:	
Accounts receivable	42 days
Inventories	60
Total trade cycle	102 days
Less: accounts payable	10
Net trade cycle	92 days

These figures indicate that Cosse's noncash assets are converted into cash in 102 days and it has the use of trade credit for only ten days. Thus the firm's investment in working capital represents an equivalent of 92 days of sales. Obviously, the higher the net trade cycle, the larger the investment in working capital is likely to be and the slower the cash flow. Cosse Supply could generate an additional $25,000 in cash balances by

237

speeding up its collection period by ten days or reducing its inventories by the amount of ten days' sales.

Composition of the Current Assets

The composition of the current assets of a firm is another good indicator of its aggregate liquidity. For example, let us examine the current position of a manufacturing firm for two consecutive years as shown in Table 13-1.

The company has a current ratio of 2:1 in both years. If the ratio alone is considered, the firm's current position appears not to have changed. However, the distribution of the current assets determines the adequacy of the current ratio. When that distribution is reviewed, it is clear that the firm has become more liquid in the second year, since a smaller proportion of its total current assets consists of the less liquid inventory asset. That can be determined simply from viewing the two statements, but for some statements the distribution might not be so evident. Hence, to help the analyst determine the distribution readily, the dollar figures are reduced to common size—that is, expressed as a percentage of total current assets. These figures are shown in Table 13-2.

Table 13-1

COMPOSITION OF CURRENT ASSETS OF A MANUFACTURING FIRM

	Year 1	*Year 2*
Cash	$ 10,000	$100,000
Accounts receivable	75,000	300,000
Finished goods	25,000	100,000
Goods in process	15,000	25,000
Raw materials	75,000	75,000
Total current assets	$200,000	$600,000
Total current debt	$100,000	$300,000
Current ratio	2.00	2.00

Table 13-2

PERCENTAGE COMPOSITION OF CURRENT ASSETS OF A MANUFACTURING FIRM

	Year 1	*Year 2*
Cash	5.00%	16.67%
Accounts receivable	37.50	50.00
Finished goods	12.50	16.67
Goods in process	7.50	4.16
Raw materials	37.50	12.50
Total current assets	100.00%	100.00%

Table 13-2 reveals that the firm made progress in some areas and slipped badly in others. It increased its proportion of cash and receivables and reduced its relatively large investment in raw materials; these facts reflect credit on management. However, the analyst will want to investigate the seemingly large investment in receivables and determine whether the investment in finished goods is in line with needs. The answers to those questions are easily determined by examining the current asset components individually, as we did earlier.

CASH

Cash balances held by a business firm are not entirely available to meet its maturing obligations. They are maintained at certain levels to (1) facilitate commercial transactions, (2) provide a reserve against unexpected cash drains, and (3) compensate banks for the services they provide. Hence the cash balance is not totally liquid.

Transactions Needs

The transactions motive for holding cash is to enable the firm to conduct its ordinary business. In industries such as utilities in which billings can be scheduled evenly throughout each month, cash inflows can be closely synchronized with cash disbursements, thereby lowering the ratios of cash to revenue and cash to current assets to minimum levels. In retail trade, by contrast, sales are less predictable, and the need for working cash balances occasioned by a relatively large volume of cash sales will result in higher ratios of cash to revenues and to current assets.

The seasonality of a business may give rise to a need for cash during certain months to purchase inventories, meet inflated payrolls, or carry a high volume of seasonally dated receivables. Such cash balances will generally be unused at fiscal year-end, when the annual statements are prepared, and therefore give the analyst the impression that the firm is highly liquid when, in fact, the apparent surplus of cash should not (and probably will not) be used to reduce current debt.

Emergency Reserves

Many firms hold cash (either on hand or readily accessible) to act as a cushion against unexpected events. Floods, work stoppages, or the failure of an important customer to pay on time are a few examples of contingencies for which such emergency reserves are held.

The amount of cash a firm must hold to provide for routine and unpredictable cash needs depends on (1) its willingness to risk running short of cash, (2) the degree of predictability of its cash flows, and (3) its available reserve borrowing power. A firm wishing absolutely to minimize risk would tend to hold very large cash balances and maintain good banking relations as a second line of defense against cash shortages. A firm willing to assume some risk for the sake of higher returns would tend to have almost all its resources—including most of its borrowing power—invested in earning assets. Management's hope, under those circumstances, would clearly be that no sudden and unexpected demand for additional funds would materialize.

The amount of income a firm is willing to forego by holding cash reserves will determine the upper limit to its investment in cash. Although some firms consistently "overinvest" or "underinvest" in cash, most follow a middle course of maintaining some excess cash on hand while keeping their bank lines of credit open, through prompt repayment of loans, so that they will be available if needed to meet unexpected demands.

Compensating Balances

Sometimes the minimum cash balances needed to meet a firm's transaction and emergency reserve requirements are not large enough to be commensurate with the volume of services its bank routinely provides. Thus, for many firms, the minimum level of cash holdings is determined by the compensating balance requirements of their banks, rather than by their own operational or precautionary needs for cash.

The size of the compensating balance that a bank may require is related to the profitability of the firm's account to the bank. Many banks determine that profitability through formulas that compare the earnings the bank can generate by investing the firm's average collected cash balances with the costs of the services the bank provides to the firm (e.g., funds transfers and check clearing). If the total cost is less than the total income from the account, the account is profitable; otherwise it is not. In any event, the minimum level of balances that will be deemed commensurate by the bank is the level at which the bank breaks even.

Measures of Cash Liquidity

As long as a firm desires to maintain good relations with its bank, the amount of cash it holds as a compensating balance will be completely illiquid. The Securities and Exchange Commission's *Accounting Series Release Number 136* proposes that a firm with outstanding bank credit segregate on its balance sheet any cash restricted under compensating balance arrangements. The adoption of that proposal would permit the analyst to determine "free" cash more closely; however, he would still have to estimate the firm's permanent investment in cash for transactions and precautionary purposes in order to measure its *true* cash surplus (or deficit) in the going concern sense. Large cash surpluses (defined in this way) suggest an inefficient use of cash, and deficits suggest the possibility of a cash flow imbalance. Both situations warrant further inquiry by the analyst.

240

Liquidity in the static sense is usually measured by *cash ratios*—cash plus marketable securities divided by total current assets or by current liabilities. Those ratios test the liquidating value of cash against (1) all current assets and (2) current obligations. The higher the ratios, the more liquid the firm's position and the better off its creditors should forced liquidation take place.

Unfortunately, cash ratios neglect to consider fixed assets and long-term debt, both of which take on significance in case of liquidation. If the firm ceases to exist as a going concern, all its long-term debt immediately becomes a current liability. Thus the static measures of liquidity do not reveal very much about the firm, either as a going concern or in liquidation.

Summary

This chapter has introduced the important concepts of liquidity and solvency as they relate to the firm as a going concern and in liquidation. It has stressed the necessity of acquiring a complete understanding of working capital and its related cash flows so that the analyst does not lose sight of the forces that create changes both in aggregate measures of liquidity and in individual components of working capital. Finally, it has examined the firm's cash balance as a largely illiquid investment in a permanent current asset.

The following chapter concludes the analysis of module one—short-term liquidity and solvency—by examining the remaining components of the firm's current position.

Questions

13-1. Explain the difference between liquidity and solvency. Why is the distinction important to the analyst?

13-2. Describe the relation between liquidity and solvency.

13-3. List some causes of illiquidity that are self-correcting and some that are not.

13-4. Discuss the importance of working capital to small business firms.

13-5. Explain the concept of permanent working capital. How should this portion of the firm's current assets be financed?

13-6. For what two reasons does a firm desire to increase the cash flow through its current assets?

13-7. What is the net trade cycle? Of what significance is it to the bank analyst reviewing an application for a short-term working capital loan?

13-8. Explain how the distribution of current assets influences a firm's liquidity.

13-9. Is cash a totally liquid asset? Explain your answer.

Chapter 14

Short-Term Liquidity and Solvency (II)

This chapter continues the discussion of module one of our basic approach to statement analysis. We shall examine in considerable detail the nature of the management problems concerned with accounts and notes receivable, inventories, and current liabilities and the implications of those problems and their solutions for financial statement analysis.

Accounts Receivable

Accounts receivable arise from the extension of open-account credit to a firm's customers in the normal course of business. When a credit sale takes place, goods previously in inventory are converted to receivables before their conversion into cash. Thus firms that extend trade credit must allocate some of their resources to support the receivables they carry. It is that allocation of funds that gives rise to a firm's investment in accounts receivable.

RATIONALE FOR EXTENDING CREDIT

Perhaps the most important reason a firm invests in accounts receivable is that the extension of credit provides it with a competitive advantage and thereby increases sales and profits. Where credit extension is an integral part of the sales program of an industry, competition requires that firms at least match one another's credit terms. The logic behind that view is that firms selling on credit are, in effect, offering the customer a package consisting of two parts: (1) the goods they manufacture or distribute, and (2) the financing of purchases for a limited period. Although credit is only one of several factors that may influence sales, a firm that adopts a conservative credit policy while its competitors are extending credit liberally may find that its conservatism has a dampening effect on sales.

243

SALES AND COLLECTION PERIOD

The level of the firm's investment in accounts receivable is determined by two interrelated factors: (1) its volume of credit sales, and (2) the length of time its receivables remain uncollected (its *collection period*). Of the two factors, the collection period is more readily subject to managerial control. To be sure, a firm's credit extension policy can affect the level of credit sales if its policy differs significantly from that of its competitors; however, in many industries, sales are generally more responsive to other factors. Therefore, management can exercise greater control over accounts receivable by establishing sound credit and collection policies and implementing them properly.

CREDIT TERMS

While the customs of an industry frequently dictate the credit terms offered, a firm can design its own credit terms as a dynamic instrument in its overall sales effort and a way of increasing the return on its investment in accounts receivable. The most important credit terms involve the *length of the credit period* and the *size of the cash discount*. Together they play a large role in determining the average collection period and hence the investment in receivables. Moreover, they affect the general quality of the accounts receivable and hence the firm's credit-worthiness.

In establishing credit terms, a firm must weigh the costs of extending credit (or changing its existing credit policies) against the benefits it expects to receive. For example, if it is considering a reduction in its credit period to speed up collections, it must compare the probable benefits from reducing its investment in receivables with the profit it will lose if the change reduces its sales volume as well. Similarly, if the firm wishes to grant cash discounts for prompt payment, it must weigh the cost of the discounts against the benefits from increased sales and a net reduction in the collection period.

MEASURES OF RECEIVABLES QUALITY AND LIQUIDITY

Accounts receivable management is no simple task. Evaluating the quality and liquidity of a firm's investment in receivables is also difficult, but the direction of the evaluation is made clearer once the analyst understands that the objective of the firm's credit and collection policies is to generate sales.

Liquidity of the Receivables

Both the quality and the liquidity of accounts receivable are affected by the rate at which they are converted into cash. That rate is measured by receivables *turnover* or *collection period*. The slower the turnover, the greater the chances of loss and hence the lower the *quality* of the receivables. The higher the turnover, the greater the flow of cash into the firm and hence the higher the liquidity of the accounts receivable.

Receivables turnover is the ratio of total net charge sales for a given twelve-month period to the average (or year-end) trade accounts receivable. That ratio may be converted into the accounts receivable collection period by dividing it into 365 (the number of days in a year). When the receivables turnover declines from one period to another (or the collection period increases), the analyst has reason to assume that receivables are being collected more slowly and are in a less satisfactory condition than before. When an upward trend in the turnover is evidenced, he has some reason to feel that payments are being made more promptly and that an improved condition exists.

The analyst must then attempt to explain the trend he discovers. For example, a decline in the ratio may reflect (1) a poor collection effort or policy, (2) a reluctance to write off uncollectible accounts, or (3) financial difficulties among the firm's customers. To lend real meaning to the size and trend of the receivables turnover, however, it is desirable to set up some theoretically ideal ratio and see how far the actual ratio varies from it. The first requirement toward this end is knowledge of the terms of sale under which the outstanding receivables were created.

Terms of Sale

It is common practice among manufacturers and wholesalers to allow an attractive cash discount on payments for credit sales made within some specified period—say ten days—after the date of the invoice. Trade debtors normally try to take advantage of this discount privilege; trade discounts received may be a significant addition to the purchaser's income account. If a business made all its charge sales subject to a 2 percent cash discount for payment within ten days and sales were reasonably uniform throughout the year, the analyst might set up an "ideal" standard collection period of only ten days. That would mean that the receivables turnover at year-end should be approximately 36.5 times. If, under the conditions mentioned, that theoretically perfect ideal were achieved, it would indicate that all outstanding receivables at year-end were within the cash discount period, suggesting that the total was owed by thoroughly responsible debtors.

As a practical matter, one could hardly hope for such an outcome; a more realistic standard might be based, not on the cash discount period, but on the period beyond which credit sales were considered past due. Thus, if selling terms were 2 percent 10 days, net 30 days (or just 30 days net, as might be true of many retail lines), the standard could be set at the equivalent of 30 days' sales, which would require a receivables turnover of approximately 12.17 at year-end. When all sales are made on the same terms and do not vary greatly from month to month, the extent of the variation above or below the "ideal" ratio indicates the weakness or strength of the actual ratio.

An abnormally high turnover of receivables, in comparison with preceding periods or with trade averages, suggests that some portion of the receivables may have been sold or discounted. That possibility should be investigated before an exceptionally high turnover figure is accepted as evidence of an exceptionally favorable collection experience. Suspiciously strong ratios are as deserving of further examination as those that are obviously weak.

Weaknesses of the Turnover Ratio

There are two primary weaknesses in the receivables turnover ratio that make it unwise to place complete dependence on its reliability.

1. The trade receivables outstanding at the close of a year usually do not arise from the sales of the whole year; they consist principally, if not entirely, of unpaid balances on accounts and of notes arising from credit sales of the last two or three months. The total receivables at year-end are determined more by the level of sales for the last quarter of the year than by the volume of business for the entire year. Therefore, an increase in the turnover of receivables, if occasioned by a drastic reduction in year-end sales, would *not* mean that the firm's collection policies had improved the quality and liquidity of the accounts receivable. The increase would merely be the result of the close relation between sales and receivables.

2. It is frequently true that a business sells different products on different terms or even the same products on different terms to different purchasers. Thus the size of trade receivables outstanding at the close of a year depends not only on how debtors comply with the terms of sale but also on the varying proportions of sales on different terms that were made during the closing months of the year. An improvement in the turnover ratio might mean only that the firm's product or customer mix had changed from prior periods and would not reflect on its credit and collection activities at all.

In addition to these inherent weaknesses, the analyst must interpret the size and trend of the ratio in light of existing business conditions. For example, a business may liberalize its trade credit terms when it introduces a new product, seizes a profitable opportunity to utilize excess capacity, or is forced to deal with special competitive conditions in its industry. Thus a "bad" trend may not necessarily reflect poor management, and a "good" trend may not always indicate improved conditions. The analyst must use his skill to interpret properly the ratios he has calculated.

Aging Accounts Receivable

A table showing the individual balances that make up accounts receivable is an essential supplement to an intelligent appraisal of this asset.

Such a table may break down the gross amount of outstanding receivables according to the months in which they were changed or the relation of the balances to their maturity dates. A breakdown according to the months in which charged might appear as in Table 14-1.

A variation of this procedure is to age the outstanding balances to show the portion of the total that is not due and the extent to which the remaining balances have passed their maturity dates. An illustration of this method is shown in Table 14-2. Both summaries are highly informative to the analyst, and one or the other should be made a routine part of every credit investigation.

It should be noted that the examples given are headed to reflect the aging of trade accounts only. If the business is such that notes or acceptances are received in payment of sales as a matter of course, they may be integrated with the aging of accounts or segregated by maturity dates in

Table 14-1

AGE OF ACCOUNTS RECEIVABLE BY MONTH CHARGED
December 31, 1978

	Amount	*Percentage of Total*
Charged during		
December	$18,000	40.9%
November	11,000	25.0
October	8,000	18.2
September	4,000	9.1
Before September	3,000	6.8
Total	$44,000	100.0%

Table 14-2

AGE OF ACCOUNTS RECEIVABLE BY DAYS PAST DUE
December 31, 1978

	Amount	*Percentage of Total*
Not due	$18,000	40.9%
1 to 30 days past due	11,000	25.0
31 to 60 days past due	8,000	18.2
61 to 90 days past due	4,000	9.1
More than 90 days past due	3,000	6.8
Total	$44,000	100.0%

247

a separate summary. The latter course seems preferable when the amounts involved are large.

There is a direct relation between the slowness of accounts receivable and bad debt losses. The longer the account is permitted to remain unpaid, the greater is the likelihood that it will not be paid in full. Table 14-3 presents evidence of this relation in terms of the probability that a retail account of a certain age will become a bad debt. The data are based on accounts receivable due to retailers of all classes.

These estimates in Table 14-3 apply to the accounts receivable of retail concerns, but it seems reasonable to suppose that the principle of deterioration in value with advancing age is equally true of the receivables of other business organizations.

Thus, by aging the accounts receivable, the analyst is able to observe their internal makeup, appraise their condition, and estimate the extent to which their balance sheet total should be adjusted to approximate a realizable value. By relating the reserve for bad debts to the proportion of accounts in the older classifications, he is able to form his own opinion of the adequacy of the reserve provided to cover probable losses. By comparing age classifications from one statement date to another, he can detect indications of developing laxness in credit and collection policies, as well as movements toward strength or weakness in the structure of the receivables shown on the balance sheet.

To provide for a running comparison of age classifications at the same date over a period of years, the analyst should transcribe account agings to columnar comparative forms, like the one shown in Table 14-4.

The subtotals in the summary enable him to compare group classifications readily. He can see at a glance that 65.9 percent of total receivables

Table 14-3

BAD DEBT PROBABILITIES OF RETAIL ACCOUNTS BY AGE CLASSIFICATION

Age of Account	Probability of Becoming a Bad Debt
30 days	5%
60 days	7
90 days	10
4 months	14
5 months	19
6 months	37
1 year	58
2 years	74
3 years	83
5 years	practically 100%

Table 14-4

COMPARATIVE SPREAD OF ACCOUNT AGING ANALYSIS

| | December 31, 1977 | | December 31, 1978 | |
	Amount	*Percentage*	*Amount*	*Percentage*
Charged during				
December	$20,000	47.0%	$18,000	40.9%
November	13,000	30.6	11,000	25.0
Subtotal	$33,000	77.6	$29,000	65.9
October	7,000	16.5	8,000	18.2
Subtotal	$40,000	94.1	$37,000	84.1
September	2,000	4.7	4,000	9.1
Subtotal	$42,000	98.8	$41,000	93.2
Before September	500	1.2	3,000	6.8
Total	$42,500	100.0	$44,000	100.0
Less: Reserve for bad debts	2,000	4.7	2,500	5.7
Net total (per balance sheet)	$40,500	95.3	$41,500	94.3

were under 60 days old at the close of 1978, compared with 77.6 percent at the close of 1977; that 84.1 percent were under 90 days old, compared with 94.1 percent for the previous year; and that 93.2 percent were under four months old, compared with 98.8 percent.

Like any tool of analysis, accounts receivable aging must be used with caution. Since the proportions of outstanding accounts in the various age classifications always add up to 100 percent, an increase in the percentage of accounts in one group means a decrease in the percentage in another group or groups. For this reason it is often difficult to determine whether a comparison of agings discloses an improved or a weakened condition of receivables as a whole.

Moreover, valuable as account agings are, they can by no means be relied upon to tell the full story. They show the quantity of outstanding receivables that fall in each age classification at the close of a period; but since they do not relate those quantities to the sales volume that created them, the percentages in each age group may have different meanings for different periods.

For example, since 65.9 percent (or $29,000) of the receivables out-standing at December 31, 1978, as listed in Table 14-4, had been charged within 60 days of the year-end compared with 77.6 percent (or $33,000) of the total in the same classification at the close of 1977, it may appear reasonable to assume that some deterioration had taken place in the quality of the receivables asset. Suppose, however, that charge sales had amounted to $100,000 for the last two months of 1977 and had risen to $116,000 for the last two months in 1978. In that case 33 percent of November and December sales remained uncollected at the close of 1977, and only 25 percent of the sales for those two months remained outstanding at the close of 1978. Obviously, that would make the analyst reconsider his conclusion that receivables quality had declined and seek further information regarding the condition of outstanding accounts.

Receivables Quality: Some Problems

The two most important questions that must be answered to assess the quality of a firm's accounts receivable are:
1. Are the receivables actually the result of open-account, commercial transactions of the usual kind, or do they include accounts that require special collection methods?
2. Does the net book value of the receivables stand a reasonable chance of being collected without unusual effort?

The answers to these questions will reveal the quality of receivables—*the likelihood of collection without loss.*

Consignment Sales.   Occasionally, a firm will transfer (rather than sell) merchandise to a customer on consignment. Under this arrangement, the seller (consignor) retains title to the goods until his customer sells them to a third party. At that time title passes to the third party, and the proceeds of the sale, less the consignee's markup, are remitted to the consignor. That kind of transaction should not create an account receivable for the consignor until the merchandise is sold to the third party; however, some firms treat consignments as sales at the time the merchandise is shipped to their customers and thereby create receivables. That will not cause the analyst any problems unless the consigned merchandise is returned unsold or otherwise reclaimed by the consignor. Under those circumstances the receivables are really inventory and not directly convertible into cash.

Other Problems.   In some industries, such as the recording, toy, and bakery industries, customers enjoy liberal merchandise return privileges. The analyst must also be aware of the possibility that receivables include installment notes collectible over more than one year, notes and accounts due from employees or officers, and similar receivables not connected with usual commercial transactions. Appropriate adjustments should be made in the value of accounts receivable when the analyst discovers such "impurities" in them. The proper adjustments are the removal of all consignment "sales" and "receivables" as well as receivables arising from other than normal commercial transactions and those that will mature in longer than one year.

Bad Debt Policy.   In considering the collectibility of receivables, the analyst must examine the bad debt policy of the firm being analyzed. Since normal bad debt losses may be considered inevitable in the conversion of receivables into cash, it follows that a reserve for bad debts should ordinarily be provided against any uncollected receivables on the books at the close of an accounting period. The reserve is necessary for two reasons:

1. The operations of the period during which the accounts originated should properly bear all the losses incurred in converting them into cash. All receivables known to be worthless at the close of the period should be charged off; in addition, a reserve should be provided against the unforeseeable losses that past experience shows are likely to be sustained in the realization of the remainder.

2. The amount at which the receivables are carried as an asset in the balance sheet should represent their probable realizable value, based on past collection experience. That is, the stated gross value of the receivables outstanding at the close of a period should be reduced by a reserve (or allowance, or "provision") for bad debts to arrive at a close estimate of realizable value.

In considering the adequacy of the reserve for bad debt losses, the analyst should attempt to determine the extent of the collection risks inherent in the firm's receivables. That risk can be measured to some extent by analyzing the following kinds of information:

1. Customer concentration, in terms of percentage of sales to the largest, five largest, and ten largest customers
2. The proportion of past due accounts remaining on the books
3. The extent to which trade discounts, returns, and other credits are reflected in the book value of the receivables
4. The nature of the credit analysis performed before extending credit to new and old customers

This type of information may be obtained directly from the firm and used to supplement, in a qualitative way, the information the analyst gathers about the liquidity of the accounts receivable. For example, a high percentage of total receivables due from one or a few customers could seriously affect cash flow from the collection of receivables if one of the large customers experienced financial difficulty. Similarly, if very little analysis is performed before the extension of credit and accounts are not reviewed periodically, bad debt loss expectations should be adjusted upward by the analyst.

Notes Receivable

Notes receivable maturing beyond one year from the date of the balance sheet should not be included in current assets, since they do not

251

conform to the suggested definition of such assets. Similarly, past-due notes should be excluded from current assets, since a note that has passed its maturity date is presumed to have been dishonored and dishonor is presumed to be evidence of questionable value. However, the condition of the notes receivable asset should not go unquestioned merely because all items are within their maturity dates. Often a business will charge back all dishonored notes to the open accounts of the debtors. Moreover, slow and questionable notes may be renewed or extended from period to period to avoid an appearance of weakness.

Trade notes receivable that are payable on demand carry their own red flag of doubtfulness; a responsible debtor will not ordinarily issue a note payable on demand for current purchases of merchandise when open accounts carry some deferment of maturity.

When it is practical to compare the unit makeup of the notes receivable from one statement date to another, the analyst can give more thorough consideration to an appraisal of value. Not only will perennial obligations be brought to his attention but, with the individual makers listed, he can institute his own investigations of their credit-worthiness when the occasion demands. Ratings can be obtained on the larger items that make up the total at each year-end, and an estimate of their collectibility can be derived.

Inventories

If retailers and wholesalers are to continue in operation as going concerns, they must keep sufficient stocks of merchandise on hand to meet the reasonable immediate demands of their trade. If manufacturers are to continue to function as producing units, they must usually carry supplies of finished merchandise for immediate delivery; they must also have stocks of raw materials for the continuing replenishment of the manufacturing process, and when the manufacturing process is continuous, they will always show an investment in work-in-process inventories. These necessary investments in inventories amount to substantial proportions of the current and total assets of the average business enterprise. The evaluation of their soundness and liquidity is one of the most difficult problems facing the analyst.

In viewing inventories on the balance sheet, it is important for the beginning analyst to remember that the total shown is the result of somebody's enumeration of quantity and estimation of value. Since a wide range of judgment may be employed in valuing inventories, an abnormally high degree of confidence in the management of a business is required if its inventory estimates are to be accepted without disinterested verification. When audited statements are being considered, inventory quantities, pricings, and salability should be of primary interest and concern to the analyst.

RELATION TO SALES AND PRODUCTION

In most businesses, a certain level of inventories must be kept on hand to support an adequate level of sales. Note that inventories should not necessarily bear a precise relation to *past* sales, except when past sales are an accurate predictor of future sales. If inventory levels are too low, lost sales or production may result; if inventories are too high, the firm may have to pay excessive storage costs, insurance premiums, and taxes. It will also run the risk of loss of inventory value through obsolescence and physical deterioration. Moreover, higher than necessary inventories tie up funds that may profitably be employed elsewhere. Consequently, determining the size of the inventory in relation to future sales is an important aspect of a firm's current asset management and an important gauge for assessing the quality of management through financial statement analysis.

In general, several kinds of balance are desirable in the inventories of a manufacturing firm:

1. Raw materials should not be excessive in relation to the time required to convert them into finished goods; supplies should not be excessive in relation to the need for them in the manufacturing process; goods in process should not constitute too great a part of total inventories and should be sufficient only to ensure a normal flow of finished products; finished goods should not be excessive in relation to the time required to convert them into cash or receivables.

2. There should be a balance within the total raw materials. Materials should tend to be found in inventories in the proportions in which they are fed to the manufacturing process or appear in the finished product. For instance, if two parts of material A are required in the manufacturing process to one part of material B, quantities of material A in inventories should tend to be twice as large as quantities of material B. When it is practical to determine the quantities of each major class of materials used in the manufacturing process during the year, it is comparatively simple to check the materials for balance by relating the year-end inventory quantity of each material to the respective quantities used.

3. The principle of balance also applies to inventories of supplies. The various classes of supplies held in stock should tend to be proportionate to the ratio in which each is required in the manufacturing process.

4. There should be a balance within the total of the finished goods. Each class of finished product should bear a reasonable relationship to its anticipated sales, as indicated by an analysis of the sales of past periods. If product A moves twice as fast as product B, quantities of product B in the inventories should be only half as great as quantities of product A. This consideration applies with equal force to the inventories of retailers and wholesalers. Each product or group of products should be proportionate to its ratio in the total volume of sales.

PROBLEMS OF INVENTORY VALUE

The effects of different methods of valuing inventories were examined in Chapter 3. There we saw that the LIFO and FIFO methods resulted in materially different ending values for inventories. While this problem is certainly significant for the analyst (and we will explore its implications later in greater depth), other problems of inventory value also exist.

Most important, the value shown on the balance sheet, regardless of the method used to arrive at it, is meaningless unless the inventories actually exist. Many instances of fraud go undetected because analysts fail to make physical checks of inventories.

Once the physical existence of the inventory has been verified, the analyst must determine whether it has been fairly valued and whether the valuation has been performed consistently from period to period. Often the analyst cannot make such assessments without expert advice on any but audited financial statements. Most published reports contain insufficient information to allow the analyst to convert an inventory figure arrived at the LIFO method to a figure reflecting the FIFO method of inventory accounting. Consequently, when inconsistent methods are applied, all the analyst can do is estimate the general impact of the change on the firm's current position and earnings.

MEASURING THE LIQUIDITY OF INVENTORY

Because of the risk involved in holding inventories and the fact that inventories are one step further removed from cash than are receivables (they must be converted into receivables before they can be turned into cash), inventories are usually considered the least liquid of the current assets. Some staple items, however—agricultural commodities; standard sizes of lumber, fasteners, and fixtures of all types; and raw materials, for example—enjoy broad and active markets in which they can be disposed of quickly and at reasonable prices. On the other hand, fashion merchandise, perishable items, and specialized equipment can rapidly lose their value unless sold on a timely basis. Hence, the *quality* of the inventory—as measured by the firm's ability to use it or dispose of it without incurring losses—is the first step in measuring its total liquidity. Knowledge of the inventory, its various uses, and its marketability is important for the analyst to acquire.

In a going concern sense, however, the liquidity of inventories can be measured by relating the cost of goods sold during a period to the average inventories—a ratio known as the *inventory turnover*. It measures the average rate at which inventories are converted into receivables (and/or cash, depending on whether the period's sales are credit sales, cash sales, or both). It thus reflects on the purchasing and merchandising efficiency of management.

A low inventory turnover by historical or trade standards suggests that the inventory may include items that are slow moving because they are obsolete, showing signs of deterioration, out of season, or otherwise unsalable. Further investigation may reveal that a slowdown in inventory turnover is the result of deliberate and commendable managerial decisions. For example, management may decide to stockpile inventory in advance of work on a future contractual commitment (remember, inventories are related to *future* sales), an anticipated price increase, a pending labor walkout, or for a number of other reasons, each of which must be investigated by the analyst.

An unusually high inventory turnover may mean that the firm is losing sales, is experiencing costly interruptions in production because of running out of raw materials, or simply has achieved a high level of efficiency in managing its inventories. Hence the level and direction of the ratio over time, while always revealing, must be interpreted only after careful analysis of the facts.

Variations by Lines and Industries

Naturally, the rate of inventory turnover varies considerably with the type of trade or industry. Retailers of perishable meats and food products, for instance, have an abnormally high turnover, while at the other extreme are retailers of jewelry and furniture and manufacturers of heavy and costly products. Comparisons between business units, therefore, should be confined to businesses that are strictly comparable in function, product, size, territory, and general operating conditions.

Effect of Changing Price Levels

Changing price levels may cause variations in the dollar turnover of inventories not based entirely on corresponding variations in the actual physical flow of merchandise through the business. Hence the dollar turnover cannot always be relied on as a dependable indicator of the relative movement of physical quantities. That is particularly true of the ratio of sales to inventories, since it is conceivable that if selling and cost prices move up continuously throughout an operating period, the average unit selling price for the year may be lower than the average unit cost value placed on inventories at the close of the year.

Advantages of Physical Quantities

Where it is practical to do so, the turnover of inventories should be computed on the basis of actual physical quantities. Tonnage sales or unit sales should be divided by average annual inventories in tons or units to determine an accurate physical turnover. Similarly, the ratio of year-end inventories to cost of sales can be more informatively expressed as the ratio of inventories in physical units to the number of physical

255

units sold during the year. The effect of varying unit prices from one period to another is thus eliminated, and a more reliable index of relative inventory quantities is made available.

The availability of unit quantities also enables the analyst to make significant comparisons among unit pricings at each statement date. Dividing the total dollar value of the inventories by the total units, he can obtain an average value per unit. By viewing that average from period to period in the light of general business conditions and the marketing outlook in the specific industry and comparing it with average unit selling prices of past periods, the analyst is able to gain unusual insight into the relative conservatism of inventory valuations. The significance of the average, of course, is weakened by variations in unit pricing resulting from variations in unit quality. Preferably, the figures should be so broken down that an average unit can be obtained for each class of product. Then comparisons of the average will truly have meaning.

Manufacturing Turnover

A better evaluation of inventory turnover for manufacturing firms can be obtained by calculating separate turnover rates for the major inventory components—raw materials, work in process, and finished goods. These turnover rates will help the analyst determine the extent and nature of actual or potential imbalances in the cash flows into and through the inventories. Table 14-5 suggests possible interpretations of the manufacturing turnover ratios. Departmental or divisional turnover ratios can similarly lead to more useful conclusions regarding inventory quality and liquidity; however, the external analyst is not likely to meet with much success in finding the data with which to calculate manufacturing and departmental turnover ratios, since they are rarely provided in published financial statements.

THE EFFECT OF ALTERNATIVE METHODS OF INVENTORY VALUATION

To illustrate the effect of alternative methods of inventory valuation on the short-run financial position of the firm, let us compare the operating results of a one-product retailer using the FIFO, LIFO, and average cost methods. Table 14-6 presents the inventory data, and Table 14-7 contains the comparative income statements produced under the three alternatives for the S. Litzky Company.

The ending inventory under the FIFO method was calculated by using the values of the last 400 units purchased: 150,000 units at $14 plus 250,000 units at $15 per unit. The LIFO inventory of $4,550,000 used 50,000 units at $10 plus 150,000 units at $11 and 200,000 units at $12. The average cost inventory of $5,156,000 was calculated at $12.89 per unit ($11,600,000/900,000) times 400,000 units.

Since Litzky's total assets on January 1 were $75 million, of which

Table 14-5

SOME INTERPRETATIONS OF MANUFACTURING TURNOVER RATIOS

Component	High Turnover	Low Turnover
Raw materials	Raw material shortages, with danger of production stoppage	Stockpiling, loss of control over purchases, or recent change in production rate
Work in process	Short production period, a recent decline in production rate, or existence of excess capacity	Long production period, recent increase in production rate, or shortage of raw materials with which to complete goods
Finished goods	Recent sales increase without proper increase in production, or possibility of lost sales	Too high a production rate, inefficient merchandising, unsalable merchandise, or stockpiling

Table 14-6

INVENTORY RECORDS OF S. LITZKY COMPANY, 1978

	Units	Price	Value
Beginning Inventory, January 1	50,000	$10	$ 500,000
Purchases: March	150,000	11	1,650,000
June	300,000	12	3,600,000
September	150,000	14	2,100,000
December	250,000	15	3,750,000
Total available for sale	900,000		$11,600,000
Ending Inventory, December 31	400,000		
Sales	500,000	25	$12,500,000

$25.5 million were current assets, and current liabilities and long-term debt totaled $12.5 million and $5 million respectively, we can use the information contained in Table 14-7 to construct three comparative balance sheets, as shown in Table 14-8. We will assume further that current liabilities increase by $3.75 million, the amount of December's purchases. Then, by computing certain ratios, we can observe the effects of the different inventory methods on the firm's current position as indicated by the statement appearing below the balance sheets.

The selected ratios clearly show that, under the circumstances assumed in the example, LIFO produced the best inventory turnover but the poorest current ratio and the lowest return on sales. More important,

257

Table 14-7

**COMPARATIVE INCOME STATEMENTS OF S. LITZKY COMPANY, 1978
(in thousands)**

	FIFO	LIFO	Average Cost
Sales	$12,500	$12,500	$12,500
Cost of sales: Beginning inventory	500	500	500
Purchases	11,100	11,100	11,100
Less ending inventory	5,850	4,550	5,156
Cost of sales	$ 5,750	$ 7,050	$ 6,444
Gross profit	$ 6,750	$ 5,450	$ 6,056
Operating expenses	2,500	2,500	2,500
Net income	$ 4,250	$ 2,950	$ 3,556

however, these figures underline the importance to the analyst of acquiring skill in interpreting comparative statements of firms using different accounting methods.

Current Liabilities

Current liabilities are those due within twelve months of the date of the balance sheet. They include notes and accounts payable, accrued taxes and other expenses, current portions of long-term debt, and a few other relatively minor classes of liability.

Not all current liabilities represent equally urgent demands for payment. At one extreme are tax liabilities and accrued wages, which must be paid promptly regardless of current conditions. At the other extreme are current liabilities owed to suppliers and notes payable to banks with whom the firm has established excellent relations. Postponement and renegotiation of such debts in periods of financial stress are both possible and rather common.

The analyst should also be aware of *unrecorded* current liabilities. Some examples are purchase commitments for inventories and fixed assets, obligations for current cash payments into employee pension funds, and current lease obligations. Finally, some long-term and intermediate-term debt arrangements call for *balloon payments* at maturity—that is, final payments of amounts larger than the usual annual debt service charges. In those cases, the analyst may assume that next year's debt payments will be the same as those of the current year; however, under balloon payment provisions, he may suddenly find that current payments on long-term debt have skyrocketed from previous periods.

Table 14-8

COMPARATIVE BALANCE SHEETS AND RATIOS OF S. LITZKY COMPANY, 1978
(dollar figures in thousands)

	Jan. 1	*FIFO*	*LIFO*	*Average Cost*
Cash and receivables	$25,000	$27,650	$27,650	$27,650
Inventory	500	5,850	4,550	5,156
Current assets	$25,500	$33,500	$32,200	$32,806
Other assets	49,500	49,500	49,500	49,500
Total assets	$75,000	$83,000	$81,700	$82,306
Current liabilities	$12,500	$16,250	$16,250	$16,250
Long-term debt	5,000	5,000	5,000	5,000
Equity	57,500	61,750	60,450	61,056
Total liabilities & capital	$75,000	$83,000	$81,700	$82,306
Selected Ratios:				
Current ratio	2.04	2.06	1.98	2.02
Inventory turnover	n.a.	1.81 times	2.79 times	2.28 times
Gross margin	n.a.	54%	44%	48%
Debt to equity	30%	34%	35%	35%
Net profit on sales	n.a.	34%	24%	28%

Many audit reports contain supplementary schedules of current liabilities that are informative to the analyst. A detailed schedule of notes payable, showing the names of the holders, the maturities and rates, and the collateral, if any, is always desirable when there are outstanding notes. This schedule not only discloses the names of other creditors, showing the relative importance of each to the company, but also reveals whether any creditor occupies a more favorable position than others.

Accounts payable are frequently itemized in a schedule, which reveals the identity of the principal suppliers of the company. The schedule can be used to obtain the names of companies with which to check the subject company's trade payment record.

Some audit reports include an itemized list of all accrued liabilities. These data are helpful and at times revealing to the analyst.

TESTING THE CONDITION OF ACCOUNTS PAYABLE

Two ratios may prove useful in testing the condition of accounts payable: the ratio of purchases to accounts payable, and the ratio of discounts earned to total purchases. If the total purchases for the year, as shown by the income statement, amount to $600,000 and accounts payable at the statement date are $30,000, the ratio of purchases to accounts payable equals 20. The ratio may be converted to days by dividing it into 365. The result in this instance is 18 days, indicating that accounts are being paid on the average within 18 days. When that figure is compared with the normal purchasing terms, it gives some idea of how the company handles its trade purchases.

Sometimes amounts owed for purchases other than inventory purchases are included in the accounts payable total. The inclusion of such accounts distorts the ratio. Moreover, special datings on purchases are sometimes given by suppliers, allowing the firm to delay paying on account for as long as six or eight months. Those arrangements likewise have a distorting influence on the ratio. The ratio of purchases to accounts payable is helpful occasionally; if it is computed annually, the trend should be revealing, suggesting improvement or retrogression in keeping current with trade obligations.

The other ratio that may be indicative of the company's manner of caring for trade debts is the ratio of discounts earned to purchases. This ratio usually has more meaning than the ratio of purchases to accounts payable since it reflects the annual dollar income brought about by paying trade obligations before the expiration of the discount period. Assume that purchases for the year, as shown by the profit and loss statement, total $300,000 and that discounts earned total $6,000. Dividing $6,000 by $300,000 gives a figure of 2 percent, showing that total discounts earned are 2 percent of total purchases. If the normal discount allowed by the trade is 3 percent, the 2 percent figure suggests that the company is discounting two-thirds of its purchases. This ratio should be informative if computed from year to year.

Summary

Management policies and practices relating to the individual components of working capital and the use of current liabilities determine both the size of the current assets (and liabilities) and the rate of cash flow through the short cycle. Unless the analyst is thoroughly familiar with the firm's operations and management's approach to decision making and control, he is likely to misinterpret the meanings of the measures of short-term liquidity and solvency he employs and reach unwarranted conclusions about the firm.

To avoid such problems, we have examined the *management* of receivables, inventories, and current liabilities before presenting the approaches useful in their analysis. The analyst should continue to place his analytical work within the context of the business environment and management practice if he hopes to achieve consistently good results from his efforts.

Questions

14-1. Why do business firms invest in accounts receivable?

14-2. What factors should a firm weigh in deciding on the terms of credit it will extend to its customers?

14-3. How is the accounts receivable collection period calculated?

14-4. Explain how an analyst should interpret the collection period once he has calculated it for a number of periods.

14-5. What is meant by aging accounts receivable? Why is this method of analysis valuable to an analyst?

14-6. Why is the correct interpretation of accounts receivable aging sometimes difficult?

14-7. What are consignment sales? Do they ordinarily create accounts receivable?

14-8. What is the purpose of holding inventories? Are there any costs associated with maintaining excessive inventories?

14-9. How is inventory quality measured? What specific measure is generally used to assess the liquidity of inventories?

14-10. What unique factor causes the inventory turnover ratio to be one of the most difficult ratios to interpret properly?

14-11. List some of the variants of the inventory turnover ratio.

14-12. Under conditions of rising inventory prices, would LIFO or FIFO produce the higher value in the following accounts and ratios?
1. total assets
2. current ratio
3. inventory turnover (year-end)
4. ratio of net profit to sales
5. retained earnings
6. ratio of debt to equity
7. current liabilities
8. gross margin

14-13. Define current liabilities. Do all current liabilities represent equally urgent demands for payment? Explain.

14-14. How is the ratio of days purchases outstanding computed? What does it measure?

Chapter 15 Module Two: Funds Flow Analysis

Preceding chapters have included many references to the *sources and uses of funds statement,* or *funds flow statement.* Chapters 5, 6, and 7 examined the operational and functional relations among the various kinds of business activity that are summarized in that statement, and Chapter 10 the technical aspects of its construction and preparation in various formats. Thus we should already be well acquainted with this important tool of analysis. Now we need to explore how the analyst can gain the greatest benefit from the information revealed in funds flow statements.

The Funds Flow Statement and the Circular Cash Flow

The discussion of the complete cash flow cycle of a manufacturing firm in Chapters 6 and 7 related changes in managerial policy and environmental factors to the circular flow of cash through a business. In several contexts, it examined the changes likely to take place both in the stocks of assets and in the rates of cash flow between various assets and liabilities, in response to internally and externally induced changes in the firm's operations. In particular, the cash flow of the growing firm and the declining firm were analyzed to show the influence of each situation on the availability of cash.

Those chapters presented a graphic analysis of cash flows; only a few numerical examples were given, to clarify the more abstract aspects of the complete cash flow cycle. The funds flow statement presents the same information conveyed graphically in the earlier chapters, but in a more precise, numerical format. Thus the funds flow statement is considered by some analysts one of the most important and useful tools of financial statement analysis. It summarizes the complete cash flow cycle of a firm and gives the analyst valuable insight into managerial ability through the observation and analysis of cash flows and, when they exist, cash flow imbalances. It also provides a bridge between the analysis of short- and of long-term liquidity and solvency by combing the short and long cash flow cycles. Finally, it serves as the necessary link between the analysis of the firm's balance sheet and the analysis of its income statement.

Dimensions of Funds Flow Analysis

The maximum amount of useful information can be obtained from the funds flow statement by recognizing that it is reporting simultaneously on three dimensions of the firm's cash flows. First, it permits the analyst to examine changes in net working capital both in aggregate form and in its individual components. Second, it helps him assess the firm's skill in managing its long-term sources and uses of funds. And finally, when used with certain other tools of statement analysis, it gives him some insight into the balance of the firm's cash flows with regard to the investment of permanent versus temporary sources of funds in permanent versus temporary uses of funds. Let us examine each of these dimensions.

CHANGES IN NET WORKING CAPITAL

Net working capital is the excess of current assets over current liabilities. Changes in the amount of net working capital over a given period are caused by the additions of new funds from long-term debt and equity capital and the applications of working capital funds to noncurrent uses. In either case, the balance sheet values of current assets, current liabilities, or both will change both absolutely and in relation to one another. If no other factors enter the picture, a dollar change in current assets will be exactly offset by a corresponding change in current liabilities, leaving the net working capital figure unchanged.

The analysis of changes in net working capital is best accomplished through the funds flow statement prepared in the working capital format. An example of that format is presented in Table 15-1 for the Timme Manufacturing Corporation. The upper portion of the statement shows how the change in the aggregate net working capital figure came about, and the schedule of working capital changes in the lower portion shows the changes that took place in the individual working capital components.

Aggregate Net Working Capital

The statement indicates that $261,000 was added to the firm's aggregate net working capital during 1978. Furthermore, the schedule of working capital changes shows that the amount of the change was not

Table 15-1

STATEMENT OF CHANGES IN NET WORKING CAPITAL
TIMME MANUFACTURING CORPORATION
for the Year Ended December 31, 1978
(000)

Factors serving to increase net working capital:			
Funds provided from operations			
Net income	$1,385		
Depreciation	571		
Loss on sale of fixed assets	20		
Deferred taxes	(100)	$1,876	
Exercise of stock options by employees		7	
Sale of company owned aircraft		86	
Total			$1,969
Factors serving to decrease net working capital:			
Purchase of tool and die machinery		$1,327	
Additions to other assets (real estate)		188	
Reduction in long-term debt		175	
Other		18	
Total			1,708
Increase (decrease) in net working capital			$ 261
Schedule of Working Capital Changes			
Additions to net working capital			
Increase in inventories		$1,850	
Increase in prepaid expenses		151	
Reduction in taxes payable		217	
Total			$2,218
Reductions in net working capital			
Reduction in cash and marketable			
securities		$ 60	
Reduction in accounts receivable		72	
Increase in the current portion of			
long-term debt		75	
Increase in accounts payable		$1,395	
Increase in other payables		355	
Total			1,957
Increase in net working capital			$ 261

simply "applied" to increasing working capital but rather was itself a "result" of changes in the firm's current assets and current liabilities over the period. Thus, unless the firm's management takes deliberate steps to increase the total investment in working capital from non-working-capital sources, it is inappropriate to consider the aggregate change in net working capital as an *application* of funds to that purpose. The change is more likely to be in the opposite direction; that is, the changes in the components of net working capital "consumed" funds from other sources, since almost all the funds were provided by normal operations and no apparent effort was made to conserve funds. That is evident from the fact that the firm purchased additional fixed assets and (nonoperating) real estate. Additional evidence in support of this proposition can be generated by examining the individual working capital components.

Working Capital Components

When the Timme Manufacturing Corporation's schedule of working capital changes is examined, two items stand out: the increase in inventories, and the increase in accounts payable. If we add the increase in other payables to the latter figure, we find that the total $1.75 million increase in short-term debt almost equals the $1.85 million increase in inventories. The transactions that produced those results are obviously related, and they suggest one of two possibilities: (1) the firm is expanding its operations and requires an additional investment in inventories, or (2) the firm did not achieve its expected level of sales, and it has made an involuntary investment in (excess) inventories. In either case, the resultant increase in accounts payable might be anticipated.

In the first instance, payables will increase spontaneously as the rate of purchases increases. In the second instance, the increase in payables results from an imbalance of cash flows and the absence of adequate cash reserves to undertake the firm's commitments to purchase fixed assets, retire long-term debt, and reduce accounts payable all at the same time.

To add further confusion to the picture, we note that accounts receivable decreased while inventories increased. If the firm's sales were growing, we would expect to see increases in both receivables and inventories, unless credit and collection policies reduced the receivables collection period. If sales were falling, however, receivables would fall, but inventories might remain unsold and increase in total dollar amount. That situation would reflect poor inventory management to the extent that management failed to reduce inventories as the rate of sales began to decline.

Of course, all these questions can easily be answered by determining whether the firm's sales increased or decreased in 1978. Once the analyst has that piece of information, he can begin to test the data and form conclusions about management's ability to formulate and implement working capital policies and decisions. We will discuss the appropriate methods later in this chapter.

LONG-TERM SOURCES AND USES OF FUNDS

As a summary of overall long-term investment and financing activities of a business, the funds flow statement is, of course, a far more reliable indicator of operating performance than the pronouncements voiced by management. It sheds light on such matters as what became of net income during the period, what assets were acquired, and how they were financed. It also draws a clear distinction between net income and funds provided by operations, as well as between financing transactions that benefit the firm and those that do not. Information of this kind is illustrated in the funds flow statement of Arvind Industries, Incorporated, shown in Table 15-2.

Financing Asset Acquisitions

Arvind Industries purchased the Ewert Oil Company during the fiscal year and paid $538,000 for the plant and equipment, $12,000 for goodwill (the excess of the purchase price over the book value of the assets), and some undisclosed amount for Ewert's inventories and accounts receivable, an amount that was absorbed into the working capital section of the statement in Table 15-2. The purchase of long-term assets totaled $550,000. The total of funds from operations plus the sale of fixed assets was only $399,000. The other long-term sources of funds, as we shall see, did not actually generate funds; consequently, Arvind Industries had to draw down its cash balances by $151,000 to complete the acquisition of the Ewert Oil Company.

The obvious next step in the analysis of this transaction is to determine whether Arvind Industries planned to use its cash reserves to complete the purchase of Ewert Oil. If this transaction (and the others) exhausted the firm's cash balances, management can be criticized for its apparent lack of financial planning. On the other hand, if the opportunity to purchase Ewert Oil occurred suddenly (and if it looks profitable), management is to be praised for its foresight in maintaining adequate cash reserves that enabled it to act quickly. Since the firm did not have to borrow money, it avoided the inevitable delays associated with arranging for a loan.

Net Income Versus Funds Provided by Operations

Normally a business firm generates a major portion of its total resources through net profits; however, as we can see in Table 15-2, Arvind Industries' net profits of $895,000 were composed largely of the profits of subsidiaries, as reported under the *equity method* of accounting for parent-subsidiary relationships. Under this accounting method, Arvind's share of its subsidiaries' profits are presented in its income statement as a line item; consequently the undistributed earnings—in this case, totaling $645,000—must be deducted as *noncash income*, leaving $250,000 of income as a cash inflow to the business.

The other $91,000 of cash flow from operations was generated through $98,000 of depreciation charges and a $7,000 addition to a

Table 15-2

STATEMENT OF CHANGES IN FINANCIAL POSITION
ARVIND INDUSTRIES, INCORPORATED
for the Year Ended June 30, 1978
(000)

Financial resources were provided by:			
Net income		$895	
Add: adjustments for noncash items			
Depreciation expense	$ 98		
Loss (gain) on sale of fixed assets	(14)		
Increase in pension reserves	7		
Equity in undistributed income of unconsolidated subsidiaries	(645)	(554)	
Resources provided by operations		$341	
Sale of fixed assets		$ 58	
Conversion of debentures into common stock		200	
Exercise of common stock options by officers		320	578
Total financial resources provided		$919	
Financial resources were used for:			
Acquisition of Ewert Oil Company:			
Purchase of fixed assets	$538		
Purchase of goodwill	12	$550	
Retirement of debentures on conversion to common stock		200	
Payment of common stock dividends		638	
Total financial resources used			1,388
Decrease in net working capital			$ 469

Analysis of increase (decrease) in net working capital:

Cash	$(683)	Accounts payable	$87
Accounts receivable	90	Federal income taxes payable	(25)
Inventories	172	Other current liabilities	(30)
Other current assets	(16)		
Increase in current assets	$(437)	Increase in current liabilities	$32

Net decrease in working capital $469

pension reserve, less the $14,000 gain on the sale of fixed assets. This last adjustment is required because it shows up on the income statement and also on the schedule of fixed assets. Since the gain is included in the $58,000 sale of fixed assets, a failure to deduct it from income would result in double counting of the profits. The net result of all these transactions is a cash inflow of only $341,000 out of a net profit of $895,000. This illustration clearly demonstrates the value of the funds flow statement in such a situation and makes it easy to explain why a firm's cash balance almost never increases by the amount of profits reported in the income statement.

Real Versus Nominal Financing Transactions

The two remaining sources of long-term funds listed on Arvind Industries' funds flow statement are the conversion of debentures into common stock and the exercise of stock options. The former transaction is obviously a *nominal* one; that is, it does not produce any actual cash inflows to the firm, since it is exactly offset by the retirement of the converted debentures, as shown in the second section of Table 15-2. The exercise of the stock options is also a nominal transaction but not so obviously as the first. Table 15-2 shows that, although $320,000 was brought into the firm by the sale of stock, $638,000 was paid out in common stock dividends. The net effect of the two transactions was a *drain* of $318,000 on both net worth and cash.

It would be interesting to discover three facts about the stock and dividends transactions: (1) how much stock the officers hold, (2) the price per common share established under the option, and (3) the dividends per share paid. With that information, the analyst could determine whether or not the cash dividend was designed to provide the officers with sufficient money to exercise their options. In addition, the common stock dividend may have persuaded the debenture holders to convert their securities into common stock to achieve a higher return on their investment; consequently, we cannot be certain what management's intentions were. We do know, however, that the firm lost a significant amount of cash as a result of these transactions.

Table 15-3

STATEMENT OF SOURCES AND USES OF FUNDS
WHITFORD IRON WORKS, INCORPORATED
for the Year Ended December 31, 1978
(000)

Sources of Funds		*Uses of Funds*	
Net income	$ 20	Purchase of fixed assets	$ 48
Depreciation	6	Dividends paid	8
Proceeds from sale of fixed assets	12	Repayment of long-term debt	3
Increase in accounts payable	50	Increase in accounts receivable	20
Increase in taxes payable	6	Increase in inventories	37
Increase in short-term notes payable	23	Increase in other current assets	1
Total sources of funds	$117	Total uses of funds	$117

269

PERMANENT VERSUS TEMPORARY SOURCES AND USES

The third dimension of the firm's cash flows that is revealed in the funds flows statement is the balance of flows relating to its permanent and temporary sources and uses of funds. The importance of this dimension arises from the proposition that permanent uses of funds (e.g., fixed assets) should be financed with long-term sources of funds and temporary assets may safely be financed with short-term sources. The funds flow statement, supplemented by certain other financial data, provides a method of examining how a business finances its operations at the margin and whether or not it has balanced its permanent funds needs with permanent sources of funds.

To illustrate, let us assume that Whitford Iron Works, Incorporated, presented the sources and uses of funds statement shown in Table 15-3. The following data were subsequently derived from its current and historical financial statements:

Increase in sales, 1978 over 1977	$180,000
Increase in cost of goods sold, 1978 over 1977	$135,000
Year-end collection period, 1977	32 days
Year-end inventory turnover, 1977	4.5 times per year
Ratio of materials to cost of goods sold	60%
Credit terms on purchase of raw materials	net 60 days

A brief examination of the statement suggests something unusual about the firm's cash flows; accounts payable and short-term notes payable appear to be out of proportion to the increases in current assets shown as uses of funds. However, we must investigate further to determine the precise nature and extent of the problem.

Uses of Funds

We can begin by examining the increases in receivables and inventories in the light of historical standards. Accounts receivable should be collected in 32 days; since the increase in sales is $180,000 (or an average of $500 per day), accounts receivable should have grown by $16,000 ($500 × 32 days). Unless evidence to the contrary is discovered, this indicates that $16,000 of the total increase of $20,000 in accounts receivable is a *permanent* use of funds and the remaining $4,000 a *temporary* use that can be recovered by returning the collection period to 32 days.

Similarly, the increase in Whitford's cost of goods sold of $135,000 should produce an increase in inventories of $30,000, based on an inventory turnover ratio of 4.5 ($135,000/4.5=$30,000). Again, unless we can justify the total inventory increase of $37,000 by further analysis, we must conclude that the growth in sales during 1978 requires a permanent increase in inventory of $30,000 and that the remaining $7,000 of inventory can be eliminated during 1979 by better inventory control.

A brief examination of the other uses of funds listed in Table 15-3 shows that the purchase of fixed assets, payment of dividends, debt repayment, and the increase in other current assets are permanent uses of funds. Consequently, of the total of $117,000 of uses, all but $11,000 represents a permanent commitment of funds by the firm; the $11,000 of "temporary uses" should be recoverable through improved management controls.

Sources of Funds

Whitford Iron Works' funds flow statement lists four permanent sources of funds: net income, depreciation, sale of fixed assets, and taxes payable. These total $44,000. In addition, at least a portion of the increase in accounts payable represents a permanent source of funds arising from the higher rate of raw materials purchases needed to support the firm's sales growth. The amount of this permanent financing is determined by calculating the increase in average daily purchases and multiplying that figure by 60 days—the length of the credit period extended to Whitford Iron Works. Average daily purchases are calculated by dividing 60 percent of cost of goods sold by 360, which equals $225—($135,000 × .6)/360. That amount times 60 days equals $13,500—the amount of the increase in permanent financing from accounts payable. The firm appears to have been "riding" its trade creditors in the amount of $36,500. That figure plus the $23,000 in short-term credit listed in Table 15-3, indicates that Whitford Iron Works is using $59,500 in temporary funds and only $57,500 in permanent funds.

Balancing Sources and Uses

Our preliminary conclusion is that Whitford Iron Works can repay only $11,000 of the $59,500 in temporary funds sources through a reduction in receivables and inventories during 1979. The firm's permanent uses exceed its permanent sources by $48,500, and it will apparently require that amount of long-term funds to retire its excess current debt.

Of course, before that conclusion becomes final, we should conduct a further analysis to determine what actually caused the apparent imbalances of cash flows. For example, the sales increase could have occurred during the last one or two months of the year. That would explain the heavy use of short-term credit; that is, if purchases of raw materials were made less than 60 days before the end of the year, the entire $50,000 increase in accounts payable would not yet be due for payment. But if

271

further inquiry reveals that the firm actually experienced cash flow problems during 1978, the analysis of the funds flow statement is an excellent way to determine the magnitude of the problem quickly and therefore aids in developing an appropriate solution.

Comparative Funds Flow Statements

A major characteristic of the flow of funds through many businesses is that inflows and outflows are more episodic than might normally be expected. Net income, dividend payments, and repayment of long-term debt may be fairly constant from year to year or change gradually over time, but large outlays of cash for plant and equipment generally take place only at intervals of several years during periods of business (and general economic) expansion. Many firms therefore seek additional funds at correspondingly irregular intervals to finance accumulated funds deficits and to provide for planned future expansion.

But even for those firms that do not experience large funds inflows and outflows on other than a regular basis, the funds flow statement—regardless of its format—is most useful when it covers several years. Moreover, a reduction in the amount of detail may prove beneficial when the analyst needs to perceive the major relations involved in the firm's financing history clearly so that he can formulate appropriate recommendations for future financing. Table 15-4 illustrates a simplified funds flow statement covering the three-year period 1975 through 1977 for the Edwards Fastener Company.

In 1975 the Edwards Company borrowed $402,000 from a life insurance company. The loan was scheduled to be repaid over 12 years in annual instalments of $48,000. The payments, due on December 31, included principal plus interest at 6 percent per annum. At the end of 1977, Edwards owed a balance of $301,000.

The figures in Table 15-4 indicate that during the period, the Edwards Company had a trend of continually rising funds retained in the business—rising from $257,000 in 1975 to $397,000 in 1977. However, the expenditures for fixed assets required to accommodate the firm's growth in sales outstripped the funds generated from operations. The result, of course, was a decline in working capital commensurate with the requirements for capital expenditures and debt retirement (and the maintenance of dividend payments). The firm's management apparently neglected to consider the needs for working capital that all growing firms experience; consequently, its financial planning efforts were incomplete. In this case, the analyst can see clearly one year into the future, assuming, of course, that the trends evidenced in the funds flow statement continue. He thus has an opportunity to advise management how to prevent the apparent cash flow imbalances from becoming worse.

Table 15-4

COMPARATIVE SOURCES AND USES OF FUNDS STATEMENT
EDWARDS FASTENER COMPANY
Years Ending December 31, 1975, 1976, and 1977
(000)

	1975	*1976*	*1977*	*Total* *1975-1977*
Funds requirements:				
Purchase of fixed assets	$284	$358	$489	$1,131
Retirement of long-term debt	48	48	48	144
Total requirements	$332	$406	$537	$1,275
Sources of funds:				
Net income adjusted for noncash items	$420	$530	$662	$1,612
Less: cash dividends	163	239	265	667
Total funds from operations	$257	$291	$397	$ 945
Decrease in working capital	75	115	140	330
Total sources	$332	$406	$537	$1,275

Summary

As we have seen from the last two illustrations in particular, the analysis of funds flow does not stand as a totally independent module. Of course, none of the modules are independent of the others. But the preceding discussion clearly describes the several links between funds flow analysis and short-term liquidity and financial forecasting. The experienced analyst will also perceive the links between this and the modules dealing with operations and long-term financial strength.

This chapter also demonstrates the importance to the analyst of acquiring specific knowledge about the operations of the firm he is analyzing. Without that knowledge, he runs a constant risk of misinterpreting the information provided by the funds flow statement.

Finally, implicit in the examination of the four funds flow statements presented is the suggestion that the analyst should choose the formats of the statements on the basis of his objectives rather than on any textbook prescription. He should feel free to cast the statement in the format that will give him the information he is seeking in its most useful form. He should also realize that the most accurate interpretation of the data from the statement usually requires additional input from other statement analysis modules.

Questions

15-1. What are the three dimensions of funds flow analysis?

15-2. What information is revealed by a decrease in aggregate net working capital?

15-3. List the direction of change you would expect to observe in accounts receivable, inventory, and accounts payable under each of the following circumstances?
   1. The firm has unexpectedly lost sales because of aggresive competition.
   2. The firm has successfully increased sales by extending more liberal credit terms to its customers.
   3. The firm's employees have remained on strike for an extended period.
   4. The delivery dates of two very large special orders are approaching.

15-4. How would you explain the fact that a firm's accounts receivable were listed as a source of funds and its inventories as a use of funds in a funds flow statement covering one year?

15-5. What information is revealed by examining the non-working-capital sources and uses of funds in the funds flow statement?

15-6. What is meant by nominal financing transactions?

15-7. Why must a firm balance its permanent uses of funds with permanent sources?

15-8. What can be learned from a comparative sources and uses of funds statement?

Chapter 16

Module Three: Analysis of Operations

The income statement is a summation, in dollar terms, of the income and expenses of a business over a specified period, with the residual amount shown as the period's profit (or loss). The statement discloses the dollar volume of the activities of the business, together with the components of the cost of acquiring and selling goods and of administering the affairs of the enterprise. It tells a story of progress or decline.

Although the balance sheet is generally considered the basic exhibit in financial statement analysis, it is, in contrast to the income statement, merely a static photograph of the financial position of a business as of the close of a given day. It discloses the existence, size, and relative proportions of the assets, liabilities, and equity capital of a business, but it does not reveal whether the assets are being used properly to produce the revenues needed to cover the firm's operating costs and provide an adequate return on the capital it employs. Nor does it reveal whether the business is a growing, thriving, sound financial risk for the future. The analysis of the income statement is thus an essential step in developing a complete financial picture of a business firm.

A primary objective of income statement analysis is to assess a firm's operating efficiency. The size of dollar sales or of gross operating income means very little unless the firm also produces net profits. The share of total revenues absorbed by operating costs and expenses is thus one of the principal concerns of business management. The credit analyst must also devote attention to it if he is to understand why and how the firm has generated profits or incurred losses and predict the future outcome of the firm's operations.

Obviously, a financial statement analyst cannot form a reasonably accurate assessment of a firm's financial condition without the information provided by a thorough examination of its operating record. But before he undertakes that examination he must satisfy himself that the data he will use are completely reliable and will yield an accurate picture of the firm's operating results. Once he is satisfied that the data are reliable, he can begin the analysis of the individual components of the income statement.

Reliability of the Data

As several preceding chapters have shown, the accounting rules dealing with measurement of revenues, costs, and income offer considerable opportunity for the exercise of judgment in arriving at a firm's net profit figure. Most variations in reporting profits from what might be termed "true" profits arise from errors in estimating the outcomes of uncertain future events. For example, the length of time over which an asset is depreciated is only an estimate of its actual useful life; revenue received from the sale of goods will not become cash until the purchaser's check clears the bank; the exact salvage value of long-lived assets remains a matter of conjecture until they are put up for sale and offers for their purchase are received.

Sometimes, however, a firm's management will deliberately set out to alter the results of its operations either (1) to record higher current profits at the expense of future profits (to please current stockholders or attract a merger partner), or (2) to report lower current profits (to reduce current tax liabilities and conserve cash). Table 16-1 contains a partial list of accounting practices management can use to benefit current income at the expense of future income. And, as has previously been stated, the effects of alternative accounting practices on operating results can be substantial.

Thus, although the income statement is indispensable for financial statement analysis, the reliability of the information it contains is sometimes open to question. The first task of the analyst in analyzing operations is to determine, to the extent that he can, the accounting practices used in preparing the income statement. The information contained in Table 16-1 will help the analyst test management's accounting practices and provide a basis for judging the reliability of the income statement data. Again, audited statements prepared by certified public accountants offer the best assurance that the deviation of reported earnings from "true" earnings is not the result of deliberate attempts to misrepresent the facts but is well within the limits governed by pure accounting risks.

Analysis of Income Statement Components

To facilitate the discussion of the individual components of the income statement we will examine the operating results of Dutch Mills, Incorporated, a manufacturer of men's hosiery. The firm manufactures

Table 16-1

ACCOUNTING PRACTICES DESIGNED TO INCREASE CURRENT REPORTED PROFITS

Area	*Accounting Practice*	*Effect on Income Statement*
Inventory	Maximizes inventory carrying values	Decreases cost of goods sold
Fixed assets	Use straight-line depreciation	Decreases cost of goods sold
	Uses maximum useful asset lives	Decreases cost of goods sold
	Capitalizes equipment installation costs and repairs	Decreases cost of goods sold
Deferred charges	Defers all kinds of costs to the future	Decreases general, selling, and administrative costs
Executive compensation	Compensates executives with stock options rather than cash	Decreases administrative expenses
Intangible assets	Amortizes costs over longest possible period	Decreases other expenses
Revenues	Accelerates income recognition under leases and contracts	Increases revenues
Taxes	Credits investment tax credits against current taxes	Decreases taxes
	Acquires "tax loss" firms	Decreases taxes

stockings from cotton, wool, and synthetic fibers. Its operating, selling, and accounting methods have not been specified, but we have been given a comparative common-size income statement covering the five-year period 1974 through 1978 (Table 16-2) and some product line data for the three-year period 1976 through 1978 (Table 16-3).

As we examine each component of these statements, we will reach tentative alternative conclusions regarding the firm's operations, which will have to be tested by inquiries addressed to management or to some outside source of information. At this point, it does not matter so much which set of conclusions will eventually be proved correct; what does matter is that the analyst be able to ask the right questions in support of his analysis. We shall attempt to formulate an exhaustive set of conclu-

Table 16-2

COMPARATIVE COMMON-SIZE INCOME STATEMENT
DUTCH MILLS, INCORPORATED
for the Years Ending December 31, 1974-1978
(dollar figures in thousands)

	1974		1975		1976		1977		1978	
Net sales	$1,838	(100.0%)	$2,098	(100.0%)	$2,337	(100.0%)	$2,354	(100.0%)	$3,091	(100.0%)
Cost of goods sold:										
Beginning inventory	241	(13.1%)	342	(16.3%)	331	(14.2%)	441	(18.7%)	393	(12.7%)
Materials used	967	(52.6%)	1,028	(49.0%)	1,280	(54.8%)	1,231	(52.3%)	1,837	(59.4%)
Direct labor	712	(38.7%)	752	(35.8%)	852	(36.5%)	799	(33.9%)	931	(30.1%)
Depreciation	28	(1.5%)	31	(1.5%)	31	(1.3%)	32	(1.4%)	40	(1.3%)
Other manufacturing expense	98	(5.3%)	94	(4.5%)	125	(5.3%)	71	(3.0%)	151	(4.9%)
Less: ending inventory	342	(18.6%)	331	(15.8%)	441	(18.9%)	392	(16.7%)	502	(16.2%)
Cost of goods sold	$1,704	(92.7%)	$1,916	(91.3%)	$2,178	(93.2%)	$2,182	(92.7%)	$2,850	(92.2%)
Gross profit	$ 134	(7.3%)	$ 182	(8.7%)	$ 159	(6.8%)	$ 172	(7.3%)	$ 241	(7.8%)
Selling expenses:										
Commissions	70	(3.8%)	83	(4.0%)	87	(3.7%)	81	(3.4%)	93	(3.0%)
Advertising	1	(0.1%)	1	(*)	2	(0.1%)	1	(*)	2	(0.1%)
Other selling expense	12	(0.6%)	13	(0.6%)	12	(0.5%)	15	(0.6%)	15	(0.5%)
Total	$ 83	(4.5%)	$ 97	(4.6%)	$ 101	(4.3%)	$ 97	(4.1%)	$ 110	(3.6%)

Administrative expenses										
Salaries	19	(1.0%)	25	(1.2%)	13	(0.6%)	25	(1.1%)	25	(0.8%)
Bad debts	2	(0.1%)	5	(0.2%)	4	(0.2%)	4	(0.2%)	2	(0.1%)
Depreciation	1	(0.1%)	1	(*)	1	(*)	1	(*)	2	(0.1%)
Other administrative expense	10	(0.5%)	12	(0.6%)	11	(0.5%)	11	(0.5%)	13	(0.4%)
Total	$ 32	(1.7%)	$ 43	(2.0%)	$ 29	(1.2%)	$ 41	(1.7%)	$ 42	(1.4%)
Total operating expenses	$ 115	(6.2%)	$ 140	(6.7%)	$ 130	(5.6%)	$ 138	(5.9%)	$ 152	(4.9%)
Operating income	$ 19	(1.0%)	$ 42	(2.0%)	$ 29	(1.2%)	$ 34	(1.4%)	$ 89	(2.9%)
Other income:										
Discounts earned	15	(0.8%)	13	(0.6%)	17	(0.7%)	16	(0.7%)	27	(0.9%)
Other expense:										
Discounts allowed	13	(0.7%)	10	(0.5%)	7	(0.3%)	11	(0.5%)	15	(0.5%)
Interest paid	9	(0.5%)	14	(0.7%)	12	(0.5%)	13	(0.6%)	12	(0.4%)
Net profit before taxes	$ 12	(0.7%)	$ 31	(1.5%)	$ 27	(1.2%)	$ 26	(1.1%)	$ 89	(2.9%)
Income Taxes	2	(0.1%)	5	(0.2%)	4	(0.2%)	4	(0.2%)	30	(1.0%)
Net profit	$ 10	(0.5%)	$ 26	(1.2%)	$ 23	(1.0%)	$ 22	(0.9%)	$ 59	(1.9%)

(*) less than 0.05 percent

Table 16-3

**PRODUCT LINE DATA
DUTCH MILLS, INCORPORATED
for the Years Ended December 31, 1976-1978
(dollar figures in thousands)**

	1976		1977		1978	
Cotton hosiery						
Net sales	$ 1,218	(52.1%)	$ 1,130	(48.0%)	$ 1,252	(40.5%)
Unit sales*	33,800	(48.7%)	29,600	(42.1%)	31,600	(30.7%)
Income contribution	77		72		74	
Wool hosiery						
Net sales	451	(19.3%)	548	(23.3%)	618	(20.0%)
Unit sales*	4,400		5,300		6,100	
Income contribution	67	(42.4%)	74	(43.3%)	96	(39.8%)
Synthetic hosiery						
Net sales	668	(28.6%)	676	(28.7%)	1,221	(39.5%)
Unit sales*	4,900		5,000		10,900	
Income contribution	14	(8.9%)	25	(14.6%)	71	(29.5%)
Company totals						
Net sales	$ 2,337	(100.0%)	$ 2,354	(100.0%)	$ 3,091	(100.0%)
Unit sales*	43,100	(100.0%)	39,900	(100.0%)	48,600	(100.0%)
Income contribution	159		172		241	
Total operating expenses	130		138		152	
Operating income	$ 29		$ 34		$ 89	

*units are expressed in gross lots (twelve dozen pairs)

sions regarding the operations of Dutch Mills to emphasize the need for complete data on the firm, its industry, and its operating environment.

SALES

The first item that should be examined in analyzing the operations of a firm is its dollar sales volume. Dollar sales are the result of a combination of two factors: the physical quantity of goods sold and the selling price per unit. An increase in dollar sales may result from an increase in the quantity sold, an increase in selling price per unit, an increase in both, or an increase in one that more than offsets a decrease in the other. A decrease in dollar sales may result from a decrease in the quantity sold, a decrease in selling price per unit, a decrease in both, or a decrease in one that more than offsets an increase in the other.

In some lines of business a reduction in selling price per unit may increase the volume of dollar sales because greater quantities may be sold. In other lines a price reduction may not result in an offsetting increase in the demand for the product, and a decline in dollar sales may result. The effect on sales, however, should not be the only guide to the determination of a pricing policy. All questions of business policy focus on the effect of a change on final earnings.

Often it may be sufficient for the analyst to know total dollar sales volume alone, without a breakdown of its makeup. When a closer analysis is desirable, however, supplementary schedules of sales should be requested and obtained, if they are not customarily given in periodic statements. Total sales should be broken down into cash sales and credit sales, and the proportion of each to the total should be followed from year to year. Needless to say, sales to affiliated concerns should be clearly segregated. If at all practicable, sales should be reported in units or physical quantities, as well as in dollars, and by division, branch, department, and even product. With these details available, the analyst is able to follow pricing policies, determine the contribution of each section of the business to its total sales volume, and detect those activities and outlets that are beginning to weaken and may eventually become problems unless corrective measures are taken.

For example, from the figures in Table 16-2, we find the annual percentage increases in Dutch Mills' total net sales:

1974-75	14.1%
1975-76	11.4%
1976-77	0.7%
1977-78	31.3%

The trend, of course, reflects favorably on the firm's marketing effort; however, the analyst should seek an explanation for the drop in the growth rate in 1977 and the substantial increase in 1978, to determine whether the firm can expect to sustain the 1978 rate. Perhaps the added sales resulted from circumstances not likely to be repeated.

The firm's product line data, presented in Table 16-3, enable us to gain a better understanding of the sales trend. The figures show that dollar sales of cotton hosiery have remained fairly constant over the past three years while sales of wool and synthetic hosiery have climbed. Moreover, synthetic hosiery accounted for most of the firm's 1978 sales increase, and the line has become dramatically more profitable since 1976.

The unit sales figures in Table 16-3 enable us to examine the effects of the firm's pricing policies on the three product lines. Table 16-4 presents the firm's average unit prices and income contributions for the three product lines over the period 1976-1978. The figures reveal that Dutch Mills steadily increased the price of cotton hosiery over the three years but cut the prices of wool and synthetic hosiery in 1978. Four explanations for the sales trends and price cuts are possible. First, the firm's pricing policy is influenced by the cost of the raw materials it purchases. Since the fibers are traded in well-structured markets that report market prices daily, it is easy to determine the average market prices for the period and compare them with Dutch Mills' selling prices. If the two sets of prices parallel each other, the analyst can accept the conclusion that the product prices are based on the cost of raw materials. Further support of that conclusion may be drawn from an examination of the income contribution per unit of sales. If fiber and hosiery prices are highly correlated, the unit income contribution should not change sharply in response to a cut in hosiery prices. The figures in Table 16-4 do not totally support the conclusion since the income contributions for wool and synthetic hosiery have fluctuated.

Second, the firm's prices may be set competitively. If that is the case, the analyst might expect to observe a tightening in the income contribu-

Table 16-4

**UNIT PRICES AND INCOME CONTRIBUTIONS BY PRODUCT LINE
DUTCH MILLS, INCORPORATED
1976-1978**

	1976		1977		1978	
	Average Price	*Contribution*	*Average Price*	*Contribution*	*Average Price*	*Contribution*
Cotton hosiery	$ 36.04	$ 2.28	$ 38.18	$ 2.43	$ 39.62	$ 2.34
Wool hosiery	102.50	15.23	103.40	13.96	101.31	15.74
Synthetic hosiery	136.33	2.86	135.20	5.00	112.02	6.50
All product lines	54.22	3.69	59.00	4.31	63.60	4.96

tions of the products whose prices have been forced down. Table 16-4 indicates that the 1978 price cuts in wool and synthetic hosiery were accompanied by increases in the income contributions per unit for both lines. While that may have resulted from economies of scale (unit sales of synthetic hosiery more than doubled in 1978 over 1977), the price cut appears to have been voluntary rather than a result of competitive pressures. At least, if it was not, it obviously should have been.

Third, fashion often plays an important role in the pricing policies of textile and clothing manufacturers. Fibers, colors, and styles come into and go out of fashion quite rapidly. Thus the large unit sales volume at historically low prices could indicate that Dutch Mills was forced to "dump" 1977's outmoded fashion goods in order to reduce inventories. Although this is a possibility, it appears unlikely because of the increased unit income contributions of wool and synthetic.hosiery in 1978.

Finally, and most likely, Dutch Mills may have achieved greater efficiency in producing synthetic hosiery, which permitted it to lower the line's selling price and increase its income contribution. The successful expansion of sales may indicate that the firm has become a price leader in its industry.

None of the four explanations individually may be sufficient to account for the firm's sales trends and price movements. Most likely some combination of them brought about the sales trends. The financial statement analyst must determine how prices are set and what external influences affect them to evaluate the firm's current and future operations fully in relation to its past results.

Aggregate Data

Table 16-4 illustrates an important characteristic of aggregate unit sales data reported by a multiproduct firm. Note that the unit price of all product lines combined rose from $54.22 in 1976 to $63.60 in 1978. That is a 17.3 percent price increase over the period; however, cotton hosiery prices increased by only 10 percent while wool and synthetic hosiery prices *fell* by 1.2 percent and 17.8 percent respectively. Thus the aggregate price increase is illusory since it was caused by changes in the product mix in the direction of the more expensive product line. Reducing aggregate sales and price data to unit equivalents in a multiproduct context can often produce misleading results. Interpretation of such data is therefore at best a risky process.

COST OF SALES FOR MANUFACTURING FIRMS

The cost of goods or services sold is the most significant cost category in the income statements of most business firms, especially manufacturing firms. The analysis of this component is important not only because the cost of sales normally consumes a greater share of total revenues than any other element of operating costs but also because it is the primary measure of a manufacturing firm's operating efficiency. Since the analyst generally must work with the available financial data, however, he may not be able to draw completely accurate conclusions about the operating efficiency of a firm because of dimensions of its cost of sales that are not revealed in the income statement, that is, technological considerations and accounting risk.

Technology

The size, composition, relation to sales, and controllability of the cost of sales are influenced in the short run more by technology than by managerial decisions and policy. When comparing the data of one firm with those of another or with industry averages, the analyst should realize that the differences revealed often result from differences in the technology employed. For example, a firm located in an area with a large, nonunionized labor force may decide that it can operate more profitably by remaining labor-intensive, than by substituting expensive automated machinery for its relatively inexpensive, manually operated equipment. When that firm is compared with a capital-intensive firm, significant differences in the proportions of direct labor and factory overhead to sales should be expected. Similarly, firms with successful research and development programs are likely to enjoy substantial short-run technological advantages in their industries.

In the long run, however, all firms are on a more equal footing, in that the management's decisions can achieve greater operational efficiency. But location and technology still limit the firm's ability to alter its cost of sales. Although management can reduce the cost of sales both in absolute terms and in relation to net sales by installing improved production, inventory, and purchasing methods and controls, its efforts will reach a point at which the firm's technology will resist further cost reduction. Unless the firm undertakes a complete overhaul of its operating facilities, its cost of sales is not likely to change significantly from period to period (barring changes in its labor or materials cost structures, of course).

Accounting Risk

The financial statement analyst must also deal with at least two dimensions of accounting risk in analyzing a manufacturing firm's cost of sales. First, since the extant body of accounting principles does not prescribe uniform cost allocation methods by which individual products of a multiproduct firm can be treated in a completely impartial way, the analysis of such data as are presented in Tables 16-3 and 16-4 must be approached with considerable caution. The allocations of depreciation, factory overhead, and occasionally even direct labor among products are based on management's judgments, which may or may not reflect the true cost burdens each should bear. It is quite possible that an increase in the production and sales of the firm's "most profitable" product will actually reduce the firm's overall profits because of a shift in real (as opposed to allocated) costs. That often happens when additional productive capacity is added to accommodate the sales growth of a particular product but other products are required to share the incremental overhead costs.

The second dimension of accounting risk—the use of accepted alternative accounting principles—has been discussed elsewhere and requires only brief mention here. Specifically, the selection of alternative methods of depreciating fixed assets and valuing inventories will influence the size and trend of each element of the cost of sales component of the income statement and thus reduce its intertemporal and interfirm comparability. While the convention of consistency reduces or eliminates the problem of intertemporal comparison, the analyst must be aware that, because of accounting risk, the firm he is analyzing may not be strictly comparable with similar firms. Consequently, industry norms that report in aggregate form data gathered from firms whose fiscal years, depreciation methods, inventory valuations, and other accounting methods differ significantly are often of little use in measuring the relative efficiency of the firm being analyzed.

Analysis of the Cost of Sales

In a manufacturing concern, operating efficiency relates primarily to the manufacturing process. The efficiency with which materials are purchased and the manufacturing process is conducted has a major bearing on the cost of the products manufactured. That cost largely determines whether the products can be sold at a gross profit sufficient to cover all operating expenses and yield a net profit.

When he lacks production figures in units or physical quantities, the analyst is handicapped in his efforts to appraise productive efficiency and to follow the trend of manufacturing costs. He is often limited to the information (in dollars only) on the cost of goods sold contained in the income statement.

Even here, however, there are certain relations and proportions that the analyst can compute and compare from period to period (or can compare with the relations and proportions shown for the same period by other manufacturers in the same line) to give him a general indication of what elements of manufacturing cost may be out of line and deserving of discussion with the management.

Each of the three major elements of manufacturing cost—cost of raw materials, direct labor, and manufacturing expenses—may be related to the total cost of goods sold (manufactured) as a preliminary check on undue proportionate heaviness in any of the three divisions of manufacturing cost. The following proportions have been computed from the income statement illustrated in Table 16-1 by dividing each of the three major elements of manufacturing cost by the total cost of goods sold.

Element of Manufacturing Costs	Percentage of Cost of Goods Sold				
	1974	*1975*	*1976*	*1977*	*1978*
Cost of raw materials	50.8%	54.3%	53.7%	58.7%	60.6%
Direct labor	41.8	39.2	39.1	36.6	32.7
Manufacturing expenses	7.4	6.5	7.2	4.7	6.7
Cost of goods sold	100.0%	100.0%	100.0%	100.0%	100.0%

The figures show that the cost of raw materials for Dutch Mills has risen while direct labor has fallen and manufacturing expenses have remained almost constant (except in 1977). Within the same firm, a change in the proportions from one period to another is difficult to interpret reliably, since it is impossible to tell which factor is responsible for the change. The decrease in the direct labor percentage, for example, may be due not to the more efficient use of labor or to a decrease in wage rates but to an increase in the cost of raw materials. The decrease in the percentage of manufacturing expenses in 1977 may be attributable not to cost economies in the necessary manufacturing expenses but to a disproportionate rise in direct labor or raw materials costs in that year.

A comparison of the proportions illustrated with those shown by another manufacturer or other manufacturers engaged in the same type of production may be more helpful and indicative than a comparison confined to the same manufacturer from one operating period to another. Changing price levels, labor costs, and manufacturing conditions should tend to have a similar effect on all manufacturers of the same type within a given period; therefore, a comparison of manufacturing cost relations of comparable concerns should give a more dependable indication of whether disproportions exist.

At best, when the components of cost of goods sold are reduced to common size and compared from period to period for the same firm, they merely provide indications that changes in proportions have occurred. Further information must be obtained to determine the cause of the changes.

By comparing breakdowns of unit costs for different companies and periods, the analyst can determine the cause of a high or an increased cost per unit. For ease of comparison and permanent reference, he can spread the unit cost figures on a comparative statement form in the credit file of each manufacturer and follow them regularly from period to period.

The breakdown of the cost of goods sold per unit for Dutch Mills for the period 1976 through 1978 is as follows:

Element of Manufacturing Costs	1976	1977	1978
Cost of raw materials	$27.15	$32.08	$35.55
Direct labor	19.77	20.03	19.16
Manufacturing expenses	3.62	2.58	3.93
Cost of goods sold	$50.54	$54.69	$58.64

Here we find that the direct labor component has remained constant while materials costs have increased. The degree of efficiency (or inefficiency) is partially masked by the change in the firm's production mix toward the presumably more costly wool and synthetic fibers. The analyst must, of course, look behind the figures to determine whether the firm's lack of success in decreasing the various components of cost of goods sold in relation to sales is the result of technological, economic, accounting, or managerial factors. For example, the rise in materials cost noted could be caused by obsolete or worn-out knitting machines, a rise in the prices of raw materials, a change in methods inventory valuation, the absence of adequate protection against loss by theft, poor handling and storage of materials, or the purchase of inferior grades of raw materials that resulted in high spoilage rates. Management must bear the ultimate responsibility for the cost increase regardless of the cause; however, the analyst will find it helpful to inquire fully into the sources of the problem. He should examine with equal vigor "favorable" trends, like that shown by the direct labor component. If the firm's employees are not receiving adequate annual wage adjustments, the favorable current trend may be reversed if the employees decide to press management for improved wages and employment benefits.

COST OF SALES FOR TRADE AND SERVICE FIRMS

The principal difference between the cost of goods sold section of the income statement of a trading firm and that of a manufacturer arises from the fact that retailers and wholesalers do not manufacture the goods they sell. The trading firms purchase their inventories in finished form; consequently, their cost of sales section is much less complex than that of a manufacturer. The principles governing the analysis of the data are the same, however, the comparative common-size statement being the most appropriate analytical tool.

The income statement of a service organization is usually presented in an entirely different form from that of a retail, wholesale, or manufacturing concern. Inventories, if any, are confined to the supplies and materials required in the service process, and they are not a major factor in the determination of profits. Labor, the exact cost of which is readily determinable, is generally the major item of operating cost. It is unnecessary to determine the cost of goods sold since no products are marketed; hence the income statement may be fairly simple in structure.

Since the other components of the income statements of trading concerns, manufacturers, and service firms are similar, their treatment in financial statement analysis is identical. We will therefore discuss the remaining income statement components under single headings.

SELLING EXPENSES

The importance of selling costs in relation to sales varies widely among industries and firms. In some firms, selling expenses tend to be fixed since sales personnel are salaried. Commission salespersons are often paid at a different rate for each product the firm produces or distributes, higher rates being associated either with products carrying a higher markup or with newly introduced products. Thus the firm's sales mix and its success in developing new products may cause year-to-year variations in the percentage of commissions paid to total net sales.

Certain selling expenses, particularly advertising, benefit future as well as current sales. The measurement of the future benefits is impossible, but the relation is nevertheless real. The ratio of current expenditures on advertising and promotion to current sales need not, therefore, be considered fixed. Indeed, there is ample reason to suggest that those expenses should rise when current sales are falling and fall to more normal levels as sales grow. Since these expenses are completely discretionary, the analyst must attempt to determine the rationale for their size and trend in his discussions with management.

Table 16-2 suggests that Dutch Mills' selling effort is minimal, especially with respect to advertising. The firm's customer list may offer some explanation for the low advertising figure. For example, if Dutch Mills has contracted with a few large retail outlets for most of its production, it will have little need to spend large sums on advertising. That is particularly true if its products carry the retailers' own brand names.

ADMINISTRATIVE EXPENSES

Most administrative expenses are fixed and are controlled by management policy. Especially during prosperous times, they tend to increase in dollar amounts, but not necessarily in relation to sales. In analyzing administrative expenses, the analyst should pay attention to both the trend and the percentage of sales revenues they consume.

In the Dutch Mills example, we see that salaries exhibited a surprising decline in 1976 and have not exceeded the $25,000 first reached in 1975. This amazing restraint on the part of management warrants further examination. Possible explanations are that officers receive compensation partly from salary and partly from selling commissions (or perhaps common stock dividends, if the company's stock is owned by the officers) and that a lender has imposed restriction on salary increases until the loan is repaid.

NONOPERATING INCOME AND EXPENSE

Miscellaneous small income and expense items are usually of no significance to the analyst. For some firms, however, that depend on *other income* for a large share of the profits they earn, the category becomes important.

Other income may include returns from investments that may alter the firm's financial picture in future years. For example, an investment in a related company may grow until the ownership level exceeds 50 percent of that firm's stock, at which time the parent company may elect to present *consolidated financial statements* that "merge" the two entities' financial statements. More important, the existence of financial and operating interrelations requires the analyst to extend his examination beyond the parent firm into the financial position and performance of each related company.

The analyst should also examine nonoperating expense categories closely to determine whether or not management has elected to put certain operating expenses into them to improve the appearance of the firm's current operations. These expenses should normally be detailed and should certainly not be netted against "other" income. The obvious loss of information resulting from such a practice should not remain unexamined.

The nonoperating income and expense categories for Dutch Mills in Table 16-2 consist of discounts earned and allowed and interest paid. The discounts allowed average only about .5 percent of sales. Discounts earned over the period ranged between .6 and .9 percent of sales; however, when we calculate the discounts earned as a percentage of materials used (in the cost of goods sold section), we find the following:

1974	1.55%
1975	1.26%
1976	1.33%
1977	1.30%
1978	1.47%

If Dutch Mills purchased its raw materials on terms of 2,10/net 30, the firm is obviously passing up cash discounts on some of its purchases. A more likely explanation is that cash discounts for cotton, wool, and synthetic materials are not uniform; consequently, the relation will vary with the product mix over time.

The size of discounts earned in relation to profits before taxes should give the analyst reason to be concerned. If Dutch Mills had been financially unable to take advantage of purchase discounts during this period, it would have lost money in 1974 and realized a return on sales before taxes of only .9, .5, .4, and 2.0 percent in the years 1975 through 1978 respectively. The firm's profitability is obviously highly dependent on purchase discounts.

INCOME TAXES

The current federal tax rate on corporate income is 22 percent of the first $25,000 of profits before tax plus 48 percent of the balance. Almost invariably, however, a quick check of the taxes shown on the income statement against this rate will reveal a discrepancy—generally in favor of the firm. For example, Dutch Mills' 1978 pretax income of $89,000, if taxed at the current rate, would produce a tax figure of $36,220 [($25,000 × .22) + ($64,000 × .48)]. Table 16-2 shows an income tax expense of only $30,000, or $6,220 less than that produced by an application of the current tax formula.

The actual effective tax rate (for Dutch Mills, $30,000/$89,000 = 33.7 percent) is influenced by various provisions in the tax law, which a firm may take advantage of to reduce its federal income tax liability. Some of the more important of those provisions are as follows:

1. Interest on municipal bonds and proceeds from life insurance are not taxed.
2. Goodwill amortization, fines imposed by courts, and certain insurance premiums are not tax deductible.
3. Capital gains and dividends paid by a subsidiary firm are taxed at lower rates.
4. Certain industries, such as shipping lines, life insurance companies, and savings and loan associations, receive special tax privileges.
5. Past losses can be carried forward to reduce taxes in the current period.
6. Tax credits for investing in production equipment are currently offered to qualifying firms.

In addition to these tax provisions, many businesses maintain two (or more) sets of books—one (or more) for reporting purposes and another for tax purposes. Consequently, a firm may use accelerated depreciation methods for tax purposes (lowering tax liability) and straight-line depreciation for reporting to the public (showing larger profits after taxes).

The most likely reasons for the $6,220 discrepancy between Dutch Mills' actual and theoretical income tax expense are (1) the provision for an investment tax credit, and (2) the use of different depreciation methods for tax and reporting purposes. Both are likely since the depreciation expense in the cost of goods sold section of Table 16-2 increased from $32,000 to $40,000 in 1978 (indicating the purchase of new equipment in 1978) and that depreciation expense had remained fairly constant over the preceding four years (indicating the likely use of straight-line depreciation for reporting purposes).

To explain the entire discrepancy by the use of accelerated depreciation for tax purposes, we can simply divide the $6,220 discrepancy by the *marginal* tax rate (48 percent) to determine how much *more* depreciation must be charged to reduce the tax expense from $36,220 to $30,000. Thus $12,958 additional depreciation ($6,220/.48), for a total of $52,958 in depreciation expenses for 1978, will explain the entire tax discrepancy. That is about 30 percent greater than the amount listed in the firm's 1978 income statement. Since it is unlikely that using accelerated depreciation would raise the annual depreciation expense that much, the lower taxes probably resulted from a combination of accelerated depreciation and the tax credit for new investment.

The reason for seeking an explanation for differences between taxable and reported income is to check on the validity of the operating results as reported to the public. In most cases, the income reported for tax purposes is more conservatively stated. For example, in its tax return, a firm may recognize revenue from sales on an instalment rather than an accrual basis, lowering sales revenue and recognizing the likelihood of noncollection of future instalments. Using accelerated depreciation and treating research and development costs as expenses (rather than deferring them) are also the more conservative accounting alternatives. However, it is highly doubtful that income declared for tax purposes is more accurate or valid than that reported to the public simply because it is more conservative. Nevertheless, reconciling the differences often reveals important information about the firm and its management.

While after-tax earnings are important, the analysis of operations relies more heavily on *pretax earnings* as a measure of operating efficiency. That is because pretax earnings are not affected by changing tax regulations and the effective tax rates, which, after all, are almost completely beyond the control of management. Thus a clearer picture of the skill and experience of a firm's management may be obtained by weighing operating income and pretax profits more heavily than after-tax profits in measuring the efficiency of its operations.

Break-Even Analysis

Once the analyst has examined the various components of the income statement in the context of the common-size statement, he can begin to form conclusions about the skill of management in dealing with the several aspects of the firm's operations. However, it is equally important to examine the firm's operations *as a whole* (as well as in their component

291

parts); at this point break-even analysis becomes useful.

Break-even analysis focuses on the location or identification of the break-even point, which is defined as "that level of sales volume that produces neither a profit nor a loss from operations." But the analysis goes far beyond merely locating this point. It is most useful in helping the analyst to understand the firm's cost variations and thus determine how changes in costs, sales volume, and the relations of sales to costs affect net profits.

COST CLASSIFICATIONS

A firm's cost structure changes because of changes in production, the passage of time, or a combination of both factors. For example, the amount of raw materials entering the production process and the cost of labor used to transform them into finished goods are directly related to the volume of production; those costs and other expenses directly related to production are considered *variable costs.*

Regardless of the volume of production, such expenses as depreciation on plant and equipment, property insurance, tax expenses, and certain other overhead costs are unavoidable, so long as the business continues to operate as a going concern. Such expenses, accordingly, vary only with time and are classified as *fixed costs.*

The amount of money spent on plant maintenance depends on the amount of wear and tear the firm's physical property receives during production, but it does not vary proportionately with output. Even at the zero level of output that may result from a labor strike, for example, a firm must continue to spend funds for maintenance if it ever hopes to resume production. Similarly, the expenses incurred for electricity, fuel, and certain administrative functions contain elements of both fixed and variable costs. Those expenses are therefore classified as *semivariable costs.*

Recording a firm's costs is a straightforward procedure; determining how they change with output and time is a challenging problem. It involves classifying the costs, calculating their rates of change, identifying their minimum fixed levels, and identifying and segregating the fixed and variable components of semivariable costs. It also involves identifying changes in the structure of costs as production rates change and estimating the probable effect of those changes on volume, costs, and profits. Obviously, an outside analyst would face considerable difficulty in forming accurate estimates of all these costs and their interrelations, but even fairly good estimates can provide valuable information relating to the firm's past and planned operations.

USES OF BREAK-EVEN ANALYSIS

Break-even analysis can be used to develop profit estimates for a firm at various levels of sales and production. Relative operational efficiency may be measured by comparing the break-even point for the firm from year to year or with those of other firms in the industry. The technique can also be applied to cover a variety of cost-volume-profit relations, such as the profitability of product lines and their contributions to the recovery of fixed costs.

The analyst may also find the breakdown of fixed and variable costs useful in establishing or reviewing a firm's pricing policies. In appraising the advisability of initiating a price cut, for example, he is able to use those relations to determine what changes in sales volume would be necessary to compensate for a given dollar reduction in price. Likewise, if a price increase is being considered, break-even analysis will help estimate the maximum reduction in volume that the firm can tolerate without reducing profits.

Two specific applications of break-even analysis are presented in the illustrations that follow. The principles brought out in the illustrations, and the mathematical operations explained in each, can be applied to many situations beyond those presented. The examples should provide sufficient evidence of the usefulness of this tool in analyzing the profit potential and operating riskiness of a business. Before discussing specific applications, let us illustrate the construction of the break-even chart and the method of computing the break-even point.

THE BREAK-EVEN POINT

Table 16-5 presents the 1978 income statement of Dutch Mills, restated from Table 16-2 in a simplified format. The statement disregards the conventional income statement format and groupings of costs and expenses. The designation "costs" is applied without distinction to items normally described as "costs," "other expenses," or "expenses." The last two columns separate the costs into fixed and variable categories. For semivariable costs, the fixed and variable components of each item have been estimated and listed in the appropriate columns. The contribution to fixed costs of $335,000 is the difference between sales ($3,091,000) and net variable costs ($2,756,000). Since sales and other revenues are generally allocated first to variable and then to fixed costs, all revenues in excess of variable costs are considered "contributions" to fixed costs and profits. In this instance, Dutch Mills earned $89,000 in profits before taxes.

The break-even volume of sales occurs at that level that produces a margin of income above variable costs that equals the amount of fixed costs incurred during the period. In terms of dollar sales, the break-even point may be calculated from the following formula:

$$\text{DBEP (dollar break-even point)} = \frac{\text{fixed costs}}{1 - (\text{variable costs/sales})}$$

Table 16-5

**SIMPLIFIED INCOME STATEMENT WITH FIXED
AND VARIABLE COSTS IDENTIFIED
DUTCH MILLS, INCORPORATED
for the Year Ended December 31, 1978
(000)**

	Total Cost	Fixed Cost	Variable Cost
Materials used	$1,769*		$1,769
Direct labor	897*		897
Depreciation	39*	$ 39	
Other manufacturing expense	145*	140	5
Commissions paid	93		93
Advertising	2	2	
Other selling expenses	15	15	
Administrative salaries	25	25	
Bad debts	2		2
Depreciation (administrative)	2	2	
Other expense	13	11	2
Discounts allowed	15		15
Interest paid	12	12	
Total costs	$3,029	$246	$2,783
Deduct:			
Discounts earned	27		27
Net costs	$3,002	$246	$2,756

Profit and Loss Summary

Sales	$3,091
Less variable costs	2,756
Contribution to fixed costs	$ 335
Less fixed costs	246
Net profit before taxes	$ 89

*Adjusted to account for the increase in inventories of $109,000 during 1978.

For Dutch Mills, the dollar break-even sales volume is

$$DBEP = \frac{\$246,000}{1-(\$2,756,000/\$3,091,000)}$$

$$= \frac{\$246,000}{1-.892} = \frac{\$246,000}{.108} = \$2,278,000$$

In other words, if Dutch Mills had achieved sales of only $2,278,000 for the year 1978, it would have earned a net profit before taxes of $0. Table 16-6 presents proof of the computation.

Table 16-6

**PROOF OF COMPUTATION OF DOLLAR BREAK-EVEN POINT
FOR DUTCH MILLS**

Sales	$2,278,000
Variable costs (89.2 percent of sales)	2,032,000
Contribution to fixed costs	$ 246,000
Fixed costs	246,000
Net profit	$ -0-

Graphic Analysis

The break-even point for any firm may be presented in graphic form. Figure 16-1 represents the break-even point for Dutch Mills.

The construction of the graph is relatively simple, provided, of course, that the relations between sales and costs is assumed to be linear (that is, can be represented by a straight line). That assumption permits the construction of the graph to be based on only two reference points: (1) the amount of fixed costs at zero sales ($246,000), and (2) the break-even point ($2,278,000).

We begin the construction of the graph by drawing the "sales" line through the origin (the intersection of the horizontal and vertical axes) and upward to the right. Since dollar sales (revenues) are measured on both axes, the sales line is drawn equidistant from each axis, that is, at à 45-degree angle. Next, we plot the two reference points on the graph. The first, fixed costs at zero sales, is plotted on the vertical axis (that is, at zero sales) at a vertical distance of $246,000. A horizontal line may be drawn from this point, as shown in Figure 16-1. The second point, the break-even point, is plotted on the graph at a horizontal *and* vertical distance of $2,278,000. This point should rest on the sales line since it is equidistant from both axes. A straight line, representing total (fixed plus variable) costs, is then drawn through those two points, completing the *basic* break-even graph.

To provide the maximum benefit from the graphic representation of the break-even point, we have added lines to Figure 16-1 that indicate the firm's current position in relation to its break-even level of sales, fixed costs, and variable costs. Those ancillary lines, though not essential to the analysis of the break-even point, highlight the basic cost-volume-profit relation and thereby aid the analyst's visual perception of them.

In interpreting the break-even graph, the analyst can visually locate the volume of the sales needed to achieve a desired level of profits. He may also point out that if the firm can lower fixed costs and thereby lower total costs at every level of sales, the break-even point can be decreased (moved to a lower point on the sales line). Similarly, if the ratio

Figure 16-1

BREAK-EVEN POINT FOR DUTCH MILLS

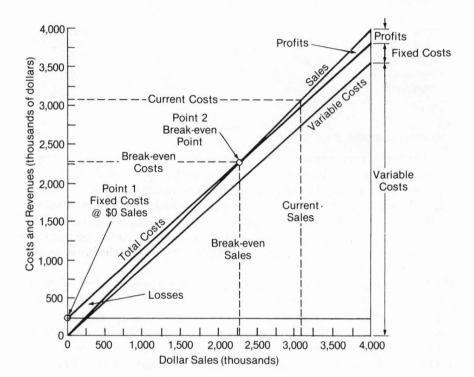

of variable costs to sales can be lowered, the total cost line will become less steep, causing the break-even point to decline to a lower level of sales and the profits earned at each sales level to increase.

In general, the higher the break-even point (that is, the higher the level of sales needed to break even), the more precarious the base underlying the company's earnings. To increase the firm's margin of safety from operations, its management may increase the selling price of the product, reduce its fixed or variable costs, or try to do both. If the gap between variable costs per unit and selling price is wide, changing either will have a modest influence on the level of the break-even point. If the gap is narrow, however, raising prices or lowering variable costs per unit will usually have a pronounced effect on the break-even level.

OPERATING LEVERAGE

The relations among costs, volume, and profits can also be expressed in terms of operating leverage. Operating leverage reflects the extent to which the use of business assets that require the payment of certain fixed costs influences operating income as output varies. At a given level of sales,

$$\text{Operating leverage} = \frac{\text{contribution to fixed costs}}{\text{operating income}}$$

$$= \frac{\text{sales} - \text{variable costs}}{\text{sales} - \text{variable costs} - \text{fixed costs}}$$

For example, at the current sales level of \$3,091,000, Dutch Mills' operating income is \$89,000, and its contribution to fixed costs is \$335,000, as shown in Table 16-5. The firm's operating leverage therefore equals 3.76 (\$335,000/\$89,000). In other words, for every 1 percent change in sales from the current level of \$3,091,000, Dutch Mills' operating income will change 3.76 percent.

Implicit in the operating leverage equation is the idea that as a firm increases its ratio of fixed costs to variable costs through, say, a capital expansion program, it likewise increases its operating leverage (by decreasing the value of the denominator in the operating leverage equation). At the same time, the firm's break-even point becomes higher, and its margin of safety from operations falls. In other words, as operating leverage and the break-even level increase, a firm's operations become more risky in the sense that a small decline in sales will lead to a greater percentage decline in operating income. A firm whose sales are highly variable may find it advantageous to keep its operating leverage (and break-even point) relatively low.

SPECIFIC APPLICATIONS OF BREAK-EVEN ANALYSIS

The following examples are based on the income statement for Dutch Mills presented in Table 16-5. As we have seen, the firm earned profits before taxes of \$89,000 in 1978; as the break-even calculations showed, the firm's sales exceeded its break-even point by \$813,000. Stated another way, sales would have to fall by more than 25 percent before Dutch Mills incurred operating losses. The two examples will illustrate other uses to which break-even analysis may be put. All calculations are rounded to the nearest thousand dollars.

Problem 1.

Dutch Mills applied for a term loan to finance recent purchases of fixed assets and working capital needs; the annual interest on the loan will be \$20,000. The lender offered a loan package that included a restriction on payment of common stock dividends unless before-tax income exceeded \$125,000. Since Dutch Mills had paid dividends for each of the past ten years, it was reluctant to accept that restriction.

297

Before giving its final answer, however, management wished to determine the level of sales needed to earn $125,000.

SOLUTION: To find the required level of sales, we treat the $125,000 in before-tax profits and the $20,000 in additional interest expense as added fixed costs. The level of fixed costs thus increases from $246,000 to $391,000. Since variable costs as a percentage of sales will remain constant at 89.2 percent, the dollar break-even point formula yields total break-even sales of about $391,000/.108, or $3,620,000. That represents a sales increase of $529,000, or about 17 percent, over 1978. The restriction does not seem unreasonable in light of the 1978 sales increase of over $700,000.

Problem 2.

Before the firm signed the term loan agreement, it learned that its closest competitors were cutting prices on hosiery by about 5 percent. Dutch Mills felt certain it would have to follow the price cut to maintain its market share. The firm also learned that costs of raw materials were expected to decline by about 15 percent as a result of competition from foreign supply sources. Management and the prospective lender were interested in what effects those changes would have on the firm's operations.

SOLUTION: The two price cuts would work in opposite directions on the firm's break-even point: the cut in selling prices would increase variable costs in relation to sales and thus increase the break-even point, and the reduction in the purchase price of raw materials would tend to lower the break-even point. To calculate the level of sales needed to reach $125,000 in before-tax profits, we must reestablish the relation between sales and costs. The following calculations are required:

To adjust sales:	
1978 sales at current price	$3,091,000
Less 5 percent price cut	155,000
1978 sales at reduced prices	$2,936,000
To adjust costs:	
1978 variable costs at current price	$2,756,000
Less 15 percent price cut on materials	265,000
1978 variable costs after price cut	$2,491,000

Variable costs as a percentage of sales under the new industry price structure become 84.8 percent ($2,491,000/$2,936,000), and the level of sales required for Dutch Mills to pay the added interest and earn $125,000 before taxes is $391,000/.152, or $2,572,000. Under these conditions, the firm's current (adjusted) sales are already more than sufficient to earn before-tax profits above the required level.

These illustrations demonstrate two of the principal uses of break-even analysis. Problems of the second kind are more commonly encountered by the analyst in an actual business setting, where very few relations remain unchanged for very long.

LIMITATIONS OF BREAK-EVEN ANALYSIS

The fact that relations among variables do change—sometimes very rapidly—has led some businessmen to conclude that break-even analysis is not particularly useful for their purposes. They cite such limitations as: (1) the complexities introduced by changes in their firm's product mix from month to month, season to season, and year to year; (2) the facts that fixed costs are not always constant and variable costs do not always increase in a straight line with output, especially when a firm's operations approach 100 percent of capacity; (3) the fiarly common practice of varying selling prices by offering cash or quantity discounts; and (4) the belief that even under perfect conditions, break-even analysis is only of short-run benefit, since it is based principally on historical experience, which may not accurately reflect future operations.

Those limitations of break-even analysis can be serious only if they are ignored by those who use it. If an analyst is thoroughly familiar with the limitations and their effects on his analyses, however, he will know that break-even graphs will become obsolete as certain changes in a firm's operations take place and new graphs based on newly determined relations will have to be constructed. He will avoid basing a five-year forecast on the current month's break-even analysis, and he will recognize that wide variations in production require that two or more sets of cost-volume relations be used. In other words, being aware of the limitations of break-even analysis permits the analyst to use the tool effectively and intelligently in financial statement analysis.

Marginal Analysis

An added refinement to the analysis of the comparative common-size income statement and break-even analysis is *marginal* income statement analysis. While it does not necessarily provide more information than the other techniques, marginal analysis generally presents information more clearly and in a more readily usable form. Table 16-7 presents a condensed marginal income statement for Dutch Mills for the period 1974 through 1978. The figures were calculated from the data presented in Table 16-2 by subtracting the earlier year's figures from the later year's; that is, 1975 minus 1974, 1976 minus 1975, and so forth.

By carefully examining Dutch Mills' marginal income statement, we can see the instability of all the expense categories in relation to sales at the margin. That instability suggests either a lack of control by manage-

Table 16-7

MARGINAL INCOME STATEMENT
DUTCH MILLS, INCORPORATED
for the period 1974-1978
(dollar figures in thousands)

	1974-75		1975-76		1976-77		1977-78	
Sales	$260	(100.0%)	$239	(100.0%)	$ 17	(100.0%)	$737	(100.0%)
Cost of goods sold	212	(81.5%)	262	(109.6%)	4	(23.5%)	668	(90.6%)
Gross profit	$ 48	(18.5%)	$(23)	(−9.6%)	$ 13	(76.5%)	$ 69	(9.4%)
Selling expenses	14	(5.4%)	4	(1.7%)	(4)	(−23.5%)	13	(1.8%)
Administrative expenses	11	(4.2%)	(14)	(−5.9%)	12	(70.6%)	1	(0.1%)
Operating income	$ 23	(8.8%)	$(13)	(−5.4%)	$ 5	(29.4%)	$ 55	(7.5%)
Other expense (net)	4	(1.5%)	9	(−3.8%)	6	(35.3%)	(8)	(−1.1%)
Net profit before taxes	$ 19	(7.3%)	$ (4)	(−1.7%)	$ (1)	(−5.9%)	$ 63	(8.5%)
Income taxes	3	(1.2%)	(1)	(−0.4%)	0	(0%)	26	(3.5%)
Net Profit	$ 16	(6.2%)	$ (3)	(−1.3%)	$ (1)	(−5.9%)	$ 37	(5.0%)

ment over operations or that the environment is not influencing operations uniformly each period. It may also indicate that management is *reacting* to patterns of change it sees developing rather than *acting* to prevent change from producing unfavorable results. This basic instability of operations is made evident in this statement because the trends and changes are amplified by the common-size figures (shown in parentheses). Here we see, for example, that the cost of goods sold as a percentage of sales increased from 91.3 percent in 1975 to 93.2 percent in 1976 (see Table 16-2) as a result of a *marginal* increase of 109.6 percent. In other words, for every additional dollar of sales in 1976 over 1975, Dutch Mills incurred an additional $1.096 in production costs. The increase in the marginal costs indicates the source of the firm's problems.

STATEMENT ACCOUNTING FOR VARIATION IN NET INCOME

Another device that permits the analyst to compare two consecutive income statements is the *statement accounting for changes in net income*. It classifies the factors affecting net income into two groups: (1) items decreasing net income, and (2) items increasing net income. It then presents those items in a format that permits the analyst to pinpoint significant factors affecting the firm's net profits. The statement for Dutch Mills is presented in Table 16-8.

The only additional information that emerges from Table 16-8 is the breakdown of the increase in gross profit into the parts caused by: (1) the increase in sales and (2) the increase in the gross margin rate. Here we see the break-even "effect" more clearly. For example, if the firm had projected profits based on a sales increase alone through break-even analysis, it would have been looking for a $54,000 profit increase from the $737,000 sales increment. However, the cost-volume-profit relations were altered somewhat in the ways shown by the statement, producing only $37,000 in added profits. In these ways, such statements can be very helpful as a supplement to break-even analysis in examining a firm's operations.

Summary

This module has examined the income statement in considerable depth. We began by examining the nature of the data, their reliability, forms of presentation, and the implications of each component to the analysis of the operating efficiency of the firm being analyzed. We then disassembled the data and reassembled them in various forms to illustrate ways in which the financial statement analyst can facilitate his task of analyzing operations.

Like the other four modules, the analysis of operations cannot stand

Table 16-8

STATEMENT ACCOUNTING FOR VARIATIONS IN NET INCOME
DUTCH MILLS, INCORPORATED
for the period 1977-1978
(dollar figures in thousands)

I. Items Increasing Net Income:
Increase in gross margin caused by:
A. an increase in sales (based on
1977 gross profit rate)

1978 sales	$3,091	
1977 sales	2,354	
	$ 737 × .073	= $54

B. an increase in the rate
(percent) of gross margin
(based on 1978 sales)

1978 gross margin rate	7.8%	
1977 gross margin rate	7.3%	
	0.5% × $3,091	= $15

Increase in other income	11	
Total		$80

II. Items Decreasing Net Income:

Increase in selling expenses	13	
Increase in administrative expenses	1	
Increase in other expenses	3	
Increase in taxes	26	
Total		43
Increase in net income		$37

alone. It is closely related to the modules dealing with financial forecasts and asset utilization, and it is related to the others as well.

Questions

16-1. What precautions should a statement analyst take before analyzing the operations of a business?

16-2. What information may be obtained from historical sales data that are reported in dollars, units, and by major products or divisions?

16-3. List four common explanations for changes noted in the unit prices of a given product.

16-4. Explain how aggregate sales data can sometimes lead to erroneous conclusions concerning multiproduct firms.

16-5. How does technology influence the results of an analysis of a manufacturing firm's cost of goods sold?

16-6. Define accounting risk as it relates to the analysis of a manufacturing firm's cost of goods sold.

16-7. Why are percentage comparisons of the elements of cost of goods sold—material, labor, and overhead—sometimes difficult to interpret reliably? How may this difficulty be overcome?

16-8. What is the principal difference between the cost of goods sold section of the income statement of a manufacturing firm and that of a trading firm? Does that difference change the principles governing the analysis of the data?

16-9. Would you expect the selling expenses of the firms in a particular industry to be uniform as a percentage of sales? Explain.

16-10. Why should an analyst expect the dollar income tax figure presented in the income statement to be different from what might be computed by multiplying before-tax income by current income tax rates?

16-11. Which is a better measure of efficiency of operations, before-tax income or after-tax income? Explain.

16-12. Define the following terms:
1. Break-even point
2. Variable costs
3. Fixed costs
4. Semivariable costs

16-13. List some of the uses of break-even analysis.

16-14. Starting from the proposition that, at zero profits, fixed costs plus variable costs equal sales (that is, $FC + VC = S$), develop the formula for the dollar break-even point (that is, $S = FC/[1-(VC/S)]$.

16-15. Define operating leverage. How is it related to break-even analysis?

16-16. Discuss the limitations of break-even analysis. Do those limitations destroy its usefulness? Explain.

16-17. What information is obtained through marginal income statement analysis?

Chapter 17

Module Four: Long-Term Financial Strength

The purposes of this chapter are (1) to examine the nature and characteristics of the various forms of intermediate- and long-term capital funds employed by business firms; and (2) on the basis of this information, to explore the means whereby the long-term financial strength of a firm may be measured and tested. We shall begin by discussing the major components of capital structure—equity (common stock, preferred stock, and retained earnings) and debt (including term loans, bonds, and leases). We shall then describe how the interaction of those components (through financial leverage) influences a firm's operational cash flows and hence its long-term financial strength. Finally, we shall illustrate the application of various coverage ratios. These may help assess the impact of management's historical long-run financing decisions on its current and future financial soundness.

Capital Structure

The capital structure of a business firm consists basically of equity funds and intermediate- and long-term debt. Its function is to supply the financial strength the firm needs to pursue its business profitably and to prosper over time. That financial strength takes the form of *permanent* funds with which the firm can acquire and *permanently* employ the stock of fixed assets and permanent working capital necessary to maintain the business as a going concern.

While the statement that all capital funds represent permanent sources of funds is generally true, certain circumstances may cause a firm's capital structure to shrink. Operating losses or the repayment of debt at maturity are two examples. If the loss of capital is very large or continues for an extended period, the firm's existence as a going concern may be threatened. Consequently, the decisions made by management regarding the acquisition and retirement (planned and actual) of capital funds are of vital concern to the financial statement analyst.

EQUITY FUNDS

All types of profit-seeking business firms—corporations, partnerships, and proprietorships—obtain some portion of their funds from investors in the form of equity capital. In fact, the equity portion of capital funds generally constitutes the first source of funds for a new firm; it also provides "support" for all types of debt the firm may subsequently acquire. Thus, besides being a source of funds, equity capital forms the foundation of the entire capital structure of a business enterprise. The holders of the equity claims, moreover, have the final responsibility for management and usually bear the greatest portion of the financial and entrepreneurial risks inherent in the operation of the business.

Equity funds may be found in four forms in a corporation—common stock, preferred stock, capital surplus, and retained earnings. In partnerships and proprietorships, only one kind of equity capital exists, generally termed *net worth*. For purposes of financial statement analysis, the major distinction between corporate net worth on the one hand and proprietorship and partnership net worth on the other is that the owners of a corporation (stockholders) enjoy *limited liability* for the debts of the corporation and the owners of unincorporated businesses generally do not.

Proprietorship and Partnership Equity

The balance sheet of a proprietorship shows the proprietor's equity in the assets as his proprietorship or capital account. The individual proprietor is obligated not only for the debts of his business but also for any outside liabilities, one being his liability for income taxes. He may have outside assets as well as outside liabilities. Those outside assets and liabilities may not be reflected in the statement of the business, but the analyst must obtain information about them to determine the real net worth of the proprietor. The payment of outside debts usually depends on the livelihood the proprietor earns from his business.

In a partnership statement, the total equity of the partners in the assets is shown in the net worth section of the balance sheet, and the capital funds of each partner are usually segregated. The outside assets and liabilities of the individual partners are not included in the business statement. The assets of the partnership are used first to discharge the obligations of the partnership, but the outside assets of an individual partner are applied first to his outside liabilities. The tax liability is generally discharged by withdrawals from the partnership. For that reason it is essential that the analyst determine the status of each partner's tax liability.

306

Except that personal and business assets and liabilities are generally inextricably bound together in proprietorships and partnerships, the function of the equity capital (or net worth) of those organizations is identical with that of the corporation. Consequently, unless otherwise noted, it is usually safe to assume that there are no substantive differences in the analysis of the capital structure of the various types of business organization.

Corporate Equity

The equity section of a corporation's balance sheet may (but need not) include the four basic forms of equity capital: common stock, preferred stock, capital surplus, and retained earnings. Because of the relative importance of the corporate form of business, the financial statement analyst should be familiar with each form of corporate equity capital.

Common Stock and Capital Surplus. The existence of common stock in the capital structure of a corporation is an absolute legal prerequisite to the creation of a corporation and an essential ingredient in its future growth. The initial contribution of capital and all subsequent contributions (either in cash or in kind) to a corporation by its owners are represented in the firm's balance sheet by the common stock and *capital surplus* (or *paid-in surplus*) accounts. The distinction between these accounts is minor from the point of view of financial statement analysis, because it represents an artificial separation of the actual cash proceeds, or the stated values of property or services, exchanged for shares of common (and preferred) stock of the corporation. The analyst may consider the sum of the common stock and capital surplus accounts as the cumulative *externally introduced* capital contributions of the common stockholders to the corporate entity. While the dollar figures listed in the balance sheet may not be particularly significant in absolute size or relative proportions, the fact that they represent residual ownership claims carries important implications for the analyst.

At the time a business is formed, the common stockholders, as the sole owners and investors in the business, possess an essentially unrestricted claim on the firm's income and assets and an essentially unchallenged voice in its management.[1] But since it is often necessary and profitable for the corporation to obtain funds from outside creditors and preferred stockholders as the business grows, the owners are generally disposed to bargain away some portion of their claims on income and assets and relinquish a portion of their control over operations in exchange for the funds those outside groups have to offer.

---

1. That also holds true for the owners of newly formed proprietorships and partnerships.

307

Consequently, in a "mature" corporation, the claims on income and assets represented by the owners' initial capital contribution tend to be diminished. However, as the corporation grows, if it is profitable and its management chooses to finance part of its long-term capital needs with internally generated funds (profits retained in the business), the stockholders' initial investment will grow—often in direct proportion to the growth of the firm.

Retained Earnings. The regular annual additions to stockholder equity resulting from the retention of earnings by the corporation are represented by the retained earnings account on the balance sheet. As we saw in Chapter 10 when we examined the statement of changes in financial position, the amount by which retained earnings will grow over a given period is determined by subtracting dividend payments from net income after taxes and adjusting that figure for certain charges or credits (tax adjustments for prior periods or changes in asset valuations, for example). While the periodic "adjustments" to retained earnings are sometimes very significant, the most important aspect of the retained earnings account for the statement analyst is management's policy on the distribution of profits between dividends and reinvestment.

American corporations have exhibited a high propensity to retain earnings and use them to finance long-term growth and expansion. Since 1900, in fact, over 85 percent of the growth in equity capital of American nonfinancial corporations has come from undistributed profits. In the last quarter-century, those funds have supplied over 20 percent of *all the funds* acquired by corporations, including short-term credit. Even greater proportions are accounted for by the undistributed profits of unincorporated businesses.

But those aggregate figures tend to mask the variations in policy and practice of individual firms; consequently, the financial statement analyst must pay close attention to the historical, current, and future dividend policies of firms in which he is interested. To the extent that current corporate earnings are distributed to stockholders as *cash* dividends, the growth in the firm's retained earnings will be slowed; and when current earnings are insufficient to cover cash dividends, a shrinkage in the firm's equity capital will occur, necessitating either a commensurate shrinkage in assets or an increase in the proportion of assets financed with debt capital. Neither situation is necessarily bad for the corporation, its owners, or its creditors unless the ability of the firm to meet its continuing financial obligations is impaired as a result.

Another dimension of corporate dividend policy should be noted here: The payment of cash dividends is clearly a drain on corporate resources and exposes the firm's creditors to added risk (although often it is almost imperceptible) by making their proportionate investment in the firm's total assets higher than it would otherwise be. However, the firm's management, by virtue of the fact that it works for the owners, is obligated to pursue the overall objective of maximizing stockholder wealth. Hence, the form into which a corporation's dividend policy finally evolves must necessarily accommodate the needs of both creditors (in terms of safety of principal and regularity of interest payments) and stockholders (in terms of realizing an adequate return on their investment). Financial statement analysts who fail to recognize the importance of dividend policy to either group of investors risk committing serious errors of judgment as they form recommendations for either credit or management advisory purposes.

Preferred Stock. As the name implies, preferred stock is a type of security through the sale of which a corporation obtains equity funds in exchange for certain kinds of preferential treatment for its holders that are not usually accorded to holders of common stock. Preferred stock occupies a position (in relation to the residual ownership claims issued by the corporation) similar to that of a limited partner (in relation to the general partners) in a partnership. Preferred stockholders and limited partners are usually given preference in the distribution of assets if a business is liquidated and priority in the distribution of income.

Preferred stock is a hybrid kind of security, possessing some characteristics of debt and some of equity. Legally it is part of the company's equity capital; preferred dividends are not a tax-deductible business expense and, unless the corporation's charter or the preferred stock indenture (the contract between the corporation and the preferred stockholders) states otherwise, preferred stockholders have almost the same rights as common stockholders.

Preferred stock carries a specified dividend rate, however, which, with its prior claims to income and assets, makes it resemble debt. Consequently, its issuance provides the common stockholders with an opportunity to gain (or lose) from the use of *financial leverage* (to be discussed later in this chapter) in the corporate capital structure.

Preferred stock may be viewed primarily as debt by an actual or potential common stockholder as he considers the impact on residual earnings of securities carrying designated charges. From the point of view of a bondholder, however, preferred stock is part of the equity cushion protecting him from loss. From the point of view of the issuing firm's management, finally, preferred stock is both debt and equity. It is debt because the firm is responsible for meeting the fixed periodic dividend payments, and sometimes the retirement of the principal amount as well; it is equity because in most cases dividend payments may legally be omitted for limited periods without penalty and the preferred stockholders share in the residual earnings and assets of the corporation.

The preferred stock indenture details the specific features of the issue, some of which may be particularly important to the financial statement analyst. For example, the issue may be *cumulative,* which means that preferred dividends must be current before any common dividends may be paid. A *participating* feature gives the preferred stockholder the right to participate in the residual earnings of the corporation, usually on an equal basis with the common stockholder, after each has received a specified dividend payment. The indenture may also provide for the ultimate redemption of the preferred stock, by establishing a sinking fund with which to retire the stock (as bonds are retired), through a *call provision* that gives the corporation the option of retiring the stock by redeeming the shares for cash, or by making the stock convertible into common stock at a specified ratio of shares. These various preferred stock features obviously affect the firm's cash flows as they are implemented; consequently, the financial statement analyst should review the indenture to determine the rights and obligations of the firm under its provisions.

DEBT CAPITAL

Debt capital is distinguished from equity capital mainly on the basis of its contractual nature; that is, debt funds are supplied to a business firm only when it promises to make periodic interest payments at a given rate and repay the principal sum at or by some specified date. Two kinds of debt are generally found in a firm's capital structure: intermediate-term debt and long-term debt. They are accorded similar treatment in financial statement analysis, but it is helpful to describe them separately.

Intermediate-Term Debt

Intermediate-term debt refers to *loans* (in contrast to securities, which are usually, but not always, marketable) with initial maturities of one to ten years. Term loans are the principal kind of noncurrent debt financing used by unincorporated businesses. The most frequent use of term financing is to satisfy requirements for permanent increases in working capital and for occasional purchases of fixed assets. Whereas short-term credit is usually repaid by seasonal reductions in accounts receivable and inventory, term debt is repaid from net profits after taxes plus depreciation (that is, from the firm's cash flow from operations).

Intermediate-term credit is ideally suited for business credit needs of moderate proportions that cannot be repaid in one year but can certainly be repaid in less than 10 years. Obviously, if a firm does not need funds for 10 to 20 years, there is little sense in its borrowing, and paying interest on, long-term funds. Furthermore, if a firm's requirements are relatively modest, it may be uneconomical to attempt to raise what those who deal in the long-term capital market would term a small amount through the issuance of bonds or new common stock. The costs of marketing both long-term debt and equity securities are likely to be considerably higher and to remain so for a considerably longer period than the costs associated with an intermediate-term loan.

Firms able to generate adequate cash flows to repay term loans can generally obtain such loans from commercial banks, insurance companies, sales finance companies, government agencies, or, in some lines of business, equipment manufacturers and suppliers. In general, as one moves down this list from banks and insurance companies to vendors, the credit standards and debt service requirements become more lenient, and the interest rate becomes higher. The ability to repay must be clearly evident under even the most liberal of credit terms, however.

Long-Term Debt

The *bond,* the basic corporate long-term debt instrument, is a long-term promissory note with an initial maturity of ten years or longer. The use of long-term debt is usually restricted to financing that part of the permanent assets of a business that cannot be (or is not) financed by the firm's owners. Previous chapters have suggested the inappropriateness of financing short-term needs with long-term funds, and we shall presently discuss such improprieties as incurring excessive debt in relation to the firm's equity base and borrowing more than actual long-term needs. At the very least, such practices tend to increase a firm's long-run financing costs, and they may be even more damaging to the firm's financial position.

The contractual terms of the debt issue are stated in the bond indenture, which may be very lengthy, since it must cover all important matters relating to the bond issue. For example, it states the precise form in which the bonds are issued, provides a complete description of the security (if any) to be pledged, and stipulates protective clauses or *covenants,* such as limitations on the borrowing corporation's total indebtedness, its ability to pay dividends, and the liquidity position it must maintain. The bond indenture also outlines any provisions for 'early redemption of the bonds (call privileges), sinking fund payments by the borrower, and penalties for nonperformance.

The bond issue may be either secured or unsecured. Secured bonds are backed by a pledge of specific assets that can be sold to satisfy creditors' claims in the event of bankruptcy and liquidation. Unsecured bonds carry no such pledge. Both kinds of bonds share a common characteristic: their payment is anticipated from the corporate borrower's earning power over the term of the bond issue.

LEASES

In general a lease is a contractual arrangement by which the owner of an asset (the *lessor*) grants the use of his property to another party (the *lessee*) under certain conditions for a specified period. The title to the property remains with the lessor, but the physical possession and control of it passes to the lessee.

The majority of manufacturing, mercantile, and service firms do not need to acquire *title* to the fixed assets they use in the operation of their businesses. What they need, of course, is the *use* of the asset, which can be obtained through a lease; that is, if acquiring title to certain assets is merely incidental to obtaining the services the assets provide, leasing should be considered as an alternative to financing the assets' purchase through other means.

Since the lease is nothing more than a financing device that is contractual, leasing must be considered an alternative to *debt* financing. Both the lease payment and the payment of principal and interest on debt are fixed obligations; the inability to meet either payment on schedule can result in serious financial problems. Consequently, the analysis of leasing as it relates to the overall long-term financial strength of the firm is very similar to the analysis of long-term debt.

Leases may be classified as either *operating leases* or *financial leases*. An operating lease is an agreement whereby the lessee acquires the use of an asset on a period-to-period basis; that is, the lease is cancelable by the lessee upon due notice to the lessor. This type of lease may have an initial term of one month or one year and is renewable for similar periods without any specified expiration date. The financial lease, in contrast, is a contractual arrangement in which the lessee agrees to make a series of payments to the lessor over a specified period in return for the use of a particular asset. During the initial term of the financial lease, the contract cannot be canceled except by mutual agreement of the parties. The length of the financial lease and the size of the payments are generally scaled so as to amortize the lessor's investment in the asset, cover his operating expenses, and return his desired rate of profit on the transaction.

The major difficulty for the financial statement analyst in analyzing lease arrangements is that the residual obligations under lease contracts do not appear on the lessee's balance sheet. In audited statements and even in unaudited ones prepared by reputable business firms, any such contractual obligation is spelled out in the notes to the financial statements; however, in many unaudited statements, outside analysts are given no clue to either the existence or the provisions of lease arrangements. Therefore, the analyst must always be alert to the possibility that the firm he is analyzing may be required to make fixed cash payments under financial lease contracts. The size of the payments, their timing, and the period over which the firm must continue to make them are necessary facts for a thorough analysis of the firm's capital structure.

Financial Leverage: Using Debt Capital

As mentioned earlier, mature business firms may often find it necessary (and profitable) to finance the purchase of permanent assets by borrowing or issuing preferred stock, or they may obtain the use of those fixed assets under leasing arrangements. Those methods of financing, of course, obligate the firm to make *fixed contractual payments* over a certain period, and the firm is willing to make such long-term commitments since it fully expects the assets so acquired to produce annual profits more than sufficient to cover the financing costs. When the assets are thus successfully employed, the outside investors receive their contractual cash payments, and the firm's owners receive the full benefits of the residual profits produced by those assets. However, if the profits generated by the new assets are insufficient to meet the fixed financing costs, earnings generated by the firm's assets that would normally accrue to the owners must be diverted to meet the fixed obligations to the outside investors. These conditions illustrate the use and the effects of *financial leverage*.

In statement analysis, financial leverage is said to exist when a firm incurs intermediate- or long-term debt, issues preferred stock, or acquires the use of an asset under a financial lease arrangement. The extent to which a firm employs financial leverage is measured by the *degree of financial leverage,* which is defined as the percentage change that occurs in a firm's earnings available to common stock (ΔEAC) as a result of the percentage change that occurs in its earnings before interest and taxes ($\Delta EBIT$).[2] It may be calculated in either of two ways: (1) definitionally as $\Delta EAC/\Delta EBIT$, or (2) given the initial level of earnings before interest and taxes (EBIT), by the formula

$$\text{degree of financial leverage} = \frac{\text{EBIT}}{\text{EBIT-interest charges}}$$

Regardless of which formula is used, the concept is the same: Financial leverage works through the fixed charges associated with debt, leasing, preferred stock, or a combination of all three that increase or decrease a firm's percentage change in EAC by a greater percentage than the corresponding change in EBIT. The following example illustrates the effects of differences in financial structure on financial leverage.

Suppose that three otherwise identical companies in a particular industry have financed their operations with different proportions of debt and equity. Company A has no debt in its capital structure, Company B employs one-fourth debt and three-fourths equity, and Company C's capital structure contains three-fifths debt and two-fifths equity. The capital structures (long-term debt and equity) of the three firms are presented in Table 17-1.

---

2. The symbol Δ in this case should be read as "percentage change in."

Suppose further that each firm has operated during the past year at identical levels of output and each has produced EBIT of $50,000. Table 17-2 shows the effects of each firm's capital structure on its earnings available to common stock and its percentage return on net worth (that is, EAC/net worth). The table also shows the degree of financial leverage employed by each firm. Note that while Company C's earnings available to common stock are the lowest of the three firms, its degree of financial leverage (and hence its return on net worth) is the highest. This illustrates the effects of differences in capital structure (leverage) on a given level of earnings before interest and taxes. In the following illustration, observe what happens to the relation between EBIT and EAC as EBIT changes.

Table 17-1

CAPITAL STRUCTURES OF THREE HYPOTHETICAL COMPANIES

	Company A	*Company B*	*Company C*
Total debt	$ 0	$100,000	$240,000
Net worth	400,000	300,000	160,000
Total capital structure	$400,000	$400,000	$400,000

Table 17-2

EARNINGS AND RETURN ON NET WORTH OF THREE HYPOTHETICAL COMPANIES AT A GIVEN LEVEL OF EBIT

	Company A	*Company B*	*Company C*
EBIT	$50,000	$50,000	$50,000
Interest on long-term debt	0	10,000	24,000
Earnings before taxes	$50,000	$40,000	$26,000
Income taxes (at 50%)	25,000	20,000	13,000
Earnings available to common stock	$25,000	$20,000	$13,000
Degree of financial leverage $\dfrac{\text{EBIT}}{\text{EBIT-int}}$	1.00	1.25	1.923
Percentage return on net worth	6.25%	6.67%	8.13%

Assume that the three firms expect labor problems during the coming year as a result of the expiration of their union contracts. A strike is almost certain, but it is not known how long it will last. All three firms will be closed during the strike. If a settlement is reached quickly, each company's expected EBIT is likely to increase by 20 percent over the previous year's (that is ΔEBIT will equal 20 percent). If the strike is long, however, each firm's EBIT will decrease by 30 percent (that is, ΔEBIT will equal minus 30 percent).

Table 17-3 shows the effects of those two possibilities on the EAC of the three firms. Note that the ratios of ΔEAC/ΔEBIT yield values for the degree of financial leverage equal to those in Table 17-2, which were calculated by the ratio EBIT/(EBIT-interest charges) at the initial level of EBIT (that is, EBIT = $50,000). For example, the ratio for Company A, whose interest charges equal zero, is $50,000/($50,000-0), and the degree of financial leverage calculated in this way equals 1. For Company C, the ratio is $50,000/($50,000-$24,000), which equals 1.923. Thus, it should be apparent that the two methods of calculating the degree of financial leverage yield the same results and that future levels of EAC (for purposes of forecasting the effects of leverage, for example) can be calculated directly from the expected percentage change in EBIT and the firm's degree of financial leverage.

More important, however, Table 17-3 clearly illustrates the riskiness that Company C's capital structure has introduced to the pattern of its earnings. While its performance during periods in which earnings are rising is clearly superior to those of Companies A and B, its return on net worth under adverse economic conditions is certainly not to be envied. The table also clearly shows the benefits (versus only the slight risks) of using a moderate amount of financial leverage as opposed to no leverage at all when Company A's percentage returns on net worth are compared to those of Company B under the two sets of economic conditions.

HOW MUCH LEVERAGE IS ENOUGH?

The question of how much leverage is enough cannot be answered definitively in either absolute or relative terms; it simply depends on the circumstances in which the firm finds itself. If the firm's sales and EBIT are expected to increase indefinitely, the firm can safely take on all the leverage it can acquire. A financial statement analyst can determine how much financial leverage is judicious for a particular firm and how much might be termed excessive only from an extensive and careful analysis of the expected growth and stability of its future sales (and EBIT). And he must make certain that he also accounts fully for the leverage effects of financial leases.

315

Table 17-3

EARNINGS, RETURN ON NET WORTH, AND FINANCIAL LEVERAGE OF THREE HYPOTHETICAL COMPANIES ASSUMING A LABOR STRIKE OF DIFFERENT DURATIONS

	Short Strike			Long Strike		
	Co. A	Co. B	Co. C	Co. A	Co. B	Co. C
EBIT	$60,000	$60,000	$60,000	$35,000	$35,000	$35,000
Interest on long-term debt	0	10,000	24,000	0	10,000	24,000
Earnings before taxes	$60,000	$50,000	$36,000	$35,000	$25,000	$11,000
Income taxes (at 50%)	30,000	25,000	18,000	17,500	12,500	5,500
EAC	$30,000	$25,000	$18,000	$17,500	$12,500	$ 5,500
Percentage return on net worth	7.50%	8.33%	11.25%	4.375%	4.167%	3.438%
Percentage change in EBIT (ΔEBIT)	20	20	20	(30)	(30)	(30)
Percentage change in EAC (ΔEAC)	20	25	38.46	(30)	(37.5)	(57.7)
Degree of financial leverage (ΔEAC/ΔEBIT)	1.00	1.25	1.923	1.00	1.25	1.923

Growth and Stability in Sales

As sales and EBIT grow, the effects of leverage diminish since, with a given (or when long-term debt is being amortized, a declining) level of annual interest charges, a larger EBIT will diminish the degree of financial leverage. For example, the degree of financial leverage of Company C, when calculated at the $60,000 level of EBIT, falls from 1.923 to 1.667—$60,000/($60,000−$24,000). Thus, the firm's risk-return trade-off in using financial leverage declines as EBIT grows. At the same time, however, the decrease in the level of financial risk inherent in the capital structure makes it easier for the firm to raise additional long-term capital from either creditors or owners and thus improves its overall long-term financial strength.

The stability of sales and EBIT is also important in analyzing the effects of leverage on the firm's operating results. With greater stability in sales and earnings, a firm can incur the fixed charges of debt with less risk that when sales and earnings are subject to periodic declines; in the latter instance, it may have difficulty in meeting its obligations of interest and principal payments on its debt as well as paying the expected dividends on its common stock. The effect of the variability of EBIT on earnings and the return on net worth for firms with varying degrees of financial leverage is clearly illustrated by examining the operating results for the three firms under the various conditions presented in Tables 17-2 and 17-3. If, for example, Company C's EBIT for three consecutive years were $50,000, $60,000, and $35,000, its percentage return on net worth would climb from 8 to 11 percent and fall dramatically to about 3.5 percent. Further, if the firm had 10,000 shares of common stock outstanding during those three years, earnings per share would equal $1.30, $1.80, and $.55 for the three years. That kind of variability would certainly cause considerable fluctuation in the market price of the stock and severely limit the firm's ability to raise additional equity capital at a favorable price.

Adjustments for Lease Obligations

Financial leases also introduce leverage into the firm's capital structure, but the data are not usually reported in a format consistent with the way intermediate- and long-term debt are reported. Thus, the analyst will have to make certain adjustments to the lease data. The adjustments include *capitalizing* the lease and imputing an interest cost to the lease payments. These adjustments will help the analyst estimate the impact of leases on the firm's capital structure and its long-term financial strength.

Capitalizing Leases. When the analyst is aware that the firm is leasing a portion of its assets, he may find it helpful, for purposes of interfirm comparisons of certain ratios (debt to net worth, for example), to *capitalize* the lease payments and adjust both sides of the firm's balance sheet to reveal the estimated long-term liability (debt equivalent) and the operating value of the leased asset created by the arrangement. For example, suppose a firm reported the following summary balance sheet:

Current assets	$100,000	Current liabilities	$ 50,000
Fixed assets	400,000	Net worth	450,000
Total assets	$500,000	Total liabilities and capital	$500,000

Assuming that the firm had contracted to pay $20,000 per year for three years for leased machinery and that the appropriate equivalent intermediate-term borrowing rate is 10 percent, we can capitalize the total amount of future lease payments by calculating their *present value*, which can then be used to make the appropriate balance sheet adjustments.

The present value of the lease payments is calculated by using the general compound interest formula,

$$C = \frac{P_1}{(1+r)^1} + \frac{P_2}{(1+r)^2} + \frac{P_3}{(1+r)^3} + \ldots + \frac{P_n}{(1+r)^n}$$

where C is the capitalized value of the lease, P_1, P_2, P_3, etc., are the lease payments made at the end of this year, the following year, and the year following that (and so forth) respectively, and r is the interest rate.[3] In our example, the capitalized value of the lease is

$$C = \frac{\$20,000}{(1+.10)^1} + \frac{\$20,000}{(1+.10)^2} + \frac{\$20,000}{(1+.10)^3}$$

$$= \frac{\$20,000}{1.10} + \frac{\$20,000}{1.21} + \frac{\$20,000}{1.331}$$

$$= \$18,182 + \$16,529 + \$15,026 = \$49,737$$

This figure, representing both the present value of the leased asset and the intermediate-term obligation incurred by the firm under the least contract, is added to both sides of the balance sheet as follows:

Current assets	$100,000	Current liabilities	$ 50,000
Leased assets	49,737	Lease obligation	49,737
Fixed assets	400,000	Net worth	450,000
Total assets	$549,737	Total liabilities and capital	$549,737

---

3. For a complete discussion of the use of compound interest in business decisions, see Clifton H. Kreps, Jr., and Richard F. Wacht, *Business Financial Management* (Washington, D.C.: American Institute of Banking, 1974) Vol. IV, Appendix I.

Hence the firm's debt-to-net-worth ratio will increase from its former level of 11.1 percent ($50,000/$450,000) to an adjusted 22.2 percent ($99,737/$450,000). And if the firm's net profit after taxes for the year totaled $50,000, its return on total assets would be adjusted downward from 10 percent to 9.10 percent as a result of recognizing that leased assets are also contributing to the firm's overall profitability and should be counted as part of the firm's total asset base.

Imputing Interest Expense. The degree of financial leverage introduced by lease arrangements, in order to be strictly comparable to that introduced by term loans, long-term debt, or preferred stock, must be calculated using an *imputed* interest expense associated with leasing. That is because the total lease expense incurred by a lessee represents to the lessor both a recovery of the cost of the asset and an interest return on his invested capital. Therefore, the annual lease payment should be separated into two parts—(imputed) interest expense and principal payment—before its debt-equivalent degree of financial leverage can be calculated.

The procedure is relatively simple, once the lease payments have been capitalized. Using the preceding example, in which the present value of the residual lease obligation was calculated to total $49,737, we find that the imputed interest expense for the year (at the 10 percent interest rate used to capitalize the lease payments) is $4,974. Thus, if the firm's EBIT was $100,000, and assuming it had no other noncurrent liabilities, its degree of financial leverage would equal

$$\frac{\text{EBIT}}{\text{EBIT}-\text{interest charges}} = \frac{\$100,000}{\$100,000-\$4,974} = 1.05$$

The preceding two adjustments will produce data that can be used to compare the risk and performance of a leasing firm either with a non-leasing firm that employs debt in its capital structure or with a firm that employs both debt and leasing to acquire the use of fixed assets. The adjustments reduce the capital structures of all three kinds of firms to a common basis. However, a strong case can be made for using the *entire* lease payment to calculate the degree of financial leverage if the leasing firm is being compared with an unlevered, nonleasing firm. In that case, the degree of financial leverage becomes

$$\frac{\text{EBIT}}{\text{EBIT}-\text{lease payments}} = \frac{\$100,000}{\$100,000-\$20,000} = 1.25$$

It is evident that the increase in the degree of financial leverage is substantial, and the element of risk introduced by the total lease payment (which is a fully tax-deductible expense) is clearly revealed for comparative purposes.

Coverage Ratios

While the figures presented in the preceding two examples provide some insight into the measurement of earnings adequacy (or inadequacy) in relation to the fixed financial charges a firm obligates itself to pay when it finances its assets in certain ways, more precise relations are obviously needed to test long-term financial strength. The following sections describe the basic tools used to measure the adequacy of earnings and cash flows to meet fixed financial obligations.

Earnings coverage ratios provide a direct measure of the relation between fixed financial charges and the earnings available to meet those charges. While the concept described in Chapter 8 is simple and straightforward, its practical implementation is complicated by the way in which the analyst chooses to define both *earnings* and *fixed financial charges*. For example, the earnings coverage ratio described in Chapter 8 is the ratio of EBIT to interest charges on long-term debt (times charges earned ratio). That basic form of the coverage ratio, though generally satisfactory for measuring the margin of safety the firm enjoys in meeting its interest payments on long-term debt out of current earnings before interest and taxes, ignores both the existence of fixed financial charges other than debt interest and the total current cash resources available for debt service.

FIXED FINANCIAL CHARGES

The legal definition of fixed financial charges generally includes only interest charges on intermediate- and long-term debt, repayment of debt principal (including amortization of deferred bond discount and premium), and payments required under financial lease obligations. Preferred stock dividends are not included in this list because, in most cases, a firm's management may choose not to declare such dividends without incurring any legal penalty. Similarly, common stock dividend payments are always made at the discretion of management.

However, a firm's management often looks on both preferred and common stock dividends as quasi-legal obligations, because of the (justified) notion that, by passing such dividend payments, the firm is implicitly admitting that it is in financial difficulty. Indeed, whether or not that is actually the case, the capital markets may interpret an omission or reduction in common dividends as a sign of financial weakness and the omission of preferred dividends as an even stronger sign. The consequences of such interpretations are obviously distasteful to management, since they interfere with its financial objective of maximizing stockholder wealth. Thus dividends are often included in the definition of fixed financial charges by analysts when the situation warrants it.

Not all debt agreements provide for sinking fund payments or other similar means of retiring the debt by periodic cash payments. Some analysts nevertheless include in fixed charges imputed sinking fund payments; however, by including such payments the analyst is adding a nonexistent burden to the firm's current operation and ignoring the large commitment the firm has assumed toward debt repayment (or replacement of existing debt with another issue) at maturity. The timing of debt principal payments is generally agreed on between the debtor firm and the creditor (or investment banker) after a careful review of the firm's continuing cash flow needs and its ability to generate cash for repayment; hence, the financial statement analyst should base his analysis of the earnings coverage ratios on the actual debt repayment schedules. Similarly, when debt (or preferred stock) is callable (or convertible into common stock), the interest and principal (or preferred dividend) payments should be adjusted to show the possible effects of those future events on the financial position of the firm. Usually that involves the removal of interest and principal payments on the callable or convertible issue from the firm's fixed financial charges as of some future date; the procedure will be illustrated later in this chapter.

AVAILABLE EARNINGS

Since fixed financial charges must be paid with cash generated from current operations unless the firm has a cash reserve out of which it can meet those obligations, the unadjusted earnings figure presented in the income statement may not be the correct measure of funds available to meet fixed charges.

As we saw in module two on funds flow, funds provided by operations include earnings after taxes and certain noncash expenses, such as depreciation. Those funds are generally available to replace depreciated assets, pay maturing liabilities, or pay dividends. In addition, since interest charges are tax-deductible, EBIT is the more appropriate earnings figure for examining the firm's ability to pay its debt *interest* charges. Thus, although the use of net income as an approximation of funds provided by operations to meet fixed obligations may in some instances be warranted, in others it may significantly overstate or understate the amount available for debt service.

Consequently, the financial statement analyst must carefully examine both the sources of funds available to meet fixed charges and the nature of the fixed charges themselves (particularly their legal and tax status) before selecting the numerators and denominators of the coverage ratios he will use in analyzing the long-run financial strength of a particular firm. The following illustrations will serve as guides to the proper use of the ratios.

ILLUSTRATIVE CALCULATIONS

Table 17-4 presents a condensed income statement of Sarah-Ann, Incorporated. The data therein are used to illustrate the computation and interpretation of several variants of the earnings coverage ratios.

Times Interest Earned Ratio

The times interest earned ratio is the simplest and one of the most widely used coverage ratios. It is computed as follows:

$$\text{times interest earned} = \frac{\text{EBIT}}{\text{interest charges}}$$

For Sarah-Ann, the ratio is

$$\text{times interest earned} = \frac{\$1,010,000 + \$360,000}{\$360,000} = 3.8 \text{ times}$$

Table 17-4

**CONDENSED INCOME STATEMENT
SARAH-ANN, INCORPORATED
for the Year Ended June 30, 1978**

Net Sales		$7,500,000
Cost of goods sold	$4,140,000	
Selling, general and administrative expenses	1,010,000	
Depreciation (excluded from above costs)	450,000	
Interest expense (on long-term debt only)	360,000	
Lease expense	530,000	
Total expenses		6,490,000
Income before taxes		$1,010,000
Income taxes		480,000
Net Income		$ 530,000
Dividends:		
On common stock	$ 220,000	
On preferred stock	110,000	330,000
To retained earnings		$ 200,000

Selected notes to the financial statements and estimates of changes in capital structure.

1. Long-term debt includes the following:

First mortgage bonds, 6%, due 1999 annual sinking fund requirement	$3,360,000
Subordinated convertible debentures, 7% conversion may take place on or after July 1, 1984	160,000
	2,240,000

2. The company leases its building and a portion of its manufacturing and administrative equipment for $530,000 annually. The leases expire at various times from 3 to 25 years from the current date. Computer lease, due to expire in 1981, will be rewritten to include hardware upgrading; the cost is likely to increase by $90,000 per year.

3. The company has a 10-year noncancelable raw material purchase commitment amounting to $56,000 annually until 1980 and $65,000 annually thereafter.

4. The interest portion of lease payments on capitalized leases totals $50,000 at present and will increase to $62,000 in 1981 when the computer lease is rewritten.

As pointed out in Chapter 8, the ratio is computed using earnings before interest and taxes because interest is tax-deductible. The value of the ratio indicates that Sarah-Ann's earnings cover its interest expense almost four times.[4]

Despite what has become common practice by some analysts, the times interest earned ratio should not be computed separately for each outstanding bond issue, giving prior claim to senior issues (e.g., first mortgage bonds) and lower claims to junior issues in descending order of priority in liquidation. The main reason for avoiding such a practice is simply that *all* outstanding bond issues must be serviced *simultaneously* out of current resources. A firm cannot survive financially by paying interest on the senior issues only while missing interest payments on other obligations; consequently, the times interest earned ratio is calculated as described regardless of the number of bond issues a firm has outstanding.

Fixed Charges Coverage Ratio

The validity of an earnings coverage ratio, such as the times interest earned ratio, that does not take all the firm's financial charges into account is open to serious question. To avoid serious financial difficulties that would accompany a missed sinking fund payment, for example, the firm's earnings must cover interest, debt principal repayment, and all other fixed financial charges.

Thus a more rigorous test of the firm's ability to service its fixed charges is the fixed charges coverage ratio. It is calculated as follows:

$$\text{fixed charges coverage} = \frac{\text{EBIT} + \text{lease expense}}{\text{total fixed charges}}$$

Of course, the items included in total fixed charges vary from firm to firm, but it is defined to include all fixed financial charges: debt interest, sinking fund payments, lease payments, and other long-term contractual commitments. Those that are deductible expenses are entered directly into the ratio's denominator; those that are not tax-deductible (e.g., sinking fund payments) must first be adjusted to a pretax equivalent basis. That is done by dividing the non-tax-deductible charge by one minus the firm's marginal income tax rate. Thus

fixed charges coverage

$$= \frac{\text{EBT} + \text{interest expense} + \text{lease expense}}{\dfrac{\text{interest}}{\text{expense}} + \dfrac{\text{lease}}{\text{payments}} + \dfrac{\text{sinking fund}}{(1 - \text{tax rate})} + \text{purchase commitment}}$$

Substituting the appropriate values from Table 17-4 and assuming a 48 percent marginal income tax rate for Sarah-Ann, we find that

---

4. The computations in this section are rounded to the nearest $1,000.

fixed charges coverage

$$= \frac{\$1,010,000 + \$360,000 + \$530,000}{\$360,000 + \$530,000 + \dfrac{\$160,000}{(1-.48)} + \$56,000}$$

$$= \frac{\$1,900,000}{\$360,000 + \$530,000 + \$308,000 + \$56,000}$$

$$= \frac{\$1,900,000}{\$1,254,000} = 1.5 \text{ times}$$

Cash Flow Coverage of Fixed Charges

The discussion earlier in this chapter pointed out that reported earnings are generally not a reliable measure of cash flows generated by current operations; a better measure of fixed charges coverage may be obtained by using EBIT plus noncash charges to income in the numerator of the ratio. Under this concept, the fixed charges coverage ratio becomes the *cash flow* coverage ratio (CFCR), which is computed as follows:

CFCR

$$= \frac{\text{EBIT} + \text{depreciation} + \text{lease expense}}{\text{total fixed charges}}$$

For Sarah-Ann, the value of the ratio is:

CFCR

$$= \frac{\text{EBT} + \text{interest expense} + \text{depreciation} + \text{lease expense}}{\dfrac{\text{interest}}{\text{expense}} + \dfrac{\text{lease}}{\text{payments}} + \dfrac{\text{sinking fund}}{(1-\text{tax rate})} + \text{purchase commitment}}$$

$$= \frac{\$1,010,000 + \$360,000 + \$450,000 + \$530,000}{\$\ 360,000 + \$530,000 + \$308,000 + \$\ 56,000}$$

$$= \frac{\$2,350,000}{\$1,254,000} = 1.9 \text{ times}$$

Earnings Coverage of Preferred Dividends

It is occasionally necessary to calculate the coverage ratios for preferred stock issues, especially when preferred dividends have not been paid for some time and the preferred stockholders appear ready to take whatever remedial action the preferred stock indenture or the courts may allow. In such cases, the claims of the creditors may be placed at least partially in jeopardy as a result of the preferred stockholders' actions.

The coverage ratio may be either *earnings* coverage or *cash flow* coverage. The earnings coverage ratio is computed by adding the preferred dividends (adjusted to their pretax equivalent basis) to the denominator of the fixed charges coverage ratio. The fixed charges coverage ratio is used as a basis for the *preferred dividends coverage ratio* since the need to continue to pay all the fixed charges associated with debt retirement and other contractual obligations is usually the principal motive for management's decision to skip payment of the preferred dividend (when that becomes necessary). Thus

preferred dividends coverage ratio

$$= \frac{\text{EBIT} + \text{lease expense}}{\text{total fixed charges} + \dfrac{\text{preferred dividends}}{(1 - \text{tax rate})}}$$

for Sarah-Ann

preferred dividends coverage ratio

$$= \frac{\$1,900,000}{\$1,254,000 + \dfrac{\$110,000}{(1-.48)}} = 1.3 \text{ times}$$

The *cash flow coverage of preferred dividends,* based on the same logic, is the same as the cash flow coverage of fixed charges ratio except for the addition of the adjusted preferred dividends to the denominator. The ratio for Sarah-Ann is

cash flow coverage of preferred dividends

$$= \frac{\$2,350,000}{\$1,254,000 + \dfrac{\$110,000}{(1-.48)}} = 1.6 \text{ times}$$

Using the Coverage Ratios

The coverage ratios, in the order presented, represent tests of increasing severity of the ability of the firm to meet its current fixed financial obligations out of current earnings or funds provided by current operations. They are, in a narrow sense, measures of how well the firm covered its *historical* obligations out of *historical* earnings, since the data used to calculate the ratios are historical. Obviously, the true test of the firm's financial strength must be forward-looking to the extent that current earnings, cash flows, and fixed charges are not mirror images of what the firm can expect in the future.

The financial statement analyst can begin testing the firm's financial strength by comparing the historical ratios with those of similar firms or the appropriate industry averages. Such comparisons will give the analyst a general notion of how other firms are managing their capital funds, but they are usually not very useful, since capital structure is largely decided by management. Thus a firm's capital structure will reflect the extent to which its management is willing to assume the financial risks that accompany the use of debt and preferred stock as sources of long-term capital.

A more fruitful approach to analyzing the firm's capital structure is to examine the behavior of the firm's cash flows over time. The more stable the earnings—that is, to the extent that the firm's earnings are free from the destabilizing effects of economic, operational, and competitive hazards—the lower its earnings and cash flow coverage ratios need to be to meet minimum acceptance. Meeting at least minimum acceptable standards of both actual and potential investors (in both debt and equity securities of the firm) means the firm will pay less for its long-term capital funds and enjoy a preferred position among lenders should it need to tap its reserve borrowing capacity.

Further, a firm whose sales and earnings have shown a constant (or at least a highly consistent) upward trend, can safely operate with very low (close to 1.0) coverage ratios, under the presumption, of course, that the past trend will continue indefinitely. If that presumption is accurate, the coverage ratios will increase in subsequent periods, other things being equal. In contrast, a declining firm or a firm with highly variable earnings will require much higher coverage ratios as minimally acceptable standards.

The intertemporal variability in the items other than earnings included in the various coverage ratios are also important in testing a firm's capital structure. Variability in sales and earnings (or at least year-to-year changes) is a fact of life for most firms. In addition, as long-term debt is gradually repaid, interest charges are reduced; leases may expire and be renewed under different terms; the firm may acquire additional debt; or other more or less significant changes may take place in a firm's capital structure. The analysis of a firm's long-term financial strength takes on dynamic characteristics that can be handled only by forecasting future sales and earnings and reviewing the terms and conditions of the firm's long-term financial obligations.

Table 17-5 presents a five-year forecast of the relevant income statement data for Sarah-Ann, Incorporated, along with the fixed charges coverage and the preferred dividends coverage ratios calculated for each year.[5] Assuming that these data were competently assembled and

---

5. The techniques used in preparing financial forecasts were presented in Chapter 11; therefore, we need not discuss the origin of the data presented in Table 17-5.

Table 17-5

FIVE-YEAR FORECAST OF EARNINGS COVERAGE RATIOS
SARAH-ANN, INCORPORATED
Selected Pro Forma Financial Data
for the Years Ended June 30, 1979-1983
(dollar figures in thousands)

	1979	*1980*	*1981*	*1982*	*1983*
EBIT	$1,500	$1,550	$1,600	$1,620	$1,650
Interest expense	349	339	330	320	310
Lease expense	530	530	530	620	620
Sinking fund (first mortgage bonds)	160	160	160	160	160
Purchase commitment	56	56	65	65	65
Preferred dividends	110	110	110	110	110
Fixed charges coverage ratio	1.63	1.69	1.73	1.71	1.74
Preferred dividends coverage ratio	1.40	1.44	1.47	1.47	1.50

that the estimates are reliable (within reasonable limits, of course), the earnings-coverage ratios presented in the table indicate that the firm will not strengthen its coverage of fixed charges by any appreciable amount over the period. The annual reduction in interest expense is offset to some extent by increases in lease expense and the raw materials purchase commitment. The figures also suggest that any instability in the firm's sales may create significant problems. For example, in 1979, the break-even level of EBIT (that is, the point at which EBIT equals *fixed charges* excluding lease payments, which are deducted before calculating EBIT), is $873,000. That means that if EBIT were to fall by 42 percent (or $627,000) to $873,000, the firm's EAC would equal zero. The firm might then not be in a position to continue last year's common stock dividends of $220,000. The analyst must assess the likelihood that EBIT will fall below the forecasted figures over time; the technique of high-low forecasting, described in Chapter 11, is the appropriate method.

Using Leverage Forecasts

The data presented thus far indicate that the degree of financial leverage employed by the firm from its debt, preferred stock, and lease arrangements is fairly high. According to Table 17-4 the total interest costs, including those imputed to the capitalized leases (see note 4 in Table 17-4), plus preferred dividends (adjusted to pretax basis) will amount to $611,000 in 1979. The degree of financial leverage (using

EBIT = $1,550,000 to reflect the interest imputed to lease payments) is therefore

degree of financial leverage

$$= \frac{EBIT}{EBIT - total\ interest - \dfrac{preferred\ dividends}{(1 - tax\ rate)}}$$

$$= \frac{\$1,550,000}{\$1,550,000 - \$399,000 - \$212,000} = 1.65$$

Consequently, a drop of 28.8 percent in adjusted EBIT from the 1979 level of $1,550,000 would result in a 47.6 percent drop in EAC. Such a drop would place EAC equal to $220,000, the amount equal to 1978's dividends on common stock. Table 17-6 shows the degree of financial leverage for Sarah-Ann for each year from 1979 to 1983.

The figures show that the degree of financial leverage for Sarah-Ann will fall only slightly over the period. The primary reasons the firm's leverage will not be appreciably reduced are (1) the increase in lease payments and (2) the existence of the unamortized convertible debenture issue in the firm's capital structure. These two factors keep the total interest costs fairly constant.

Note 1 in Table 17-4 indicates that the debentures may be converted to common stock in 1984. The bondholders, of course, will convert if the market value of the shares they will receive upon conversion is greater than the value of the bonds they hold or if the expected returns from the common stock investment are greater than the returns they are realizing on the bonds. If we assume that the conversion will take place in 1984 and Sarah-Ann's 1984 adjusted earnings before interest and taxes will be $1,750,000, the firm's degree of financial leverage will fall as a result of the reduction in interest paid on the debentures. In 1984 the first

Table 17-6

PRO FORMA DEGREE OF FINANCIAL LEVERAGE, 1979 to 1983
(dollar figures in thousands)

	1979	*1980*	*1981*	*1982*	*1983*
Adjusted EBIT	$1,550	$1,600	$1,650	$1,682	$1,712
Total interest plus preferred dividends	611	601	592	594	584
Degree of financial leverage	1.65	1.60	1.56	1.55	1.52

mortgage bond principal outstanding will total $2,400,000 as a result of the $160,000 per year sinking fund payments. Thus:

Interest on first mortgage bonds	$144,000
Interest on capitalized leases	62,000
Tax-adjusted preferred dividends	212,000
Total fixed charges	$418,000

degree of financial leverage in 1984

$$= \frac{\$1,750,000}{\$1,750,000 - \$418,000} = 1.31$$

If conversion does not take place, however, the firm will continue to operate with a higher degree of financial leverage, and it will continue to be vulnerable to cyclical and competitive fluctuations in sales and earnings.

Implications For Analysis

The calculations relating to both leverage and the coverage of fixed financial charges are designed basically to help the financial statement analyst assess the amount of risk the firm is facing in managing the long-term capital funds it has decided to acquire. Since management has total discretion as to how it will finance its firm's permanent assets, the analysis of the capital structure is an analysis of management's attitude toward financial risk and its competence in making and implementing long-range financial plans.

The most telling measures of risk are those relating to the pro forma coverage ratios and degree of financial leverage. If the analyst is satisfied that earnings and cash flows are not likely to fall to levels at which the firm would be forced to lower its dividend rates, violate the protective covenants in its preferred stock or debt contracts, or, worse, default on an interest or sinking fund payment, the coverage ratios may be termed at lease minimally adequate.

Further, if the analyst feels that future earnings will be sufficient to service additional long-term debt, preferred stock, or financial lease arrangements, the firm's long-run financial condition can be termed sound. Such a condition not only implies that all investors are involved in an essentially risk-free venture but also indicates that the firm possesses reserve borrowing power to see it through periods of temporary financial stress. That is probably the best of all possible worlds when the analyst is (or represents) a potential long-term creditor.

Finally, when the firm's capital structure is completely made up of equity funds—the safest kind of capital structure from the standpoint of financial risk—managerial competence may be open to question, especially in light of the advantages to the owners of the use of a judicious degree of financial leverage. Such conservatism on the part of management should not be commended (or condemned, for that matter) until the reasons for the decision to eschew debt have been ascertained. At one extreme, management may indeed be conservative in relation to financial risk; at the other extreme, it may be planning a large expansion program and preparing to load the firm's capital structure all at one time with all the debt it can support.

Analysis of a firm's long-term financial strength must thus take full account both of the firm's present operating environment and of its management's future plans.

Summary

The major task of this chapter has been to describe the ways in which the long-term financial strength of a business firm may be tested. The discussions have included brief descriptions of the major components of capital structure—equity, debt, and leases—and thorough analyses of financial leverage and of the various earnings and cash flow coverage ratios.

Financial leverage—using debt, preferred stock, and leases to boost rates of return on equity over returns available on assets—was shown to be favorable when earnings increase and unfavorable when earnings decline. Consequently, although leverage may be used to increase stockholder returns, it is used at the risk of increasing losses if the firm's sales decline.

The earnings and cash flow coverage ratios present an alternative method of examining the effects of using a leveraged capital structure. The ratios enable the financial statement analyst to test the firm's ability to meet its fixed financial commitments (both contractual and to the owners) out of funds provided from current operations. The ratios are more properly used to test pro forma financial strength, however, because of the dynamic nature of all the variables that enter the coverage ratios.

Questions

17-1. Define capital structure. What is its function in the context of the going concern?

17-2. How do the equity bases of partnerships and proprietorships differ from the equity base of the corporation?

17-3. What account or accounts measure the growth in the equity contribution of the firm's owners in a corporation's balance sheet?

17-4. How does dividend policy affect corporate growth?

17-5.   Explain why preferred stock is considered debt by the common stockholders and management.

17-6.   What are the principal differences between short- and long-term debt?

17-7.   Why must leasing an asset be considered an alternative to financing its purchase by borrowing?

17-8.   Define operating lease and financial lease. Which appears in the body of the lessee's balance sheet as a financial obligation?

17-9.   What is financial leverage? How is the degree of financial leverage calculated?

17-10. What characteristics must a business firm possess if it is to avoid the risks associated with acquiring a high degree of financial leverage? Explain.

17-11. Briefly explain the two adjustments an analyst must make before he can estimate the impact of lease arrangements on the firm's capital structure.

17-12. List all the items included in the definition of fixed financial charges.

17-13. How are available earnings defined for use in coverage ratios?

17-14. What is the most significant defect of the coverage ratios? How may it be overcome?

17-15. What is the purpose of calculating the degree of financial leverage and the coverage of fixed financial charges?

Chapter 18

Module Five: Asset Utilization

This chapter is concerned with asset utilization, or the efficiency with which a firm uses its assets to produce a profit (or a return on invested capital). The primary measures we will examine are the so-called *turn-over ratios* as indicators of efficient asset utilization, *gross* and *net profit margins,* and, more important, the *return on investment* (ROI), which combines the turnover and profit margin concepts into a single performance measure. In addition, we will reexamine the ways in which operating and financial leverage influence decisions on asset utilization and illustrate their combined effects on the firm's overall profitability. First, however, let us examine the importance of the analysis of asset utilization to the owners and creditors of a business firm.

Importance of Resource Management

The business financial manager's primary concern is to plan the efficient use of the funds the firm acquires from its owners and its creditors. The firm's major objective, of course, is to build maximum sustainable values for the ownership claims (that is, to maximize stockholder wealth); however, to do so, the management must invest all the funds at its disposal in that combination of earning assets that will achieve the highest possible returns in relation to the scale of resources (or funds) used to produce them. In other words, management attempts at all times to maximize the firm's *return on investment.*

The implications of measuring and analyzing the efficiency with which management employs the firm's resources are thus clearly established with respect to the owners of the firm; the objective of maximizing the ROI recognizes that the stockholders are relying on the firm's resources being efficiently managed to produce a constant increase in the value of their personal financial investment in its shares. Relating the firm's net income to its invested capital allows the owner-analyst to compare the performance of his investment in that business with the returns available from alternative financial ventures subject to a similar degree of risk.

The firm's intermediate- and long-term creditors are also interested in its ability to produce adequate returns on invested capital through skillful asset management. Since the contractual periodic interest payments and the ultimate repayment of the principal of the firm's outstanding debt depend on the firm's ability to generate profits over an extended period, intermediate- and long-term creditors are interested in its ability to employ *new* funds profitably. That is, to be judged credit-worthy by participants in the capital market, a firm must demonstrate that it is able to earn a sufficient return on newly acquired assets to cover the costs of the capital those assets consume, including the provision of a reasonable return to the owners. If profits are expected to grow apace or ahead of the firm's asset growth, debt service coverage is also likely to increase and thereby reduce the riskiness of lending large amounts of money to the firm for extended periods.

Finally, short-term creditors (bankers and suppliers, for example) rely heavily for the ultimate satisfaction of their claims on the firm's ability to maintain its status as a going concern. A major factor in the firm's continued operation is the level of efficiency it achieves in managing its assets. As long as the firm remains financially viable—that is, as long as its assets remain sufficiently productive to enable it to meet all its financial obligations—short-term creditors need not become unduly alarmed by minor delays in the repayment of their claims.

Assessing the strength and productivity of the firm's assets is therefore important for all who supply funds to the business. The ROI as a measure of overall efficiency of asset utilization and individual asset turnover ratios as measures of efficiency of use of specific kinds of assets reflect on the quality of management and, because asset structure and operating efficiency are basically long-run concepts, on the future prospects of the firm as well.

Turnover Ratios

Chapter 8 introduced three turnover ratios: accounts receivable turnover, inventory turnover, and operating asset turnover. They are calculated as follows:

$$\text{accounts receivable turnover} = \frac{\text{credit sales}}{\text{average accounts receivable}}$$

$$\text{inventory turnover} = \frac{\text{cost of goods sold}}{\text{average inventory}}$$

$$\text{operating asset turnover} = \frac{\text{net sales}}{\text{operating assets}}$$

Some analysts add two other turnover ratios to that list: fixed asset turnover and working capital (or current asset) turnover. These are calculated as follows:

$$\text{fixed asset turnover} = \frac{\text{net sales}}{\text{net fixed assets}}$$

$$\text{working capital turnover} = \frac{\text{net sales}}{\text{current assets}}$$

The turnover ratios are occasionally referred to as *efficiency* or *activity* ratios, since some measure the rate at which (or the efficiency with which) the assets are being converted into other asset forms (i.e., receivables, inventory, and working capital turnover) and others measure the assets' ability to sustain or support the sales activity of the firm (i.e., the operating and fixed asset turnover ratios). Each ratio, when subjected to intertemporal and interfirm analysis, provides the financial statement analyst with significant insight into the efficiency with which a particular aspect of the firm is being managed.

To illustrate, we will examine the data in the balance sheet and income statement of Webster and Company, Incorporated, presented in Tables 18-1 and 18-2. The firm manufactures plastic containers, which it sells to local dairies and to several local chemical manufacturers. Webster was organized in 1976 and, mainly because of its limited production facilities, has experienced almost no growth in sales since January 1977. The firm's average turnover ratios are almost equal to its year-end ratios since its asset values have remained virtually constant. The values of the five turnover ratios for Webster and Company are compared with those of the industry in Table 18-3.

RECEIVABLES TURNOVER

Webster's accounts receivable turnover is equal to $59,315/$10,924, or 5.4 times per year. Its credit terms are net 60 days; that is, the receivables ideally should be turned (collected) 6 times per year. Since the actual turnover is below the ideal standard, Webster has, in effect, excessive cash invested in its accounts receivable. That overinvestment suggests that the firm's receivables management is less efficient than it should be (other things being equal, of course), and consequently the firm's overall efficiency tends to suffer.

The extent of the overinvestment in receivables is easy to measure. If we assume that the ideal standard of 6 times per year is both desirable and feasible, we can calculate the "ideal" investment in receivables by

Table 18-1

BALANCE SHEET
WEBSTER AND COMPANY, INCORPORATED
December 31, 1978

Assets		*Liabilities and Capital*	
Cash	$ 6,976	Notes payable, banks	$ 2,200
Marketable securities	2,100	Accounts payable	8,451
Accounts receivable (net)	10,924	Taxes payable	2,708
Inventories	10,796	Accrued expenses	335
Other current assets	110	Current portion of term loan	1,000
Total current assets	$30,906	Total current liabilities	$14,694
Fixed assets (net)	19,030	Term loan payable	4,000
Goodwill	3,500	Common stock	20,000
Long-term investments	2,603	Retained earnings	17,345
Total assets	$56,039	Total liabilities & capital	$56,039

Table 18-2

INCOME STATEMENT
WEBSTER AND COMPANY, INCORPORATED
for the Year Ended December 31, 1978

Sales		$59,315
Cost of goods sold		35,589
Gross profit		$23,726
Selling expenses	$6,125	
Administrative expenses	3,693	
Other operating expense	965	
Total operating expense		$10,783
Operating income		12,943
Interest expense		2,120
Nonoperating expense (income)		(1,485)
Income before taxes		$12,308
Income taxes		2,708
Net income		$ 9,600

dividing sales by the turnover of 6 times, which yields $9,886 ($59,315/6). Since 1978 year-end receivables figure of $10,924 is $1,038 greater than the ideal, Webster has over a thousand dollars in *nonproductive funds* tied up in accounts receivable.

This interpretation, as well as the interpretations we will suggest for the other turnover and the profit margin ratios to be discussed in this

Table 18-3

FIRM AND INDUSTRY AVERAGE TURNOVER RATIOS
WEBSTER AND COMPANY, INCORPORATED
Year-end 1978

Ratio	Webster and Co.	Industry Average
Accounts receivable turnover	5.4	6.1
Inventory turnover	3.3	9.0
Working capital turnover	1.9	3.0
Fixed asset turnover	3.1	2.7
Operating asset turnover	1.2	2.0

chapter, should be considered merely tentative conclusions, subject to modification if contradictory evidence arises from, say, another financial statement analysis module. These conclusions, therefore, should not be automatically applied to similar situations without careful analysis of the complete financial picture of the firm being studied.

INVENTORY TURNOVER

Webster's inventory turnover for 1978 is equal to $35,589/$10,796, or 3.3 times per year (or once in every 110 days). Unlike the receivables turnover, however, the inventory turnover has no *internal* standard that can serve as a convenient benchmark with which actual turnover can be compared. Historical standards are inappropriate because the firm is new; the financial statement analyst must therefore use an industry average or a ratio computed from the statements of another similar firm. Alternatively, if the analyst is familiar with the production process or is able to inspect the firm's facilities, he may be able to form some independent judgment regarding the appropriate size of the inventory in relation to the firm's sales volume.

In this case, the industry's average inventory turnover ratio for firms of similar size is 9 times per year. During his visit to Webster's factory, the analyst saw what he considered a very large number of plastic bottles apparently awaiting shipment. Both facts suggest that Webster's inventory management is somewhat inefficient. Whether the analyst will accept the industry average turnover of 9 times per year as an "ideal" standard for Webster will depend on a judgment based on external comparison and his discussions with management about how it is managing the firm's production and inventories. Assuming that he accepts 9 times as the proper standard, Webster's ideal inventory level should be $35,589/9, or $3,954—$6,842 less than the 1978 year-end level of $10,796. Here again, Webster has overinvested in inventory and consequently impaired its overall operational efficiency.

337

WORKING CAPITAL TURNOVER

Since we have already determined that the firm has overinvested in receivables and inventories by almost $8,000, the working capital turnover ratio should do little more than confirm the fact. If, however, Webster is also holding excessive cash balances, the working capital turnover ratio will reveal that as well.

The firm's ratio for 1978 is equal to $59,315/$30,906, or 1.9 times per year; the industry average ratio is 3.0 times per year. Using the industry average as an ideal standard (a somewhat dangerous practice under most circumstances, as mentioned frequently in earlier chapters), we find that the firm's "ideal level" of current assets should be $19,772 ($59,319/3), or $11,134 lower than the 1978 balance sheet figure. Since we have determined that the firm's investment in receivables and inventories is about $8,000 more than is required for efficient operation, it would appear that the firm is carrying, in addition, $3,000 in excess cash balances (that is, $11,000−$8,000, using rounded figures).

If the industry average ratio of 3.0 times per year is an appropriate standard by which to judge Webster's performance, the implications of this analysis are that Webster's management is wasting funds by carrying an excessive amount of current assets in relation to its sales revenues. Further, if the firm could increase its efficiency, funds would be released that could be used to purchase additional productive capacity and increase sales and profits, all without having to increase liabilities or capital funds.

FIXED ASSET TURNOVER

Like the preceding turnover ratios, fixed asset turnover permits the analyst to assess how efficiently the firm is using its assets to produce sales revenues; in this case, however, the ratio relates to the firm's fixed assets. Other things being equal, a high ratio is preferred to a low one.

Webster and Company's fixed asset turnover ratio for 1978 is $59,315/$19,030, or 3.1 times per year. Since fairly elaborate and expensive equipment is required to produce the plastic bottles, Webster's ratio compares favorably with that of the trade, which for 1978 is 2.7 times per year. Of course, the financial statement analyst should look into the ratio in detail to determine what is responsible for Webster's good showing in this area. For example, differences in depreciation methods, the age of the assets (Webster may have purchased second-hand equipment), and the existence of leased assets may destroy the usefulness of comparing this ratio with those of other firms in the trade. But assuming that the trade comparison is appropriate, we must conclude that the firm is managing its plant and equipment rather efficiently in generating sales.

OPERATING ASSET TURNOVER

The last turnover ratio we will examine is the operating asset turnover, which employs as the denominator the total value of only those assets used in the operation of the business. Excluded are "nonproductive" assets, such as intangibles, facilities under construction, and investments unrelated to the production of sales revenues. The ratio for Webster is calculated using total assets less goodwill and long-term investments (\$56,039−\$3,500−\$2,603=\$49,936); its value is \$59,315/\$49,936, or 1.2 times per year, which does not compare favorably with the industry average of 2.0 times per year. This result is to be expected since Webster is carrying an excessive investment in current assets that overrides the success the firm has achieved in using its fixed assets.

USING THE TURNOVER RATIOS

The turnover ratios, in the order presented here, measure the activity of the firm (that is, its sales) as it relates to progressively larger segments of the firm's assets. They permit the analyst to examine the efficiency with which management is employing the firm's assets in generating sales revenues and to reach conclusions concerning management's competence in those areas to which the several ratios relate.

However, like the conclusions suggested by any single ratio or group of ratios, the conclusions drawn by the analyst from evidence supplied by the turnover ratios must remain tentative until the facts behind the ratios are fully investigated and all information obtained is integrated into the complete financial statement analysis. The ratios should be used, therefore, only to help the analyst either to uncover areas in which the firm may be weak or to confirm or disprove evidence obtained through other means relating to asset utilization. This point cannot be emphasized too strongly.

A major deficiency in the turnover ratios is that they measure only the efficiency of the firm in producing sales revenues. To obtain a complete picture of the firm's asset utilization, the analyst must also measure (1) the efficiency with which sales revenues are converted into profits, (2) the relation of profits to the total resources used to produce them, and (3) the impact that the firm's capital structure has on its overall profitability. Analytical approaches to the measurement of the firm's performance in each of those areas are discussed in the following sections.

Profit Margins

A firm's ability to generate profits has long been held the ultimate measure of performance. The importance of profits to the firm's owners and creditors and to its ability to grow and prosper is well documented.

However, for financial statement analysis, the dollar figure found at the bottom of the income statement—the "bottom line"—carries only a limited amount of useful information. To determine whether or not the firm's net income is "sufficiently large," the analyst obviously must relate that figure to one or more other figures taken from the financial statements. He will then be able to judge, for example, whether profits are sufficiently large in *relation* to sales.

The analyst may use three ratios to measure the efficiency with which a firm's management is able to convert sales revenues into profits: the gross profit margin, the operating ratio, and the net profit margin. Each is an *indirect* measure of asset utilization, since the firm's assets (and the efficiency with which they are employed) generally determine the rate and volume of production and establish the patterns in which costs are incurred. Of course, the efficiency of the firm's work force also affects its profitability; consequently the profit margin ratios should be thought of as measures of *overall* efficiency. Let us illustrate the computation and use of those ratios by using the Webster and Company data presented in Table 18-2. A comparison of Webster's 1978 profit margins with those of the industry is contained in Table 18-4.

GROSS PROFIT MARGIN

The gross profit margin is the ratio of gross profit to sales; Webster and Company's gross profit margin is $23,726/$59,315, or 40 percent. In other words, 60 percent of Webster's 1978 sales revenues was consumed by the cost of goods sold. That figure may be compared with the firm's past performance or an industry standard. In this case, the industry ratio is 33 percent, which appears to reflect favorably on Webster's performance.

Of the three profit margin ratios, the gross profit margin provides the most direct measure of a firm's asset utilization—especially for manufacturing firms—because the firm's assets are used primarily in the produc-

Table 18-4

**FIRM AND INDUSTRY AVERAGE PROFIT MARGINS
WEBSTER AND COMPANY, INCORPORATED
Year Ending December 31, 1978**

Ratio	Webster and Co.	Industry Average
Gross profit margin	40.0%	33.0%
Operating ratio	78.2	73.0
Net profit margin:		
before taxes	20.8	19.8
after taxes	16.2	11.1

tion of the goods it offers for sale. The more efficient the production process and the use of the assets involved therein, the higher the gross profit margin will be.

OPERATING RATIO

The operating ratio, as we saw in Chapter 8, is calculated by dividing total operating expenses, including cost of goods sold, by net sales. It measures the percentage of each sales dollar that is consumed by the firm's operations. Nonoperating income and expense are excluded from the ratio; since they play no role in generating sales revenue, they cannot be used in measuring efficiency of *operations*.

Webster's operating ratio is $46,372/$59,315, or 78.2 percent, indicating that 78.2 cents of each dollar of sales were spent on operations. Alternatively, it means that the firm realized 21.8 cents ($1.00−$.782) of operating profit from each sales dollar. When Webster's operating ratio of 78.2 percent is compared with the industry average of 73 percent, the firm's operations appear to be somewhat less efficient; while its cost of goods sold (as measured by the gross profit margin) appears to be well controlled, its selling, general, and administrative expenses are out of line with industry averages.

NET PROFIT MARGIN

Net profit margin can be measured either before or after taxes. As mentioned in Chapter 8, the before-tax figure is often considered a better measure of the firm's profit performance since management has little or no control over the rate at which profits are taxed. On the other hand, management has the opportunity to lower the firm's tax liability by selecting from among several alternative accounting conventions relating to the management of its assets and operating expenses (see Chapter 3); consequently, taxes can be "managed," though usually only marginally.

On an after-tax basis, Webster's net profit margin is $9,600/$59,315, or 16.2 percent; before taxes it is $12,308/$59,315, or 20.8 percent. The industry averages are 11.1 percent and 19.8 percent respectively, indicating, first, that Webster's nonoperating expenses are significantly lower than those of the average firm in the industry. The following comparison suggests that Webster's ratio of nonoperating expenses to sales is 6.2 percentage points lower than the industry's.

	Webster	*Industry Average*	*Difference*
Operating profits/sales	21.8%	27.0%	5.2%
Less net profit margin before taxes	20.8	19.8	−1.0
Nonoperating expense/sales	1.0%	7.2%	6.2%

Figure 18-1

RETURN ON INVESTMENT (ROI) MEASURED BY THE DUPONT SYSTEM OF FINANCIAL ANALYSIS

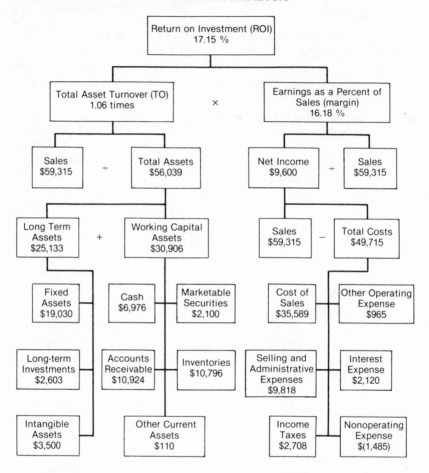

Second, the net profit margin on an after-tax basis (16.2 percent for Webster compared with 11.1 percent for the industry) is probably influenced by the fact that Webster is among the smallest firms in the industry, or at least its dollar profits are among the smallest. Its effective tax rate, calculated by the formula [1 − (net profit margin after taxes/net profit margin before taxes)], is 1 − (.162/.208) = 1− .78, or 22 percent. The industry's average marginal tax rate is 1 − (.111/.198) = 1 − .56, or 44 percent, twice that of Webster. That fact places Webster's net profit margin in a very favorable light when compared with industry averages, perhaps unfairly so.

Return on Investment

The turnover ratios measure the efficiency with which the firm uses its assets to produce sales revenues; profit margins measure the efficiency with which the firm converts those sales revenues into profits; together, the turnover and profit margin ratios measure the total efficiency with which the firm is operated. A popular method of combining those two measures to produce a single performance measure—return on investment (ROI)—is the *duPont System of Financial Analysis.*

The application of the duPont system to Webster and Company's 1978 operations is illustrated in Figure 18-1. The left side of the figure develops the total asset turnover ratio for Webster; it shows how working capital assets (cash, marketable securities, accounts receivable, inventories, and other current assets), when added to long-term assets (fixed assets, investments, and intangible assets), equal total assets. And when sales are divided by total assets, the result is the total asset turnover ratio.

Total assets, rather than operating assets, are used in this system because the firm's management is given the authority and responsibility for deciding on where to invest *all* the funds the owners and creditors have provided to the firm. If management chooses to invest those funds in assets that yield no return, it should be held accountable for that decision. Thus the profitability of *total* assets is a better measure of performance than others that exclude assets from the investment base merely because they are not productively employed.

The right side of Figure 18-1 develops the net profit margin on sales. The figure uses net profits after taxes, although in many instances a strong case can be made for using before-tax profits. It summarizes the total operating and nonoperating expenses and produces the net profit margin as the ratio of net income to sales.

The figure represents the firm's ROI as the product of two components:

$$\text{TURNOVER} \times \text{MARGIN} = \text{ROI}$$

$$\frac{\text{Sales}}{\text{Total Assets}} \times \frac{\text{Profit}}{\text{Sales}} = \frac{\text{Profit}}{\text{Total Assets}}$$

$$1.06 \quad \times \quad 16.18 \quad = \quad 17.15$$

By looking at ROI in this way, the analyst can quickly pinpoint the principal areas in which the firm's performance has either improved or deteriorated over time or in relation to similar firms. For example, Webster's ROI, which was 17.15 percent in 1978, compares favorably with the industry average ROI of 16.65, as calculated by the formula

$$\text{Turnover} \times \text{Margin} = \text{ROI}$$

$$1.5 \quad \times \quad 11.1 \quad = 16.65$$

When the components of the ROI for Webster and the industry are compared, we find that Webster's 1978 turnover is lower than the industry's but its margin is higher. The analyst, starting from this point, should pursue the analysis downward through both sides of Figure 18-1 to determine the underlying causes for the relatively poor asset turnover (and high net profit margin). These analyses, illustrated in the earlier discussions of turnover ratios and profit margins, suggest that Webster's investment in current assets is too large and its margin is being artificially maintained at a high level because of its relatively low tax rate. Consequently, we must conclude that Webster and Company is among the less efficient firms in its industry, despite maintaining comparatively superior control over its cost of goods sold. If it can improve its turnover of inventories and receivables and reduce its operating expenses, its overall financial performance, as measured by the duPont system, will achieve a superior rating. That, however, may be a rather large order.

Effects of Leverage on Asset Utilization

An important aspect of asset utilization not accounted for directly by the duPont System of Financial Analysis is the effect of leverage—both operating and financial—on the firm's overall performance. Chapter 16 introduced and discussed the concept of operating leverage, and Chapter 17 presented financial leverage. In this section we will see how operating and financial leverage influence the firm's overall performance both individually and in concert.

OPERATING LEVERAGE

An alternative algebraic expression to that given in Chapter 16 permits the calculation of the degree of operating leverage from the percentage changes in sales and operating earnings over a single year (or other period):

$$\text{degree of operating leverage} = \frac{\text{percentage change in operating income}}{\text{percentage changes in sales}} = \frac{\Delta OI}{\Delta Sales}$$

Note that this ratio and the operating ratio measure two similar aspects of efficiency. The operating ratio, calculated by dividing *operating expenses* by *sales* for a given period, measures the percentage of each sales dollar that is consumed by operating expenses during the period. The degree of operating leverage measures the *change in operating earnings* in relation to the *change in sales* from one period to the next.

Although both measure operating efficiency, the degree of operating leverage is a more direct measure in that it shows the profitability of the incremental sales dollar.

To illustrate, let us return to the Webster and Company example. Table 18-5 summarizes the firm's income statements for the years 1977 and 1978 and shows the percentage change for each of the accounts over the period. By substituting the appropriate figures from the table into the preceding equation, we find that

$$\text{degree of operating leverage} = \frac{\Delta OI}{\Delta Sales} = \frac{16.0}{2.0} = 8.0$$

Thus, for every 1 percent increase in sales, Webster can expect an 8 percent increase in operating income. Moreover, from the percentage change column in Table 18-5, we can see that most of the increase in operating income is accounted for by the firm's increase in gross profit (12.5 percent); therefore, its operating efficiency is being enhanced through operating leverage supplied largely by the fixed costs inherent in its production process (e.g., depreciation expense).

Table 18-5

COMPARATIVE SUMMARY INCOME STATEMENT
WEBSTER AND COMPANY, INCORPORATED
for the Years Ended December 31, 1977 and 1978

	1977	*1978*	*% change*
Net sales	$58,152	$59,315	2.0%
Gross profit	21,090	23,726	12.5
Operating income	11,158	12,943	16.0
Earnings before interest and taxes	12,438	14,428	16.0
Interest expense	2,120	2,120	—
Earnings before taxes	10,318	12,308	19.3
Earnings available for common stock	8,048	9,600	19.3

FINANCIAL LEVERAGE

When a firm employs debt in its capital structure, it is able to take advantage of the effects of financial leverage. As explained in Chapter 17, the fixed interest payments associated with debt supply the leverage that permits the firm to increase or decrease its earnings available for common stock by a percentage greater than the percentage increase or decrease in its earnings before interest and taxes (EBIT). In algebraic terms, degree of financial leverage

$$= \frac{\text{percentage change in earnings available for common stock}}{\text{percentage change in earnings before interest and taxes}}$$

$$= \frac{\Delta EAC}{\Delta EBIT}$$

Webster and Company's degree of financial leverage, using the figures from Table 18-5, is

$$\text{degree of financial leverage} = \frac{\Delta EAC}{\Delta EBIT} = \frac{19.3}{16.0} = 1.2$$

For every 1 percent increase in EBIT, Webster can expect a 1.2 percent increase in EAC.

Note that Webster's nonoperating earnings remained constant for the two years (that is, the percentage increases in its operating income and EBIT are the same). That situation is not unusual among business firms, whose nonoperating earnings and expenses (other than interest expense) often are nonexistent, of nominal dollar amounts, or fairly constant over time. Consequently, the degree of financial leverage can often be calculated using the percentage change in either operating income or EBIT.

The degree of financial leverage does not measure efficiency in the use of *assets*, but it often has a very great impact on net income and therefore on the overall performance measure, ROI. Since it is important that the analyst be able to distinguish between the effect of asset utilization and the effect of financial leverage on the firm's performance measures, the measurement of the degree of financial leverage becomes an important tool of financial statement analysis.

COMBINED EFFECTS OF OPERATING AND FINANCIAL LEVERAGE

The *margin* in the duPont System was defined earlier as

$$\frac{\text{profits}}{\text{sales}}$$

which measures the efficiency with which management converts current sales into profits. The discussions of operating and financial leverage have demonstrated how *changes* in earnings are influenced by changes in sales and the existence of fixed operating and financial charges. When these measures are combined, we obtain an overall measure of leverage that relates directly to the profit margin ratio. Thus degree of total leverage

= degree of operating leverage × degree of financial leverage

$$= \frac{\Delta OI}{\Delta Sales} \times \frac{\Delta EAC}{\Delta EBIT}$$

If, as in most cases, ΔOI is approximately equal to $\Delta EBIT$, then

$$\text{degree of total leverage} = \frac{\Delta EBIT}{\Delta Sales} \times \frac{\Delta EAC}{\Delta EBIT}$$

$$= \frac{\Delta EAC}{\Delta Sales}$$

This ratio will permit the financial statement analyst to predict how changes in the firm's sales will influence its profit margin and hence its ROI.

For example, Webster's operating and financial leverage were found to be 8.0 and 1.2 respectively; the firm's degree of total leverage is therefore 8.0 × 1.2, or 9.6. For every 1 percent change in sales, the firm can expect its profits (earnings available for common stock) to change by 9.6 percent. If we assume that Webster's total asset turnover will remain constant at 1.06 during 1979 but its sales will increase by 2 percent, its profits will increase by 2 percent times 9.6 (the degree of total leverage), or 19.2 percent. Webster's margin for 1979 may be calculated as follows (given that the 1978 margin was 16.18 percent):

$$\text{1979 margin} = \frac{\text{1979 profits}}{\text{1979 sales}} = \frac{16.8\% \times (1 + .192)}{100\% \times (1 + .02)}$$

$$= \frac{16.18\% \times 1.192}{100\% \times 1.02} = \frac{19.29\%}{102\%} = 18.91$$

The firm's ROI for 1979 will be

ROI = turnover × margin = 1.06 × 18.91 = 20.04,

which is almost a 3 percentage point increase over the 1978 ROI.

Finally, to illustrate that leverage is indeed a "two-edged sword," as many have characterized it, Webster's margin and ROI for 1979 with a 2 percent *decrease* in sales will be:

$$\text{1979 margin} = \frac{\text{1979 profits}}{\text{1979 sales}} = \frac{16.18\% \times (1 - .192)}{100\% \times (1 - .02)}$$

$$= \frac{16.18\% \times .808}{100\% \times .98} = \frac{13.07\%}{98} = 13.34$$

and

$$\text{ROI} = \text{turnover} \times \text{margin} = 1.06 \times 13.34 = 14.14$$

Thus Webster, or any other firm, will find that its ROI will be affected by the degree of operating and financial leverage it employs. More important, however, the approaches to measuring the effects of leverage discussed in this section will permit the financial statement analyst to examine the firm's efficiency of asset utilization separately from the influences of its capital structure. In the Webster illustration, operating leverage is by far the more important factor in the firm's total leverage (8.0 as compared with the degree of financial leverage of only 1.2). As a result, when the firm's ROI increases, most of the increase can be attributed to efficiencies in the use of assets (and other nonfinancial factors of production) rather than to the uses of borrowed funds.

Summary

The efficiency with which a firm employs its assets is an important consideration for many financial statement analysts. The measures generally employed in judging the firm's efficiency are the several turnover ratios—including receivables, inventory, working capital, fixed asset, and operating asset turnovers. Taken individually and as a group, the turnover ratios measure how efficiently the firm's assets are being employed to generate sales revenues.

To measure the firm's efficiency in converting sales into profits, financial statement analysts often rely on the profit margin ratios, including the gross profit margin, operating ratio, and net profit margin.

A useful framework for analyzing the firm's overall performance is the duPont System of Financial Analysis. That system, coupled with measures of the effects of operating and financial leverage on the firm's overall profitability, provides a complete picture of how well a firm employs its assets and capital structure to produce sales and convert those sales into net profits.

Questions

18-1. Which group is most concerned with efficient asset utilization by a firm—its stockholders, long-term creditors, or short-term creditors? Explain.

18-2. List the five basic turnover ratios. What does each measure?

18-3. What information must be used to supplement the turnover ratios when examining asset utilization?

18-4. List the three ratios generally used to measure the efficiency with which sales are converted into profits. Why are they termed indirect measures of asset utilization?

18-5. Explain the basis for the duPont System of Financial Analysis.

18-6. What does the degree of operating leverage measure? What does the degree of financial leverage measure?

18-7. How is the degree of total leverage related to the margin in the duPont System of Financial Analysis?

Bibliography
Index

Bibliography

Some of the following materials are available on loan from the American Bankers Association library.

GENERAL ACCOUNTING

Accounting Trends and Techniques. New York, American Institute of Certified Public Accountants, annual.

"An annual cumulative survey of the accounting aspects of the annual reports of 600 industrial and commercial corporations to which are added excerpts from, and comments upon, unusual accounting treatments."

American Bankers Association. *Accounting Principles and Applications,* Parts I and II, 3rd ed. Washington, D.C., ABA, 1974.

Part I, the basic text, covers, among other topics, the analysis of transactions, the accounting cycle, payables and receivables, and valuation of other assets. Part II builds on the foundation developed in Part I.

Andersen, Arthur & Co. *The Public Interest in Public Accounting.* Chicago, 1977.

Contains comments on the issues and problems of current interest as well as the future of accounting. Topics covered include professional functions and relations with clients, accounting standards, auditing standards, and ethical standards and performance.

Briloff, Abraham J. *More Debits Than Credits; the Burnt Investor's Guide to Financial Statements.* New York, Harper and Row, 1976.

Geared toward the nonaccountant, the author uses examples of corporate nonaccountability to instruct the reader in corporate accounting.

Davidson, Sidney, and Weil, Roman. *Handbook of Modern Accounting,* 2nd ed. New York, McGraw-Hill, 1977.

Designed to help both the accountant and the receivers of accounting information. Provides a simple but comprehensive explanation of the meaning of accounting terms and of financial statements.

Edwards, James Don, and Black, Homer A., eds. *The Modern Accountant's Handbook.* Homewood, Ill., Dow Jones-Irwin, 1976.

A "one-volume, up-to-date compendium of current knowledge on accounting policies."

Kohler, Eric L. *A Dictionary For Accountants,* 5th ed. Englewood Cliffs, N.J., Prentice-Hall, 1975.

Lurie, Adolph G. *Working with the Public Accountant; a Guide for Managers at All Levels.* New York, McGraw-Hill, 1977.

Directed toward managerial personnel, this book discusses the function of the accountant and the auditor in layman's language.

Novak, Stephen R. *Accounting Desk Book,* 5th ed. Englewood Cliffs, N.J., Institute for Business Planning, 1977.

A reference tool for financial accounting and reporting standards and principles.

Wixon, Rufus, ed. *Accountants' Handbook,* 5th ed. New York, Ronald Press, 1970.

INTERNATIONAL ACCOUNTING

Rueschhoff, Norlin G. *International Accounting and Financial Reporting.* New York, Praeger, 1976.

Serves as an introduction to international accounting. Major topics covered include accounting for international activities, multinational enterprise accounting control, comparative international accounting principles, and international financial reporting to investors.

ANALYZING FINANCIAL STATEMENTS

American Bankers Association. *Financial Statement Analysis.* Washington, D.C., ABA, 1976.

Investigates lending officer fundamentals used to analyze a borrower's financial statement.

Boyer, Patricia A., and Gibson, Charles H. *Financial Statement Analysis.* Boston, CBI, 1978.

Written for the layman with only a basic understanding of accounting, this text covers definitions and descriptions of basic accounts, summaries, and an analysis of FASB and SEC pronouncements.

Coit, David M. "Automated Financial Analysis: A New Tool for Commercial Lending," *Journal of Commercial Bank Lending,* March 1977, pp. 43–53.
Describes how computers can aid commercial lenders in pricing loans, monitoring a company's performance, recognizing bad credits, and ultimately reducing the loan loss account.

Dearden, John, and Shank, John. *Financial Accounting and Reporting; A Contemporary Emphasis.* Englewood Cliffs, N.J., Prentice-Hall, 1975.
Discusses the preparation of the basic financial statement, with emphasis on the interpretation of the statement, from the point of view of the person preparing it, then reviews the published financial report from the point of view of the outsider who reads the published statement.

Graham, Benjamin, and McGolrick, Charles. *The Interpretation of Financial Statements.* New York, Harper and Row, 1975.
A basic work on interpreting corporation balance sheets and income accounts for those involved in analyzing financial statements.

Helfert, Erich A. *Techniques of Financial Analysis,* 4th ed. Homewood, Ill., Richard D. Irwin, 1977.
This guide covers such topics as funds flow analysis, ratio analysis, cash budgets, break-even analysis, and basic capital expenditure analysis.

Ketchum, John A. *A Lender's Approach to the Analysis of a Bank Holding Company.* New Brunswick, N.J., Stonier Graduate School of Banking, 1976.
This analysis of lender considerations includes how to analyze the financial statements of the bank, the parent holding company, and the subsidiaries. Includes a general discussion of bank holding company financing.

Kristy, James E. *Analyzing Financial Statements: Quick and Clean.* Buena Park, Cal., Books on Business, 1977.
Covers ratio analysis, collateral and guarantees, cash flow analysis, and the delta-flow statement in 22 pages of text and illustrations.

Lev, Baruch. *Financial Statement Analysis: A New Approach.* Englewood Cliffs, N.J., Prentice-Hall, 1977.
The book's major purpose is to bridge the gap "between traditional

financial statement analysis and modern economic and finance theories." Geared toward financial analysts, accountants, researchers in finance and accounting, and students.

Merrill Lynch, Pierce, Fenner & Smith. *How to Read a Financial Report.* New York, 1973.

A basic "how to" approach to understanding corporate reports.

O'Malia, Thomas J. *Banker's Guide to Financial Statements.* Boston, Bankers Publishing Co., 1976.

Covers five major subject areas: the statements, the mechanics of analyzing, the meaning and use of ratios, the source and application of funds, and case studies.

Perry, James E. "Analyzing the Borrower's Situation," *Banking,* June 1977, pp. 118–120.

Discusses an alternative financial statement that reflects net cash flow.

Scott, George M., and Ward, Bart H. "The Internal Audit—a Tool for Management Control," *Financial Executive,* March 1978, pp. 32–37.

Provides a framework for the audit staff and for corporation management.

FINANCIAL REPORTING

Duff & Phelps, Inc. *A Management Guide to Better Financial Reporting.* Chicago, Arthur Andersen & Co., 1976.

Describes ideas to strengthen annual and quarterly reports to shareholders, evaluates the reports, and covers current accounting issues.

Ernst & Ernst. *Financial Reporting Trends: Banking 1977.* Cleveland, 1977.

"A survey of banking industry reporting practices as disclosed in the published annual reports and filings with the Securities and Exchange Commission."

Levers, Herbert H., and Winsten, Irwin. "How Credible is That Financial Statement?" *Credit and Financial Management,* August 1977, pp. 14–15+.

Covers the role of the accountant who prepares the financial statement, the difference between an audited and an unaudited statement, and the amount of credibility that can be given to a company's statement.

Peat, Marwick, Mitchell & Co. *Principles and Presentation: Banking.* New York, 1977.

The seventh annual edition, which presents the results of a study of financial reporting practices and accounting principles used by domestic banking organizations in the preparation of their annual reports.

AUDITING

Albrecht, William Steve. "Toward Better and More Efficient Audits," *Journal of Accountancy,* December 1977, p. 48.

Discusses how improved audit methods can help keep audit fees down.

American Institute of Certified Public Accountants. Industry Audit Guides. New York, AICPA, 1973.

Guides in series include: *Audits of Investment Companies, Audits of Savings and Loan Associations,* and *Audits of Finance Companies.* Practical guides to examining financial statements of various types of financial companies.

American Institute of Certified Public Accountants. *Statement on Auditing Standards.* New York, AICPA, 1973.

A "codification of auditing standards and procedures" issued by the Committee on Auditing Procedures.

Bank Administration Institute. *Statement of Principles and Standards for Internal Auditing in the Banking Industry.* Park Ridge, Ill., 1977.

The standards provide a guide to evaluating audit performance.

Dwyer, John N. *Modern Bank Accounting and Auditing Forms.* Boston, Warren, Gorham, & Lamont, 1970.

Provides bank accountants and auditors with suggestions for, and assistance in, developing forms for use in their own institutions.

Fisher, Walter S. "Building a Better Audit Program," *Bank Administration,* August 1977, pp. 17–21.

Author describes four essential "building-blocks" of a good audit program: competent individuals; proper positioning of audit personnel in the bank; creation of a set of realistic auditing goals; and the formation of standards, programs, schedules, and reporting systems that will help achieve the goals.

Froehlich, Willard R. "Developing an Internal Audit Program," *Bank Administration,* February 1978, pp. 22–24.

Defines three main objectives for internal auditors and explains ways of accomplishing them.

Ingram, Robert W., and others. "Disclosure Practices in Unaudited Financial Statements of Small Business," *Journal of Accountancy,* August 1977, pp. 81–86.
This survey of the unaudited financial statements of a number of small businesses uncovers some inadequacies in current procedures.

Tinkham, Leo V., and Jones, Seymour. *The Banker's Guide to Audit Reports and Financial Statements.* New York, Coopers & Lybrand, 1975.
Includes an explanation for the banker of the auditor's function, his responsibility, and the standards and procedures he follows. Also explains significant aspects of the meaning of auditors' reports for the banker.

Vance, Lawrence, and Boutell, Wayne. *Principles of Auditing.* Hinsdale, Ill., Dryden Press, 1975.

Wendell, Paul J. *Modern Accounting and Auditing Checklists.* Boston, Warren, Gorham, & Lamont, 1975.
The purpose of the book is to provide the accountant, auditor, and financial analyst with a collection of checklists that cover a variety of corporate and professional problems.

Willingham, John J., and Carmichael, D. R. *Auditing Concepts and Methods,* 2nd ed. New York, McGraw-Hill, 1975.
Provides a basic yet comprehesive framework of auditing with emphasis on concept rather than procedure.

PRICE-LEVEL ACCOUNTING

Chippindale, Warren, and Defliese, Philip L., eds. *Current Value Accounting; A Practical Guide for Business.* New York, AMACOM, 1977.
This text covers issues, alternatives, advantages, and problems of current value accounting and is geared toward the nonfinancial executive.

National Association of Accountants. *Managing Price-Level Accounting.* New York, 1975.

Revsine, Lawrence, and Thies, James B. "Price Level Adjusted Replacement Cost Data," *Journal of Accountancy,* May 1977, pp. 71–75.
Discusses "the impact of general price level adjustments superimposed on replacement cost financial statements."

Shank, John K. *Price Level Adjusted Statements and Management Decisions.* New York, Financial Executives Research Foundation, 1975.

COMMERCIAL CREDIT ANALYSIS

American Bankers Association. *A Banker's Guide to Commercial Loan Analysis.* Washington, D.C., ABA, 1977.
Covers all aspects of credit decision making from how to judge principals, to analysis of financial statements, to analysis of ability to generate cash.

Anderson, Gary G. "The Role of Economic Information in Commercial Lending Analysis," *Journal of Commercial Bank Lending,* December 1977, p. 30 +.
Discusses the information about a company that is relevant and suggests ways of using the economic information in connection with a specific loan applicant.

Feinstein, Richard L., and Leykum, Charles A. "Footnotes Tell the Story," *Credit and Financial Management,* August 1977, pp. 28–31.
Through the use of a fictitious example, the authors present important issues to be considered by the credit grantor.

Fox, Harold W. "A Dynamic Perspective for Credit Analysis," *Credit and Financial Management,* January 1977, pp. 30–31 +.
The author offers his views on applying the product life cycle concept to credit decisions.

Haskell, N. "What to Look for When Extending Credit to a New Business," *Credit and Financial Management,* September 1976, p. 33 +.
Details the experiences of First Boston Corporation, which segregated its new business accounts into a special department.

Houget, George R. "Techniques of Term Loan Analysis," *Journal of Commercial Bank Lending,* March 1975, pp. 30–36.
Looks at term lending from three perspectives: analyzing the borrower's credit-worthiness, structuring the credit, and pricing the loan.

Kreps, Clifton H., Jr., and Wacht, Richard F. *Credit Administration.* Washington, D.C., American Bankers Association, 1972.
Discusses factors influencing and determining loan policy based on time-tested lending principles and practices, as well as methods of credit investigation and analysis, credit techniques, and specific problems.

MacDonald, D. J. "Problem Loans: Their Prevention, Handling and Cures," *Journal of Commercial Bank Lending,* December 1977, pp. 54–64.

Discusses areas of concern in negotiating a loan, provides a checklist for appraising company operations, and offers procedures to be followed when the loan becomes a problem.

Orgler, Yair E. *Analytical Methods in Loan Evaluation.* Lexington, Mass., Lexington Books, 1975.

Redding, Harold T., and Knight, Guyon H., III. *The Dun and Bradstreet Handbook of Credits and Collections.* New York, T. Y. Crowell, 1974.

A handbook for the credit manager and business executive that covers, among other topics, credit investigation, the credit executive, specific credit systems, financial analysis, the Fair Credit Reporting Act, and setting credit limits.

Wantland, Calvin A. "How a Banker Evaluates a Credit Risk," *Credit and Financial Management,* September 1977, pp. 16–17.

Explains the role of three key factors in evaluating a credit risk: the prevailing economic climate, the management of the company, and the financial well-being of the company.

RATIO ANALYSIS

Kristy, James E. "New Techniques in Financial Statement Analysis," *Credit and Financial Management,* August 1977, p. 16.

Covers ratio analysis, credit scoring systems, and cash flow. The author outlines the ratios he finds most helpful in analyzing financial statements.

Melicher, Ronald W., and others. "Industry Concentration, Financial Structure and Profitability," *Financial Management,* Autumn 1976, pp. 48–53.

The authors examine equity rates of return in relation to their appropriate concentration ratios and financial leverage ratios by degree of industry concentration.

Miller, Donald E. *The Meaningful Interpretation of Financial Statements; The Cause and Effect Ratio Approach.* New York, American Management Association, 1972.

Geared toward providing basic financial information for the business manager so that he can make effective use of analytical techniques.

Monroe, John S. "A Look at 1975 Bank Performance Through Ratio Analysis," *Bank Administration,* August 1976, pp. 15–18. (For the "Top 50 Income Producing Banks 1976"—see October 1977 issue, p. 26.)

The author reviews those ratios he feels are essential to reviewing performance.

Sanyo, Richard. *Ratio Analysis for Small Business.* Washington, D.C., Small Business Administration, 1977.

Provides information on standard or typical ratios and on the evaluation and interpretion of ratios. Includes a case history.

Swift, John R. "Using Ratios in Analyzing a Commercial Finance Company," *Mid-Western Banker,* October 1976, p. 14 + .

Weston, Fred, and Brigham, Eugene. *Managerial Finance,* 5th ed. Hinsdale, Ill., Dryden Press, 1975.

A basic textbook on the subject of finance. See especially Chapter 2, "Ratio Analysis."

FINANCIAL FORECASTING

Evans, Michael K., and Norris, John F. "International Business and Forecasting," *Columbia Journal of World Business,* Winter 1976, pp. 28–35.

Discusses the Chase Econometrics International Model System of international economic forecasting.

Hennessy, J. H., Jr. *Financial Manager's Handbook.* Englewood Cliffs, N.J., Prentice-Hall, 1977.

See Chapter 3, "Achieving Corporate Objectives Through Efficient Financial Forecasting."

Lebell, Don, and Krasner, O. J. "Selecting Environmental Forecasting Techniques from Business Planning Requirements," *Academy of Management Review,* July 1977, pp. 373–383.

The authors discuss the selection of appropriate forecasting techniques.

Mandel, Joseph D., and Altschul, David E. "Financial Forecasts and Projections: A Pitfall for the Uninitiated Accountant," *Journal of Accountancy,* May 1977, p. 46 + .

The authors describe legal restrictions the accountant must be aware of in preparing and reviewing financial statements.

O'Malley, Charles A., III. "Financial Forecasting and the Credit Decision," *Journal of Commercial Bank Lending*, November 1977, pp. 42–48.

Identifies and discusses three key questions regarding financial forecasts: why ask for one? what do you do once you get it? and what confidence can you have in a forecast?

Van Horne, James C. *Fundamentals of Financial Management.* Englewood Cliffs, N.J., Prentice-Hall, 1977.

See especially Chapter 4, "Source and Use Statements and Financial Forecasting."

Wheelwright, Steven C., and Clarke, Darral G. "Corporate Forecasting: Promise and Reality," *Harvard Business Review*, November-December 1976, pp. 40–42 +.

Results of a survey on the status of forecasting in major U.S. corporations.

Wheelwright, Steven C., and Makridakis, Spyros. *Forecasting Methods for Management*, 2nd ed. New York, John Wiley and Sons, 1977.

A review of the various methods used in business forecasting and their application to problem solving and planning.

BUSINESS FINANCIAL MANAGEMENT

Brigham, Eugene F. *Financial Management.* Hinsdale, Ill., Dryden Press, 1977.

Donaldson, Elvin F., and others. *Corporate Finance,* 4th ed. New York, Ronald Press, 1975.

A basic textbook covering, among other topics, the role of the finance function in business, financial statement analysis, financial management practice, working capital management, and financing alternatives.

Hempel, George H., and Yawitz, Jess B. *Financial Management of Financial Institutions.* Englewood Cliffs, N.J., Prentice-Hall, 1977.

Emphasizes management of the assets and liabilities of major U.S. financial institutions.

Hennessy, J. H., Jr. *Financial Manager's Handbook.* Englewood Cliffs, N.J., Prentice-Hall, 1977.

Discusses 100 ideas for profit improvement for companies, regardless of size or product.

Kreps, Clifton H., Jr., and Wacht, Richard F. *Business Financial Management.* Washington, D.C., American Bankers Association, 1974.
A five-volume set that serves to acquaint the student with the principles of finance as applied to operations of a profit-seeking firm.

McConkey, Dale D., and Vander Weele, Ray. *Financial Management by Objectives.* Englewood Cliffs, N.J., Prentice-Hall, 1976.
Geared toward the manager or supervisor in finance, this text provides a financial management by objective checklist, then highlights each facet of the MBO system.

Soldofsky, Robert M., and Olive, Garnet D. *Financial Management.* Cincinnati, South-Western Publishing, 1974.
Emphasizes financial decision making and is geared toward the student who has little or no background in financial management.

Summers, Edward L. *Profits, Growth, and Planning; Techniques of Modern Financial Management.* Homewood, Ill., Dow Jones-Irwin, 1974.
Written to aid the reader in the use of accounting information for decision making and control. Also covers forecasts, planning capital investments, inventory management, and cost analysis.

Van Horne, James C. *Fundamentals of Financial Management.* Englewood Cliffs, N.J., Prentice-Hall, 1977.
Covers primarily the allocation of funds within a business enterprise and the raising of funds.

Zwick, Jack. *A Handbook of Small Business Finance.* Washington, D.C., Small Business Administration, 1975.
Describes the concepts and tools of financial analysis so that the small business manager can more easily interpret the financial data of his business.

COMMERCIAL BANK LENDING

American Bankers Association. *A Banker's Guide to Small Business Loans.* Washington, D.C., ABA, 1975.
Describes the how and why of small business loans. Covers the initial loan interview, the credit investigation, the credit decision, and closing the loan.

American Bankers Association. *Comprehensive Compliance Manual, Regulation B of the Equal Credit Opportunity Act.* Washington, D.C., ABA, 1977.

Provides an overview of Reg. B and how it pertains to all steps of the lending process from the application and interview to the questions on records retention.

American Bankers Association. *Loan Officer Development,* 2 vols. Washington, D.C., ABA, 1973.

A programmed training kit for the new loan officer. Topics covered include the loan interview, loan development decisions, loan documentation, and problem loans.

Belew, Richard C. *How to Negotiate a Business Loan.* New York, Van Nostrand Reinhold, 1973.

Outlines financial planning techniques for obtaining funds. For the business student, engineer, bank officer, and public accountant.

Fiorentini, Walter G. *Communicating Credit Judgement.* New Brunswick, N.J., Stonier Graduate School of Banking, 1975.

The author's main objective is to explore how an experienced loan officer can pass on his knowledge of the many factors involved in making a credit judgment to the trainee. Chapter II examines the basic elements of the teaching process from a theoretical standpoint and applies them to the credit training situation.

Grisanti, Frank. "Ten Ways to Improve the Handling of Problem Loans," *Banking,* December 1976, pp. 38–39.

Some of the ten ways mentioned include proper use of a problem loan committee, insisting on a thorough look at the company's viability, and monitoring the performance of the company closely.

Johnson, William B. "Regulation B as It Affects Business Credit," *Credit and Financial Management,* May 1977, pp. 12–14.

Summarizes the main sections of Reg. B and spells out certain sections where the business creditor is exempt.

Mueller, P. Henry. "The Most Challenging Issues Facing Bank Lending," *Journal of Commercial Bank Lending,* March 1977, pp. 16–24.

Focuses on the dos and don'ts of the lender's job.

Pace, E. A., and Collins, F. "Bankers-Accountants-Financial Statements: Their Relationship to Small Business Loan Decisions," *Journal of Small Business Management,* October 1976, pp. 16–22.

Written for the small businessman, this article discusses the type of information banks need from prospective borrowers. Especially concerned with the role of the financial statement and how a CPA can aid in its preparation.

U.S. Small Business Administration. *Bank/SBA Loans: A Partnership for Small Business Programs.* Washington, D.C., GPO, 1973.

A handbook for the banker who wants to participate in the SBA program, it describes all aspects of SBA lending from who may apply for a loan, to questions of loan administration, to SBA training programs and publications available. Includes sample forms.

Wells, John W. "Credit Training—A Systematic Approach," *Journal of Commercial Bank Lending,* February 1976, pp. 18–29.

The author details the experiences of Seattle-First Bank in setting up a training program for new personnel and practicing lending officers.

Zweibel, Joel B. "Work-Out Problems and Solutions," *Bankers Magazine,* Spring 1976, pp. 87–96.

Reviews several questions involved in various stages of the problem loan situation, from determining that the loan is a "problem loan," to whether to seek new or additional collateral and when to declare a default, to the lender-management relationship.

RETURN ON INVESTMENT

Boberski, Irving V. "Don't Strike Out on the Yield Curve," *Savings and Loan News,* October 1977, pp. 86–90.

The author suggests basing investment decisions on the concept of total return to improve portfolio performance.

Cramer, Robert H., and Seifert, James A. "Measuring the Impact of Maturity on Expected Return and Risk," *Journal of Bank Research,* Autumn 1976, pp. 229–235.

"Discusses the formulation of the expected return equations for bank portfolio assets."

Peters, Robert A. *ROI; Practical Theory and Innovative Applications.* New York, AMACOM, 1974.

Discusses the downward trend of corporate return on investment, then suggests methods managers can use to receive a favorable ROI.

Wyman, H. E., and MacFarland, J. E. "Financial Investments and the True Rate of Return," *Management Accounting,* August 1977, pp. 41–45.

See also appropriate chapters in texts listed under *Business Financial Management.*

OPERATING AND FINANCIAL LEVERAGE

Beard, Larry H. "Economic Profit Maximization and Break-Even Analysis," *University of Michigan Business Review,* September 1977, pp. 18–22.
Discusses the break-even function and its benefits.

Harris, Clifford C. *Break-Even Handbook: Techniques for Profit Planning and Control.* Englewood Cliffs, N.J., Prentice-Hall, 1978.

Harris, Clyde E., Jr., and Hilliard, Jimmy E. "Switchover for Bigger Profits," *Sales and Marketing Management,* November 8, 1976, pp. 47–48.
Discusses break-even or switchover analysis using a sales company as an example.

Lusht, Kenneth M. "A Note on the Favorability of Leverage," *Real Estate Appraiser,* May-June 1977, pp. 41–44.
Discusses the effect of leverage on the rate of return on individual real estate investments and also tests to determine whether leverage is favorable.

Martin, John D., and others. "Bank Leverage Really Does Pay," *Bankers Magazine,* Spring 1977, pp. 70–76.
The authors comment on an earlier study of bank leverage and present new evidence indicating a favorable use of leverage by commercial banks.

Siegel, Joel, and Atkinson, Robert. "Break-Even Analysis: A Tool for Banks," *Bank Administration,* June 1976, pp. 32 +.
"Describes break-even analysis as a framework for profit planning in banks."

Weston, J. Fred, and Brigham, Eugene F. *Managerial Finance,* 5th ed. Hinsdale, Ill., Dryden Press, 1975.
See Chapter 3, "Profit Planning."

See also appropriate chapters in texts listed under *Business Financial Management.*

Index